EMDR Therapy
for Schizophrenia
and Other Psychoses

Paul William Miller, MD, DMH, MRCPsych, is a senior psychiatrist specializing in general adult and old-age psychiatry and a member of the Royal College of Psychiatrists. He is an accredited EMDR consultant and an EMDR institute facilitator. Dr. Miller has served on the Council of the EMDR UK and Ireland Association and chaired the training subcommittee. He introduced EMDR to psychiatry in the Northern Ireland National Health Service (NHS), setting up EMDR clinics across the region. He left the NHS in April 2009 to pursue a full-time private practice and founded Mirabilis Health in January 2011, the first private psychiatrist-led clinic specializing in EMDR in Northern Ireland with an active research interest. Dr. Miller is a popular national and international speaker on topics including schizophrenia and EMDR, and he has been an Honorary Lecturer in Mental Health at the University of Birmingham and at Queen's University Belfast. Dr. Miller is the recipient of the Galloway Award presented by the National Schizophrenia Fellowship (2000), the International Society for Psychiatric Genetics Travelling Scholarship (2001), and the Northern Ireland Section of the Royal College of Psychiatrists Research Prize (Irish Division: 2002). Dr. Miller is affiliated with the EMDR research group at Worcester University. He has spoken on EMDR in schizophrenia and other psychoses in Europe and was an invited speaker at an EMDRIA workshop in Minneapolis (2010) and at EMDRIA Anaheim (2011), where he was also a plenary speaker. Dr. Miller has published scholarly articles in peer-reviewed journals on psychological reactions to trauma, schizophrenia, and EMDR.

EMDR Therapy for Schizophrenia and Other Psychoses

Paul William Miller, MD, DMH, MRCPsych

SPRINGER PUBLISHING COMPANY
NEW YORK

Springer Publishing Company, LLC
11 West 42nd Street
New York, NY 10036
www.springerpub.com

Acquisitions Editor: Sheri W. Sussman
Composition: S4Carlisle Publishing Services

ISBN: 978-0-8261-2317-6
e-book ISBN: 978-0-8261-2318-3

15 16 17 18 19 / 5 4 3 2 1

The author and the publisher of this Work have made every effort to use sources believed to be reliable to provide information that is accurate and compatible with the standards generally accepted at the time of publication. The author and publisher shall not be liable for any special, consequential, or exemplary damages resulting, in whole or in part, from the readers' use of, or reliance on, the information contained in this book. The publisher has no responsibility for the persistence or accuracy of URLs for external or third-party Internet websites referred to in this publication and does not guarantee that any content on such websites is, or will remain, accurate or appropriate.

Library of Congress Cataloging-in-Publication Data
Miller, Paul William, MD, author.
  EMDR therapy for schizophrenia and other psychoses / Paul William Miller.
     p. ; cm.
  Includes bibliographical references and index.
  ISBN 978-0-8261-2317-6 — ISBN 978-0-8261-2318-3 (e-book)
  I. Title.
  [DNLM: 1. Schizophrenia—therapy. 2. Eye Movement Desensitization Reprocessing—methods.
  3. Psychotic Disorders—therapy. WM 203]
  RC514
  616.89'80651—dc23

                                                                        2015027617

Printed in the United States of America by Gasch Printing.

Ad Dei Gloriam (To the Glory of God)

For my family: Dad, who taught me the meaning of hard work, love, and perseverance; my wife Nicola and children Jessica and Joshua, my heart, my home, and my safe place. Thank you for giving me the space and time for this project.

For Helen and Rosie: without you this book would never have been written; thank you for all your support.

E Pluribus Unum

An individual having unusual difficulties in coping with his environment struggles and kicks up the dust, as it were. I have used the figure of a fish caught on a hook: his gyrations must look peculiar to other fish that don't understand the circumstances; but his splashes are not his affliction, they are his effort to get rid of his affliction and as every fisherman knows these efforts may succeed.

—*Karl Menninger, psychiatrist*
(Asylum to Action, *Helen Spandler, 2006*)

Contents

Foreword by Uri Bergmann, PhD   ix
Preface   *xiii*
Acknowledgments   *xxi*
Introduction   *xxiii*

1. The Link Between Trauma, Psychosis, and
   Schizophrenia   *1*

2. The Phenomenology of Dissociation, Psychosis, and
   Schizophrenia   *23*

3. History Taking and Mental State Examination in
   Psychosis   *43*

4. Psychotherapy for Psychosis and Schizophrenia:
   The "Wizard of Oz Fallacy"   *63*

5. Eye Movement Desensitization and Reprocessing (EMDR)
   Therapy   *75*

6. EMDR for Schizophrenia and Other Psychoses:
   Rationale and Research to Date   *101*

7. An End to Therapeutic Nihilism   *123*

8. Case Formulation and Treatment Planning:
   EMDR Therapy + ICoNN Model   *145*

9. EMDR Therapy + ICoNN 1 Category Case Examples   *163*

10. EMDR Therapy + ICoNN 2 Category Case Examples   *173*

11.   EMDR Therapy + ICoNN 3 Category Case Examples   *191*

12.   EMDR Therapy + ICoNN 4 Category Case Examples   *207*

The INCBLOT Archive   *231*
Appendix   *239*
Index   *257*

Foreword

No psychiatric disorder is more shrouded in mystery, misunderstanding, and fear than schizophrenia. As Paul Miller notes, the original intention of Eugen Bleuler was for the diagnosis of "the schizophrenias" to represent a *group* of disorders. Upon examination of our contemporary scientific assumptions regarding schizophrenia in 2015, it is apparent that we may need to come *full circle* and carefully revisit the ideas Bleuler published in 1911.

The pendulum of mainstream psychiatry has, since the 1950s, swung overwhelmingly in the direction of endogenous and genetic models of schizophrenia. This mode of thinking has persisted despite the fact that the scientific data do not support a primarily genetic cause. As a specific genetic identifier is yet to be discovered, the current gold standard of evidence for genetically induced traits is monozygotic concordance. The classic twin study design relies on observing sets of twins raised together in the same family environment. Monozygotic ("identical") twins share 100% of their genes, whereas dizygotic ("fraternal") twins share only approximately 50% of their genes. Therefore, if a researcher compares the similarity for a particular trait between a set of identical twins to the similarity for said trait between a set of fraternal twins in that same family, then any excess resemblances between the identical twins should be attributed to genetics rather than to the environment.

So, for example, if we examine traits that are obviously genetic, such as race, eye color, or gender, we find 100% monozygotic concordance. Similarly, in medical diseases that have clearly shown genetic causation, such as Huntington's chorea, cystic fibrosis, and Tay-Sachs disease, we also find 100% monozygotic concordance. In studies examining schizophrenia, in contrast, we find only 30% monozygotic concordance. In fact, more recent studies with refined methodologies have found only approximately 22.4% concordance. Thus, the data do not support the claims that schizophrenia is predominantly genetic in origin. They support the conclusion that 22.4% to 30% may have genetic causation, whereas 70% to 78% of schizophrenia's causation is, therefore, nongenetic. This calls into question the confidence with which the medical and scientific communities continue to make these claims despite decades of empirical evidence to the contrary.

Although Eugen Bleuler's stature as one of the fathers of the schizophrenia field has endured, his descriptions of schizophrenia have been forgotten. Many of his phenomenological descriptions are almost identical to modern portrayals of dissociative identity disorder (DID); for example, what Bleuler defines as "splitting" is synonymous with today's definition of dissociation. He was furthermore aware that this group of schizophrenias also contained cases wherein a formal thought disorder, rather than splitting/dissociation, was manifest. Bleuler observed that in the cases that he described as dissociative, histories of trauma were often evident. In contrast, some cases that he described as manifesting florid thought disorders were not overwhelmingly driven by traumatic histories. We've celebrated Bleuler, and honored many of his conceptualizations, but have managed to completely forget some of his most cogent and important observations.

Further examination of the amnesia and confusion in our medical and scientific communities requires an exploration of the mainstream criteria for the diagnosis of schizophrenia: Schneider's first rank symptoms. First rank symptoms (FRS) were first defined by Kurt Schneider as diagnostic of schizophrenia in 1959, at which point in time schizophrenia was already considered to be a purely genetic, endogenous thought disorder. Bleuler's phenomenological descriptions of splitting, dissociation, and trauma were forgotten, whereas his classifications of schizophrenia were still considered the gold standard.

To date, despite the lack of consistent empirical support, modern diagnostic criteria of schizophrenia continue to give particular emphasis to Schneider's FRS. Recent empirical explorations have noted numerous methodological flaws in previous studies that supported the diagnostic strength of FRS. The overwhelming majority of said studies suffered from insufficient sampling and methods of interview. An example: When examining whether FRS are predominantly features of schizophrenia, empirical standards dictate that it is necessary to examine whether the symptoms under examination are also found in nonschizophrenic patients, yet the overwhelming majority of studies lacked such a nonschizophrenic control group.

So, let's examine what this means in real life. Although Schneider, in the original German text, did not explain in detail his 11 FRS, they are considered to be as follows: voices commenting, voices arguing, made feelings, made impulses, made actions, made influences on the body, thought withdrawal, thought insertion, voice or thought broadcasting, delusions, and hallucinations.

Reflecting on the foregoing, it should come as no surprise to anyone at this point that people properly diagnosed with DID consistently exhibit a majority of the first eight FRS (i.e., voices commenting, voices arguing, made feelings, made impulses, made actions, made influences on the body, thought withdrawal, thought insertion). They would thus appear to be symptoms of dissociation, not psychosis. They are often manifestations of alters speaking and of uncontrolled switching. In contrast, people properly diagnosed with the nondissociative schizophrenia thought disorder tend to overwhelmingly exhibit the FRS of voice or thought broadcasting, delusions, and hallucinations.

If this is known in the trauma and dissociation field, why is it ignored in the mainstream of psychiatry? Why do diagnostic interviews omit phenomenological explorations, such as "tell me about your life... what happened to you?" Is there some societal pressure causing us to cast a *blind eye*?

The author notes that Rolf Carriere, formerly of the United Nations, UNICEF, and the World Bank, has spoken of the "staggering global burden of trauma." Indeed, recent epidemiological studies suggest that with the increasing rates of trauma worldwide, posttraumatic stress disorder (PTSD) is on track to become a major global public health problem. Despite its wide prevalence, PTSD continues, nonetheless, to be ignored or relatively underrecognized, with proper diagnoses complicated by stigma, comorbidity and symptom overlap, rigid onset criteria, and questionably high diagnostic thresholds.

Frank Putnam has argued that the study of dissociation, and DID in particular, appears to have been held to a different standard than that of any other disorder. Nowhere else has such a body of research, consisting of clinical case histories, series studies with structured interview data, and studies of memory, prevalence, neurobiology, and neuroimaging, utilizing samples of children and adolescents from North America, Europe, Latin America, Turkey, and Asia, been so entirely discounted.

Richard Lowenstein has opined that when viewed within a larger sociopolitical context, dissociation theory intersects with many of the most controversial social issues of modern times. The role of trauma in our culture, particularly intergenerational violence and sexual abuse, intersects with historically taboo subjects such as rape, incest, child abuse, and domestic violence, and their actual pervasiveness in our society. In addition, the study of trauma forces us to confront greater legal, social, and cultural questions related to peace and war, the implications of violence in our society, the meaning of good and evil, and even divergent religious views about the relationship between men, women, children, and the nature of the family.

Bessel van der Kolk, McFarlane, and Weisaeth (2007) contend,

> A hundred years of research have shown that patients often cannot remember, and instead reenact their dramas in interpersonal misery. The professionals attending to these patients have had similar problems with remembering the past, and thrice in this century have drawn a blank over the hard-earned lessons. It is not likely that these amnesias and dissociations will be things of the past; they are likely to continue as long as we physicians and psychologists are faced with human breakdown in the face of overwhelming stress, which flies in the face of our inherent hubris of imagining ourselves as masters of our own fate, and as long as we need to hide from the intolerable reality of "man's inhumanity to man." (p. 67)

Thus, the understatement of the impact of the vast epidemic of world PTSD—driven by centuries of history written in the blood of colonialism, wars, slavery, pogroms and holocausts, global economic and natural disasters—should hardly surprise us. Is it any wonder that on a global level, science ignores Bleuler's observations regarding trauma and dissociation, and their relationship to psychotic processes?

From a clinical perspective, several questions are raised. If we reach back to Bleuler and bring his phenomenology forward to the present, how would this affect our diagnoses of schizophrenia? One possibility is that Bleuler was referring to both what are currently considered cases of DID as well as nondissociative schizophrenic thought disorders. Another possibility, as Colin Ross has suggested, would be that Bleuler was addressing a whole spectrum of disorders, such as nondissociative schizophrenia, dissociative schizophrenia, schizodissociative disorder, and DID. A third possibility, also proposed by Colin Ross, suggests that Bleuler intended to distinguish between dissociative schizophrenia and nondissociative schizophrenia; this would imply that we may not need the diagnosis of DID—we would simply follow Bleuler and discuss the various forms of *schizophrenias*. That would truly honor Bleuler's recommendations.

The good news is that we need not immediately answer these questions in order to implement Dr. Miller's clinical recommendations. We need only, as Colin Ross recommends, to begin to view these cases through a new lens, without necessarily reaching a definitive conclusion about their diagnoses. If we abide by Bleuler's emphasis on a careful phenomenological exploration, it becomes rather clear as to what specific treatment these different cases require.

Dr. Miller notes that, with respect to eye movement desensitization and reprocessing (EMDR) treatment, the following presentations can be discerned: people diagnosed with psychosis who are affected by identifiable trauma that appears etiologically linked; people diagnosed with psychosis who experience the psychotic phenomena and/or their treatment as traumatic; and those in whom the PTSD and psychosis are comorbid, with the comorbidity acting as a perpetuating factor in their presentation. In this book, perhaps the most seminal and promising recommendation that Paul Miller makes is that EMDR treatment can address psychotic symptoms without needing to identify a dysfunctional memory network, but rather by processing directly the core beliefs that are driving the psychosis.

This scholarly offering is a clarion call for us to listen to our patients and to let their stories inform their treatment. This book is a major contribution to furthering the understanding of trauma in general, and the schizophrenias in particular. It is written with a wonderful warmth and an ever-so-subtle twinkle of humor that lurks just below the surface. Paul Miller's ideas bring a healing sunlight to an area that has been encased for so long in darkness, and will open the doors to tens of thousands of people suffering from schizophrenia and other psychoses who have been denied effective comprehensive treatment. It is with the greatest of pleasure and admiration that I write this foreword.

Uri Bergmann, PhD
Past president, EMDR International Association
Author, *Neurobiological Foundations for EMDR Practice*

REFERENCE

van der Kolk, B. A., McFarlane, A. C., & Weisaeth, L. (Eds.). (2007). *Traumatic stress: The effects of overwhelming experience on mind, body, and society.* New York, NY: Guilford Press.

Preface

I asked a dear friend and mentor to comment on what he thought of this book, and with his consent I share what he sent to me in reply:

Readers of this text will eventually end up in two categories:

1. Finally! A new approach, something radically different.

2. No! This is too radical, too different, too unproven.

My hope for the reader is that you avoid either category!

Let this text create arguments leading to a constructively improved adjunctive therapy for those who suffer and have not received sufficient help through traditional treatments.

Bring forward the doubts, the questions, the arguments: the constructive differentiations of these diagnostic categories.

Bring on the good that comes forth as you tentatively explore, implement, and personalize some of these ideas.

Stay united, as well, on the goal of all healers: to bring understanding, adaptation, comfort—a sense of wholeness—to those for whom suffering has been so poorly understood, so difficult for both the individual and for those whom he loves.

Walter Bahn, MSW

The biggest impact of any person on my clinical practice as a psychiatrist was a patient I will call *Janus*, for he was the ending of my thinking that schizophrenia and psychoses were untreatable with psychotherapy and the beginning of my journey that witnessed a person heal and get better, who met the strict *DSM-III-R* (*Diagnostic and Statistical Manual of Mental Disorders* [3rd ed., revised]—the diagnostic "bible" used for classifying mental illness) criteria for schizophrenia, which I learned to use as a member of Professor Kenneth Kendler's Irish Schizophrenia Triad Study. At the time of writing, Janus is approaching 8 years symptom-free and medication-free; he has restarted his working life and is contented. I hope that these pages will entice you to make a similar journey.

I have always loved stories, and one of my mentors in psychiatry taught me that good psychotherapists are often good storytellers. Have a beginning, middle, and end . . . and have a point (i.e., meaning): These are the essential rules of narrative and they never need to be learned. We know them intuitively—from our earliest days we do not need to be taught how to understand or follow a story; we are simply able to do so. This ability to generate narrative is a core part of the human condition and one that wreaks havoc when it ceases to function as designed.

I want to invite you to join me in a story, a journey through knowing and understanding a narrative that is in general about psychosis and in particular schizophrenia. If I follow the innate "rules" of narrative, then this journey will have a beginning, middle, and end and it will have meaning. I hope you will agree that I have stuck to this model when we finish our journey together. This story, like all good stories, has a number of subplots that create something that is bigger than any individual element: the story of psychosis and schizophrenia; the story of a client who changed my practice; the story of a woman, a "walk in a park," and a community of open-hearted healers—Francine Shapiro and the EMDR therapy community.

This community introduced me to a wonderful and powerful psychotherapy that I have witnessed helping people in my community who have suffered from the internecine violence of what we in typically understated Ulster terminology called "the Troubles." I have also seen it help bring wholeness and healing to clients with anxiety disorders, phobias, obsessive-compulsive disorder, and depression, but the most powerful impact on me was when I realized its efficacy in schizophrenia and psychosis.

One day, while listening to a radio program on my commute to work, I heard the host interview an expert who made the following comment: "We wanted Jack, who was a six-year-old boy, to ask some of the big questions about the universe and life; so that we could record them." But they were unable to get the boy to do so, as he simply wanted to tell them what he thought the answers to such questions were. Jack already had a narrative in place that explained the universe as he saw it, "the sky isn't black; it is just, really . . . really blue." This process of narrative generation is what we do throughout life and it begins when we are children. We are born to narrate the world around us; this is what allows us to feel our way through life and to place ourselves in the world. Random observations and data taken into the mind are sorted and assimilated to generate meaning, and this process helps us to orientate and feel safe. This is essentially the *adaptive information processing* (AIP) system that Francine Shapiro describes, which underpins *eye movement desensitization and reprocessing* (EMDR) therapy (Shapiro & Maxfield, 2002). AIP is a natural, inborn system, and the AIP model is the soil in which we sow the stories of our clients. The AIP mechanism is like a cartographer making a map, which allows us to navigate our way through the unknown landscape of life ahead, and AIP is the map-making system with which we are all born. People and societies have always told stories to help understand themselves and to allow them to find their place in the world. Dáithí O'Suilleabhain, a friend of mine who is a cartographer, once explained how many indigenous peoples have stories and songs that teach them about their environment (O'Suilleabhain, personal communication, 2013). Often, as an elder walks a person through the landscape, the elder will sing his or her journey. These songs orientate individuals, allowing them to find their way, and also teach them how to look after the land.

Dáithí explained to me, following a trip to Belfast,

When place, story, and song come together, indigenous people call it singing the land. We sing it into existence by story and song. It then fills our awareness. We can sing it as we journey through naming all the features we see left and right as we pass, Slieve Scroob & Dromara, Slievenaboley & Aughnaskeagh, Lappoges & Dromore Donaghcloney & Maheralin, Moira, Hillsborough & The Maze, Lisburn & Lambeg, Ballynahatty's Giant's Ring, Belvoir Forest. Queen's City, hidden Blackstaff River and The Docks. Mountains and hills of Collin, White, Divis, Black, Wolf, Squires, Cave and Knockagh, and Mariners naming each rocky crag of coastline Lough. Singing it into existence, singing a journey through, singing it back to health. (O'Suilleabhain, personal communication, 2013)

However, what happens when the narrative process fails or flounders? Do we get meaningless jibber-jabber, or do we get a different form of narrative? In 1913, Jaspers built the foundation of psychiatric nosology on the dichotomy of neuroses and psychoses (Jaspers, 1913). For a long time, in the post-Jaspers age, we viewed psychosis as unintelligible and meaningless babble spewed out from the "broken mind" of the psychotic individual. No more worthy of study than spilled milk; all it represents was that a spillage had occurred. However, for those of us who are prepared to really listen, we discover that there is symbol and meaning in the psychotic material; this can at times be understood, and often it can provide access to the place where healing can be found. Schizophrenia is generally considered the most disabling form of psychosis; however, contrary to the assumptions of Jaspers, the mind of a person suffering with schizophrenia is not just a complex, broken machine with meaningless output; there is meaning in the symbols contained in the phenomena (delusions and hallucinations), and I believe that this principle is the key to seeing the negative cognitions and dysfunctional memory networks in psychosis as amenable to the psychotherapies such as EMDR therapy. We are creatures of symbols; they give us meaning, form the basis of language, and facilitate connection with each other. I want to invite us to think of the phenomena in psychosis as Indicating Cognitions of Negative Networks (ICoNN), and it is these negative networks that the EMDR therapist ultimately wants to reprocess; they are what Shapiro calls "dysfunctional memory networks" (DMNs) in her AIP model.

Example:

A man who comes to the clinic with a dog phobia presents his phenomena, and its functional impact, as an icon (ICoNN) of his underlying problem: the dysfunctional memory network relating to a time in childhood when a dog attacked him. Thus in EMDR therapy, considering his presentation within an AIP formulation, we identify and target the dog attack with the resulting functional outcome being that he is no longer afraid of dogs in the present.

In the standard eight-phase treatment model of EMDR therapy, the target is the past event that connects us to the dysfunctional memory network, its affect and negative cognition. In the previous example, the target would be an aspect of the original dog attack. Yet, as the EMDR therapy model has been evolving clinically, we see authors delineating protocols when the target is in the present. We see this in Elan Shapiro's Recent-Trauma Episode Protocol (R-TEP; Shapiro & Laub, 2013) and Robert Miller's Feeling-State Addiction Protocol (FSAP; Miller, 2010).

The R-TEP is an adaptation of the basic EMDR therapy protocol for treating recent traumatic memories—it is useful when the traumatic memory has not yet been consolidated or integrated into memory. The R-TEP protocol is a brief intervention (possibly on successive days) that may be used not only to treat acute distress, but also to provide a window of opportunity to prevent future complications from occurring and to strengthen resilience. Early intervention with EMDR therapy seems to reduce the sensitization and accumulation of trauma memories by means of rapid reduction of intrusive symptoms and a de-arousal response. R-TEP incorporates and extends existing EMDR therapy protocols together with additional measures for containment and safety.

The FSAP allows clinicians to work with substance and behavioral addictions, such as gambling compulsions, sex addictions, and smoking, that have been notoriously resistant to treatment. The feeling-state theory (FST) of addiction presents a new understanding of the etiology of addiction, hypothesizing that addictions are caused by a fixation of a positive feeling event. Afterward, whenever the person wants to experience that feel-good feeling, the link with that particular behavior is triggered. By utilizing this model of addictive behavior, Robert Miller has delineated the FSAP as a modified form of EMDR therapy that helps the client to break the fixation, resulting in the resolution of behavioral addictions with the elimination of the urges and cravings of substance addictions.

This book introduces the ICoNN approach, which is an adaptation to the standard eight-phase protocol that is helpful in working with psychosis. The ICoNN approach is similar to the R-TEP and FSAP, as the modification of the standard eight-phase, three-pronged protocol is in respect to target identification, which allows psychotic phenomena to be used as targets for reprocessing by a clinician using EMDR therapy. Once we repatriate schizophrenia into the spectrum of disorders with which it was originally associated, which is to say, "those which can be interpreted by a dissociation model" (Moskowitz, Schäfer, & Dorahy, 2008, p. 62), we can more understandably apply a trauma-focused formulation to schizophrenia in particular and psychoses in general; then the potential effectiveness of the psychotherapies, such as EMDR therapy, in psychotic disorders becomes all the more apparent.

We have been speaking about psychosis and are also mentioning dissociation, seemingly interchangeably, and I have spoken of returning schizophrenia to the category of dissociative disorders. Dr. Colin Ross looks at the clinical phenomenological conundrum of "psychosis or dissociation" and states, "Because of the way the two disorders are defined in the *DSM-IV-TR* and the clinical and research literatures, they cannot be separated into two discrete categories. They are too much and too often the same thing" (Ross, 2004, p. 16). I concur with his opinion.

Essentially, from a psychological perspective, if trauma results in a failure of narrative generation, this results in the formation of a DMN; this in turn is adapted to through dissociation, which suggests that if the DMN driving the dissociative (psychotic) psychopathology can be processed, then the pathology should resolve. This theory is in keeping with the AIP model of EMDR therapy. We will see from the small amount of case material that is presently available and from current international research that this is indeed what can be observed clinically in some, and those patients who respond positively can achieve long-term symptom control without the need for medication. Despite having more than 100 years of experience with the mental disorder formulated as schizophrenia, only a minority of cases can be said to make a full recovery; this observation invites us as clinicians and scientists to be, at the very least, curious about the apparent response to psychotherapeutic interventions. In many fields of science we have suffered from a them-and-us form of trench warfare: psychology versus psychiatry, nature versus nurture, and drug therapy versus talk therapy. I want to invite us to be more integrative and to consider allowing the content of this book's journey to inform a third space where we can allow dissonance to form and, I hope, to eventually bring clarity. Richard Rohr describes such a position well, and I share a section from a recent daily contemplation from his blog to give us a context for the "third space" in which I am inviting you to join me:

> The House that Wisdom Builds—"Paradox" comes from two Greek words: *para* + *doksos*, meaning beyond the teaching or beyond the opinion. A paradox emerges when you've started to reconcile seeming contradictions, consciously or unconsciously. Paradox is the ability to live with contradictions without making them mutually exclusive, realizing they can often be both/and instead of either/or. G. K. Chesterton said that a paradox is often a truth standing on its head to get our attention! "Dialectic" is the process of overcoming seeming opposites by uncovering a reconciling third. The third way is not simply a third opinion. It's a third space, a holding tank, where you hold the truth in both positions without dismissing either one of them. It often becomes the "house that wisdom builds" (Proverbs 9:1–6). It's really the fruit of a contemplative mind. (Rohr, 2014)

So, with this in mind, let us indulge our curiosity in our own third space.

> "Curiosity has its own reason for existing. One cannot help but be in awe when he contemplates the mysteries of eternity, of life, of the marvellous structure of reality."
> —*Albert Einstein*
> (*Recollection of a statement to William Miller, an editor,*
> *as quoted in* LIFE *magazine, May 2, 1955*)

My own professional journey with EMDR therapy began in 1997 when a colleague, Dr. Michael Curran, invited me to attend an EMDR therapy training organized by Humanitarian Assistance Programs (HAP), which was being run to help the local mental health professionals in Northern Ireland in dealing with the violence of the previous decades: "the Troubles." The training was delivered in the city of my birth, its very name a shibboleth—Derry/Londonderry—as it remains so for many, and I have witnessed too many people who have been attacked and injured just for calling it the "wrong" name. All these things meant that it was a very appropriate birthplace for an area of my professional practice that is responding to the pain and hurt of the violence of the Troubles and for trauma in general. In that training I was excited to hear and experience this "new" therapy that was linking in with a developing neurobiological understanding of the psychological impact of a traumatic event. It also appeared readily scalable, as it built upon the existing professional skills of mental health professionals and has at its core the innate information processing of the human mind. I believed that it could provide much-needed treatment for posttraumatic stress disorder (PTSD) and the other psychological sequelae of trauma to a community that needed healing. EMDR therapy's potential as a readily scalable psychotherapy for the treatment of posttraumatic psychological conditions was to be later picked up famously by Rolf Carriere, a development economist who worked for the United Nations and the World Bank. After he read Dr. Shapiro's book, while a UNICEF representative in Bangladesh in the 1990s, he saw EMDR therapy's potential for the people of Bangladesh who had been traumatized through a violent war of independence; 54 Bangladeshi psychiatrists and psychologists were initially trained after he serendipitously picked up Dr. Shapiro's first book on the therapy (Carriere, 2013).

As in the United States (Manfield, 1998), Northern Irish psychiatry in the early 1990s was not generally accepting of EMDR therapy, which was treated with much suspicion; many viewed it as a dressed-up and repackaged form of cognitive behavioral therapy (CBT) at best. I recall a time, while at a revision course for my exams for membership in the Royal College of Psychiatrists, when trainers were asking with which psychotherapy models we had experience; they looked with derision on EMDR therapy. I was repeatedly told that EMDR therapy was just a technique, and a colleague recently told me that a senior colleague had once told him that as a practitioner of EMDR he ought not to consider himself a psychotherapist.

At the same time, in the field of psychotherapy, CBT was the rising star, and there was little space for other modalities. Nonetheless, I began to see people recovering from their traumas as I applied an EMDR therapy paradigm to their presenting problems, which largely consisted of PTSD. One of my favorite quotes that characterizes that period in my professional development is by Dag Hammarskjöld, a Swedish diplomat, the second United Nations Secretary-General, and Nobel Peace Prize recipient: "Never, 'for the sake of peace and quiet,' deny your own experience or convictions" (Hammarskjöld, 1966, p. 84). When working with victims of the violence of the Troubles and of civilian trauma—road traffic collisions and childhood sexual abuse, for example—I began to see remarkable healing: I witnessed patients' recovery and was powerfully impacted by this. Whereas some mental health professionals were negative or merely apathetic, Dr. P. S. Curran was supportive and encouraged me, saying, "the patients don't read the textbooks." As a consequence, they didn't know that they were not supposed to improve, and so despite there being no strong published evidence at that time, I found my patients getting better. As I write this, there are now more than 30 randomized controlled trials (RCTs) worldwide examining EMDR therapy; the patients still haven't read them.

The battle for the recognition of the efficacy and validity of EMDR therapy was led in Northern Ireland by pioneers in the field such as Dr. Des Poole, who brought EMDR therapy to Northern Ireland; and the advocacy of Dr. Michael Paterson OBE was key in having the Clinical Resource Efficiency Support Team (CREST) include EMDR therapy in its 2003 guidance for the psychological treatment of PTSD, guidance that preceded the wider UK National Institute for Health and Care Excellence (NICE) Guidelines. Many people are now benefiting because of these endeavors. The EMDR therapy community in the island of Ireland is now healthy and growing, with many active and openhearted participants.

We are also at a time of a highly significant paradigm change for the EMDR therapy community. Pathfinders forge ahead and make the path easier for those who follow. In the United Kingdom (UK), enormous efforts and commitment by Dr. Derek Farrell have resulted in the development and delivery of the first university-based EMDR therapy training at the University of Worcester, where it is delivered as a Masters in Science course (MSc). I am fortunate to be in the first group of EMDR Europe Trainers-in-Training who are being mentored by Dr. Farrell; the group has been drawn from the UK, Ireland, Greece, and Pakistan, and as a group we will be endeavoring to develop the research and further study and growth of EMDR therapy through academic training. We as trainers will be contributing to the teaching of the course, and many of us believe that this shift from an essentially entrepreneurial model of EMDR therapy training to an academically focused one will mark a paradigm shift for EMDR therapy training that is as vital and as important as the delineation of EMDR therapy itself. These are exciting times, and this book is written for such a time as this, where innovation can be tested and cupellated in the crucible of academia for the benefit of humankind and not for seeking fame, reward, or a bigger bank balance.

I have now had the great honor to hear Dr. Francine Shapiro, the originator of EMDR therapy, speak many times, and she has been a source of great support and encouragement for me. She has called me the "father" of this area of development for EMDR therapy: the application of EMDR therapy in schizophrenia and psychosis. If I am the father, she must surely be the "mother," for I could never have birthed this area of innovation without her. At the start of her keynote addresses, she asks the audience to indicate with a show of hands to which areas of clinical practice they are applying EMDR therapy. I have witnessed responses that cover depression, obsessive-compulsive disorders, addictions, pedophilia, the reduction of self-harming behaviors, and, of course, psychosis; her response is always the same: "publish." There is now a solid research literature examining EMDR therapy for PTSD, but the other clinical areas continue to lag behind. This is something that I believe will change fundamentally as we move EMDR therapy training and study into mainstream academia. I hope that this book will further encourage the exploration and research of the clinical applications of EMDR therapy, and to achieve that goal I believe that we need to take some "radical" approaches. I believe that this radical change will come through a return to the roots of the phenomenology of schizophrenia, with a repatriation of "the schizophrenias" into the category of psychiatric illnesses that can be framed within a dissociation model (Moskowitz et al., 2008) that allows a trauma-focused formulation of cases to be made (Miller, 2014). Such a formulation sits readily within the architecture of the AIP model if we postulate that trauma leads to a derailment and failure of the AIP system, resulting in a dysfunctional memory network. I propose that by targeting and reprocessing the dysfunctional memory network through the biological facilitation of memorial processing, by the actions of dual attention stimulation/bilateral stimulation (DAS/BLS) acting via stochastic resonance (SR), we can achieve resolution of the psychotic phenomena; this is indeed what I have observed. As the AIP model is the central paradigm upon which EMDR therapy is built, I wish to look at it in more detail next, and we will similarly explore how the proposed innate mechanism of SR, which is believed to be ubiquitous throughout nature, has a key role too.

REFERENCES

Carriere, R. (2013). Healing trauma, healing humanity. *TEDxTalks*. Retrieved from http://www.ted.com

Hammarskjöld, D. (1966). *Markings*. London, England: Faber and Faber.

Jaspers, K. (1913). *Allgemeine psychopathologie* [General psychopathology]. Berlin, Germany: Springer.

Manfield, P. (Ed.). (1998). *Extending EMDR: A casebook of innovative applications*. New York, NY: W. W. Norton.

Miller, P. W. (2014). *Psychosis/dissociation—a rose by any other name* [eLetter]. Retrieved from http://bjp.rcpsych.org/content/202/6/428.e-letters#psychosis—dissociation—a-rose-by-any-other-name

Miller, R. (2010). The feeling-state theory of impulse-control disorders and the impulse-control disorder protocol. *Traumatology, 16*(3), 2–10. doi:10.1177/1534765610365912

Moskowitz, A., Schäfer, I., & Dorahy, M. J. (2008). *Psychosis, trauma, and dissociation: Emerging perspectives on severe psychopathology*. Chichester, England: Wiley-Blackwell.

Rohr, R. (2014). *The house that wisdom builds*. Daily Meditation. Retrieved from http://stjohnsquamish.ca/richard-rohrs-daily-meditation-244/

Ross, C. A. (2004). *Schizophrenia: Innovations in diagnosis and treatment*. Binghamton, NY: Haworth Maltreatment and Trauma.

Shapiro, E., & Laub, B. (2013). The Recent Traumatic Episode Protocol (R-TEP): An integrative protocol for early EMDR intervention (EEI). In M. Luber (Ed.), *Implementing EMDR early mental health interventions for man-made and natural disasters: Models, scripted protocols and summary sheets*. New York, NY: Springer Publishing Company.

Shapiro, F., & Maxfield, L. (2002). Eye movement desensitization and reprocessing (EMDR): Information processing in the treatment of trauma. *Journal of Clinical Psychology, 58*(8), 933–946. doi:10.1002/jclp.10068

Acknowledgments

My early experience in psychiatry attracted me to the multidisciplinary team environment of psychogeriatrics (the psychiatry of old age), with the integration of mind and body formulations and treatments. Psychiatric colleagues such as E. Anne Montgomery, Stephen Compton, Jill Gilbert, and Noel Scott, to name a few, stoked my love for working with the over-65-years age group, and I am grateful for that. I found the field of old-age psychiatry to be richly multidisciplinary, maintaining a healthy connection with the brain, thus retaining a holistic approach.

The first consultant psychiatrist under whom I worked was Peter S. Curran, a local Northern Irish expert in psychological trauma, based at the Mater Hospital. I am grateful for his support and mentorship across the years. He taught me to respect every member of the team when I started in the Mater, Belfast. Subsequently, F. A. (Tony) O'Neill and Professor Kenneth Kendler gave me a wonderful opportunity within the GEMINI team, the Northern Irish arm of the Irish Schizophrenia Triad Study. This was a genetic epidemiological exploration of schizophrenia on the island of Ireland, and the training in the phenomenological assessment of schizophrenia that these men and the wider team gave me continues to be a wonderful gift.

To my many friends and colleagues in the EMDR therapy community—where to start and end is nearly as big a challenge as writing this book, but I must name a few: Francine Shapiro, Robbie Dutton, Udi Oren, Uri Bergmann, Mark Dworkin, Jim Cole, Robin Shapiro, Jim Knipe, Frank Corrigan, Arne Hofmann, Ulrich Lanius, Carol Forgash, Katie O'Shea, Zona G. Scheiner, Derek Farrell, Derek McLaughlin, Anabel Gonzalez Vazquez, Des Poole, John Swift, Mary Mitchell, Marshall Wilensky, Sue Genest, and Peter Mulhall. My fellow EMDR Europe Trainers-in-Training at the University of Worcester have also been wonderful team members who have walked alongside me throughout this project; they are Saleem Tareen, Rashid Qayyum, Lorraine Knibbs, Lynn Keenan, Paul Keenan, Gus Murray, Penny Papanikolopoulos, and Tessa Prattos—thank you all.

I have been encouraged greatly by those in the EMDR therapy and wider trauma community who are utilizing psychotherapy for psychosis and schizophrenia: Akiko Kikuchi, Anabel Gonzalez, Andrew Moskowitz, Colin Ross, Daeho Kim, Jim Knipe, Karen Forte, and Martin Dorahy. You are an inspiration. In particular I must mention Colin Ross; he opened my eyes to the potential role of EMDR therapy for people diagnosed with schizophrenia. I stand on the shoulders of giants.

This journey has led me to explore how we, as humanity, have approached these experiences. I am especially grateful to the following people who were gracious enough to give me time and the benefit of their experience. I was blessed to talk with the following about their work and gained some wonderful insights: Phil Borges, Walter Bahn, Hal Stone, Sidra Stone, and Professor Marius Romme. I must also thank in particular some people whose writing has greatly influenced me in my journey: Joseph Campbell, Richard Rohr, M. Scott Peck, and Robert Johnson.

To those who proofread and helped with shaping the chapters—Helen Harbinson, Alastair Clarke-Walker, Aaron Brady, and Derek McLaughlin—thank you for giving so generously of your time. I am especially grateful to those who coauthored chapter sections with me: Remy Aquarone, Mark Dworkin, and Derek Farrell. Of course, none of this input would have been necessary were it not for Marilyn Luber and her kind introduction to Sheri W. Sussman at Springer Publishing Company. Sheri has "tickled" me over the years this project has taken, with the recent assistance of Alina Yurova. Thanks for your patience with me and for your tenacity with this project.

This book is a testament to a community of people; I hope that you find something in it that is of value. My prayer is that in the crucible of clinical practice and peer review, the "hay and straw" will burn up and the "gold and silver" remain as a good work, well done.

> "The way to get things done is not to mind
> who gets the credit."
> *Benjamin Jowett (1817–1893, English clergyman,*
> *educator, and classicist, quoted in John Gross,*
> The Oxford Book of Aphorisms)

Introduction

EYE MOVEMENT DESENSITIZATION AND REPROCESSING (EMDR) THERAPY AND THE ADAPTIVE INFORMATION PROCESSING (AIP) MODEL

Eye movement desensitization and reprocessing (EMDR) therapy is an integrative psychotherapy developed by Dr. Francine Shapiro (Shapiro, 2001). In 1989, she published the first research data examining and delineating the therapy, while a Senior Research Fellow in Palo Alto, California (Shapiro, 1989). Through the endeavors of the clinical community, EMDR therapy has gained recognition as an efficacious therapy for the treatment of posttraumatic stress disorder (PTSD). In the United Kingdom (UK), it has been recommended as a gold standard in the psychological treatment of those suffering from PTSD, being first recommended by the Clinical Resource Efficiency Support Team (CREST) in its document that gave guidance on the psychological management of PTSD, *The Management of Post-Traumatic Stress Disorder in Adults* (CREST, 2003). CREST operated in Northern Ireland, a UK region that has seen substantial loss of life and experienced severe trauma within its relatively small community of around 1½ million people. This was due to the internecine violence colloquially referred to as "the Troubles." The work of CREST was duly followed in the rest of the UK with a similar recommendation by the National Institute for Health and Care Excellence (known as NICE; NICE, 2005); and most recently the World Health Organization (WHO) published *WHO Guidelines on Conditions Specifically Related to Stress*, which recommends the use of EMDR therapy in the treatment of PTSD for children, adolescents, and adults—see specifically recommendations 14 and 15 (WHO, 2013).

ADAPTIVE INFORMATION PROCESSING, PSYCHOPATHOLOGY, AND MALADAPTIVE ENCODING OF TRAUMATIC LIFE EXPERIENCES

Rolf Carriere has spoken of the "staggering global burden of trauma" (Carriere, 2013), and I believe that it is our duty to respond to this huge area of need. I have heard this articulated in many forms, but essentially it comes down to the same thing: hurt people, hurt people. As we will see later from the discussion of the epigenetics and neurobiological effects of trauma on the body, this cycle need not continue (Pembrey et al., 2006; Waterland & Jirtle, 2003; Weaver et al., 2004). A foundational postulate of the AIP model and of EMDR therapy is that we are all born with an innate information processing system that takes the experiential data of our lives and processes it into a cohesive, coherent, and contiguous narrative that allows us to make sense of the world around us and of our place in it. This system need not be learned or studied by the patient before he or she can benefit from its functioning. However, it is this same information processing system that can get derailed in a trauma, resulting in dysfunctionally stored material, which results in the pathologies we see clients presenting with in our offices and clinics. In the late 1880s, pioneering French psychologist, philosopher, and psychotherapist Pierre Janet developed detailed and comprehensive models of dissociation and traumatic memories (van der Hart & Dorahy, 2006). Although some have sought to erroneously state that he came to later repudiate his theories on dissociation, the evidence does not support this (Dorahy & van der Hart, 2006). Janet stated that traumatic memories are distinct from normal "bad" memories and postulated that they are stored differently in the brain and have differing properties—something that to my mind is very much a foundational aspect of the AIP model. These unprocessed, state-specific, frozen memories are conceptualized as *dysfunctional memory networks* (DMNs) by Shapiro (2007), and I believe that just as Jung's "complex" derives from Janet's "fixed idea," the DMNs of the AIP model belong to the same lineage. Consider Jung's description of a complex in his 1934 review, quoted by Moskowitz (2006, p. 14),

> What then, scientifically speaking, is a "feeling-toned complex"? It is the *image* of a certain psychic situation which is strongly accentuated emotionally. . . . This image has a powerful inner coherence, it has its own wholeness, and in addition, a relatively high degree of autonomy . . . and therefore behaves like an animated foreign body in the sphere of consciousness. (Jung, 1934/1960)

In this same review in 1934, Jung describes complexes as having a trauma at their genesis: "The aetiology of their origin is frequently a so-called trauma, an emotional shock or some such thing, that splits off a bit of the psyche (Jung, 1934/1960)" (Moskowitz, 2006, p. 14). This is also how Janet described the formation of his "fixed idea," and Jung acknowledges his debt to Janet, as I believe we must do too in regard to the DMN.

PIERRE JANET—ONE OF PSYCHOTRAUMATOLOGY'S GIANTS

I believe that we stand on the shoulders of giants; indeed, it is our duty to do so, and one such giant in the area of psychotraumatology is undoubtedly Pierre Janet. We will learn later in the book that Janet's work had a significant influence on Bleuler and Jung (Moskowitz, 2006; Moskowitz, Schäfer, & Dorahy, 2008). The AIP model allows us to see further along this course of study, as it explains the basis of pathology, predicts successful clinical outcomes, and guides the clinician in case conceptualization (*formulation*) and treatment procedures (Shapiro, 2007). Within this innate information processing system, we take the experiences of the outside world and process them, stripping them of extraneous data, automatically linking the perceptions of current situations with associated memory networks already in existence.

Everyone reading this book will know that one plus one equals two—it forms a part of our mathematical understanding—but very few of us, if any, will recall where we were and who we were with when we learned it. We simply do not need that level of information. When the AIP system processes new experiences, the incoming sensory perceptions are integrated and connected to related information that is already stored in the person's memory networks. This conceptualization informs the intention and sequencing of the eight phases of EMDR therapy, and we know that the more closely treatment adheres to the eight-phase protocol, the better the clinical outcome (Maxfield & Hyer, 2002).

THE DOG BITE

If we explore a clinical example, this will aid our understanding of how the AIP model benefits us. Think of an individual who has had the experience of being bitten by a dog as a young boy; such an experience can be sufficiently negative and emotionally charged to overwhelm the innate processing system, resulting in unprocessed material. This material, we conceptualize, becomes stored as a DMN containing emotions and perceptual information in state-specific form. This DMN is cut off from the processed, functionally encoded, coherent memories that already exist in the person's mind—perhaps happy memories of playful interaction with a dog—but it also remains cut off in the person's future experiences. The unprocessed material can remain walled off like an abscess within a patient's body, and it is this "psychic abscess" that can be triggered by idiosyncratic present experiences, manifesting disorder. The boy grows into a man and the DMN remains walled off from any new learning. So when he sees a dog of the same breed that bit him as a boy, this acts as a trigger to summon the DMN. The key characteristics of this DMN are that it exists outside of context and chronology and is stored in state-specific form—meaning it is frozen in time in its own neural network, unable to adaptively connect with other memory networks (Solomon & Shapiro, 2008). In this unprocessed form, it is relived rather than remembered, in line with Pierre Janet's model for dissociated traumatic memories (Janet). So considering our current example, even if a strong adult male was bitten by a very small dog such as a Chihuahua when he was a boy, the DMN—with its strongly negative state-specific perceptions, feelings, and cognitions—is triggered in the present by seeing a Chihuahua; this results in an intense emotional response. He may become frozen in fear in the presence of this breed of dog even though the actual risk to him is negligible in the present. In this example we can see how the AIP model predicts pathology and helps us to understand the client's current presentation—that is, a severe fear response to and avoidance of Chihuahuas. The DMN is fear-laden and associated with "adaptive" avoidant behaviors triggered by this specific breed of dog.

GETTING THE RIGHT TARGET FOR EMDR THERAPY

The AIP model directs the clinician to target the original trauma, which, like a pollutant entering a river, poisons everything downstream of its point of entry. In this metaphor of a polluted river, we can see that the best response is to remove the pollution at the source, rather than to merely decontaminate the river downstream, and this is what the AIP model directs us as EMDR clinicians to do; we do so within the eight phases of the treatment model. The processing of the original trauma (the source of pollution) links the previously unprocessed material with existing functional memory networks and so removes the drive for pathology in the present and future, and this is indeed what we observe (Shapiro, 2007; Shapiro & Forrest, 1997; Shapiro & Maxfield, 2002). In EMDR we examine the past, present, and future within what is called the "three-pronged process." This three-pronged process sits within the AIP model, and essentially the clinician processes the *past* "unmetabolized" DMN that generates the presenting pathology, processes the *present* situations that cause disturbance, and generates an adaptive *future* template to allow the individual to facilitate effective future action (Manfield, 1998). As already mentioned, the growing neurobiological understanding of memory processing and the effects of trauma help us to understand the nature of the eight phases in the standard protocol and the logic for their sequencing. We can unpack this further if we consider the neurobiology of normal information processing according to the AIP model. Those wishing a deeper understanding of the current research on the neurobiological foundations of EMDR practice are directed to read Uri Bergmann's book *Neurobiological Foundations for EMDR Practice*, which I consider a seminal text in this area of study and that I recommend to you (Bergmann, 2012).

SCHIZOPHRENIA/PSYCHOSIS AND THE TRAUMA MODEL

As the nature/nurture debate continues, I hope that we can hold both these considerations in a "third space," as ultimately this will provide clarity and give the best hope of healing to this patient group. When we examine schizophrenia by formulating it within a trauma model, this allows us to consider the application of psychotherapies with a trauma focus. EMDR therapy is one of the current international gold-standard psychotherapies for PTSD, and early outcomes of its application to schizophrenia have been encouraging (Kim et al., 2010; Miller, 2010, 2014); however, more work is warranted. Of course, by holding to the principle of third space we can choose not to get stuck in the debate of talking therapy versus drug therapy (*either/or*), and instead we can embrace a *both/and* approach. This makes sense clinically, as psychotherapy will not necessarily exclude the need for drug therapy completely in all cases. As clinicians we commit ourselves to lifelong learning; psychiatrists and doctors refer to our work as a medical "practice"—we are not yet getting it perfectly right. If you think you are, perhaps you ought to think again.

LIFELONG LEARNING

Francine Shapiro and the works of Colin Ross (2004, 2013), Jim Knipe (personal communication, 2014; 2015), and Carol Forgash (Forgash & Copeley, 2008) have been extremely influential. Their work encourages me to explore this area of EMDR therapy. I still recall the conversation that Jim Knipe and I had in Philadelphia, sitting outside in the sun during an EMDR International Association

(EMDRIA) conference. Research is not a simple and straightforward endeavor; it is difficult, complex, and challenging. However, seeing the commitment of individuals like Tony O'Neill and Kenneth Kendler encouraged me to take the risks and work toward getting the necessary research done and published. At the start of my research MD thesis (Miller, 2007), I quoted the words of Barbara W. Tuchman (American author and two-time Pulitzer Prize winner): "Research is endlessly seductive: writing is hard work" (Tuchman, 1979, p. 34).

Research and the statements based upon it have consequences— unintended as well as intended. We see this in the nosological journey that the *Diagnostic and Statistical Manual of Mental Disorders (DSM)* itself has taken with disorders such as PTSD. I believe that it is in community that we heal and can be healers; therefore, we need to understand mental disorder as it is experienced within and through a community context. The importance of the intersubjective within the EMDR therapy method is greatly enriched through the teaching of Mark Dworkin (2005). We are required to be fully present and connect with one another to undertake good therapy. It will therefore come as no surprise that I believe that healing takes place, in psychosis, schizophrenia, and dissociative disorders, within the intersubjective space. This is where we connect in the milieu of the very nature of our consciousness. At the start of a book that explores shell shock, the following appears: "A French doctor has said, 'Il n'y a pas de maladies' [*There are no sicknesses, there are only sick people*]" (Smith & Pear, 1917). I have been taught that those who are wounded in the crucible of community must heal in community, and this is an important consideration for the people who seek my help. The EMDR therapy community is eclectic, and, like the function of rapid eye movement (REM) sleep, I found that upon reaching out and forming new associations, I was able to advance the development of the Indicating Cognitions of Negative Networks (ICoNN) model. The other communities where I have witnessed healing work are mythopoetic support groups, the community of faith, and the ManKind Project (MKP). These communities are all rich with story, and I have come to appreciate through them the power of mythos as a healing dynamic. When we complete research, as we ought to, or even reflect upon our clinical work, we should share the outcomes—not keep the research to ourselves, because that is shortsighted. We need to share it, present it at conferences, and publish it, so that it can be examined and debated. I am committed to lifelong learning and continuing professional development. Colleagues teach me much; books and journals teach me something else, but it is the journeys that I make with people, like Janus, that teach me the most. I see their courage to share and seek healing in a safe community. This, more than anything, encouraged me to explore EMDR therapy's applicability to schizophrenia and psychosis.

LIGHTING A BEACON FIRE

I have, within these pages, the opportunity to explain and articulate my position on EMDR therapy for schizophrenia and the other psychoses. EMDR therapy is a powerful psychotherapy, but it is not a panacea. Neither ought it to be undertaken by those unfamiliar with the treatment of schizophrenia/psychosis. As the motto of the Royal College of Psychiatrists states, "Let Wisdom Guide." This work in the area of psychosis and schizophrenia is fledgling and requires more research and critical examination. I heard the following story about a theologian who once visited a university chaplain:

> The theologian observed that the chaplain would preach to the students by standing on a soapbox and haranguing them. At dinner that night in the University College the theologian was critical of the chaplain's "style" and method of communication. In response the chaplain asked the theologian how he preached the Gospel. The theologian responded that he did not preach the Gospel at all; he lectured on the theology of scripture. The chaplain responded then if that was the case, he liked the way he did it, better than the way the theologian didn't do it.

This book is not a declaration of complete and final knowledge as it pertains to the application of EMDR therapy for the treatment of psychosis and schizophrenia. This book is a beginning. When I lecture, I always begin with the following quotation:

> "The mind is not so much a vessel to be filled,
> as a fire to be kindled."
>
> —*Plutarch*

I hope that this book will act as academic kindling, and I hope that researchers and clinicians will add their wisdom and clinical experience to this fire. Hopefully, the light of this beacon will illuminate a path through the fog of battle.

THE ROAD AHEAD

In the first chapter we will explore the links between trauma, psychosis, and schizophrenia. This connection is one that was known and accepted from the earliest days of the characterization of the mental disorder (Bleuler, 1911, 1950; Kraepelin, 1881; Kraepelin, Barclay, & Robertson, 1919) that we now know as "schizophrenia" (Moskowitz et al., 2008). Then, with the passage of time, nosologically we lost our way for a season, choosing to see schizophrenia as an entirely organic illness that was psychologically incomprehensible (Jaspers, 1913, 1963). However, the wheel turns and we are returning once again to acknowledge the connection between trauma and psychosis/schizophrenia (Knipe, 2015; Lanius, Paulsen, & Corrigan, 2014; Moskowitz, 2006; Moskowitz et al., 2008; Ross, 2004, 2013).

Next, we look into the phenomenology and diagnostic entities of dissociation, psychosis, and schizophrenia. This is important because I believe that if we can see beyond and through the current labels of diagnosis, we can apply the healing power that EMDR therapy can bring to people with these experiences. I hope to guide you through the limitations of the current categorical diagnostic nosology of the *DSM* and *International Classification of Diseases* (*ICD*) systems, as I believe we need to move through the current focus on diagnostic labels. By refocusing on the phenomenology beyond a mere label and through a therapeutic awareness of the intersubjective nature of these disorders, it is my belief that we will be more capable of helping the people who present to us seeking assistance. Will it help all people with these experiences? I doubt that. Will it help some? In my opinion, it will. I hope that this book will make people think about for whom it might be helpful and why. We ought not to be so wedded to our research or clinical "findings" that we cannot reappraise them in the light of new knowledge. Sticking to a position in the face of new experience may be the same dynamic that we propose occurs in the information processing system when overwhelmed by trauma: No new learning occurs. Sometimes we simply see research from a different perspective, one that comes from having traveled some distance further down the road of experience. It is not so much that I am suggesting that the current diagnostic labels are wrong as saying that they are mere labels. They are pale representations of the complex person who has joined us in therapy. We need labels at some level. Indeed, we can think of language itself as a collection of labels that we use to bring narrative to life. Language is the externalization of the inner experience of our minds and consciousness.

The next chapter explores the phenomenology of dissociation and psychosis. This naturally leads on to a suggested model for gathering the necessary information and thus assisting the person seeking our help. This is done through the outlining of a semistructured model of history taking and a review of how to examine the mental state.

After equipping ourselves with what to look for and how to look for it, we will look briefly at the current psychotherapies that are applied to psychosis and schizophrenia. In the light of these other paradigms, we will then explore in particular the work around EMDR therapy for psychosis and schizophrenia. All good structures need a sound foundation, and so we will recap the standard EMDR therapy model first (Shapiro, 1989; Shapiro & Maxfield, 2002; Solomon & Shapiro, 2008). The ICoNN paradigm is a methodology that adapts and adds to the standard EMDR therapy model, so knowing where and why we are making a change is professionally and clinically important. As we have seen in the important work done by the Dutch team, there are occasions when EMDR therapy can be applied in psychosis without any modification to the standard eight-phase, three-pronged protocols (van den Berg & van der Gaag, 2012; van den Berg, van der Vleugel, Staring, de Bont, de Jongh, 2014; van der Vleugel, van den Berg, & Staring, 2012). There is a small but growing literature around the use of EMDR therapy in and for the treatment of psychosis/schizophrenia; this is reviewed and summarized for the reader. This literature and clinical experience are used to present the logic and argument in favor of performing EMDR therapy in people with these experiences. I will also provide some guidance on how to identify those who are most likely capable of engaging with and benefiting from EMDR therapy. The next chapter will assist in the step from academic exploration to the clinical environment: the so-called "translational step." We will look at how to generate a case formulation and develop a treatment plan in general before looking at the specifics of the ICoNN model's methodology, which we will do with the aid of clinical examples. There are four key cases:

1. In the first case, we will explore a formulation in which the trauma is clearly known and believed to be etiologically connected to the psychosis that is manifesting (Miller, 2010). It is a case of Cotard's syndrome (also known as

"walking corpse syndrome")—this is not specifically contained in the *DSM-5* (American Psychiatric Association, 2013). In the *ICD-10* we can diagnose this as F32.3: "Severe depressive episode with psychotic symptoms" (World Health Organization [WHO], 1992, 1993). We will see that the case formulation allows the application of the standard model with a resulting resolution of psychotic phenomena and depression. Interestingly, during a dip in mood during the recovery, there was no return of psychosis (Miller, 2010).

2. The second case (Miller, 2010) is one of a body dysmorphic disorder, which the *ICD-10* classifies under the rubric of F45, "Somatoform Disorders." Specifically, it is coded as F45.2, "Hypochondriacal Disorder" (WHO, 1992, 1993). In this case, a young man presents with the belief that he has female breasts; in his case this was a delusional belief. Here I treat the emotional impact of the belief within EMDR therapy rather than challenging its veracity. The specifics of targeting and processing within the ICoNN method are described and discussed.

3. The third case is one of complex PTSD with marked dissociation. There are heard voices that can be engaged in dialogue—these are the "peopled wound" (McCarthy-Jones, 2012), and talking with them acts as a proxy for accessing the DMN.

4. The fourth and final case (Miller, 2010) is the one that prompted me to write this book. I introduced Janus to you in the preface. Janus fulfilled the strict *DSM-III-R* criteria for schizophrenia used by the GEMINI team (American Psychiatric Association & American Psychiatric Association Work Group to Revise *DSM-III*, 1987). Janus was given the usual medication for the treatment for schizophrenia, but failed to respond over a suitable duration of time. Sensing that Janus possessed the capacity to engage in psychotherapy, we discussed the possible benefit of EMDR therapy, to which Janus consented. We outline the formulation and treatment plan as delivered. Janus is now 8 years symptom-free and medication-free and has been able to reenter the workplace successfully.

THE PERSON IN THERAPY

Those who live with experiences of trauma, dissociation, and psychosis and those who have been given the label of schizophrenia are, first and foremost, people. The most human thing in our life journey is our innate desire to tell stories, to find meaning in our lives (Frankl, 1988, 1992). If we are to find a solution to the challenge of mental disorder, then I believe that we need to have all the information before us. A diagnosis is epistemologically a reduction and characterization of the complex phenomena of a person's conscious experience. How on earth would a label fully encapsulate that? I believe it cannot. So, am I saying that we should eschew labels altogether? No, but we must never forget that they are labels. In the ICoNN model, the labels can lead us to the real material that needs to be targeted in therapy. I use the analogy of talking to "the man behind the curtain" in the scene where Dorothy goes to meet the Wizard of Oz. We will never solve the problem fully by talking to the big scary green face of the "wizard"; that will send us on quests to do battle with witches and flying monkeys, but we will not reach home until we look behind the curtain. It is the little dog that leads

Dorothy to look behind the curtain. I believe that in the treatment of psychosis the little dog can be EMDR therapy when applied through the methodology of the ICoNN model. So let us begin our journey as Dorothy and Toto did: one step at a time. The journey continues.

Journey Well.

REFERENCES

American Psychiatric Association. (2013). *Diagnostic and statistical manual of mental disorders* (5th ed.). Washington, DC: Author.

American Psychiatric Association & American Psychiatric Association Work Group to Revise *DSM-III*. (1987). *Diagnostic and statistical manual of mental disorders: DSM-III-R* (3rd ed.). Washington, DC: American Psychiatric Association.

Bergmann, U. (2012). *Neurobiological foundations for EMDR practice*. New York, NY: Springer Publishing Company.

Bleuler, E. (1911). *Dementia praecox, oder Gruppe der Schizophrenien* [Dementia praecox; or, The group of schizophrenias]. Leipzig, Germany: Deuticke.

Bleuler, E. (1950). *Dementia praecox; or, The group of schizophrenias*. New York, NY: International Universities Press.

Carriere, R. (2013). Healing trauma, healing humanity. *TEDxTalks*. Retrieved from http://www.ted.com

Clinical Resource Efficiency Support Team. (2003). *The management of post-traumatic stress disorder in adults*. Belfast, Northern Ireland: Author.

Dorahy, M. J., & van der Hart, O. (2006). Fable or fact?: Did Janet really come to repudiate his dissociation theory? *Journal of Trauma and Dissociation: The Official Journal of the International Society for the Study of Dissociation (ISSD)*, 7(2), 29–37.

Dworkin, M. (2005). *EMDR and the relational imperative: The therapeutic relationship in EMDR treatment*. New York, NY: Routledge.

Forgash, C., & Copeley, M. (2008). *Healing the heart of trauma and dissociation with EMDR and ego state therapy*. New York, NY: Springer Publishing Company.

Frankl, V. E. (1988). *The will to meaning: Foundations and applications of logotherapy* (Expanded ed.). New York, NY: New American Library.

Frankl, V. E. (1992). *Man's search for meaning: An introduction to logotherapy* (4th ed.). Boston, MA: Beacon Press.

Janet, P. M. F. (1889). *L'automatisme psychologique. Essai de psychologie expérimentale sur les formes inférieures de l'activité humaine* [Psychological automatism. Experimental psychological tests on lower forms of human behaviour]. Paris, France: Evreux.

Jaspers, K. (1913). *Allgemeine psychopathologie* [General psychopathology]. Berlin, Germany: Springer.

Jaspers, K. (1963). *General psychopathology* (Trans. from the German 7th ed.). Manchester, England: Manchester University Press.

Jung, C. G. (1960). Experimental researches. In *On the doctrine of complexes* (R. F. C. Hull, Trans., pp. 598–604). London, England: Routledge & Kegan Paul. (Original work published 1934)

Kim, D. C., Choi, J., Kim, S. H., Oh, D. H., Park, S.-C., & Lee, S. H. (2010). A pilot study of brief eye movement desensitization and reprocessing (EMDR) for treatment of acute phase schizophrenia. *Korean Journal of Biological Psychiatry*, 17(2), 93–101.

Knipe, J. (2015). *EMDR toolbox: Theory and treatment of complex PTSD and dissociation*. New York, NY: Springer Publishing Company.

Kraepelin, E. (1881). *Ueber den einfluss acuter krankheiten auf die entstehung von geisteskrankheiten* [On the influence of acute diseases on the emergence of mental illness]. (n.p.).

Kraepelin, E., Barclay, R. M., & Robertson, G. M. (1919). *Dementia praecox and paraphrenia.* Edinburgh, Scotland: E. & S. Livingstone.

Lanius, U. F., Paulsen, S. L., & Corrigan, F. M. (Eds.). (2014). *Neurobiology and treatment of traumatic dissociation: Towards an embodied self.* New York, NY: Springer Publishing Company.

Manfield, P. (Ed.). (1998). *Extending EMDR: A casebook of innovative applications.* New York, NY: W. W. Norton.

Maxfield, L., & Hyer, L. (2002). The relationship between efficacy and methodology in studies investigating EMDR treatment of PTSD. *Journal of Clinical Psychology, 58*(1), 23–41.

McCarthy-Jones, S. (2012). *Hearing voices: The histories, causes, and meanings of auditory verbal hallucinations.* Cambridge, England: Cambridge University Press.

Miller, P. W. (2007). *The genetic epidemiology of tardive dyskinesia in Northern Ireland.* Doctoral dissertation, Queen's University Belfast, Belfast, Ireland.

Miller, P. W. (2010). *EMDR in psychosis—2 year follow-up of a case series of severe depression, with psychosis; delusional dysmorphophobia and schizophrenia, treated with EMDR.* Paper presented at the EMDR UK and Ireland meeting, Dublin, Ireland.

Miller, P. W. (2014). *Psychosis / dissociation—a rose by any other name* [eLetter]. Retrieved from http://bjp.rcpsych.org/content/202/6/428.e-letters#psychosis—dissociation—a-rose-by-any-other-name

Moskowitz, A. (2006, February). *Pierre Janet's influence on Bleuler's concept of schizophrenia.* Paper presented at the Trauma, Dissoziation, Persönlichkeit, Pierre Janets Beiträge zur modernen Psychiatrie, Psychologie und Psychotherapie, Lengerich.

Moskowitz, A., Schäfer, I., & Dorahy, M. J. (2008). *Psychosis, trauma, and dissociation: Emerging perspectives on severe psychopathology.* Chichester, England: Wiley-Blackwell.

National Institute for Health and Care Excellence (NICE). (2005). *Post-traumatic stress disorder (PTSD): The management of PTSD in adults and children in primary and secondary care. Clinical Guideline 26.* London, England: Author.

Pembrey, M. E., Bygren, L. O., Kaati, G., Edvinsson, S., Northstone, K., Sjostrom, M., . . . Team, A. S. (2006). Sex-specific, male-line transgenerational responses in humans. *European Journal of Human Genetics, 14*(2), 159–166. doi:10.1038/sj.ejhg.5201538

Ross, C. (2013). *Psychosis, trauma, dissociation, and EMDR.* Paper presented at the 18th EMDR International Association Conference, Austin, TX.

Ross, C. A. (2004). *Schizophrenia: Innovations in diagnosis and treatment.* Binghamton, NY: Haworth Maltreatment and Trauma.

Shapiro, F. (1989). Eye movement desensitization: A new treatment for post-traumatic stress disorder. *Journal of Behavioral Therapy and Experimental Psychiatry, 20*(3), 211–217.

Shapiro, F. (2001). *Eye movement desensitization and reprocessing (EMDR): Basic principles, protocols, and procedures* (2nd ed.). New York, NY: Guilford Press.

Shapiro, F. (2007). EMDR, adaptive information processing, and case conceptualization. *Journal of EMDR Practice and Research, 1*(2), 68–87.

Shapiro, F., & Forrest, M. S. (1997). *EMDR: The breakthrough therapy for overcoming anxiety, stress, and trauma* (1st ed.). New York, NY: Basic Books.

Shapiro, F., & Maxfield, L. (2002). Eye movement desensitization and reprocessing (EMDR): Information processing in the treatment of trauma. *Journal of Clinical Psychology, 58*(8), 933–946. doi:10.1002/jclp.10068

Smith, G. E., & Pear, T. H. (1917). *Shell shock and its lessons.* Manchester, England: Manchester University Press.

Solomon, R. M., & Shapiro, F. (2008). EMDR and the adaptive information processing model. *Journal of EMDR Practice and Research, 2*(4), 315–325.

Tuchman, B. W. (1979). *A distant mirror: The calamitous 14th century.* London, England: Macmillan.

van den Berg, D. P., & van der Gaag, M. (2012). Treating trauma in psychosis with EMDR: A pilot study. *Journal of Behavioral Therapy and Experimental Psychiatry, 43*(1), 664–671. doi:10.1016/j.jbtep.2011.09.011

van den Berg, D. P. G., van der Vleugel, B. M., Staring, A. B. P., de Bont, P. A. J., & de Jongh, A. (2014). [EMDR in psychosis: Guidelines for conceptualization and treatment]. *Journal of EMDR Practice and Research, 8*(3), E67–E84. doi:10.1891/1933-3196.8.3.E67

van der Hart, O., & Dorahy, M. (2006). Pierre Janet and the concept of dissociation. *American Journal of Psychiatry, 163*(9), 1646; author reply 1646.

van der Vleugel, B. M., van den Berg, D. P., & Staring, A. B. P. (2012). Trauma, psychosis, post-traumatic stress disorder and the application of EMDR. *Rivista di Psichiatria, 47*(2, Suppl. 1), 33S–38S. doi:10.1708/1071.11737

Waterland, R. A., & Jirtle, R. L. (2003). Transposable elements: Targets for early nutritional effects on epigenetic gene regulation. *Molecular and Cellular Biology, 23*(15), 5293–5300.

Weaver, I. C. G., Cervoni, N., Champagne, F. A., D'Alessio, A. C., Sharma, S., Seckl, J. R., . . . Meaney, M. J. (2004). Epigenetic programming by maternal behavior. *Nature Neuroscience, 7*, 847–854.

World Health Organization. (1992). *The ICD-10 classification of mental and behavioural disorders: Clinical descriptions and diagnostic guidelines.* Geneva, Switzerland: Author.

World Health Organization. (1993). *The ICD-10 classification of mental and behavioural disorders: Diagnostic criteria for research.* Geneva, Switzerland: Author.

World Health Organization. (2013). *WHO guidelines on conditions specifically related to stress.* Geneva, Switzerland: Author.

ONE

The Link Between Trauma, Psychosis, and Schizophrenia

Intention: *To equip the reader with a working knowledge of the relationship between trauma, schizophrenia, and the other psychoses.*

TRAUMA

The word *trauma* comes from the Greek term meaning "to wound." The one thing that we all experience is wounding. I was born in Northern Ireland at the start of the internecine violence known colloquially as "the Troubles," a phrase concocted by the stoic Ulster personality. I grew up in a city whose very name was a shibboleth—Derry/Londonderry—and I later treated people assaulted just for calling it the "wrong" name. As a medical student I witnessed the aftermath of the Shankill Road bombing, carried out by the Provisional Irish Republican Army (IRA), and during the following week, while on rotation in psychiatry in Londonderry, I saw the psychological aftermath of the retaliatory Ulster Defence Association (UDA) shootings that occurred at the Rising Sun Pub in Greysteel. After initially qualifying as a doctor, I completed my general training and joined a central surgical training rotation, but was soon to return to my first love: psychiatry. My first consultant, whom I worked under, was Dr. Peter S. Curran, a local expert in the psychological impact of trauma, and I gained from him a deep and abiding interest in this area of psychiatry (Curran & Miller, 2001).

THE HISTORY OF THE NOMENCLATURE
OF THE PSYCHOLOGICAL IMPACT OF TRAUMA

Trauma and its consequences have been a part of society for a very long time. It is a central theme in the archetypal hero's journey (Campbell, 2004), occurring time and time again throughout the myths and stories of humanity. Herodotus describes an Athenian soldier, Epizelus, who had been "behaving with valor" (Herodotus, 1837, p. 118) at the Battle of Marathon (490 BCE). The historian describes Epizelus

1

as suddenly losing his sight in the midst of the fight, although he had not been wounded. We would frame this as a somatic response to trauma. Such things have occurred throughout military history, but unfortunately the people who experienced them have not always received a sympathetic response. Herodotus goes on to tell us about the Spartans, who were known to be fierce warriors and made more famous still by their exploits at the Battle of Thermopylae (480 BCE). He mentions Aristodemus, who, although one of the elite "300" warriors, was so affected by the battle that he chose not to rejoin the fray; as a consequence, he was judged by the people as "being faint-hearted" (Herodotus, 1837, p. 235). Upon his return home he became known as "Aristodemus the Trembler." He was to later redeem himself at the Battle of Plataea (Herodotus, 1837). Others, too, have experienced rejection and have had negative judgments made upon their character when really they were suffering a mental illness. The Caesars chose the bravest of their men to be standard-bearers, but even these men could break down, demonstrating that, as in the case of Epizelus, personal valor is not protective against "war neurosis" (Sargant, 1976). In 1678 Swiss physician Hofer coined the term *nostalgia*—an illness that afflicted soldiers on campaign—and by 1755 one directory of diseases stated that it was found most often in the Swiss, as they were exceptionally fond of their country (Anderson, 2010; Babington, 1997; Wilson & Hohman, 1959). Larry, who was a surgeon in Napoleon's army, thought nostalgia to be a form of madness and stated so in a paper published in 1821, but many of his contemporaries believed it to be a severe form of melancholia (Babington, 1997). Nostalgia was also recognized and diagnosed during the American Civil War period (Anderson, 2010; Wilson & Hohman, 1959). In the early part of the 20th century, World War I was raging, and hundreds of men fighting on the Western Front were being diagnosed with "irritable heart." The psychological impact of the trauma of war became most widely known as "shell shock" in World War I (Babington, 1997; Myers, 1940). In the United Kingdom (UK), Wilson named this "soldier's heart" and focused on the cardiac symptoms and signs of the malady (Wilson, 1916). MacCurdy, who came from the United States and made a study of men suffering shell shock on the Western Front, thought it was a form of anxiety neurosis, given that heart function could be affected by anxiety (MacCurdy, 1918a, 1918b). These developments in nomenclature were occurring in the context of a society that was deep in the thrall of the psychological repercussions of the war. Jacoby in Russia and British-based Salmon remarked on the increase in asylum admissions for insanity during wartime (Babington, 1997; Metcalf, 1940; Raftery, 2003). Experts began to conceptualize that these disorders could be the physical consequences of the war environment and proposed that perhaps it only *seemed* that no physical injury had occurred. This was similar in thinking to the concept of "railway spine" that had been described by Sir John Erichsen, who postulated a physical concussive injury as the mechanism of injury in railway accidents (Erichsen, 1875). However, the theory of railway spine was linked neither with the developing concept of soldier's heart nor with that of shell shock. Charcot was critical of Erichsen and stated that he believed railway spine to be nothing more than hysteria (Babington, 1997). The British medical establishment was becoming increasingly confronted by the psychological impact of battle from the time of the Boer War (Anonymous, 1904). War neurosis was mostly diagnosed as neurasthenia or hysteria before Myers coined the term *shell shock* in 1915, assuming that there was a form of brain damage resulting from the concussion of exploding shells. This was a delicate time, during which investigation and professional discussions about shell shock were difficult. The authorities were so worried about Myers writing on this sensitive subject that they insisted on a delay in his book being printed; it finally reached publication many years after World War I (Myers, 1940). First in the post of consulting neurologist and later as consulting psychologist to the British Army, the then-Colonel Myers stated as late as 1916 that there were only one of two options for men presenting as deserters: the asylum or the firing squad (Babington, 1997). By the 1920s the British public was unsettled by the military executions during the 1914–1918 war. However, it was not until 2007 that the Armed Forces Act of 2006 passed an order that allowed soldiers to be pardoned posthumously (*The Guardian*'s corrections & clarifications column, 2007), although section 359(4) of the act states that the pardon "does not affect any conviction or sentence." Society is changing: In 2009, in commemoration of the first Armed Forces Day in the UK, the Bolton council added the name of Private James Smith to the Roll of Honor. Private Smith had been executed in 1917 for military misconduct, but had been suffering from shell shock (Reid, 2010).

MODERN NOSOLOGICAL CLASSIFICATIONS

Wartime features heavily in the development of the nomenclature of the psychological impact of trauma. William C. Menninger was a member of the famous Menninger family of psychiatrists and the director of the Psychiatry Consultants Division in the Office of the Surgeon General of the U.S. Army. He chaired the committee that produced "Medical 203" (Lieberman, 2015), which defined psychiatric nomenclature and became hugely influential in the development of subsequent classification systems (Medical 203, 1946). This document acknowledged the psychological impact of trauma, but framed it as largely due to a *diathesis*—that is, predisposing factors in the person who is presenting with the disorder. The first edition of the *Diagnostic and Statistical Manual of Mental Disorders* (DSM-I) in 1952 acknowledged the role of trauma in psychological reactions (Blashfield, Keeley, Flanagan, & Miles, 2014; Conti, 2014). However, the *DSM-II* completely ignored the concept of trauma resulting in psychological disorders. This has been attributed to the Vietnam War that was raging at the time (Lieberman, 2015). It may well have remained the case for the *DSM-III*, were it not for the lobbying undertaken by Chaim F. Shatan, a Polish-born Canadian psychiatrist. Shatan realized that in 1972, the nomenclature *gross stress reaction*, which was used to classify psychological reactions to trauma, had been removed from the *DSM*. Moved to action by this observation, he and a group of colleagues began to tirelessly advocate for a return of this nosological concept. Among others, they reached out to Mardi J. Horowitz, who was a renowned researcher in the area of stress reactions (Horowitz, 1973, 1975a, 1975b; Horowitz & Becker, 1973; Horowitz, Becker, & Malone, 1973; Horowitz, Becker, Moskowitz, & Rashid, 1972). However, it was apparently Shatan's lobbying of the influential Robert Spitzer, chair of the task force of the *DSM-III* (American Psychiatric Association, 1980) that made the difference. Spitzer is surely the "master builder" of the modern nosology of mental disorders, but even he has been critical of what he feels have been the excesses of the later iterations of the *DSM* (Carey, 2008; First & Spitzer, 2003).

THE "BIRTH" OF PTSD

The *DSM-III* saw a paradigm change with the creation of posttraumatic stress disorder (PTSD), which appeared after Spitzer appointed Nancy Andreasen to scrutinize Shatan's proposed "post-Vietnam syndrome" (Lieberman, 2015). Given her own experience of treating the psychological impact of severe burns, she found his ideas very resonant, and the *DSM-III* ushered in PTSD. Instead of the focus of the diathesis–stress model being on the diathesis, the *DSM* was now saying that the essential criterion for making a diagnosis of PTSD was something that lay outside the person, an experience "outside the normal range of experience" (American Psychiatric Association [APA], 1980). This was Criterion A, and it became known as the "gatekeeper" criterion. PTSD was also delineated in the *International Classification of Diseases* (*ICD-10*; World Health Organization, 1993, F43.1). Rather than the problem being an innate weakness in the person experiencing the disorder, the *DSM* was now stating that the event was so devastating that it was sufficient to overwhelm a person's normal coping strategies. This was not referring to the normal vagaries of everyday life, such as divorce or losing your job; the authors were thinking of events of such magnitude as the Nazi Holocaust, the atomic bombs' devastation in Hiroshima and Nagasaki, war, torture, sexual abuse, natural disasters, and other disasters such as severe industrial injuries and road traffic collisions (Friedman, 2007). The latest version, *DSM-5* (APA, 2013), retains this "gatekeeper" criterion for PTSD. The other criteria fall into four symptom clusters: *intrusion, avoidance, negative alterations in cognitions and mood,* and *alterations in arousal and reactivity.* A sixth criterion details the duration of symptoms required to make the diagnosis, the seventh considers whether there is functional impairment, and the eighth makes clear that the symptoms are not attributable to a substance or co-occurring medical condition (APA, 2013). It is clear that the evolution of the understanding of the psychological effects of trauma has been largely driven by our experiences of war. This has, unsurprisingly, led to the evolution of the diagnosis of PTSD. A person who is involved in a trauma may, however, as a consequence, suffer from a range of affective disorders, or none, and not reach case criteria for PTSD. For example, an electrician I saw following an accidental electrocution, in which he was thrown several feet across the room he was working in, did not fulfill all of the criteria necessary for a diagnosis of PTSD to be made. He did, however, fulfill all of the criteria for a specific phobia because he was terrified of even seeing electrical wiring when I first met with him. Indeed, this event had a severe functional impact upon him, for he was unable to do his job. The recognition of the diagnosis of PTSD in 1980 came after Congress finally passed Senator Alan Cranston's bill in 1979, which saw the creation of outreach centers for Vietnam veterans suffering from the psychological sequelae of their service. PTSD is, at least in the public mind, the archetypal response to a traumatic event, and the concept soon expanded from the military to all of society as potential sufferers. In my opinion, much of this has been driven by a culture of compensation and legal actions, more so than any public health endeavor. The only disorders in our current diagnostic systems that have an etiological factor specified in their diagnostic criteria are PTSD and the substance misuse/addictions. This is because the traditional emphasis of the diathesis–stress model is upon the diathesis and not the stress. We will see this as we examine schizophrenia.

SCHIZOPHRENIA: A GROUP OF DISORDERS

The evolution of the diagnosis of schizophrenia was characterized by a move away from a trauma/dissociation model (Moskowitz, 2006; Moskowitz, Schäfer, & Dorahy, 2008) and toward a biological diathesis model, which resulted in schizophrenia's phenomena being viewed as psychologically incomprehensible (Jaspers, 1913, 1963). We will explore this further in the next chapter when we examine the phenomenology of schizophrenia. This view of schizophrenia as a mental disorder with a pathophysiological predisposition that interacts with psychological factors returns us to the same considerations that were being debated in 1908, around the time of the first public mention of "the schizophrenias" by Bleuler (1906, 1911). Moskowitz observed that Jung compared his work to Bleuler's, stating, "The chief difference between us is as to whether the *psychological disturbance* should be regarded as primary or secondary in relation to the *physiological* basis [italics added]" (Jung, 1960/1914, p. 155; quoted in Moskowitz, 2006). As we see in more detail in the following chapter, Bleuler's original intention was to describe a group of disorders (Bleuler, 1911), and a return to the dissociative origins of this group of disorders is also being called for (Gonzalez, Mosquera, & Moskowitz, 2012; Moskowitz et al., 2008). Ross, for example, proposes the following spectrum: from nondissociative subtypes of schizophrenia, to dissociative schizophrenia, through schizodissociative disorder, to dissociative identity disorder (DID) (see Figure 1.1) (Ross, 2007; Ross & Halpern, 2009).

• **FIGURE 1.1 The Dissociative Spectrum of the Schizophrenias. Includes 'Grid 1' (Oil on canvas, 48" X 72") by Julie Leff (2008). Owned by the Author.**

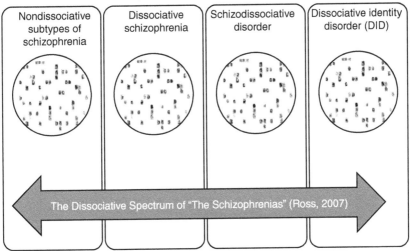

Source: Ross (2007).

This is a very important realignment of our current paradigm. Schizophrenia is *not* one disorder; it is a *group* of disorders.

POSITIVE AND NEGATIVE "SCHIZOPHRENIAS"

In 1980 Tim Crow published a landmark work delineating two syndromes of schizophrenia: positive and negative (Crow, 1980; Crow, Cross, et al., 1980; Crow, Frith, Johnstone, & Owens, 1980; Crow & Johnstone, 1980). Essentially he described an acute "positive" syndrome that consists of active delusions, hallucinations, and thought disorder. He proposed that this was related to a pathological process involving increased numbers of dopamine receptors, and thus it would be responsive to antipsychotic drugs (Crow, 1981), which are largely antidopaminergic (Frith, 1992). The negative syndrome is a chronic syndrome characterized by poverty of speech and flattened or "wooden" affect with social constriction. He stated that it is associated with structural brain abnormalities (Crow, 1995) and has a generally poor response to antipsychotic drugs (Crow, 1981; Frith, 1992).

THE DISSOCIATIVE HEART OF "THE SCHIZOPHRENIAS"

This group of disorders has at its core the dynamic of dissociation, and the force that drives this is trauma. Ross opines that toward the nondissociative-subtypes-of-schizophrenia end of the spectrum there are more negative and fewer positive symptoms, with less psychological trauma and less responsiveness to psychotherapy, with the voices becoming much less interactive. At the other end of this spectrum we have DID, with the voices manifesting as distinct ego-states, with more positive and fewer negative symptoms of schizophrenia (Ross, 2007; Ross & Halpern, 2009). This is clinically what people who have been working with this group of individuals see; as Japanese researcher Akiko Kikuchi noted, "the hallucinations of the hi-DES [Dissociative Experiences Scale] patients are more understandable. I don't hear devils and gods as common interpretations of their voices. The origin of voices are [sic] thought by the patients to be someone from the past, such as the bully" (Kikuchi, personal communication, 2012).

OVERVIEW OF THE NOSOLOGY OF SCHIZOPHRENIA

Bentall suggests that the orthodox position of believing that mental illness is capable of characterization as a discrete number of diagnoses is wrong (Bentall, 1992, 2003, 2009). He makes a similar statement about the erroneous assertion that "madness" cannot be understood in terms of the psychology of the person (Bentall, 1992, 2003, 2009). This latter statement is an inheritance from the work of Karl Jaspers (1913). Bleuler first mentioned the term "the schizophrenias" in a public lecture in April of 1908, and in print shortly thereafter (Moskowitz, 2006). He had continued the discussion group at the Burghölzli that his junior, C. G. Jung, had run while there (1900–1909) and demonstrated an interest in both the biological and psychological etiologies of his patients' symptoms (Bleuler, 1906, 1911, 1931). However, Jaspers's influence was to forge the mold for "modern nosology," and Kurt Schneider, of "First Rank Symptoms" fame, also stated something similar when he emphasized that the clinician ought to pay more attention to the "form" rather than to the actual "content" of a patient's experience (Schneider, 1950, 1957). There were those who still emphasized the dissociative mechanisms at play in schizophrenia and took an active interest in their phenomena, as we see from this passage:

> In that most frequent and disastrous of all the mental disorders, namely, *dementia praecox* or *schizophrenia,* this condition becomes confirmed; the patient lives apart in his dream-world, loses all emotional rapport with his fellows, and interprets such impressions as he continues to receive from the world about him in terms of the world within. (Emphasis in original text; McDougall, 1935, p. 249)

When we return to the dissociative roots of schizophrenia and psychosis, we are inextricably also drawn to examine the relationship with trauma. For if there is a dissociation of the mental processes, something must be causing that to happen, and trauma has long been acknowledged as the key that opens that door (Foote & Park, 2008).

EPIGENETICS

Many have thought that genetic epidemiology has come to the aid of biological psychiatry—a cavalry charge to fight off those who would seek to assail the edifice of schizophrenia as a biological entity. The models for the genetic transmission of schizophrenia have become increasingly complex since the realization that we were not going to find a single gene of major effect in causing it. The International Schizophrenia Consortium described an oligogenic model for schizophrenia in 2009 (i.e., lots of genes of small effect working together), but noted that very large numbers of genes were required to make the model work: 1000 genes only explained 30% of the liability for schizophrenia. It has been estimated that the human genome has 26,000 genes. Modeling also considers how the expression of one gene can be modified by one or more other genes, referred to as *epistasis* (Khoury, Beaty, & Cohen, 1993). This epistatic effect works in addition to any other physiological and epigenetic force (Sapolsky, Uno, Rebert, & Finch, 1990; Sweatt, 2009; Weaver et al., 2004). Epigenetics can involve a variety of various mechanisms, including the methylation of DNA, which can affect gene stability and has been observed to switch gene expression on or off (Habl et al., 2012; Kuang, Sun, Zhu, & Li, 2011; Shifman et al., 2008; Teixeira et al., 2011; Wedenoja et al., 2010; Yang, Kang, Liu, & Yang, 2013). However, the most recent work on genetics that includes epigenetics demonstrates further how a person's experiences can result in biological change (Tsankova, Renthal, Kumar, & Nestler, 2007; Yehuda et al., 2014). These marks, which influence the expression of the person's genetic code, have also been shown to be capable of being passed on to subsequent generations (Sweatt, 2009). As an identical twin, genetics has always fascinated me. The effects of epigenetics are one of the factors that mean genetically identical individuals can look different. In work carried out on mice it was shown that genetically identical mice appear different in color and size (brown and thin cf. yellow and obese) because of epigenetic effects on the agouti gene, which is turned "off" by methylation in the thin mice and "on" in the obese ones (Duhl, Vrieling, Miller, Wolff, & Barsh, 1994). In my opinion, the focus on heritability research has not given adequate consideration to the environmental factors, and I believe that epigenetic forces may be much more significant and substantial than once thought. However, are we "mice or men" (*sorry—couldn't resist that*)? We are, of course, the human race—so what do we know of epigenetic marks in humans?

EARLY-LIFE CHOICES, EXPERIENCES, AND EPIGENETIC TRANSMISSION OF RISK

Consider that each cell in the body—apart from the sperm and the egg—contains the same complement of genetic material. If we stretched out the DNA from one cell into a long string, it would be over 6 feet of linear DNA. The problem of packaging this into each cell is solved by winding this DNA around "spools" called histones that, with the DNA, form chromatin. Although each cell has the same DNA, one becomes a neuron, for example, and the other a muscle cell; how is this happening? This is related to environment in two senses of that term. There is the immediate environment that the cell is in, but there is also the wider environment: the milieu that the embryo is developing within. As we will see, a father can pass on "epigenetic marks" in his sperm (Pembrey et al., 2006; Pembrey, Saffery, & Bygren, 2014), and these marks can switch "on" or "off" gene expression. A mother can affect the developing child epigenetically too—through lifestyle choices, such as smoking and diet, as well as through her experiences, such as stress levels, depression, and the like.

SMOKING AND DIET

Long-term studies have now demonstrated that children and grandchildren can be affected epigenetically by the choices that a predecessor makes. In one study of the sons and grandsons of men who chose to smoke and who had poor diets in their prepubescent years, researchers found that those offspring had shorter life spans than their peers (Pembrey et al., 2006, 2014). Here we see the epigenetic risks being passed down through the *paternal* line.

THE CHILDREN OF HOLOCAUST SURVIVORS

Rachel Yehuda, a professor of psychiatry and neuroscience and director of the Traumatic Stress Studies Division, and her team at the Mount Sinai School of Medicine have completed work that looks at the intergenerational effects of the trauma of the Nazi Holocaust on subsequent generations. As we have already observed, methylation is an epigenetic mechanism that can switch "on" or "off" genes, controlling what of the genome is expressed. The levels of PTSD in Holocaust survivors were evaluated, and the degree of methylation of a gene-promoter region of the glucocorticoid receptor (GR-1F) gene (NR3C1) was assessed. These measures were then examined against data on the glucocorticoid receptor sensitivity in the offspring (Yehuda et al., 2014). This work built upon the important glucocorticoid receptor work of Michael Meaney's team in Canada, completed on rats (Weaver et al., 2004). His team had found that better nurturing by the mother (e.g., licking of the pups by the rat mother) resulted in a lower level of methylation of a gene-promoter region (i.e., a region that enables gene expression for the glucocorticoid receptor). They found that the rat pups were born with a number of epigenetic silencing marks that can be removed through nurturing, grooming, and licking, and this change stays with the pups throughout their lives. (See also TEDxOU Talk by Courtney Griffins at https://www .youtube.com/watch?v=JTBg6hqeuTg; Griffins, 2012.) Yehuda's team, which was also looking at glucocorticoid receptors, proposed that PTSD in the father resulted in higher levels of methylation and consequently a decrease in receptors. This would lead to higher circulating levels of cortisol that could in turn be associated with higher risk of developing depression or "chronic stress responses" (Yehuda et al., 2014). The team noted a different effect when the mother had PTSD. In these cases the researchers noted an increased attachment of the mother to the child, which they propose is due to the mother's fear of a loss of attachment. The presence of maternal PTSD alongside paternal PTSD was found to be associated with lower levels of methylation, and Yehuda proposes that the epigenetic forces in the mother may be preconception as well as in utero (Yehuda et al., 2014). She argues that the epigenetic marks could not have been simply laid down in childhood, as a consequence of experiencing a parent with PTSD, because that would fail to explain the different findings that depend on whether it was the mother or the father with PTSD. It is acknowledged that more work is needed, but remember that you can positively affect your epigenome.

TRAUMA AND SCHIZOPHRENIA

When those in our field speak to members of the general public about the relationship between a history of exposure to trauma and the development of psychosis/schizophrenia, they generally express the belief that adverse life events can lead to the development of these disorders (Tarrier et al., 2004). Indeed, when I asked my wife this question she stated exactly that. Work by John Read's research group has found that people in the following countries believe that mental health disorders are caused primarily by adverse life events and therefore enter mental health services with this set of beliefs in their minds (Read & Dillon, 2013):

South Africa	China	Egypt	Turkey	Fiji
India	Mongolia	Japan	Malaysia	Switzerland
Ethiopia	Greece	Australia	Russia	Bali
Brazil	England	Ireland	Germany	Italy
New Zealand				

Although many people, like my wife, generally believe that this connection appears obvious, Kingdon found that for every one psychiatrist who agreed with the thinking of the general public, there were 115 who thought it primarily due to biological factors (Kingdon, 2004; Tarrier et al., 2004). The issue is then compounded by the behavior of professionals within the system of treatment. People receive psychoeducation that they are "biologically broken" as a consequence of a genetically inherited set of risk factors. As professionals, by doing so, we make them *passive* and *incapable*. We essentially tell them that they are not able to be responsible for their illness, and medical paternalism steps in and medicates this broken biology. People, as a consequence, fail to be given the opportunity to talk about the adverse life events. However, if we give people the opportunity, I have found that they are willing, and with time and the right assistance, able to do so. In medical school I was taught that the biological and indeed genetic etiology of schizophrenia was a universally accepted "fact." I had the honor and great opportunity to work as a small part of the team that Professor Kenneth Kendler led in Ireland that examined the genetic epidemiology of schizophrenia and poor-outcome schizoaffective disorder. However, as we are learning, the nature/nurture debate is not a straightforward one. It is in every sense a Gordian knot, and pulling loose one piece seems only to tighten others.

"AM I CRAZY?"

I want to introduce at this point a concept that might be new to many: the healthy-voice-hearer. A substantial proportion of psychotic phenomena are auditory verbal hallucinations (AVHs). If we explore AVHs, the following figures have been quoted in the literature: 34% of voice-hearers have been given a diagnosis of *schizophrenia*, 31% have been diagnosed with *borderline personality disorder*, 21% have *no psychiatric diagnosis* (*healthy-voice-hearers*), and 10% have *PTSD* (McCarthy-Jones, 2012). Romme argues that hearing voices is not the pathology; rather, it is the failure to adapt to the experience of hearing voices that results in mental illness (Romme & Escher, 1993).

THE WIZARD OF OZ FALLACY

I agree with Romme that the "psychotic" material need not be viewed as the problem; it is actually how a person is adapting to the core pathology of the dysfunctional memory network (DMN): The DMN is the *real* problem. In the introduction I referred to the *Wizard of Oz fallacy*. I define this as the situation where we focus our treatment solely on the psychotic material rather than working to psychologically "metabolize" the DMN. In the Indicating Cognitions of Negative Networks (ICoNN) model, we view psychotic material as a bridge that connects us to the DMN, which is the primary target for our therapeutic endeavors. I have already said that we need to focus on "the man behind the curtain" (DMN) because only "talking to the big scary green face of the wizard" (psychosis) results in being sent on expeditions to battle witches and flying monkeys. This is misspent time in therapy, as getting "home to Kansas" requires us to look behind the curtain, and that is what we do by reprocessing the DMN through ICoNN methodology. Toto, the little dog that leads Dorothy to look behind the curtain, is eye movement desensitization and reprocessing (EMDR) therapy applied using the ICoNN model's methodology.

ALLEGORY: "LET ME TELL YOU A STORY"

The function of the adaptive information processing (AIP) model of EMDR therapy is to generate a healthy memory network. A healthy memory is a coherent and contiguous narrative of the experience; this is in keeping with what we hypothesize in the AIP model (Shapiro, 2001, 2007; Solomon & Shapiro, 2008). The generation of narrative, as an adaptive response to one's surroundings and experience, is a normal phenomenon. Once we discard the fallacy that psychotic phenomena are psychologically unintelligible, we begin to see the meaning and symbolism in them (Jaspers, 1913, 1963). We see this archetype in the allegory presented in *Life of Pi*, where a boy tells a story of being in a boat with a tiger, when what he really experienced was the horrors of having seen another person do terrible things to their shipmates (Martel, 2011). We see clearly that the generation of his version of his experience was adaptive. I believe that this is also what I observe in people who present with these experiences and who have been diagnosed with psychosis. These are adaptations to the experience of living. As Ross has indicated, there is a range of disorders within "the schizophrenias," with differing levels of dissociative force. McCarthy-Jones offers the following paradigm shift: "It may be that the important transition is not from patient-voice-hearer to non-voice-hearer but from patient-voice-hearer to healthy-voice-hearer" (McCarthy-Jones, 2012, p. 148).

THE ROLE OF TRAUMA

PTSD and DID are known and accepted to have trauma as an etiological factor. We will also see that schizophrenia was born of dissociative mechanisms and trauma accepted as a causative force (Moskowitz, 2006; Moskowitz et al., 2008). The AIP model proposes that trauma derails this normal innate mechanism and generates a DMN. It is my hypothesis that this is then adaptively expressed as psychotic material. If, however, we remember that there is meaning in the "ICoNN-ography" of the psychosis, then I believe that by telling the person that there is meaning that can be decoded, we give them hope. When we assume this position as professionals, this is not an extremist position when the whole population is considered; it may be extreme for those of us who are psychiatrists, but I certainly think these data are compelling and confirm something that we appear to have known intuitively. Hope flows when meaning is present, and the mind is all about meaning (Campbell, 2004). At a lecture he gave in Cork, John Read described a story from his experiences of working in a U.S. hospital while in his 20s (Read, 2013). He told of a man, whom he called Bob, who had been admitted and was walking around with his eyes closed; he was "black and blue" as a consequence. At the end of his tale, Read explains that being naturally inclined to engage with the other man, and not being trained at the time, he did what came naturally: He asked him why he was keeping his eyes closed. Note that this "intervention" came from what Read felt natural to do, and I believe this is a nice example of working with an awareness of the intersubjective. Healing is a very relational endeavor; or, rather, it ought to be. The man opened his eyes and got right into Read's face and angrily stated that it was about time someone had asked him that question. His answer: "My family put me in here to get insight and that's what I am doing!" We can see in this example that the man was *adapting*, albeit concretely. He had to get insight; so he closed his eyes and cast his "sight" inward—literally, in-sight. Psychosis and the associated behaviors are not meaningless; they are iconic.

> "Neither can embellishments of language be found without arrangement and expression of thoughts, nor can thoughts be made to shine without the light of language."
> —*Cicero (unknown source, 106–43 BCE)*

I have had the fortune to hear both John Read and Richard Bentall speak, and my recollection is that they both used the same phrase to cameo the work that they have been undertaking. There is meaning in the psychosis, and they sum up the connections that they are shining a light upon through their publications as follows: "Bad things happen and can drive you crazy!"

Currently a large amount of research has been completed and published that confirms a link between adverse life events and trauma and the later development of psychosis/schizophrenia. This research is not saying that these trauma cause the psychosis; rather, research indicates that there is a very important relationship between the two. If we examine psychiatric inpatients with psychosis, we find that 59% will have experienced either childhood sexual abuse (CSA) or childhood physical abuse (CPA) (Read, Fink, Rudegeair, Felitti, & Whitfield, 2008). When people diagnosed with schizophrenia are examined, we find that 47% have experienced emotional abuse, 51% have experienced neglect, and 41% have experienced CPA (Read, 2013; Read & Dillon, 2013). These authors are not making extreme statements. Some people consider them "radicals" in making the connections noted earlier. Perhaps if we return to the origins of the word *radical*, which has been getting some bad press of late, people can feel better about this accusation. *Radical* comes from the Latin word *radix*, which means "root." I think that we ought to go back to the fundamental root of psychosis, and that, as we shall see in the next chapter, is dissociation.

REMEMBER THE PERSON SEEKING HELP

There is no single cause of psychosis (Read & Dillon, 2013), just as there is no single gene (Owen, Cardno, & O'Donovan, 2000). Some have even gone as far as to say that there is no evidence of a genetic predisposition to psychosis and schizophrenia (Hamilton, 2008). As I have already noted, there is little to be gained in fighting from entrenched positions. At this point I want to move forward and keep in mind the needs of the person who is asking for assistance. We see that there is a growing modern literature linking adverse life events with increased risk of developing pathology-level psychosis (Read & Dillon, 2013). The strongest predictive factor for psychosis is actually poverty, or, more specifically, relative poverty (Pickett & Wilkinson, 2009). When biological psychiatrists were examining this phenomenon, they proposed that the biological illness preceded the social drift downward rather than poverty being the primary factor. However, when the relationship is examined, we see that higher rates of psychiatric disorder are found first, before poverty. Higher rates of mental disorder were also observed for those who were members of an ethnic minority, or of a colonized indigenous people (Pickett & Wilkinson, 2009). The research into this area of inquiry now consistently shows the importance of attachment and healthy interpersonal functioning in the intersubjective space. When 390 people who were diagnosed with first-episode psychosis were studied, the researchers found that they were 2.4 times more likely to have been separated from one or both parents before the age of 16 years, they were 3.1 times more likely to have had a parent die, and they were 12.3 times more likely to have had their mother die (Morgan et al., 2007). Attachment is not an optional extra for us; it is a need, and needs are nonnegotiable. Attachment is so important that when a child is confronted by abuse at the hands of a parent, the child will dissociate in order to maintain the attachment (Freyd & Birrell, 2013). The importance of a nurturing attachment is seen in the research with Romanian orphans. Romanian orphanages were known for their harsh and overcrowded conditions. After the fall of the Romanian Communist politician Nicolae Ceaușescu, the plight of the orphans came to wider international awareness. In follow-up studies it was observed that those orphans who went to foster homes and had loving, nurturing mothers had hippocampal volumes that were 10% larger than those of the children whose mothers were not so nurturing, and these children suffered more wide-ranging neurocognitive impairments (Almas et al., 2012; Bos et al., 2011; Bos, Fox, Zeanah, & Nelson, 2009; Bos, Zeanah, Smyke, Fox, & Nelson, 2010; Gleason et al., 2011; Johnson et al., 2010; Levin, Zeanah, Fox, & Nelson, 2014; Marshall, Reeb, Fox, Nelson, & Zeanah, 2008; McGoron et al., 2012; McLaughlin, Fox, Zeanah, & Nelson, 2011; McLaughlin et al., 2010; McLaughlin, Zeanah, Fox, & Nelson, 2012; Moulson, Westerlund, Fox, Zeanah, & Nelson, 2009; Nelson, Fox, & Zeanah, 2013; Nelson et al., 2007; Slopen, McLaughlin, Fox, Zeanah, & Nelson, 2012; Smyke et al., 2007; Troller-Renfree, McDermott, Nelson, Zeanah, & Fox, 2014; Windsor et al., 2011; Windsor, Moraru, Nelson, Fox, & Zeanah, 2013). In 2004, a team led by Jim van Os published its findings that experiences of childhood abuse increase the likelihood of pathology-level psychosis (Janssen et al., 2004). Over a 3-year follow-up, the team found that children who had been abused had 9 times the likelihood of developing a pathology-level psychosis, but, most important, it identified that severe abuse increased this to 48 times (Janssen et al., 2004). This demonstrates a dose–response relationship and is a highly significant finding. Although this finding was received with some skepticism, the evidence is mounting in support. A later study that examined the sample group for the presence or absence of five types of trauma also found a dose–response relationship: For those who had experienced three traumas, the increased likelihood of being psychotic was 18 times; for those who had experienced *five traumas,* that increased likelihood went up to *193 times* (Shevlin, Dorahy, & Adamson, 2007).

THE EFFECT OF TRAUMA ON THE BRAIN

If we acknowledge this important effect of exposure to trauma, then we will naturally consider the nature of the impact. We have touched upon there being physical changes to the brain; so, are there any similarities between the impact of trauma on the developing brain and the changes seen in psychosis? Original work by Read et al. reported a huge similarity between the pattern of brain abnormalities in people with schizophrenia and the changes found in the developing brains of individuals who had gone through traumatic events (Read, Perry, Moskowitz, & Connolly, 2001):

1. Overactivity of the hypothalamo-pituitary-adrenal (HPA) axis, the body's stress regulation system
2. Abnormalities in the neurotransmitter systems (especially dopaminergic systems)
3. Hippocampal damage
4. Cerebral atrophy
5. Reversed cerebral asymmetry

(Read, 2013)

TRAUMAGENIC NEURODEVELOPMENTAL MODEL OF SCHIZOPHRENIA

Read's team described a traumagenic neurodevelopmental (TN) model of schizophrenia based upon the findings (Read et al., 2001; Read, Fosse, Moskowitz, & Perry, 2014). The TN model also helped in the development of models for how cognitive impairment and the positive and negative symptom clusters (Crow, 1981, 1995) occur as a consequence of exposure to trauma. Although Read discusses the relationship between dissociation and psychosis, as we will see in the following chapter, Ross believes it is not so much an issue of either/or versus both/and, because in his opinion they are frequently describing the same thing (Ross, 2004). Following publication of the TN model there has been much interest in this area of research, and when the same team revisited the model in 2014 they noted that 125 subsequent publications indirectly supported or directly confirmed their hypothesis (Read et al., 2014). As a consequence, they made the recommendation that clinicians and researchers should endeavor at all times to gather a comprehensive history that details a person's experience of trauma, neglect, and loss. They argue that the implications for primary prevention are profound, given the role of trauma in the development of later mental conditions (Read et al., 2014). As already stated, this represents a return to the clear connection between trauma and psychosis that was acknowledged in the days of Bleuler (Bleuler, 1911; Moskowitz, 2006). Rather than the stress–diathesis model, with the emphasis being on constitutional vulnerabilities, conferred through an oligogenic model of risk (Fanous et al., 2005; Straub et al., 2002), they are proposing that the focus be on the stressor. Of 11 studies that have looked for a dose–response relationship, 8 have found it to be present (Read et al., 2008). This same group advocates a return to the *stress–vulnerability model* (Zubin & Spring, 1977), noting that the vulnerability need not be inherited genetically; the original work stated that the vulnerability may also be acquired through life events. The observation that more than 337 publications now demonstrate a link between trauma and increased likelihood to developing psychosis, and that many note a dose–response relationship, would appear to support this acquired vulnerability. Researchers such as Read and Bentall have invited the geneticists to now turn their attention toward the epigenome and cease looking for genes of small effect, to add to the oligogenic models, which in the end of it all will still require thousands of interactions to explain the increased vulnerability in only a fraction of cases. We ought also to ask, what will we do if we identify all the genes of risk in any case? Compare this to the finding that people who have experienced five traumas have a 193-times-increased likelihood of developing psychosis (Shevlin et al., 2007). The work in the area of epigenetics is increasingly opening doors to understanding how these increased levels of vulnerability might occur. To continue to insist that mental illness requires an underlying genetic vulnerability is simply no longer in alignment with the research. When Read's team looked at 41 of the most rigorous of studies in a meta-analysis, they found that people who had experienced childhood adversity were 2.8 times more likely to develop psychosis than the general public (Varese et al., 2012). In the 10 studies that looked for a dose–response relationship, nine found it to be present (Varese et al., 2012).

DOOMED FROM THE START

When we examine the nosological origins of schizophrenia, we see that psychiatry has struggled to hold out any hope for healing in the area of psychosis in general, but this is especially so for schizophrenia. Kraepelin actually included as part of the *dementia praecox* concept the statement that if someone got better, they could not really have had *dementia praecox* in the first place. This is precisely what some people have said about the Janus case study. Given how well Janus has done (now more than 7 years posttreatment and symptom- and medication-free), surely the original diagnosis could not have been correct. However, Janus was assessed with the same rigor and instruments that we used in the Irish Schizophrenia Triad Study—I completed his ratings and another colleague reviewed the Structured Clinical Interview for *DSM-IV* (SCID). Had we been recruiting for the genetic study, he would have been included. Now is the time to end our therapeutic nihilism for schizophrenia and psychosis.

HOPE SPRINGS FROM MEANING

Jim van Os, in his TEDx talk, spoke of the need for us to give people who are being given diagnoses of psychosis a "perspective of hope and the possibility of change" (van Os, 2014). This is the opposite of how many professionals are looking at psychoses. The population attributable risk for psychosis has been calculated as 33% for people who have experienced six childhood adversities while under the age of 5 years (Varese et al., 2012). This means that from a primary prevention perspective, if we can eliminate those six childhood adversities, we would reduce the incidence of psychosis by one third. By acknowledging the link between trauma and psychosis, we also naturally come to examine treatment, and where better to look than among the psychotherapies with a trauma-based formulation and a trauma-focused methodology of therapeutic intervention? Researchers exploring EMDR therapy in patients with psychosis have found that it is safe and efficacious in these people (de Bont et al., 2013). As clinicians and researchers who are working with people who are experiencing psychotic disorders, it is very important that we have a high index of suspicion for the presence of early adverse life events. Our assessers need to form a strong therapeutic rapport, listen well, and gather information in a comprehensive manner, from a position of therapeutic neutrality. Our journey continues.

REFERENCES

Almas, A. N., Degnan, K. A., Radulescu, A., Nelson, C. A., III, Zeanah, C. H., & Fox, N. A. (2012). Effects of early intervention and the moderating effects of brain activity on institutionalized children's social skills at age 8. *Proceedings of the National Academy of Sciences, 109*(Suppl. 2), 17228–17231. doi:10.1073/pnas.1121256109

American Psychiatric Association. (1980). *Quick reference to the diagnostic criteria from DSM-III.* Washington, DC: Author.

American Psychiatric Association. (2013). *Diagnostic and statistical manual of mental disorders* (5th ed.). Washington, DC: Author.

Anderson, D. (2010). Dying of nostalgia: Homesickness in the Union Army during the Civil War. *Civil War History, 56*(3), 247–282.

Anonymous. (1904). Madness in armies in the field. *British Medical Journal (Clinical Research Ed.), 2,* 30.

Babington, A. (1997). *Shell shock: A history of the changing attitudes to war neurosis.* London, England: Leo Cooper.

Bentall, R. P. (1992). *Reconstructing schizophrenia.* London, England: Routledge.

Bentall, R. P. (2003). *Madness explained: Psychosis and human nature.* London, England: Allen Lane.

Bentall, R. P. (2009). *Doctoring the mind: Is our current treatment of mental illness really any good?* New York, NY: New York University Press.

Blashfield, R. K., Keeley, J. W., Flanagan, E. H., & Miles, S. R. (2014). The cycle of classification: *DSM-I* through *DSM-5. Annual Review of Clinical Psychology, 10,* 25–51. doi:10.1146/annurev-clinpsy-032813-153639

Bleuler, E. (1906). *Affektivität, suggestibilität, paranoia* [Affectivity, suggestibility, paranoia]. Halle a. S., Germany: Marhold.

Bleuler, E. (1911). *Dementia praecox, oder Gruppe der Schizophrenien* [Dementia praecox, or the group of schizophrenias]. Leipzig, Germany: Deuticke.

Bleuler, E. (1931). *Mechanismus, vitalismus, mnemismus* [Mechanism, vitalism, and the memory as a transcendent regulative function]. Berlin, Germany: J. Springer.

Bos, K. J., Fox, N., Zeanah, C. H., & Nelson, C. A., III. (2009). Effects of early psychosocial deprivation on the development of memory and executive function. *Frontiers in Behavioral Neuroscience, 3,* 16. doi:10.3389/neuro.08.016.2009

Bos, K. J., Zeanah, C. H., Fox, N. A., Drury, S. S., McLaughlin, K. A., & Nelson, C. A. (2011). Psychiatric outcomes in young children with a history of institutionalization. *Harvard Review of Psychiatry, 19*(1), 15–24. doi:10.3109/10673229.2011.549773

Bos, K. J., Zeanah, C. H., Jr., Smyke, A. T., Fox, N. A., & Nelson, C. A., 3rd. (2010). Stereotypies in children with a history of early institutional care. *Archives of Pediatric and Adolescent Medicine, 164*(5), 406–411. doi:10.1001/archpediatrics.2010.47

Campbell, J. (2004). *The hero with a thousand faces* (Commemorative ed.). Princeton, NJ: Princeton University Press.

Carey, B. (2008, December 18). Psychiatrists revise the book of human troubles. *New York Times,* p. A1.

Conti, N. A. (2014). [Classifications in psychiatry: From Praxeos Medicae to *DSM-I*]. *Vertex, 25*(113), 73–78.

Crow, T. J. (1980). Molecular pathology of schizophrenia: More than one disease process? *British Medical Journal, 280*(6207), 66–68.

Crow, T. J. (1981). Positive and negative schizophrenia symptoms and the role of dopamine. *British Journal of Psychiatry, 139,* 251–254.

Crow, T. J. (1995). Brain changes and negative symptoms in schizophrenia. *Psychopathology, 28*(1), 18–21.

Crow, T. J., Cross, A. J., Johnstone, E. C., Longden, A., Owen, F., & Ridley, R. M. (1980). Time course of the antipsychotic effect in schizophrenia and some changes in postmortem brain and their relation to neuroleptic medication. *Advances in Biochemical Psychopharmacology, 24,* 495–503.

Crow, T. J., Frith, C. D., Johnstone, E. C., & Owens, D. G. (1980). Schizophrenia and cerebral atrophy. *Lancet, 1*(8178), 1129–1130.

Crow, T. J., & Johnstone, E. C. (1980). Dementia praecox and schizophrenia: Was Bleuler wrong? *Journal of the Royal College of Physicians, 14*(4), 238, 240.

Curran, P. S., & Miller, P. W. (2001). Psychiatric implications of chronic civilian strife or war: Northern Ireland. *Advances in Psychiatric Treatment, 7*(1), 73-80. doi:10.1192/apt.7.1.73

de Bont, P. A., van den Berg, D. P., van der Vleugel, B. M., de Roos, C., Mulder, C. L., Becker, E. S., . . . van Minnen, A. (2013). A multi-site single blind clinical study to compare the effects of prolonged exposure, eye movement desensitization and reprocessing and waiting list on patients with a current diagnosis of psychosis and comorbid posttraumatic stress disorder: Study protocol for the randomized controlled trial Treating Trauma in Psychosis. *Trials, 14,* 151. doi:10.1186/1745-6215-14-151

Duhl, D. M., Vrieling, H., Miller, K. A., Wolff, G. L., & Barsh, G. S. (1994). Neomorphic agouti mutations in obese yellow mice. *Nature Genetics, 8*(1), 59–65. doi:10.1038/ng0994-59

Erichsen, J. E. S. (1875). *On concussion of the spine, nervous shock, and other obscure injuries of the nervous system, in their clinical and medico-legal aspects.* (n.p.).

Fanous, A. H., van den Oord, E. J., Riley, B. P., Aggen, S. H., Neale, M. C., O'Neill, F. A., . . . Kendler, K. S. (2005). Relationship between a high-risk haplotype in the DTNBP1 (dysbindin) gene and clinical features of schizophrenia. *American Journal of Psychiatry, 162*(10), 1824–1832. doi:162/10/1824 [pii] 10.1176/appi.ajp.162.10.1824

First, M., & Spitzer, R. L. (2003, April 1). The *DSM*: Not perfect, but better than the alternative. *Psychiatric Times.*

Foote, B., & Park, J. (2008). Dissociative identity disorder and schizophrenia: Differential diagnosis and theoretical issues. *Current Psychiatry Reports, 10*(3), 217–222.

Freyd, J. J., & Birrell, P. (2013). *Blind to betrayal: Why we fool ourselves we aren't being fooled.* Hoboken, NJ: Wiley.

Friedman, M. J. (2007). *PTSD history and overview.* Retrieved from http://www.ptsd.va.gov/professional/pages/ptsd-overview.asp

Frith, C. D. (1992). *The cognitive neuropsychology of schizophrenia.* Hillsdale, NJ: Erlbaum.

Gleason, M. M., Zamfirescu, A., Egger, H. L., Nelson, C. A., III, Fox, N. A., & Zeanah, C. H. (2011). Epidemiology of psychiatric disorders in very young children in a Romanian pediatric setting. *European Child and Adolescent Psychiatry, 20*(10), 527–535. doi:10.1007/s00787-011-0214-0

Gonzalez, A., Mosquera, D., & Moskowitz, A. (2012). *EMDR in psychosis and severe mental disorders [EMDR en psicosis y trastorno mental severo].* Paper presented at the annual meeting of EMDR Europe Association, Madrid, Spain.

Griffins, C. (2012, February 23). Epigenetics and the influence of our genes. *TED Talks.* Retrieved from https://www.youtube.com/watch?v=JTBg6hqeuTg

Habl, G., Schmitt, A., Zink, M., von Wilmsdorff, M., Yeganeh-Doost, P., Jatzko, A., . . . Falkai, P. (2012). Decreased reelin expression in the left prefrontal cortex (BA9) in chronic schizophrenia patients. *Neuropsychobiology, 66*(1), 57–62. doi:10.1159/000337129

Hamilton, S. P. (2008). Schizophrenia candidate genes: Are we really coming up blank? *American Journal of Psychiatry, 165*(4), 420–423. doi:10.1176/appi.ajp.2008.08020218

Herodotus. (1837). [The nine books of the History of Herodotus, translated from the text of . . . T. Gaisford. With notes illustrative and critical, a geographical index, an introductory essay and a summary of the History. By P. E. Laurent.] [electronic resource]. Retrieved from https://books.google.co.uk/books?id=Mts9AAAAYAAJ&printsec =frontcover&source=gbs_ge_summary_r&cad=0 - v=onepage&q&f=false

Horowitz, M. J. (1973). Phase oriented treatment of stress response syndromes. *American Journal of Psychotherapy, 27*(4), 506–515.

Horowitz, M. J. (1975a). A cognitive model of hallucinations. *American Journal of Psychiatry, 132*(8), 789–795.

Horowitz, M. J. (1975b). Intrusive and repetitive thoughts after experimental stress. A summary. *Archives of General Psychiatry, 32*(11), 1457–1463.

Horowitz, M. J., & Becker, S. S. (1973). Cognitive response to erotic and stressful films. *Archives of General Psychiatry, 29*(1), 81–84.

Horowitz, M. J., Becker, S. S., & Malone, P. (1973). Stress, different effects on patients and nonpatients. *Journal of Abnormal Psychology, 82*(3), 547–551.

Horowitz, M. J., Becker, S. S., Moskowitz, M., & Rashid, K. (1972). Intrusive thinking in psychiatric patients after stress. *Psychological Reports, 31*(1), 235–238. doi:10.2466/pr0.1972.31.1.235

Janssen, I., Krabbendam, L., Bak, M., Hanssen, M., Vollebergh, W., de Graaf, R., & van Os, J. (2004). Childhood abuse as a risk factor for psychotic experiences. *Acta Psychiatrica Scandinavica, 109*(1), 38–45.

Jaspers, K. (1913). *Allgemeine psychopathologie* [General psychopathology]. Berlin, Germany: Springer.

Jaspers, K. (1963). *General psychopathology* (Trans. from the German 7th ed.). Manchester, England: Manchester University Press.

Johnson, D. E., Guthrie, D., Smyke, A. T., Koga, S. F., Fox, N. A., Zeanah, C. H., & Nelson, C. A., III. (2010). Growth and associations between auxology, caregiving environment, and cognition in socially deprived Romanian children randomized to foster vs ongoing institutional care. *Archives of Pediatric and Adolescent Medicine, 164*(6), 507–516. doi:10.1001/archpediatrics.2010.56

Khoury, M. J., Beaty, T. H., & Cohen, B. H. (1993). *Fundamentals of genetic epidemiology.* New York, NY: Oxford University Press.

Kingdon, D. (2004). Cognitive-behavioural therapy for psychosis. *British Journal of Psychiatry, 184*, 85–86; author reply 86.

Kuang, W. J., Sun, R. F., Zhu, Y. S., & Li, S. B. (2011). A new single-nucleotide mutation (rs362719) of the reelin (RELN) gene associated with schizophrenia in female Chinese Han. *Genetics and Molecular Research, 10*(3), 1650–1658. doi:10.4238/vol10-3gmr1343

Levin, A. R., Zeanah, C. H., Jr., Fox, N. A., & Nelson, C. A. (2014). Motor outcomes in children exposed to early psychosocial deprivation. *Journal of Pediatrics, 164*(1), 123–129. e1. doi:10.1016/j.jpeds.2013.09.026

Lieberman, J. (2015). *Shrinks: The untold story of psychiatry* (1st ed.). New York, NY: Little, Brown.

MacCurdy, J. T. (1918a). *The psychology of war.* New York, NY: E. P. Dutton.

MacCurdy, J. T. (1918b). *War neuroses.* Cambridge, England: Cambridge University Press.

Marshall, P. J., Reeb, B. C., Fox, N. A., Nelson, C. A., 3rd, & Zeanah, C. H. (2008). Effects of early intervention on EEG power and coherence in previously institutionalized children in Romania. *Developmental Psychopathology, 20*(3), 861—880. doi:10.1017/S0954579408000412

Martel, Y. (2011). *Life of Pi.* Edinburgh, Scotland: Canongate.

McCarthy-Jones, S. (2012). *Hearing voices: The histories, causes, and meanings of auditory verbal hallucinations.* Cambridge, England: Cambridge University Press.

McDougall, W. (1935). *The energies of men: A study of the fundamentals of dynamic psychology* (3rd ed.). (n.p.).

McGoron, L., Gleason, M. M., Smyke, A. T., Drury, S. S., Nelson, C. A., 3rd, Gregas, M. C., . . . Zeanah, C. H. (2012). Recovering from early deprivation: Attachment mediates effects of caregiving on psychopathology. *Journal of the American Academy of Child and Adolescent Psychiatry, 51*(7), 683–693. doi:10.1016/j.jaac.2012.05.004

McLaughlin, K. A., Fox, N. A., Zeanah, C. H., & Nelson, C. A. (2011). Adverse rearing environments and neural development in children: The development of frontal electroencephalogram asymmetry. *Biological Psychiatry, 70*(11), 1008–1015. doi:10.1016/j.biopsych.2011.08.006

McLaughlin, K. A., Fox, N. A., Zeanah, C. H., Sheridan, M. A., Marshall, P., & Nelson, C. A. (2010). Delayed maturation in brain electrical activity partially explains the association between early environmental deprivation and symptoms of attention-deficit/hyperactivity disorder. *Biological Psychiatry, 68*(4), 329–336. doi:10.1016/j.biopsych.2010.04.005

McLaughlin, K. A., Zeanah, C. H., Fox, N. A., & Nelson, C. A. (2012). Attachment security as a mechanism linking foster care placement to improved mental health outcomes in previously institutionalized children. *Journal of Child Psychology and Psychiatry, 53*(1), 46–55. doi:10.1111/j.1469-7610.2011.02437.x

Medical 203, Office of the Surgeon General, Army Service Forces War Department Technical Bulletin. (1946). Nomenclature of psychiatric disorders and reactions. *Journal of Clinical Psychology, 2,* 289–296.

Metcalf, T. (1940). *War neurosis in the civil population* (An address delivered to the clergy, ministers, doctors and teachers of Keighley). London, England: Epworth Press.

Morgan, C., Kirkbride, J., Leff, J., Craig, T., Hutchinson, G., McKenzie, K., . . . Fearon, P. (2007). Parental separation, loss and psychosis in different ethnic groups: A case-control study. *Psychological Medicine, 37*(4), 495–503. doi:10.1017/S00332917060 09330

Moskowitz, A. (2006, February). *Pierre Janet's influence on Bleuler's concept of schizophrenia.* Paper presented at the Trauma, Dissoziation, Persönlichkeit, Pierre Janets Beiträge zur modernen Psychiatrie, Psychologie und Psychotherapie, Lengerich.

Moskowitz, A., Schäfer, I., & Dorahy, M. J. (2008). *Psychosis, trauma, and dissociation: Emerging perspectives on severe psychopathology.* Chichester, England: Wiley-Blackwell.

Moulson, M. C., Westerlund, A., Fox, N. A., Zeanah, C. H., & Nelson, C. A. (2009). The effects of early experience on face recognition: An event-related potential study of institutionalized children in Romania. *Child Development, 80*(4), 1039–1056. doi:10.1111/j.1467-8624.2009.01315.x

Myers, C. S. (1940). *Shell shock in France, 1914–18.* Cambridge, England: Cambridge University Press.

Nelson, C. A., 3rd, Fox, N. A., & Zeanah, C. H., Jr. (2013). Anguish of the abandoned child. *Scientific American, 308*(4), 62–67.

Nelson, C. A., 3rd, Zeanah, C. H., Fox, N. A., Marshall, P. J., Smyke, A. T., & Guthrie, D. (2007). Cognitive recovery in socially deprived young children: The Bucharest Early Intervention Project. *Science, 318*(5858), 1937–1940. doi:10.1126/science.1143921

Owen, M. J., Cardno, A. G., & O'Donovan, M. C. (2000). Psychiatric genetics: Back to the future. *Molecular Psychiatry*, 5(1), 22–31.

Pembrey, M. E., Bygren, L. O., Kaati, G., Edvinsson, S., Northstone, K., Sjostrom, M., . . . Team, A. S. (2006). Sex-specific, male-line transgenerational responses in humans. *European Journal of Human Genetics*, 14(2), 159–166. doi:10.1038/sj.ejhg.5201538

Pembrey, M. E., Saffery, R., & Bygren, L. O. (2014). Human transgenerational responses to early-life experience: Potential impact on development, health and biomedical research. *Journal of Medical Genetics*, 51(9), 563–572. doi:10.1136/jmedgenet-2014-102577

Pickett, K. E., & Wilkinson, R. G. (2009). Greater equality and better health. *British Medical Journal*, 339, b4320. doi:10.1136/bmj.b4320

Raftery, J. (2003). *Marks of war: War neurosis and the legacy of Kokoda*. Adelaide, Australia: Lythrum Press.

Read, J. (2013). *Childhood adversity and psychosis*. Retrieved from https://www.youtube.com/watch?v=Y6do5bkUEys

Read, J., & Dillon, J. (Eds.). (2013). *Models of madness: Psychological, social, and biological approaches to psychosis* (2nd ed.). New York, NY: Routledge.

Read, J., Fink, P. J., Rudegeair, T., Felitti, V., & Whitfield, C. L. (2008). Child maltreatment and psychosis: A return to a genuinely integrated bio-psycho-social model. *Clinical Schizophrenia and Related Psychoses*, 2(3), 235–254.

Read, J., Fosse, R., Moskowitz, A., & Perry, B. (2014). The traumagenic neurodevelopmental model of psychosis revisited. *Neuropsychiatry*, 4(1), 65–79.

Read, J., Perry, B. D., Moskowitz, A., & Connolly, J. (2001). The contribution of early traumatic events to schizophrenia in some patients: A traumagenic neurodevelopmental model. *Psychiatry*, 64(4), 319–345.

Reid, F. (2010). *Broken men: Shell shock, treatment and recovery in Britain, 1914–1930*. London, England: Continuum.

Romme, M., & Escher, S. (1993). *Accepting voices*. London, England: MIND Publications.

Ross, C. A. (2004). *Schizophrenia: Innovations in diagnosis and treatment*. Binghamton, NY: Haworth Maltreatment and Trauma.

Ross, C. A. (2007). *The trauma model: A solution to the problem of comorbidity in psychiatry*. Richardson, TX: Manitou Communications.

Ross, C. A., & Halpern, N. (2009). *Trauma model therapy: A treatment approach for trauma, dissociation and complex comorbidity*. Richardson, TX: Manitou Communications.

Sapolsky, R. M., Uno, H., Rebert, C. S., & Finch, C. E. (1990). Hippocampal damage associated with prolonged glucocorticoid exposure in primates. *Journal of Neuroscience*, 10(9), 2897–2902.

Sargant, W. (1976). *Battle for the mind: A physiology of conversion and brain-washing*. London, England: Heinemann.

Schneider, K. (1950). [Suicide and schizophrenia as service-connected liabilities in veterans; opinions in three cases]. *Nervenarzt*, 21(11), 480–483.

Schneider, K. (1957). [Primary & secondary symptoms in schizophrenia]. *Fortschritte de Neurologie Psychiatrie*, 25(9), 487–490.

Shapiro, F. (2001). *Eye movement desensitization and reprocessing (EMDR): Basic principles, protocols, and procedures* (2nd ed.). New York, NY: Guilford Press.

Shapiro, F. (2007). EMDR, adaptive information processing, and case conceptualization. *Journal of EMDR Practice and Research*, 1(2), 68–87.

Shevlin, M., Dorahy, M. J., & Adamson, G. (2007). Trauma and psychosis: An analysis of the National Comorbidity Survey. *American Journal of Psychiatry*, 164(1), 166–169.

Shifman, S., Johannesson, M., Bronstein, M., Chen, S. X., Collier, D. A., Craddock, N. J., . . . Darvasi, A. (2008). Genome-wide association identifies a common variant in the reelin gene that increases the risk of schizophrenia only in women. *PLoS Genetics*, 4(2), e28. doi:07-PLGE-RA-0891 [pii] 10.1371/journal.pgen.0040028

Slopen, N., McLaughlin, K. A., Fox, N. A., Zeanah, C. H., & Nelson, C. A. (2012). Alterations in neural processing and psychopathology in children raised in institutions. *Archives of General Psychiatry*, 69(10), 1022–1030. doi:10.1001/archgenpsychiatry.2012.444

Smyke, A. T., Koga, S. F., Johnson, D. E., Fox, N. A., Marshall, P. J., Nelson, C. A., . . . Group, B. C. (2007). The caregiving context in institution-reared and family-reared infants and toddlers in Romania. *Journal of Child Psychology and Psychiatry*, 48(2), 210–218. doi:10.1111/j.1469-7610.2006.01694.x

Solomon, R. M., & Shapiro, F. (2008). EMDR and the adaptive information processing model. *Journal of EMDR Practice and Research*, 2(4), 315–325.

Straub, R. E., Jiang, Y., MacLean, C. J., Ma, Y., Webb, B. T., Myakishev, M. V., . . . Kendler, K. S. (2002). Genetic variation in the 6p22.3 gene DTNBP1, the human ortholog of the mouse dysbindin gene, is associated with schizophrenia. *American Journal of Human Genetics*, 71(2), 337–348. doi:S0002-9297(07)60479-0 [pii] 10.1086/341750

Sweatt, J. D. (2009). Experience-dependent epigenetic modifications in the central nervous system. *Biological Psychiatry*, 65(3), 191–197. doi:10.1016/j.biopsych.2008.09.002

Tarrier, N., Lewis, S., Haddock, G., Bentall, R., Drake, R., Kinderman, P., . . . Dunn, G. (2004). Cognitive-behavioural therapy in first-episode and early schizophrenia. 18-month follow-up of a randomised controlled trial. *British Journal of Psychiatry*, 184, 231–239.

Teixeira, C. M., Martin, E. D., Sahun, I., Masachs, N., Pujadas, L., Corvelo, A., . . . Soriano, E. (2011). Overexpression of reelin prevents the manifestation of behavioral phenotypes related to schizophrenia and bipolar disorder. *Neuropsychopharmacology*, 36(12), 2395–2405. doi:10.1038/npp.2011.153

The Guardian. (2007, February 21). [Corrections & clarifications column.] *Soldiers shot at dawn honoured after 90 years*. Retrieved from http://www.theguardian.com/uk/2007/feb/19/military.uknews4

Troller-Renfree, S., McDermott, J. M., Nelson, C. A., Zeanah, C. H., & Fox, N. A. (2014). The effects of early foster care intervention on attention biases in previously institutionalized children in Romania. *Developmental Science*, 18(5), 713–722. doi:10.1111/desc.12261

Tsankova, N., Renthal, W., Kumar, A., & Nestler, E. J. (2007). Epigenetic regulation in psychiatric disorders. *Nature Reviews Neuroscience*, 8(5), 355–367. doi:http://www.nature.com/nrn/journal/v8/n5/suppinfo/nrn2132_S1.html

van Os, J. (2014). *Connecting to madness*. Retrieved March 22, 2015, from https://www.youtube.com/watch?v=sE3gxX5CiW0

Varese, F., Smeets, F., Drukker, M., Lieverse, R., Lataster, T., Viechtbauer, W., . . . Bentall, R. P. (2012). Childhood adversities increase the risk of psychosis: A meta-analysis of patient-control, prospective- and cross-sectional cohort studies. *Schizophrenia Bulletin*, 38(4), 661–671. doi:10.1093/schbul/sbs050

Weaver, I. C. G., Cervoni, N., Champagne, F. A., D'Alessio, A. C., Sharma, S., Seckl, J. R., . . . Meaney, M. J. (2004). Epigenetic programming by maternal behavior. *Nature Neuroscience*, 7, 847–854.

Wedenoja, J., Tuulio-Henriksson, A., Suvisaari, J., Loukola, A., Paunio, T., Partonen, T., . . . Peltonen, L. (2010). Replication of association between working memory and reelin, a potential modifier gene in schizophrenia. *Biological Psychiatry*, 67(10), 983–991. doi:10.1016/j.biopsych.2009.09.026

Wilson, R. M. (1916). Discussion on the soldier's heart. *Proceedings of the Royal Society of Medicine*, 9(Ther. Pharmacol. Sect.), 37–39.

Wilson, W. P., & Hohman, L. B. (1959). The nostalgia syndrome: With a reference to its occurrence in the Union Army in the Civil War. *Southern Medical Journal, 52,* 1449–1453.

Windsor, J., Benigno, J. P., Wing, C. A., Carroll, P. J., Koga, S. F., Nelson, C. A., 3rd, . . . Zeanah, C. H. (2011). Effect of foster care on young children's language learning. *Child Development, 82*(4), 1040–1046. doi:10.1111/j.1467-8624.2011.01604.x

Windsor, J., Moraru, A., Nelson, C. A., Fox, N. A., & Zeanah, C. H. (2013). Effect of foster care on language learning at eight years: Findings from the Bucharest Early Intervention Project. *Journal of Child Language, 40*(3), 605–627. doi:10.1017/S0305000912000177

World Health Organization. (1993). *The ICD-10 classification of mental and behavioural disorders: Diagnostic criteria for research.* Geneva, Switzerland: Author.

Yang, X. B., Kang, C., Liu, H., & Yang, J. (2013). Association study of the reelin (RELN) gene with Chinese Va schizophrenia. *Psychiatric Genetics, 23*(3), 138. doi:10.1097/YPG.0b013e32835d705c

Yehuda, R., Daskalakis, N. P., Lehrner, A., Desarnaud, F., Bader, H. N., Makotkine, I., . . . Meaney, M. J. (2014). Influences of maternal and paternal PTSD on epigenetic regulation of the glucocorticoid receptor gene in Holocaust survivor offspring. *American Journal of Psychiatry, 171*(8), 872–880. doi:10.1176/appi.ajp.2014.13121571

Zubin, J., & Spring, B. (1977). Vulnerability—a new view of schizophrenia. *Journal of Abnormal Psychology, 86*(2), 103–126.

TWO

The Phenomenology of Dissociation, Psychosis, and Schizophrenia

Paul William Miller and Remy Aquarone

Intention: *To equip the reader with a working knowledge of dissociation and schizophrenia from a phenomenological perspective.*

PHENOMENOLOGY

In this chapter we look at dissociation, psychosis, and schizophrenia from a phenomenological standpoint. Phenomenology is the lens through which psychiatrists look at mental illness, and psychiatry as a specialty has looked at people in this way from its earliest days. Rather than looking at illness/disorder through definitive tests and specialized investigations, as other medical specialties do, we look at mental health through the person's report of what he or she is experiencing (Bürgy, 2008; Wing, 1983). In other medical specialties we name these experiences *symptoms*; in psychiatry/mental health we refer to them as *phenomena*. This emphasizes that we are framing mental disorder as *syndromes*, that is, groups of experiences, within a phenomenological model. Some have described the phenomenological approach to schizophrenia as analogous to a physician diagnosing a "cough disorder" (Kendell, 1975).

NOSOLOGY

However, before we expand upon the phenomenological aspect of our journey we must note the nosological limitations that psychiatric diagnoses have. In 1913 Jaspers built the foundation of psychiatric *nosology* (i.e., the classifying of diseases) on the separation of neuroses and psychoses (Jaspers, 1913). He stated that whereas neuroses represented a psychologically understandable disorder, psychoses were the result of *somatic (physical) illness* and so were only explainable as a biological *process*, and as such were psychologically unintelligible. This position held sway in the minds of psychiatrists, and as a consequence little attention has been historically given to psychotherapies for the treatment of psychosis; this is now, thankfully, changing (Arseneault et al., 2011; Kim et al., 2010; Moskowitz, Schäfer, & Dorahy, 2008; Ross, 2004), with interest and research once again turning to the application of psychotherapy to psychosis in general and schizophrenia in particular (Kim et al., 2010).

THE HISTORY OF NOMENCLATURE IN MENTAL DISORDER

In mental health, *diagnoses* are groups of symptoms/phenomena that are grouped together into what we believe are valid and discrete illnesses. Psychiatrists have been the guardians of diagnosis; we are the alchemists who compound this mysterious thingamajig—or is it a thingamabob, or a hoojamaflip? The validity of this approach is now increasingly being challenged in some quarters. The British Psychological Society published a document in the United Kingdom (UK) that encouraged a fuller psychological understanding of psychosis and schizophrenia. It was critical of what is generally referred to as the *medical model* of mental disorders (Basset et al., 2014). This clarion call is a reiteration of the thoughts of those who have previously sought to abolish diagnosis in the area of mental disorders, such as Karl Menninger (Kendell, 1975). Interestingly, Karl was the brother of William C. Menninger, a psychiatrist whom we have already met on our journey through our exploration of the links between trauma, dissociation, and schizophrenia. Menninger was the director of the Psychiatry Consultants Division in the Office of the Surgeon General of the U.S. Army and was the chair of the committee that produced "Medical 203," which greatly influenced the later *International Classification of Diseases* (ICD) and *Diagnostic and Statistical Manual of Mental Disorders* (DSM) classification systems (Lieberman, 2015). The brothers appear, at least in this regard, to be at opposite ends of a spectrum, with one generating diagnostic systems and the other assuming the position of an abolitionist, in respect to diagnosis. Another influential psychiatrist in this arena spent two of his earliest professional years as a military psychiatrist: R. D. Laing. Although Laing's name is synonymous with the anti-psychiatry movement (Crossley, 1998), he was never against the application of therapeutic endeavors to ease mental suffering. His paradigm shift away from the psychiatric orthodoxy of his day was seen as heresy by many, as it shifted away from a diathesis–stress model and toward a model that placed the etiology of "mental illness" as being situated within the crucible of social, intellectual, and cultural dimensions (Crossley, 1998). The concept of people having a vulnerability to developing illness (*diathesis*) was not new in medicine. However, in regard to mental disorders the interaction between external stressors and these internal vulnerabilities was termed the *diathesis–stress model*, and this was first applied to schizophrenia in 1960 (Ingram & Luxton, 2005). Modern psychiatric thinking reflects this same paradigm. In taking a phenomenological view of dissociation and psychosis, I hope to reiterate some of the dissonance brought by Laing when he invited people to understand schizophrenia as a theoretical model and not a biological entity (Laing, 1964; Laing & Esterson, 1967). Laing believed that Jaspers was wrong to say that psychosis was unintelligible and insisted that when we listened, with the right attitude, to what people with these experiences were saying, we could find meaning in their discourse (Laing, 2010). As I wrote this I was reminded of a phrase my grandmother would often say, "there's method in his madness." It would appear she got that one from Shakespeare:

> Polonius (to himself): "There's a method to his madness . . ."
> —*Hamlet (Shakespeare, 1770, 2.2.195)*

LABELS ARE FOR JARS, NOT PEOPLE

One point that rings true with me is that all too often diagnostic labels create a false sense of comfort—a veneer of knowing where nothing much is known, or where it is at the very least a partial "knowing." Generally we believe that if we name a thing, we gain some degree of power over it; this is an ancient, archetypal theme (Campbell, 2004). This reminds me of the story about a patient who went to see a physician friend of mine. The patient was seeking more painkillers and was, with good reason, refused. On hearing this, the patient threw the doctor's paperwork across the room. When things had been de-escalated and the doctor was talking the patient through boundaries and the reasoning behind the refusal, the patient blurted out, "Well, what do you expect; I'm euthymic!" The patient had seen this in his most recent clinic letter from his treating psychiatrist and taken it as "proof" of a diseased state; ironically, it had been a declaration of the exact opposite. I myself am not taking up an abolitionist's position, as I believe diagnostic labels can be a useful characterization of the experiences being brought to us in the clinical context. However, as the meme states, labels are for jars, not for people. We must look beyond the diagnostic label and investigate the phenomenology. I believe we need to do so because the phenomena are not the problem, but are the fruit of the problem. They are the icons of the ICoNN (Indicating Cognitions of Negative Networks) model, and this model provides a methodology that helps to target the dysfunctional memory networks (DMNs) within eye movement desensitization and reprocessing (EMDR) therapy.

DISSOCIATION

For our journey through this phenomenological landscape, an expert in dissociation joins us: past president of the European Society for Trauma and Dissociation (ESTD) Remy Aquarone.
    Definition:

> The state of affairs in which two or more mental processes
> co-exist without becoming connected or integrated.
> *(Rycroft, 1968)*

Every day, dissociation—or *altered consciousness*, as it is now more generally called—is something we all engage with even if we are unaware of doing so. There is a pleasurable side to this phenomenon as well as, at times, an appropriately defensive reaction needed in order to protect us from becoming overwhelmed.

Let me give you a few examples of altered consciousness:

The ability to drive on a familiar road and let your mind wander on other matters

A lot of drivers can find themselves doing this. Part of them is driving on the road, and another part might be thinking about a problem at work or thinking of a holiday that lies ahead. When something makes them focus completely on the road ahead, such as a red light, several miles may have gone by without them apparently being aware of this.

The ability to be absorbed in a film or play

The pleasure of the experience is increased by only focusing on the play or the actors, without any apparent awareness of your surroundings. You become, in a sense, lost in the story. At the end of the film or play, the lights go on and you reorient yourself to the room, to people around you.

In both of these examples the individuals have the element of choice and the ability to reconnect with surroundings as appropriate.

The ability to protect yourself from overwhelming psychic pain

This occurs more at an unconscious level, as a means of protecting yourself from becoming overwhelmed or traumatized. An example of this might be watching a newsreel of starving children on the African continent. You only take in what you can tolerate emotionally and filter out the gruesome details; otherwise you would not survive the secondary trauma. Ambulance drivers are an example of a professional group that needs to do this to some degree to survive and function. This is not a lack of compassion but a means of continuing to be present in a functional way that allows these professionals to deal with crisis. In the example of the starving children, there is a temporary split between the cognitive functioning and the emotional impact of the stimuli.

The ability to bypass fear

This occurs at a more primitive, animal level (similar to an involuntary muscle that gets you to withdraw your hand from a hot iron before you have had time to think what action is needed to minimize the burn). An example of this would be a mother who, when in charge of her small child, rushes up to a threatening adult (*out of character*) and finds herself aggressively telling the person to get the hell away. The need to protect her young bypasses her normally passive personality with no thinking time involved. Only afterward, when the danger is gone, might she tremble, reacting emotionally with the realization of what she had done.

> "Pathological dissociation is a post-traumatic defence
> mobilized by a person as protection from overwhelming
> pain and trauma."
> *(Ross, Norton, & Wozney, 1989)*

Extreme dissociation is the most primitive form of survival, where a human being is confronted with events that are impossible to process. For the most part this is as a result of early childhood trauma (emotional, physical, and/or sexual abuse). At its root is the disruption of the most basic survival need for an attachment to another human being. This need for attachment is innate, which is to say we are born with it, and is similar to attachment in other animals, such as ducklings that, without a mother, will turn to the first moving object—human or animal.

From birth, the baby's need to attach to an adult is paramount. At that point in time there is no distinction between a good or bad attachment. It is much more basic. The primitive, innate need is for an attachment of any kind in order to survive. Thus, where the baby's experience fluctuates between abandonment (e.g., left alone, no stimulation, no ability to gain a sense of self, no chance to regulate his or her own affect, experiencing this like being in an abyss) and periods of overstimulation (through physical or sexual abuse), the attachment is with the active overstimulation. This can lead, in adulthood, to individuals who only feel attached within abusive relationships; at other times they may be left with a deep sense of pointlessness and strong suicidal ideation. More often than not, extreme forms of dissociation such as dissociative identity disorder (DID) occur as a result of a person unconsciously needing to separate out different experiences from conscious thought; these separated-out experiences have often occurred in their childhood. Let me give you an example.

A 4-year-old girl is brought up by her single parent. During the week he (the father) does everything you would want a good parent to do: He makes sure she is fed and clothed, and keeps to a good routine. He cares for her emotional well-being, reading to her at bedtimes, comforting her when she is distressed, and so forth. Every Friday on his way home from work, he gets drunk in a pub, comes home, and abuses her. In order to keep her attachment to (in this case) her good father, she has to separate those two experiences. This is not a conscious process. She splits those two experiences. As soon as he gets home she can immediately know which state of mind he is in and can switch in order to fit in with what is needed. If he comes home drunk, she dissociates into the little girl who will deal with the abuse. This will be kept very separate from the little girl who deals with the father during the week. Dissociation works because there is no leakage between the two. There is an amnesic wall between the two parts of her. In this case the dissociation is adaptive, as it allows the girl to maintain her attachment to her father. This is consistent with the betrayal trauma theory of Jennifer J. Freyd that was first outlined in 1996 (Freyd & Birrell, 2013), which states that the degree of dissociation, as an adaptation, can be predicted by the level of threat that is being brought to the person's system of attachment (DePrince & Freyd, 2014). In this case, if we presume that the father is the only attachment figure for the girl, the level of dissociation is likely to be profound, as the risk to the system of attachment is high.

As time goes on, the part of her present at nonabusive times becomes more of a functional, nonemotive aspect of her being. The role of this part is to meet the need to keep up the appearance of "normality," termed the apparent normal part (ANP) in the structural dissociation model (Nijenhuis, Van der Hart, & Steele, 2004). The part that deals with the abuse, termed the emotional part (EP), has to absorb the emotional trauma of her psychological and physical state (Nijenhuis et al., 2004). None of the emotional trauma is processed at the time, and in effect this brings about an "arrested development." In the EMDR therapy paradigm, the adaptive information processing (AIP) model refers to this unprocessed traumatic material as a dysfunctional memory network (DMN) (Shapiro & Maxfield, 2002). Multiple traumatic experiences can lead to multiple splits occurring in an attempt to deal with multiple situations that are impossible to process. This would lead to a system of EPs that all relate in some manner to the ANP.

Historical Context

The last few years have seen an exponential growth in the knowledge of, acceptance of, and interest in extreme symptoms of dissociation and dissociative disorders (Armstrong, Putnam, Carlson, Libero, & Smith, 1997; Dorahy, 2010; Frewen & Lanius, 2006; Heber, Fleisher, Ross, & Stanwick, 1989; Johnston, Dorahy, Courtney, Bayles, & O'Kane, 2009; Knipe, 2015; Lanius, Paulsen, & Corrigan, 2014; Moskowitz, 2004; Moskowitz et al., 2008; Putnam et al., 1996; Ross, 1991; Ross et al., 2008; van der Hart & Dorahy, 2006; Watkins & Watkins, 1990; Xiao et al., 2006). This has especially been the case within the medical world, which, for years, has either dismissed the condition as "attention seeking," "fantasy," and "suggested by therapists," or, if it has been accepted, has seen it as an extremely rare condition that most clinicians are unlikely to encounter over their working lives.

Yet, this condition has been recognized in both diagnostic psychiatric manuals for more than 30 years (currently the *ICD-10* and *DSM-5*). Furthermore, most studies place the incidence within the general population with a prevalence of between 1% and 3%, compared to 1.1% for schizophrenia, although this can vary up to three-fold depending on the diagnostic criteria. In studies of the general population, a prevalence rate for DID of 1% to 3% of the population has been described (Johnson, Cohen, Kasen, & Brook, 2006; Ross, 1991; Sar, Akyuz, & Dogan, 2007; Waller & Ross, 1997). So why is it the case that the diagnosis of DID is so controversial? I believe there are a number of reasons that contribute to the reluctance to accept this condition within our culture. It is only relatively recently that our culture has accepted the notion of trauma and abuse existing within our "developed" society. For a long time, abuse was considered an abhorrence that existed only in third-world countries. Gradually it was accepted as occurring within poor sections of our society, and now as a society we finally accept that abuse can occur in all sections of the population—celebrities and noncelebrities alike. Furthermore, within the psychoanalytic fraternity all reported occurrences of abuse used to be analyzed as childhood fantasies having to do with the child's Oedipal conflicts. This was still the case 10 years ago; a lot has since changed.

Both Freud and psychiatry may have contributed to this denial of reality. Charcot and, more specifically, Pierre Janet were pioneers in the knowledge, acceptance, and treatment of dissociation (Janet, 1907). Freud studied under both of them. Furthermore, early on in his career Freud accepted the stories he was hearing from his adult patients about their childhood traumas. However, cultural and professional career reasons made him shift his focus away from an acceptance that abuse and incest were taking place in Austrian society. This was because of the realization that he would need to be cautious in the Austrian society of his day, which was not prepared to accept that such abuse was occurring any more than our society has been in the past. A lot has been written about Freud's change, his expansion of the notion of a child's development through the stages that included the Oedipal stage, which thus required analyzing patients in terms of their sexual fantasies toward their parents. This, unfortunately, allowed the denial of abuse to be made with alacrity.

Last, in order to accept the notion of dissociation, clinicians need to accept the idea that none of us can ever be certain that our sense of identity and self is absolute. It fluctuates depending on the environment and our individual life circumstances. In the face of overwhelming trauma, our sense of identity often becomes redundant, and most people experience a temporary loss of identity. Trauma and dissociation are intimately related, as we have noted, and as we shall now see, so too are trauma and psychosis (Moskowitz et al., 2008).

PSYCHOSIS AND SCHIZOPHRENIA

Schizophrenia is viewed as the most serious syndrome among the psychotic disorders. Its impact and psychiatric morbidity can be substantial, and despite more than 100 years of experience in treating schizophrenia, it is still only a minority of individuals who make a full recovery (Kurihara, 2010). Schizophrenia is termed a severe enduring mental illness (SMI), and although the diagnostic boundaries have extended and retracted over the years the core disturbances remain conceptualized as disorders of thinking, of perception, and of the emotions. It is accepted as having a heavy burden, with significant effects on those suffering from the experience of psychosis, as well as upon their families and caregivers (Perlick et al., 2010).

Schizophrenia as a Dissociative Disorder

Nosologically we are being invited to repatriate schizophrenia (Scharfetter, Moerbt, & Wing, 1976) into the spectrum of disorders that it was associated with when Bleuler first hypothesized it (Bleuler, 1911, 1950)—in other words, to return it to a category of disorders that can be formulated within a dissociative model (Moskowitz et al., 2008). When we examine the research of the historical figures who were active at the time the schizophrenia "brand" was created, we find that the core concepts of Bleuler's schizophrenia (Bleuler, 1911, 1950) have a stronger relationship with dissociation theory and parallel the work of Janet and Paulhan rather than the work of Freud, whose model was focused on repression (Moskowitz et al., 2008). It is notable that at the time Bleuler coined the term *the schizophrenias*, there were in existence four other terms that all drew explicitly on the dissociation model in an attempt to explain the phenomena as a diagnostic entity: Wernicke's *sejunctionpsychose*, or "dissociation psychosis"; Otto Gross's *dementia sejunctiva*, or "insanity of dissociation"; Stransky's *dissoziationsprozess*, or "process of dissociation"; and Zweig's *dementia dissecans*, or "insanity of dissociation" (Moskowitz et al., 2008). It has also been proposed that psychoanalyst C. G. Jung was "reading Freud with Janetian eyes" (Haule, 1984, p. 649) as he attempted to discuss schizophrenia. Jung's perspective is important to note, as

Freud was said to have been at the peak of his influence on Bleuler during the writing of his seminal book (1907–1908) *Dementia praecox, oder Gruppe der Schizophrenien* (Bleuler, 1911), through his relationship with Jung. As Moskowitz observes, the channel for Freud's influence over Bleuler was his contact with Jung, who was at that time fascinated with Freud (Moskowitz, 2006; Moskowitz et al., 2008). "Jung often wrote to Freud during this time about conversations he and Bleuler had had about Freud's ideas" (Moskowitz, 2006, p. 2). Although Bleuler described his concept of "the schizophrenias" as being a result of the application of the ideas of Freud to Kraepelin's *dementia praecox*, it appears to owe more to Janet's ideas and dissociation. However, because of the interpersonal dynamic between the men, Freud got the credit rather than Janet (Moskowitz et al., 2008). The detailed examination of the historical record of the time by researchers such as Moskowitz has done a great deal to set the record straight.

Historical Context

First we need to take a brief historical step back. The journey to conceptualize schizophrenia really begins to gather pace when Emil Kraepelin popularizes the diagnosis of *dementia praecox*, which first started the nosological journey that leads to an understanding of what modern-day schizophrenia is (Kraepelin, 1881; Kraepelin, Barclay, & Robertson, 1919). Bleuler develops it further and coins the term *the schizophrenias* (Bleuler, 1911, 1950). In naming it in the plural he was underlining the notion that this was a group of disorders and not a single disease entity. Perhaps we now see in retrospect that schizophrenia's definition was more influenced by the gregarious personality and proselytizing of Freud, compared to the quieter and less avuncular Janet, whose model was fundamentally dissociative (Moskowitz, 2005, 2006; Moskowitz et al., 2008). Sometimes research and conventional science take a path that has more to do with who is speaking than with what is said.

Schizophrenia and Genetic Epidemiology

As modern psychiatry has sought to deal with the nosological issues of schizophrenia, genetic epidemiology has energized the drive to elucidate a clearer, more workable diagnostic *phenotype*, which is defined as the set of observable characteristics of an individual resulting from the interaction of its genetic code (genotype) with the environment. These genetic epidemiological studies have found that people with schizophrenia, or a poor-outcome schizoaffective disorder, appear to have the same disorder from a genetic viewpoint (Kendler, Maguire, Gruenberg, & O'Hare, 1993; Kendler, McGuire, et al., 1993; Kendler, Spitzer, & Williams, 1989). The diagnostic difficulty experienced with schizophrenia is similar to that with all mental illness, as the current classification systems are phenomenological, as we have already observed. This challenge of obtaining "good enough" diagnostic criteria for mental illness was still very much with us as we entered the new millennium. The "Millennium Article" in *Molecular Psychiatry* reminded readers that psychiatric illness phenotypes are still best viewed as syndromes rather than clearly demarcated disease entities

(Owen, Cardno, & O'Donovan, 2000). However, even with these difficulties, studies utilizing operational research diagnoses have reportedly been success-ful in demonstrating that genes have a role to play in the current syndromes defined by current psychiatric models (Owen et al., 2000), and this is argued to support the validity of applying the operational approach to phenomena. However, as the genetic model becomes increasingly complex, there has yet to be a clear associated pathophysiology described and agreed upon that links the genes to the ultimate expression of the mental disorder. The models for the genetic transmission of schizophrenia evolved from a single-major-locus model to a better fit, polygenic modeling of which there are two types: the oligogenic model (where the discrete number of loci is described) and the multifactorial polygenic model (where there are a large unspecified number of loci). None of the models in and of themselves is a "best fit" for schizophrenia. However, a combination of the single-major-locus model with components of the multifac-torial polygenic model is the most precise, especially when epistasis is included in the modeling (Farone, Taylor, & Tsuang, 2002). *Epistasis* is a situation where the expression of one gene is modified by one or more genes that assort inde-pendently (i.e., gene–gene interaction) (Khoury, Beaty, & Cohen, 1993). This is in addition to any physiological and epigenetic effects of cortisol that have been discussed by researchers such as Sapolsky (Sapolsky, Uno, Rebert, & Finch, 1990) and Weaver (Weaver et al., 2004).

Schizophrenia on the Emerald Isle

As I have noted, research into the genetic epidemiology of schizophrenia fuels the study and evolution of the diagnostic criteria for schizophrenia. The case-controlled epidemiological family study led by Professor Ken-neth Kendler, the Roscommon Family Study, was completed in Ireland be-cause of the relative genetic homogeneity of its population. This made the study easier to complete, as it avoided the issue of population stratification (Miller, 2007). Kendler observes that although the diagnostic boundaries of schizophrenia have expanded and contracted several times from the time of Emil Kraepelin (Kendler, Maguire, Gruenberg, et al., 1993), most diagnostic systems do agree on the "core" group of symptoms. This core group includes *negative symptoms, auditory hallucinations, bizarre delusions, the absence of promi-nent affective components*, and *a poor functional outcome*. So-called "marginal" cases, such as "brief psychosis with schizophrenia-like symptoms and good outcome," have been described, and these are not easily categorized within existing classification systems. Historically the *DSM-II* included most of them under the heading of schizophrenia, whereas the *DSM-III* and the *DSM-III-R* tended to include these cases in categories such as schizophreniform disorder (Miller, 2007). In the most recent diagnostic rendering, the *DSM-5* (American Psychiatric Association, 2013), the previously described subtypes of schizo-phrenia have been omitted, and it is believed that *ICD-11* is set to do the same. The argument for removal is that they lack reliability, prognostic validity, and pragmatic implications for treatment (Howes & Kapur, 2014), so why retain them? In these newest diagnostic iterations, rather than utilizing the previous subtypes, clinicians will be encouraged to use a multidimensional assessment covering the severity of positive, negative, affective, and cognitive symptoms (Howes & Kapur, 2014). This seems an interesting, if not counterintuitive, approach, as Bleuler himself considered schizophrenia to be a *group* of heterogeneous disorders, hence the name *the schizophrenias*—plural. Indeed, recent research looking at groups of genetic differences rather than single genes has concluded that schizophrenia is a group of heritable disorders, which could be best characterized as a number of discrete clinical syndromes (Arnedo et al., 2014). Members of this research group believe they are capable of identifying eight syndromes that have their own genetic patterns (Arnedo et al., 2014). Thus, thinking appears inconsistent between the phenomenologists and the genetic epidemiologists. I believe that this apparent inconsistency may be epistemological, as current diagnostic "labels" are generalizations, whereas phenomenological characterizations are the individual's experiences of disorder of the intersubjective—distortions of consciousness and being.

DISSOCIATION, PSYCHOSIS, AND SCHIZOPHRENIA

If we bear in mind that schizophrenia is a group of disorders, consisting of closely related syndromes, I believe that we can adopt a paradigm where it is reasonable to assume that some of these syndromes are more dissociative than others. Furthermore, by recognizing that there is a dose–response relationship between exposure to trauma and psychosis (Laferriere-Simard & Lecomte, 2010), we can understand that the greater the trauma exposure has been, the more dissociative the syndrome. If we return to the nosological roots of schizophrenia, within the dissociation model, it is logical therefore to deduce that psychotherapy will have a range of effectiveness for the different forms of schizophrenia. Experts such as Ross have flagged the phenomenological closeness of the dissociative disorders and schizophrenia and found that two-thirds of people who meet the diagnostic criteria for DID also meet structured interview criteria for schizoaffective disorder or schizophrenia (Ross, 2004). Individuals in this group have been found to respond well to the type of psychotherapy utilized in dissociative disorders, and the result is the long-term remission of their psychoses. On this basis Ross argues for the classification of a subphenotype of schizophrenia that he refers to as *dissociative schizophrenia*. A similar assertion is made by a French group of experts that proposes the designation *reactive dissociative psychosis* (or *La psychose dissociative réactive* in French) (Laferriere-Simard & Lecomte, 2010) in order to put an emphasis on the traumatic etiology of the condition and the principal role dissociation has in these experiences. As a consequence of these phenotypes having causative environmental factors, they ought to be amenable to psychotherapeutic intervention. Ross has stated that his argument is in part a political and strategic one, as he notes that patients with a diagnosis of schizophrenia are much less likely to receive psychotherapy of the type that is known to benefit patients with dissociative disorders (Ross, 2004, 2013). Both of the chapter's authors have witnessed this in our clinical and advocacy work. Ross states that the concept of dissociative schizophrenia is consistent with the literature stemming from the time of Eugen Bleuler (Bleuler, 1911) and according to the *DSM-IV-R* (American Psychiatric Association & American Psychiatric Association Task Force on *DSM-IV*, 1994, 2000), DID and schizophrenia are not mutually exclusive. He has proposed diagnostic criteria for dissociative schizophrenia, and found that 25% to 40% of those people who currently have a diagnosis of schizophrenia would meet his criteria for dissociative schizophrenia (Ross, 2004)—these criteria are outlined in full in Chapter 5. So why is this even important? The French group proposes that reactive dissociative psychosis results when exposure to traumatic events becomes overwhelming for an individual. Based on several case studies and theoretical assumptions building on the concept of dissociative psychosis, van der Hart claimed that psychotic features mitigate or would disappear once the traumatic origins have been identified (van der Hart & Nijenhuis, 1993). Ross (2004) makes a similar assertion, and this is also what I have found in my clinical practice with psychosis (Miller, 2010, 2014). Treating schizophrenia by formulating it within a trauma and dissociation paradigm allows for the application of EMDR therapy, which is one of the current international gold-standard psychotherapies for posttraumatic stress disorder (PTSD). The outcomes to date have been encouraging (Kim et al., 2010; Miller, 2010, 2014), but much more work is needed. Of course, if we continue to hold to the intention of having a "third space," we avoid the internecine violence of pitching talking therapy against drug therapy in an "either/ or" way and can embrace a "both/and" approach to the problem of treatment. This allows for a complete biopsychosocial treatment plan.

Something Doesn't Feel Right

Josef Parnas (2012) has expertly discussed the core Gestalt of schizophrenia (Henriksen & Parnas, 2012; Parnas, 2011, 2012). Epistemologically, the concept of mental illness in general and of schizophrenia in particular is inadequate because of the difficulty of defining what consciousness is. As mental illness is currently characterized within a phenomenologically based diagnostic system, and therefore founded on descriptions of a person's experience, belief, and expression, these are correspondingly abnormalities of consciousness; thus, the question of the nature of consciousness ought to be at the very heart of the concept of schizophrenia. An attempt to define the abnormality of consciousness has been present from the earliest days of experts wrestling to define *dementia praecox*/schizophrenia.

Rümke, a Dutch psychiatrist, talked of a characteristic "schizophrenic taint" and coined the phrase *praecox-feeling* (*praecox Gefühl*). He acknowledged that for him to say that certain phenomena were characteristic of schizophrenia, but only if they had a characteristic schizophrenic taint, was a tautology. Interestingly, although he accepted that his statement was a scientific absurdity, he noted that it is a concept that the experienced clinician is no stranger to (Parnas, 2012). I believe that most experienced clinicians still understand what he is saying here. This "schizophrenic taint" is a phenomenological X-factor, and it can be best thought of as a core Gestalt of schizophrenia (Parnas, 2012). We can define *Gestalt* as "a salient unity or intrinsic organisation of diverse phenomenal features, based on reciprocal part-whole interactions" (Parnas, 2012, p. 67). We are reminded that before the arrival of operational psychiatry a person was not merely the sum of a list of phenomena; there was a "depth" to the presentation that was in the intersubjective space (Parnas, 2011). The core Gestalt of schizophrenia is *trait* and not temporally fluctuating *state* phenomena (i.e., psychotic symptoms), and it cannot be merely deconstructed to a list of constituent phenomena. This is what Rümke tells us in his tautological statement (Rümke, 1960; Rümke & Neeleman, 1990); certain illusions and hallucinations (state phenomena) are characteristic of schizophrenia because of their "schizophrenic taint" (core Gestalt/trait). We need to ensure that this concept of a core Gestalt for schizophrenia is not confused with the idea of pathognomonic symptoms for schizophrenia. The core Gestalt, it is argued, is a trait feature; although it is a developing aspect of the disorder, it does not arise abruptly out of nowhere, but is preceded by what we would perhaps now term a prodrome. Also, as Bleuler told us from the start, there is a spectrum of schizophrenias that are characterized by their additional state phenomena (Bleuler & Kline, 1952). This way of phenomenologically understanding schizophrenia matches very well with the IConN model, which informs formulation and the clinical understanding of the condition, facilitating treatment planning. As we will see outlined in the descriptions of the IConN methodology, the state phenomena—hallucinations, for example—are a result of the trait phenomena, which in EMDR therapy we conceptualize as a DMN. This is why we will have difficulty in achieving any long-term efficacy with paradigms that only process the state phenomena; we need to process the DMN—the dissociated/psychotic material that we model as having resulted from trauma. Parnas refers to the trait phenomena as "a trait alteration of the very structure of consciousness" (Parnas, 2012, p. 68). This "alteration" becomes a lens through which the person experiences our shared world and that results in profound dissociative experiences: the state phenomena. Parnas further reminds us that the state phenomena place a person along a spectrum from preonset vulnerability through schizotypy to full-fledged schizophrenia. I will not further elucidate the phenomena found in people with these experiences, nor repeat the content of the *DSM-5* or *ICD-10* criteria here because these are, first, something the reader should already know if planning to work with this client group, and, second, the more important message that I wish to convey is about our need to become experienced in recognizing the "schizophrenic taint." This experience can only be gained through an apprenticeship to the only master who can teach us such a thing: an expert through lived experience. In my opinion, this core Gestalt is deeply dissociative. When I completed research interviews with people for the Irish Schizophrenia Triad Study led by Kendler, I came to know the feeling of that core Gestalt of schizophrenia. In the intersubjective we do not experience the normal feeling of "we," which ought to be felt by the therapist. The person caught up in these experiences is deeply dissociated, which results in a severely impaired capacity for attunement (Schore, 2012). This recapitulates a failure in the person's attunement with the world around him or her. In the IConN model, negative symptoms that are well recognized as a part of the disorder of schizophrenia are not so much a psychological defense as an out-working of the trait phenomena/DMN. At this level the DMN results in a fundamentally changed subjectivity (Parnas, 2012), which results in state phenomena manifesting in all of the person's mental domains: affect, appearance and behavior, speech patterns and prosody, thought form and content, perception and insight. The DMN is the lens through which the entire mental state is distorted. This, however, also holds out to us the hope of healing—as with any lens, if we get the prescription correct, things can quickly come into focus. As already mentioned, this is what has been reported when traumatic material is processed; the DMN is removed and psychoses (state phenomena) remit or are ameliorated (Ross, 2004).

The Loss of Language

Sadly, as psychiatry moved away from seeing the importance of and meaning in phenomena, and embraced operational criteria, there was a resulting decrease in psychopathological competence and scholarship (Andreasen, 1982). Nancy Andreasen, who had been a professor of Renaissance literature before training as a psychiatrist, examined the use of language found in the first-person accounts of people diagnosed with schizophrenia; she found characteristic language defects (Andreasen, 1982). Schizophrenia was proposed to result in a destruction of language resulting in a permanent language deficit. This was illustrated by an observation of the poet Ivor Gurney, who experienced impairment in his capacity for creative thought following a psychotic episode. It was noted that all of his best work had been before the psychosis and that after his episode, little work of literary merit was produced in those 11 years (Jones, 2015). Another example of this is the author Charles Dickens, who, following the Staplehurst railway accident in which 10 people died and 40 were injured, suffered emotionally and became gripped by anxiety when traveling by train. All but one of the first-class carriages had plunged into the ravine, and that was the one that Dickens was on (Matus, 2001). He was never as prolific a writer thereafter. The fundamental phenomena of schizophrenia overlap and do include formal thought disorder, reflected in language deficits, but the prime fundamental symptom is that of autism.

> The . . . schizophrenics, who have no more contact with the outside world, live in a world of their own. They have encased themselves with their desires and wishes . . .; they have cut themselves off as much as possible from any contact with the external world. This detachment from reality with the relative predominance of the inner life, we term "autism." (Bleuler, 1911)

Henry Ey, a famous French psychiatrist, described five clinical manifestations of this autism, which also expertly demonstrate the dissociative nature of schizophrenia (Ey, 1975).

The Intersubjective Space

The considerations described thus far make us aware that for the individuals experiencing psychosis, there is a profound problem with their intersubjective functioning. This, for me, is where the consequences of the DMN are most disabling. It is also important to remind ourselves that EMDR therapy has a vital relational element, which is most clearly articulated by Mark Dworkin, the "father of relational EMDR therapy" (Dworkin, 2005). The intersubjective aspect of EMDR therapy is a key component in the IConn methodology. Parnas reflects on the dissociative nature of the core Gestalt of schizophrenia and demonstrates that this same appreciation is found in the works of Kraepelin, Schneider, Bleuler, Gruhle, Blankenburg, and Minkowski (Parnas, 2011). Upon close examination, Parnas helps us to see that dissociation is writ large throughout the phenomeno-logical elucidation of schizophrenia: from the writings of Kraepelin to his own in the present age (Henriksen & Parnas, 2012; Parnas, 2011, 2012). *Praecox-feeling* (*praecox Gefühl*), as depicted by the Dutch psychiatrist Rümke, sits clearly in the territory of the intersubjective (Rümke, 1958), and although this concept forms no part of the modern-day diagnostic systems, the capacity of an experienced cli-nician to make an intuitive diagnosis is recognized. In one famous study, Essen-Möller (a Swedish expert on schizophrenia spectrum conditions) was asked to make a binary choice: schizophrenia spectrum condition, present or absent. He was blind to the person and could only use the case vignettes of the Maudsley Schizophrenia Twin Study to inform his decision (Gottesman, Shields, & Meehl, 1972; Shields & Gottesman, 1972). When the monozygotic (MZ) concordance rate was examined, comparing those diagnosed according to the operational crite-ria of Gottesman and Shields and those given a blind diagnosis, Essen-Möller's schizophrenia spectrum group had a 90% MZ concordance rate (without inflat-ing the dizygotic [DZ] concordance), compared with an MZ concordance rate of 50% obtained by Gottesman and Shields using their operationalized diagnostic criteria for schizophrenia. However, Parnas notes that Essen-Möller was unable to distill his choice-making process into a symptom list and proposes that this is most likely due to his decision making having been based on his capacity to recognize the core Gestalt, which would be irreducible to an operational list for-mat (Parnas, 2011). I believe there is much that we can gain from a return to recognition of the epistemological and conceptual importance of the *praecox feel-ing*. It could restore a deeper understanding of what the diagnosis really means to schizophrenia research. Henriksen and Parnas revisited the "clinical mani-festations of self-disorders and the Gestalt of schizophrenia" in their paper of the same title (Henriksen & Parnas, 2012). I believe that these trait phenomena, which constitute essential aspects of the schizophrenia spectrum, are clearly dis-sociative, and we see this in the prototypical case examples that Henriksen and Parnas provide for us in their paper (Henriksen & Parnas, 2012).

TAKE HOME

We have come full circle from Bleuler's "schizophrenias" to find schizophre-nia firmly grounded in and secured by its dissociative roots (Bürgy, 2008; Miller, 2014; Moskowitz, 2005; Moskowitz et al., 2008; Read, Mosher, & Bentall, 2004; Ross, 2004; Shevlin, Dorahy, & Adamson, 2007; van der Hart & Dorahy, 2006). I believe that this is good news for clinicians and for those who seek our assistance with these experiences. The acknowledgment of the fundamen-tally dissociative roots of schizophrenia holds out hope for healing through psychotherapy, especially those therapies with a trauma focus. An EMDR therapy approach can achieve healthy metabolism of the DMN, resulting in trait change and the possible long-term resolution of psychosis. We have been speaking of schizophrenia in particular, and as we can consider it the archetypal psychotic disorder, I believe that what we have modeled specifically for schizophrenia is likely to be applicable for psychotic phenomena in general. In other words, psychotic phenomena, when considered within the AIP model, can be understood as resulting from dissociated, unprocessed material. This material is proposed to exist in a DMN with associated trait-specific feelings and cognitions. We will explore this theory later in the book with clinical correlates.

When we consider Chapters 1 and 2 together, I hope that we can acknowledge a link between trauma, dissociative mechanisms, and psychotic disorders, including schizophrenia. This acknowledgment is important if we are to encourage clinicians and service commissioners to make the psychotherapies available as possible treatments for people laboring under these experiences. Next we will explore an overview of the psychotherapies that are currently available and actively being used with psychosis and schizophrenia.

REFERENCES

American Psychiatric Association. (2013). *Diagnostic and statistical manual of mental disorders* (5th ed.). Washington, DC: Author.

American Psychiatric Association & American Psychiatric Association Task Force on *DSM-IV*. (1994). *Diagnostic and statistical manual of mental disorders: DSM-IV* (4th ed.). Washington, DC: American Psychiatric Association.

American Psychiatric Association & American Psychiatric Association Task Force on *DSM-IV*. (2000). *Diagnostic and statistical manual of mental disorders: DSM-IV-TR* (4th ed.). Washington, DC: American Psychiatric Association.

Andreasen, N. (1982). There may be a "schizophrenic language." *Behavior and Brain Sciences, 5*, 588–589.

Armstrong, J. G., Putnam, F. W., Carlson, E. B., Libero, D. Z., & Smith, S. R. (1997). Development and validation of a measure of adolescent dissociation: The Adolescent Dissociative Experiences Scale. *Journal of Nervous and Mental Disease, 185*(8), 491–497.

Arnedo, J., Svrakic, D. M., Del Val, C., Romero-Zaliz, R., Hernandez-Cuervo, H., Fanous, A. H., . . . Zwir, I. (2014). Uncovering the hidden risk architecture of the schizophrenias: Confirmation in three independent genome-wide association studies. *American Journal of Psychiatry, 172*(5), 441–449. doi:10.1176/appi.ajp.2014.14040435

Arseneault, L., Cannon, M., Fisher, H. L., Polancyk, G., Moffitt, T. E., & Caspi, A. (2011). Childhood trauma and children's emerging psychotic symptoms: A genetically sensitive longitudinal cohort study. *American Journal of Psychiatry, 168*, 65–72.

Basset, T., Bentall, R., Boyle, M., Cooke, A., Cupitt, C., Dillon, J., . . . Weaver, Y. (2014). In A. Cooke (Ed.), *Understanding psychosis and schizophrenia: Why people sometimes hear voices, believe things that others find strange, or appear out of touch with reality, and what can help*. A report by the Division of Clinical Psychology. Leicester, England: British Psychological Society, Division of Clinical Psychology.

Bleuler, E. (1911). *Dementia praecox, oder Gruppe der Schizophrenien*. Leipzig, Germany: Deuticke.

Bleuler, E. (1950). *Dementia praecox; or, The group of schizophrenias*. New York, NY: International Universities Press.

Bleuler, E., & Kline, N. S. (1952). *Synopsis of Eugen Bleuler's dementia praecox; or, The group of schizophrenias*. New York, NY: International Universities Press.

Bürgy, M. (2008). The concept of psychosis: Historical and phenomenological aspects. *Schizophrenia Bulletin, 34*(6), 1200–1210. doi:10.1093/schbul/sbm136

Campbell, J. (2004). *The hero with a thousand faces* (Commemorative ed.). Princeton, NJ: Princeton University Press.

Crossley, N. (1998). R. D. Laing and the British anti-psychiatry movement: A sociohistorical analysis. *Social Science and Medicine, 47*(7), 877–889.

DePrince, A. P., & Freyd, J. J. (2014). Trauma-induced dissociation. In M. J. Friedman, T. M. Keane, & P. A. Resick (Eds.), *Handbook of PTSD: Science and practice* (2nd ed., pp. 219–233). New York, NY: Guilford Press.

Dorahy, M. J. (2010). The impact of dissociation, shame, and guilt on interpersonal relationships in chronically traumatized individuals: A pilot study. *Journal of Trauma and Stress, 23*(5), 653–656. doi:10.1002/jts.20564

Dworkin, M. (2005). *EMDR and the relational imperative: The therapeutic relationship in EMDR treatment.* New York, NY: Routledge.

Ey, H. (1975). *Psychophysiologie du sommeil et psychiatrie* [Psychophysiology of sleep and psychiatry]. Paris, France: Masson.

Farone, S. V., Taylor, L., & Tsuang, M. T. (2002). The molecular genetics of schizophrenia: An emerging consensus. *Expert Reviews in Molecular Medicine, 02*(00475-1a), 1–13. Retrieved from http://www.expertreviews.org/02004751h.htm

Frewen, P. A., & Lanius, R. A. (2006). Toward a psychobiology of posttraumatic self-dysregulation: Reexperiencing, hyperarousal, dissociation, and emotional numbing. *Annals of the New York Academy of Sciences, 1071,* 110–124. doi:1071/1/110 [pii] 10.1196/annals.1364.010

Freyd, J. J., & Birrell, P. (2013). *Blind to betrayal: Why we fool ourselves we aren't being fooled.* Hoboken, NJ: Wiley.

Gottesman, I. I., Shields, J., & Meehl, P. E. (1972). *Schizophrenia and genetics: A twin study vantage point.* New York, NY: Academic Press.

Haule, J. R. (1984). From somnambulism to the archetypes: The French roots of Jung's split with Freud. *Psychoanalytic Review, 71*(4), 635–659.

Heber, A. S., Fleisher, W. P., Ross, C. A., & Stanwick, R. S. (1989). Dissociation in alternative healers and traditional therapists: A comparative study. *American Journal of Psychotherapy, 43*(4), 562–574.

Henriksen, M. G., & Parnas, J. (2012). Clinical manifestations of self-disorders and the Gestalt of schizophrenia. *Schizophrenia Bulletin, 38*(4), 657–660. doi:10.1093/schbul/sbs033

Howes, O. D., & Kapur, S. (2014). A neurobiological hypothesis for the classification of schizophrenia: Type A (hyperdopaminergic) and type B (normodopaminergic). *British Journal of Psychiatry, 205*(1), 1–3. doi:10.1192/bjp.bp.113.138578

Ingram, R. E., & Luxton, D. D. (2005). Vulnerability-stress models. In B. L. Hankin & J. R. Z. Abela (Eds.), *Development of psychopathology: A vulnerability-stress perspective* (pp. 32–46). Thousand Oaks, CA: Sage.

Janet, P. (1907). *The major symptoms of hysteria: Fifteen lectures given in the Medical School of Harvard University.* New York, NY: Macmillan.

Jaspers, K. (1913). *Allgemeine psychopathologie* [General psychopathology]. Berlin, Germany: Springer.

Johnson, J. G., Cohen, P., Kasen, S., & Brook, J. S. (2006). Dissociative disorders among adults in the community, impaired functioning, and axis I and II comorbidity. *Journal of Psychiatric Research, 40*(2), 131–140. doi:10.1016/j.jpsychires.2005.03.003

Johnston, C., Dorahy, M. J., Courtney, D., Bayles, T., & O'Kane, M. (2009). Dysfunctional schema modes, childhood trauma and dissociation in borderline personality disorder. *Journal of Behavior Therapy and Experimental Psychiatry, 40*(2), 248–255. doi:S0005-7916(08)00080-3 [pii] 10.1016/j.jbtep.2008.12.002

Jones, E. (2015). Invited commentary on . . . Word use in first-person accounts of schizophrenia. *British Journal of Psychiatry, 206*(1), 39–40. doi:10.1192/bjp.bp.114.149476

Kendell, R. E. (1975). *The role of diagnosis in psychiatry.* Oxford, UK: Blackwell Scientific.

Kendler, K., McGuire, M., Gruenberg, A., Spellman, M., O'Hare, A., & Walsh, D. (1993). The Roscommon Family Study II. The risk of nonschizophrenic nonaffective psychoses in relatives. *Archives of General Psychiatry, 50,* 645–652.

Kendler, K., Spitzer, R., & Williams, J. (1989). Psychotic disorders in *DSM-III-R. American Journal of Psychiatry, 146,* 953–962.

Kendler, K. S., Maguire, M., Gruenberg, A. M., & O'Hare, A. (1993, July). The Roscommon Family Study I. Methods, diagnosis of probands, and risk of schizophrenia in relatives. *Archives of General Psychiatry, 50,* 527–539.

Khoury, M. J., Beaty, T. H., & Cohen, B. H. (1993). *Fundamentals of genetic epidemiology.* New York, NY: Oxford University Press.

Kim, D. C., Choi, J., Kim, S. H., Oh, D. H., Park, S.-C., & Lee, S. H. (2010). A pilot study of brief eye movement desensitization and reprocessing (EMDR) for treatment of acute phase schizophrenia. *Korean Journal of Biological Psychiatry, 17*(2), 93–101.

Knipe, J. (2015). *EMDR toolbox: Theory and treatment of complex PTSD and dissociation.* New York, NY: Springer Publishing Company.

Kraepelin, E. (1881). *Ueber den einfluss acuter krankheiten auf die entstehung von geisteskrankheiten* [On the influence of acute diseases on the emergence of mental illness]. (n.p.).

Kraepelin, E., Barclay, R. M., & Robertson, G. M. (1919). *Dementia praecox and paraphrenia.* Edinburgh, Scotland: E. & S. Livingstone.

Kurihara, T. (2010). No differences in mortality and suicide between treated and never-treated people with schizophrenia. *Evidence-Based Mental Health, 13*(2), 46. doi:10.1136/ebmh.13.2.46

Laferriere-Simard, M. C., & Lecomte, T. (2010). [Does dissociative schizophrenia exist?]. *Santé Mentale au Québec, 35*(1), 111–128.

Laing, R. D. (1964). Is schizophrenia a disease? *International Journal of Social Psychiatry, 10,* 184–193.

Laing, R. D. (2010). *The divided self: An existential study in sanity and madness* (New ed., with an introduction by Anthony David [Ed.]). London, England: Penguin.

Laing, R. D., & Esterson, A. (1967). Families and schizophrenia. *International Journal of Psychiatry, 4*(1), 65–71.

Lanius, U. F., Paulsen, S. L., & Corrigan, F. M. (Eds.). (2014). *Neurobiology and treatment of traumatic dissociation: Towards an embodied self.* New York, NY: Springer Publishing Company.

Lieberman, J. (2015). *Shrinks: The untold story of psychiatry* (1st ed.). New York, NY: Little, Brown.

Matus, J. L. (2001). Trauma, memory, and railway disaster: The Dickensian connection. *Victorian Studies, 43*(3), 413–436.

Miller, P. W. (2007). *The genetic epidemiology of tardive dyskinesia in Northern Ireland.* Doctoral dissertation, Queen's University Belfast, Belfast, Ireland.

Miller, P. W. (2010). *EMDR in psychosis—2 year follow-up of a case series of severe depression, with psychosis; delusional dysmorphophobia and schizophrenia, treated with EMDR.* Paper presented at the EMDR UK and Ireland meeting, Dublin, Ireland.

Miller, P. W. (2014). *Psychosis/dissociation—a rose by any other name* [eLetter]. Retrieved from http://bjp.rcpsych.org/content/202/6/428.e-letters#psychosis—dissociation—a-rose-by-any-other-name

Moskowitz, A. (2004). Dissociation and violence: A review of the literature. *Trauma, Violence, and Abuse, 5*(1), 21–46.

Moskowitz, A. (2005). *Pierre Janet's influence on Bleuler's concept of schizophrenia.* Paper presented at the First Symposium of the Pierre Janet Gesellschaft, Freiburg, Germany.

Moskowitz, A. (2006, February). *Pierre Janet's influence on Bleuler's concept of schizophrenia.* Paper presented at the Trauma, Dissoziation, Persönlichkeit, Pierre Janets Beiträge zur modernen Psychiatrie, Psychologie und Psychotherapie, Lengerich.

Moskowitz, A., Schäfer, I., & Dorahy, M. J. (2008). *Psychosis, trauma, and dissociation: Emerging perspectives on severe psychopathology.* Chichester, England: Wiley-Blackwell.

Nijenhuis, E. R. S., Van der Hart, O., & Steele, K. (2004, January). *Trauma-related structural dissociation of the personality.* Retrieved from http://www.trauma-pages.com/a/nijenhuis-2004.php

Owen, M., Cardno, A., & O'Donovan, M. (2000). Psychiatric genetics: Back to the future. *Molecular Psychiatry, 5,* 22–31.

Parnas, J. (2011). A disappearing heritage: The clinical core of schizophrenia. *Schizophrenia Bulletin, 37*(6), 1121–1130. doi:10.1093/schbul/sbr081

Parnas, J. (2012). The core Gestalt of schizophrenia. *World Psychiatry, 11*(2), 67–69.

Perlick, D. A., Rosenheck, R. A., Kaczynski, R., Swartz, M. S., Canive, J. M., & Lieberman, J. A. (2010). Impact of antipsychotic medication on family burden in schizophrenia: Longitudinal results of CATIE trial. *Schizophrenia Research, 116*(2–3), 118–125. doi:10.1016/j.schres.2009.09.026

Putnam, F. W., Carlson, E. B., Ross, C. A., Anderson, G., Clark, P., Torem, M., . . . Braun, B. G. (1996). Patterns of dissociation in clinical and nonclinical samples. *Journal of Nervous and Mental Disorders, 184*(11), 673–679.

Read, J., Mosher, L. R., & Bentall, R. P. (2004). *Models of madness: Psychological, social and biological approaches to schizophrenia.* Hove, England: Brunner-Routledge.

Ross, C. A. (1991). Epidemiology of multiple personality disorder and dissociation. *Psychiatric Clinics of North America, 14*(3), 503–517.

Ross, C. A. (2004). *Schizophrenia: Innovations in diagnosis and treatment.* Binghamton, NY: Haworth Maltreatment and Trauma.

Ross, C. A. (2013). *Psychosis, trauma, dissociation, and EMDR.* Paper presented at the 18th EMDR International Association Conference, Austin, TX.

Ross, C. A., Keyes, B. B., Yan, H., Wang, Z., Zou, Z., Xu, Y., . . . Xiao, Z. (2008). A cross-cultural test of the trauma model of dissociation. *Journal of Trauma Dissociation, 9*(1), 35–49.

Ross, C. A., Norton, G. R., & Wozney, K. (1989). Multiple personality disorder: An analysis of 236 cases. *Canadian Journal of Psychiatry, 34*(5), 413–418.

Rümke, H. C. (1958). [Clinical differentiation within the group of schizophrenias]. *Nervenarzt, 29*(2), 49–53.

Rümke, H. C. (1960). Contradictions in the concepts of schizophrenia. *Comprehensive Psychiatry, 1,* 331–337.

Rümke, H. C., & Neeleman, J. (1990). The nuclear symptom of schizophrenia and the praecox feeling. *History of Psychiatry, 1*(3, Pt. 3), 331–341.

Rycroft, C. (1968). *A critical dictionary of psychoanalysis.* London, England: Nelson.

Sapolsky, R. M., Uno, H., Rebert, C. S., & Finch, C. E. (1990). Hippocampal damage associated with prolonged glucocorticoid exposure in primates. *Journal of Neuroscience, 10*(9), 2897–2902.

Sar, V., Akyuz, G., & Dogan, O. (2007). Prevalence of dissociative disorders among women in the general population. *Psychiatry Research, 149*(1–3), 169–176. doi:10.1016/j.psychres.2006.01.005

Scharfetter, C., Moerbt, H., & Wing, J. K. (1976). Diagnosis of functional psychoses. Comparison of clinical and computerized classifications. *Archiv für Psychiatrie und Nervenkrankheiten, 222*(1), 61–67.

Schore, A. N. (2012). *The science of the art of psychotherapy* (1st ed.). New York, NY: W. W. Norton.

Shakespeare, W. (1770). *Hamlet, Prince of Denmark. A tragedy*. Edinburgh, Scotland: A. Donaldson.

Shapiro, F., & Maxfield, L. (2002). Eye movement desensitization and reprocessing (EMDR): Information processing in the treatment of trauma. *Journal of Clinical Psychology, 58*(8), 933–946. doi:10.1002/jclp.10068

Shevlin, M., Dorahy, M. J., & Adamson, G. (2007). Trauma and psychosis: An analysis of the National Comorbidity Survey. *American Journal of Psychiatry, 164*(1), 166–169.

Shields, J., & Gottesman, I. I. (1972). Cross-national diagnosis of schizophrenia in twins. The heritability and specificity of schizophrenia. *Archives of General Psychiatry, 27*(6), 725–730.

van der Hart, O., & Dorahy, M. (2006). Pierre Janet and the concept of dissociation. *American Journal of Psychiatry, 163*(9), 1646; author reply 1646.

van der Hart, O., & Nijenhuis, E. (1993). [Dissociative disorders, especially multiple personality disorder]. *Nederlands Tijdschrift voor Geneeskunde, 137*(37), 1865–1868.

Waller, N. G., & Ross, C. A. (1997). The prevalence and biometric structure of pathological dissociation in the general population: Taxometric and behavior genetic findings. *Journal of Abnormal Psychology, 106*(4), 499–510.

Watkins, J. G., & Watkins, H. H. (1990). Dissociation and displacement: Where goes the "ouch?" *American Journal of Clinical Hypnosis, 33*(1), 1–10; discussion, 11–21.

Weaver, I. C. G., Cervoni, N., Champagne, F. A., D'Alessio, A. C., Sharma, S., Seckl, J. R., . . . Meaney, M. J. (2004). Epigenetic programming by maternal behavior. *Nature Neuroscience, 7*, 847–854.

Wing, J. K. (1983). Use and misuse of the PSE. *British Journal of Psychiatry, 143*, 111–117.

Xiao, Z., Yan, H., Wang, Z., Zou, Z., Xu, Y., Chen, J., . . . Keyes, B. B. (2006). Trauma and dissociation in China. *American Journal of Psychiatry, 163*(8), 1388–1391. doi:163/8/1388 [pii] 10.1176/appi.ajp.163.8.1388

THREE

History Taking and Mental State Examination in Psychosis

"Not everything that a man knoweth can be disclosed, nor can everything that he can disclose be regarded as timely, nor can every timely utterance be considered as suited to the capacity of those who hear it."

—*Bahá'u'lláh*

Intention: *To equip the reader with information on how to gather a relevant history and clinical examination in schizophrenia and the other psychoses.*

LISTEN

I have already noted that I believe the adage stating that good therapists are good storytellers. Good therapists also help their patients to tell their own stories. The Rule of St. Benedict was a document that led to a powerful reform of monastic practice in the 1st century, and under its influence monasticism grew and flourished. It has been used for more than 15 centuries and to this day it remains an influential and pragmatic document for all those who want to live well in a community context. In my opinion it is full of useful guidance and is not just for monks. The very first word of the Rule is "Listen," and that is an appropriate place for us to start as we examine how we engage with the people who seek our help. Listening ought to be our guiding principle in the areas of history taking and mental state examination. As therapists we journey with the person from assessment, through treatment, to outcome—hopefully a good outcome at that. Within the therapy room we are seeking to understand individuals: who they are, where they have come from, and why they are here at this point in time. By listening attentively to them in a safe and loving environment, we facilitate this process.

IRISH SCHIZOPHRENIA TRIAD STUDY

In this chapter I offer guidance on how to use a semistructured approach to taking a person's history and provide practical advice on how to complete a mental state examination. This guidance is based on my own psychiatric training. My specific training in the examination of psychosis is shaped by my time working and training under Professor Kenneth Kendler and Dr. Tony O'Neill. I worked with both men as a member of the Genetic Epidemiology of Mental Illness in Northern Ireland (GEMINI) Study Team, which was a part of the Irish Schizophrenia Triad Study (ISTS). ISTS is part of an illustrious pedigree of genetic epidemiological studies investigating schizophrenia. These studies help to clarify the modern-day phenotype of schizophrenia. Professor Kendler selected Ireland for this form of research, as, in genetic terms, Ireland is relatively homogeneous. In other words, there is not a lot of genetic mixing from other ethnicities, which makes such research more complex. Although the Irish diaspora is spread throughout the world, historically there has been relatively little immigration.

FAMILIALITY

In studying the genetics of a psychiatric disorder, one of the initial methods of investigation is an exploration of familiality. This is the study of illness and its patterns of occurrence within family groups. An understanding of the patterns of illness through the gathering of large family pedigrees can inform psychiatric nosology, and this facilitates the development of a phenotype for any disorder being studied. The Roscommon Family Study was a case-controlled epidemiological family study that produced a series of papers that has yielded important data relevant to the diagnostic boundaries of schizophrenia. These diagnostic boundaries have expanded and contracted several times from the time of Kraepelin (Kendler, Maguire, Gruenberg, & O'Hare, 1993). However, if we ask experienced clinicians to describe the syndrome that they identify as schizophrenia, most will consistently describe the core symptoms that current diagnostic systems agree upon. These core symptoms include negative symptoms, auditory hallucinations, bizarre delusions, no prominent affective components, and poor functional outcome. What some clinicians consider "marginal" cases, such as "brief psychosis with schizophrenia-like symptoms and good outcome," do exist and cause diagnostic challenges. The challenge lies in respect to where they should be conceptualized within the classification systems. The second edition of the *Diagnostic and Statistical Manual of Mental Disorders* (*DSM-II*) included most of these cases under the rubric of schizophrenia, whereas the third edition (*DSM-III*) and third edition text revision (*DSM-III-R*) included these in categories such as schizophreniform disorder. In examining the evolution of the *Diagnostic and Statistical Manual of Mental Disorders* (*DSM*), we observe that since the American Psychiatric Association published the first edition in 1952, the *DSM* has grown into a multimillion-dollar enterprise. After the appointment in 1974 of Robert Spitzer, a psychiatrist and retired professor of psychiatry at Columbia University in New York City, as chairman of the *DSM-III* Task Force, the *DSM* grew rapidly. Professor

Kenneth Kendler was to be similarly influential in the area of schizophrenia. His choice of Ireland as the location for this research was to be one of the reasons that I found myself benefiting firsthand from his experience and training. I consider myself fortunate indeed to have received my training in how to interview people using the Structured Clinical Interview for *DSM-III-R* (SCID) from Professor Kendler himself.

GENETIC EPIDEMIOLOGY ON THE ISLAND OF IRELAND

The first Irish epidemiological study of schizophrenia by Professor Kendler's team was the Roscommon Family Study, which commenced in June 1984 and ran until November 1989. This was followed by the Irish High-Density Schizophrenia Family Study, which commenced in April 1987 and ran until November 1992. The analysis of the data commenced in 1993 and helped shape the ISTS of which GEMINI was the Northern Irish arm. The Roscommon Family Study looked at the vulnerability to schizophrenia that was transmitted within families and found that the vulnerability was not limited to the "core"' symptoms; rather, it could be conceptualized as a risk for what the team referred to as "nonaffective psychosis"—in other words, not psychotic depression or mania. Members of the Kendler research group went on to state their belief that the "narrow" definition of schizophrenia according to the *DSM-III-R* was too narrow. However, *DSM-III* and *DSM-III-R* have been argued to have validity, as they produced a definition for the disorder of "schizophrenia with a strong tendency for a poor outcome" (Kendler, Spitzer, & Williams, 1989) that is scientifically reliable and clinically pragmatic. This genetic epidemiological work is extremely important in the development of a phenotype for schizophrenia, and the work of Kendler and his associates has been at the forefront of this.

SCHIZOPHRENIA—A "BIOLOGICAL BRAIN DISEASE"

Although the precise pathophysiology of schizophrenia is not known, it is now generally accepted that there is some form of discrete neuropathology present in individuals with schizophrenia. Neuroimaging is now vastly sophisticated, and over the past 25 years, developments in computed tomography (CT) and magnetic resonance imaging (MRI) scanning have led to the description of a number of structural brain changes in the disorder of schizophrenia. Anatomically, there are consistent findings with respect to the thalamus, hippocampus, and dorsal prefrontal cortex, and enlargement of the ventricles is also described (Johnstone et al., 1989). The debate between the demonstrable changes being neurodevelopmental rather than neurodegenerative has raged, with support for the former being largely built upon a lack of evidence for the latter (Harrison & Lewis, 2003). However, the fact remains that, as there is no reliable physical test for schizophrenia, or for psychosis, clinicians must resort to their primary clinical skills that look at the patient phenomenologically. In other words, we take detailed histories and complete an examination of the mental state of the person sitting with us in the office. We listen to the individual's symptoms and elicit the available signs, after which we make a diagnosis and case formulation. In many ways the phenomenological approach to illness is the diagnostic method that was in use in the early days of the elucidation of tuberculosis (TB). If you had a cough productive of blood-stained sputum in the morning and it was like that every morning for a certain number of days, then you had TB. It was only when the bacterium that causes the illness was identified and cultured that we could develop specific tests for the disease. In many ways the phenomenological diagnosis of schizophrenia is like that "diagnostic tree" for TB, and schizophrenia is analogous to calling a disease a "cough disorder" in physical medicine.

STRUCTURED CLINICAL INTERVIEW FOR THE *DSM*

To improve this phenomenological approach to diagnosing schizophrenia, Professor Kendler refined the SCID, informed by the Irish research. I will not seek to reiterate the SCID here; rather, I will underline the intention of each section of the history and suggest some sample questions. Ultimately, as clinicians, you are already completing this process in one way or another. We know that in genetic epidemiology one of the most difficult aspects of psychiatric research is the definition of phenotype (McGuffin, Owen, & Gottesman, 2002), but it is, basically, a summation of the genotype, plus the effects of the environmental milieu the person lives in, plus the gene–environment correlations, plus the gene–environment interactions.

As a matter of first importance, the genetic epidemiological study of psychiatric illness requires an effective and accurate definition of the phenotype of the condition being studied. As we ended one millennium and started another, researchers in the field of genetic epidemiology and clinicians remained all too aware of this ongoing difficulty where mental illness is concerned (Owen, Cardno, & O'Donovan, 2000). If a phenotype is too wide or indefinite there is a danger of picking up false results; likewise, if the definition is too narrow then we run the risk of missing them. However, even with these difficulties associated with phenotype definition, studies utilizing operational research diagnoses proved to be successful in demonstrating that genes have a role to play in the current syndromes defined by psychiatric nosology (Owen et al., 2000). In other words, researchers and clinicians in this area believe that we have "good enough" pragmatic descriptions for schizophrenia to allow for a genetic search for genes of risk for schizophrenia. The SCID is one method of gathering the information to see if a person meets these operational research diagnoses.

The SCID is a semistructured interview, meaning that there are stem questions and further probe questions that the interviewer reads. There is also nonscripted discussion that informs the ultimate answer recorded. I recommend that clinicians consider training in the use of the SCID, as it can provide you with a very useful lexicon of questions. When I was in my first psychiatry post, my mentor gave me a copy of the Present State Examination (Wing, 1976; Wing & Nixon, 1975). This was the history-taking schedule used in the U.S./U.K. Diagnostic Project (Gurland, 1976; Zubin & Gurland, 1977); these exemplars are a great addition to our clinical toolkits.

A completed SCID allows a clear diagnosis to be made according to whether the person meets the strict diagnostic criteria for schizophrenia or not. Use of the phenotype developed by Kendler, based on the Irish epidemiological studies, led to the identification of what was believed to be the first gene of risk for developing schizophrenia: the 6p22.3 gene DTNBP1, the human ortholog of the mouse dysbindin gene (Straub et al., 2002). Following this, it was believed that even though over time there has been expansion and contraction in the phenotype of schizophrenia, the phenotype delineated by Kendler is valid. We will consider the lessons learned by this pedigree of studies to inform our patient assessments. Those who are from disciplines that do not form diagnoses will note that as the focus is on phenomena, the methods described within this chapter are of value in a general sense and not just limited to doctors who may be focused in part on making a diagnosis.

A CORD OF THREE STRANDS

To assist us in forming the best understanding of the person presenting for assistance, I invite you to think of the method for obtaining a client's history and the examination of the client's mental state as being formed by weaving three strands together. These three strands, once they are woven together, provide a clear and unified understanding of the case. Sometimes you will hear this unified understanding and analysis of the client's presenting problems called a *case formulation*. The three strands that form it are as follows:

1. An exploration of current presenting problems and the story of their development
2. A background contextual history and the person's "life story" up to the current day
3. An examination of the person focusing on the here and now and usually looking at signs and symptoms (phenomenology) that have been manifesting over the past 2 weeks (this includes the examination of the client's mental state, which will include a cognitive assessment, *to some degree*)

I will illustrate this process through the example of a model client and the client's specimen answers. This is not one single patient, but represents a combination of a number of people whom I have seen and interviewed across my career, who have presented with these complaints. We can further structure the history and examination into the following sections:

1. Presenting Problems
2. History of Presenting Problems
3. Past Psychiatric History
4. Past Medical History
5. Family Psychiatric History
6. Medication (Current)
7. Family History
8. Social History
9. Forensic History

10. Personal History
11. Mental State Examination
12. Case Formulation/Diagnosis

CURRENT PRESENTING PROBLEMS
AND THE STORY OF THEIR DEVELOPMENT

Intention of this section: *To explore why the person is here at this time and to ascertain what goals he or she has for this therapeutic relationship. This covers the first two sections listed: "Presenting Problems" and "History of Presenting Problems."*

It is important to use active listening as a guiding principle throughout the entire interview. If the client feels "heard," then he or she is more likely to settle into the examination and thus generate a good-quality interview that can be relied upon. A strong therapeutic rapport allows clients to go to a place of vulnerability where they can describe the phenomena that are distressing them. If their answers are probed too vigorously or if they are compelled to challenge their beliefs and thoughts too forcefully at this stage, clients may choose not to engage and may simply not return for any further appointments. Colin Ross directs us to be actively neutral when obtaining the necessary information from the client (Ross, 2004)—good advice. I find that active listening by the therapist, with appropriate empathy, when carried out in an actively neutral stance, best facilitates the disclosure of psychotic material.

So what does this look like? In one instance I have empathized with a client who was distressed and felt terrible shame about having female breasts, despite being a flat-chested teenage boy. On another occasion I empathized with someone as I acknowledged how painful and upsetting it must be to be experiencing all of his internal organs as rotting, while he was still able to walk around—a sort of a living shell. I found that I did not need to actively challenge the veracity of these clients' beliefs, nor convince them of the delusional nature of their beliefs, to create the space to carry out effective therapy together. I journeyed with both to a successful resolution of their conditions.

When we listen to the patients and show that we accept as "real to them" the phenomena that have plagued their desire for peace and contentment, we forge a collaborative bond. We are modelling nonjudgmental understanding, and so it is no longer solely them against the problem; rather, it becomes us and them against the problem. As Dan Siegel states, "in the therapy space we aim for a sense of 'we' rather than a sense of 'I'" (Siegel & Buczynski, 2014). It is from this place of connection and collaboration that we move forward together, toward health.

I routinely start my assessment by giving an overview of the assessment process and allowing clients to ask any questions that they might have. I describe the three strands of the assessment noted previously and give explicit permission for them to interrupt and ask me to clarify anything that they need me to as we go along. Although we, as clinicians, may be following this paradigm for the third time that day, we must remember that this is not a terrain that is familiar to clients, and they may often be terrified. It is more than likely their first time through such a process. We are to be their guide through this unfamiliar terrain and not their inquisitor.

SPECIMEN PATIENT: ADAM

1. Presenting Problems

Guidance: In this section you are aiming to list the issues flagged by Adam, which he describes as being his reasons for meeting with you. The story of these issues will develop during the interview, and be mindful that some additional "presenting problems" may surface in the course of the assessment.

Sample Questions
First, consider using the "WWW" questions:

I. Why are you here today? What has been troubling you that led to you arranging this assessment today?

   [Sample response] "I have come today in the hope that you will be able to help me understand what is happening to me. I believe that I am losing my mind and that I am crazy. No one appears to understand what is happening to me. I spoke to my doctor and she recommended that I come to see you. Please, can you help?"

II. What do you hope to gain through therapy?

   [Sample response] "Answers to the questions that I need answered. If I am losing my mind, maybe I can get back to health again with therapy of some kind. I want to be able to go to work and be capable of doing the job I love. I want to be able to be with my family and go to the park or the restaurant without being afraid."

III. Why are you seeking out therapy at this time? What has been happening recently in your life that has led to you coming here today?

   [Sample response] "I just couldn't hold it together anymore. My boss insisted I go on some leave and 'get sorted out' after I ran out of an important meeting suddenly, in a panic. My wife and kids are worried sick. I want to be able to get the help I need and I want to find out if there is anything I can do for myself too."

As you will note from the specimen answers given by way of example, these questions give us a sense of why this person is sitting with us in our office at this point. It is useful to ascertain whether clients are actively seeking therapy on their own initiative, or whether they have been compelled to attend under any form of duress. The nature of this dynamic will substantially affect how much work we have to do in respect to forging a good enough therapeutic rapport. We need a strong link with the client to be able to do therapy well. Please remember that although some people come initially only to keep a spouse or employer happy, it is still possible to engage such individuals. For others, it is their psychotic or dissociative phenomena that act against us as we seek to forge a good therapeutic rapport. In both cases the therapist needs to be actively tuning in to what is taking place in the room: both for the client and within himself or herself. Once clients feel that you are there for them and that you are making them the number one priority during your sessions together, you have laid a firm foundation to build therapy upon.

Now we move on to deepening our understanding of what is troubling the client. Please remember to utilize open questions. These are questions that cannot be answered with a simple "yes" or "no."

It may be necessary to use some questions that give clients some options that will help them to answer. The giving of options in this case, rather than limiting the response, can begin to help clients tell their stories—much like an essay plan for a written piece of work. The narrative that clients provide at this point and the manner in which they deliver it will also give you a sense of where they are in the progression of their illness (i.e., Has the episode only started or is the client beginning to recover?). Someone near the start of an episode may have a very chaotic and disjointed narrative as compared with someone in recovery who is able to present a contiguous and coherent narrative with a clear and easy-to-follow flow.

Here are some examples:

I. "If 10 is normal good mental health and 0 is as far away from that as you can imagine, where would you score yourself between 0 and 10—(a) today, and (b) as an average for the past 2 weeks?"

II. Once the client has given you a score out of 10 (e.g., 5 out of 10), a very useful question that will help to identify symptoms and obtain the relevant narrative is: "Why is that not a 6?"

III. "When were you last perfectly well as far as you are concerned?" This is a useful question to get a sense of timing and an idea of how long the episode has been manifesting.

For Adam, we record the following presenting problems

I. "People are following me"; "They wish me harm" [Persecutory beliefs]

II. "People are spying on me"; "Cannot go out of the house with family" [Persecutory/paranoid beliefs]

III. "There are things that they have in my body that are bad. They are influencing me through what they put into me" [Passivity/control beliefs]

2. History of Presenting Problems

Guidance: This section gathers the story of the development of the issues flagged in the first section, and it develops the timeline of their occurrence. Relevant information is sought out and collated to explore what has been happening: before the onset of symptoms, at the onset of illness, and up to the present day.

Sample Questions
Consider using the following questions (or similar):

I. When were you last completely well, as far as you are concerned?

II. Take me from that time (of complete wellness) to the present day; what occurred?

III. Do you ever feel that people are persecuting you or plotting against you? Tell me about that. Please unpack what you mean by that for me.

Some negative responses by our composite client Adam, presented here to guide you through some possible themes for delusional material, are as follows:

I. Definite history of delusions of persecution: "hidden cameras in the mirror," which was manifest just prior to his turning up at the office where he worked. He made a scene there by accusing people of invading his privacy. He also told me that for 3 years, "people have been terrorizing me. The man brought trouble into my life. They wanted me to do things but I refused." I note that he moved to a different house each year for 3 years in a row, to avoid the negative influences he believed people were having on him. I note that this is consistent with the history of a delusional system previously articulated and contained within his notes and documents that were made available to me.

II. There was no clear evidence of delusions of influence/passivity.
Consider using the following question (or similar):
Have you ever felt that someone or something outside of yourself was controlling your body?

III. No delusions of grandiosity were described.
Consider using the following question (or similar):
Have you ever been famous? Tell me about that please.

IV. No somatic delusions were described.
Consider using the following question (or similar):
Have you ever felt something in your body that you could not explain? Please tell me more about that experience.

V. No religious delusions were described.
Consider using the following question (or similar):
Have you ever felt especially important from a religious point of view? Please describe that time fully to me, in your own words.

VI. He describes clinically significant delusions of persecution, which are focused on a man called "Red Curtains," and he alludes to activity, which he describes as "dirty." These thoughts are of a nonbizarre nature and he believed them to be true at the time they were manifesting most strongly. When most convinced by the beliefs, they had a major effect on his behavior.

Consider the following:
Once delusional material is identified or suspected to be present, it is very useful to gain a sense of the functional impact of it at the time it was manifesting most strongly.

VII. At the interview today he currently believes that this delusional system "came from something a friend's father did," which he asserts as being a real occurrence. He no longer is totally convinced that he is being monitored and observed, but does now hold these beliefs at the level of an overvalued idea.

Consider the following:
If the belief is held with unshakable belief and is outside the person's normal social, spiritual, and environmental milieu, then we consider it to be a

delusion. At the point that the person becomes capable of challenging the belief at some level, it is considered to be *an overvalued idea.*

VIII. He denied any hallucinatory experiences.

Consider the following:
A hallucination may occur in any of the sensory modalities and is described as an abnormal perception that is occurring in the *absence* of external stimulus. An abnormal perception occurring in the *presence* of an external stimulus is classified as an *illusion.* Terminology for hallucinations is as follows:

Perceptual Modality	Terminology for Hallucinations
Sight	Visual hallucinations
Hearing	Auditory hallucinations
Touch	Somatic hallucinations
Taste	Gustatory hallucinations
Smell	Olfactory hallucinations

IX. He reports the persecutory delusions as being active for a 3-year period at their longest.

Consider the following:
Understanding how long these phenomena have been active is very important. A longer period of untreated psychosis is thought by many to herald a poorer prognosis (Addington et al., 2015; Lyne, Joober, Schmitz, Lepage, & Malla, 2015; Srihari et al., 2014; Ucok & Ergul, 2014).

X. He denied any prodromal period of symptoms, stating that the year prior to his admission he was "very active looking for jobs. Doing very well at interviews. I had three interviews; got three job offers."

Consider the following:
Ask about the period leading up to the time when clients consider themselves becoming unwell. Pay particular attention to functioning in the different arenas of their life and also to the quality of their interpersonal dynamics.

XI. He believes that the precipitating factors to his current episode of illness came in the form of "unwanted sexual attention, threats, and violence from a man in town"; he notes, "had in mind they would come again." He also describes regular heavy cannabis use at the time of the onset of illness.

Consider the following:
You are able to ask what clients' thoughts are regarding why they have become well, in addition to the history and information you garner from them and through collaborative information sources (e.g., family, partner, etc.).

XII. There is no history of major depressive episodes and he described himself as, "If I'm working and have money I'm a very happy person. A positive person."

Consider using the following question (or similar):
Have you ever been depressed or low every day for at least 2 weeks, where it has had an impact on your ability to function in your life? Tell me about that time in your life.

XIII. No history of mania.

Consider using the following question (or similar):
Have you ever felt "better than good" most days for at least 10 days in a row, when people may have thought you were not acting as your normal self? What was happening in your life at that time?

XIV. He does report a brief period of excessive alcohol intake (more than 14 alcoholic drinks in a week); his heaviest intake was around the age of 21 years and he noted in particular that on his 21st birthday he got very drunk, as he had consumed spirits, but had such a negative experience that he decided not to drink spirits "ever again." During this incident he ended up being admitted to a local hospital because, as he informs me, "I was dancing naked in the bar at one point." He noted a general aversion to excessive alcohol intake currently, as he reflected in regard to his stepfather, "He is drinking too much alcohol and can't work. I can't stand what alcohol does." He described now only drinking occasional wine with a meal. He would not meet criteria for alcohol dependence or harmful use of alcohol currently.

XV. He describes the longest episode of psychosis with persecutory delusional beliefs as having a significant functional impact. He was unable to continue with work and failed in his duties when his boss had delegated important tasks to him.

XVI. Psychosis was not associated with failure to achieve expected level of social relations or work performance.

Consider the following:
A useful question is one that assesses whether there has been some failure in attaining expected levels of achievement.

3. Past Psychiatric History

Guidance: This section aims to capture all of the client's contact with mental health professionals up to the present day. It is also useful in some cultures and ethnic groups to ask whether pastoral support or counseling has been undertaken, as some people seek out this form of assistance in preference to a mental health professional, often because of stigma or imagined bias against their faith background.

Adam

I. No previous psychiatric admissions prior to this current episode of illness.

II. Referral letter from his primary care physician noted that he had been responding poorly to antipsychotic medication that had been tried to date in the community.

III. The letter from his family physician also listed that he attended a psychologist for anger issues, several years ago. He denied any recollection of having done so.

IV. He acknowledges a brief admission for psychiatric evaluation in the emergency room (ER) following dancing naked in a bar, which occurred, as noted earlier, on his 21st birthday after he became very intoxicated due to having consumed spirits, which he has since avoided. He stated he believed he was taken to the ER as a police cell was felt not to be appropriate at the time. He declined any psychiatric follow-up.

4. Past Medical History

Guidance: This section captures all of the client's contact with health professionals up to the present day, including surgeries and any regular attendances at hospital clinics.

Adam's notes for this section are as follows

I. He gave a vague history of a head injury as a child, which he described as, "as a 7-year-old my stepfather hit my head during a game and knocked me out"; he also noted, "that didn't affect my life." There are no clinical notes available to corroborate the details of the head injury, other than that one possibly occurred.

Consider the following:
There are a variety of physical pathologies that can exacerbate or even cause mental illness. If there is an extensive history of physical illness, an inquiry as to what is being actively reviewed and the date of last review by the client's medical team is useful. If in doubt, a recommendation to get a checkup is wise. When members of my medical school tutorial group were doing our pediatric placement, we were taught how to check newborns for a rare but very problematic birth defect: an imperforate anus, a condition where the bowel has failed to create the access to the "outside world." We were taught the adage, "Better to put your finger in it, so you don't put your foot in it!" If in doubt, seek advice and referral for a medical opinion.

II. He denied any significant ongoing active physical illness.

5. Family Psychiatric History

Guidance: This section captures information on whether any *blood relatives* of the client have required contact with mental health professionals up to the present day. As with the inquiry about the client's own history of contact with mental health professionals, it will also be useful to inquire about pastoral support or counseling that has been undertaken, as some people seek out this form of assistance in preference to a mental health professional.

Notes for Adam are as follows

I. Adam denied any awareness of a positive psychiatric history.

II. Corroborative history from Adam's father, obtained with his consent, noted the presence of an aunt with prolonged psychiatric admissions; the diagnosis was unknown.

Consider the following:
There are often cases where the client is unaware of a family history of mental illness, and this is where collateral history (*gathered with the client's consent*) can be very useful.

6. Medication (Current)

Guidance: This section captures information on the client's current medication. You may also wish to obtain information on what has previously been prescribed to treat the client.

Notes for Adam are as follows

I. Lorazepam: He noted 4 mg is prescribed, "but I used to take 2 mg," and he asserts that recently he has not needed it at all.

7. Family History

Guidance: This section captures information on the client's family of origin. Remember that some people may have been adopted and know little or nothing of their birth family. However, it is also necessary to examine the same information as it relates to the adoptive family as well.

Notes for Adam are as follows

I. His birth father separated from the family when Adam was 4 years of age and Adam had no contact with him thereafter.

II. His stepfather came into his life when Adam was 6 years of age and Adam describes him as an alcoholic who worked as a laborer.

III. Adam has a younger sister, who is 6 years his junior. They have never been close.

IV. He reports being raised by maternal grandparents because of the demanding nature of his parents' work that often needed them to travel. He was with his grandparents until the age of 13, when he returned to live with his mother and stepfather, following the death of his grandfather. This change in environment appears to be associated with a loss of some degree of perceived freedom, and it appears to have been quite traumatic for the young man.

V. He describes his father as the person he confides in the most, and when asked about close friends it is his close family that he considers within this category.

8. Social History

Guidance: This section captures information on the client's social context. Think of it as building a word picture that you can tell to someone that would allow that person to understand where the client lives and who the client lives with, whether the client is in a romantic/emotional relationship, how the client is financially, and how the client earns an income or whether the client receives government benefits. This category will also ask about substance use: legal ones such as alcohol and tobacco, illicit drugs, and the nonmedical use of prescription medications.

Notes for Adam are as follows

I. Alcohol: He is currently a nondrinker.

Consider using the following questions (or similar):
A. Do you drink alcohol?
B. At what age was your first drink?

C. At what age were you drinking most? Please describe how much you were drinking at that time. Was that all the time—what was the pattern of your drinking?
D. When was your last drink?
E. Have you ever had a problem with alcohol or were worried about your drinking?
F. Have you ever sought out treatment for alcohol abuse?

Please note that we may use the same areas of questioning when gathering information about illicit drug use, as follows:

II. Illicit drug use:
   A. Cannabis: He first used cannabis at age 26; he was using it most by age 31, when he states he was using it on a daily basis. He now clearly and strongly links his cannabis use to the persecutory delusional system described at his admission and, given his history, it may well have had a likely sustaining role.
   B. He has never been in receipt of treatment or counseling or gone to self-help groups because of his drug use.
III. Social/relational functioning:
   A. He states that in the past year he has met with friends about once every 2 weeks, but on further detailed questioning these "friends" were in fact mostly close family. Although he does describe close intimate friends, it appears that he is actually relatively socially isolated.
   B. He describes these family relationships as "moderately close." He states that he would tend to see his father as his main confidante but does note that he hid his cannabis use from his father.
IV. In the last year he describes being employed through agencies and temporary jobs for about half of the year's working hours. He reports that he has not received any complaints in regard to workplace functioning.
V. Subjectively he described no impairment with respect to activities of daily living and believed himself to be competent.
VI. His appraisal of his own life is that he lives a generally full life.

9. Forensic History

Guidance: The intention of this section is to gather information about the client's experience of any interface with the legal system. This could include the client's involvement in compensation claims or criminal cases, such as those involving alcohol or interpersonal difficulties.

Notes for Adam are as follows
   I. Nothing of note.

10. Personal History

Guidance: The intention of this section is to gather information about the client's life story to date. It should lead from birth to the present and include the following areas: birth, developmental milestones, schooling, educational achievement, trauma, relationships (including sexual history), and work history.

Notes for Adam are as follows

I. He was born May 12, 1982, in Belfast, Northern Ireland, and grew up in the Carrickfergus region.

II. He attended education in Belfast to the age of 18 and commenced higher education but had to leave halfway through his second year of study for what he says were "financial problems."

III. He has never been in or lived in a marriage-like relationship, by his own report.

IV. Work most recently was for a large retail chain, with his last job being as a trainee manager in the company's Belfast store. He states that his feedback and appraisals have all been positive to date and there were no problems or complaints until his outburst that led to his being placed on sick leave.

V. Reflecting on his upbringing, he noted that a return to his parental home around the age of 13 was a difficult adjustment for him, and around this period of time he got in with what he referred to as "a bad crowd." He believes their influences led him into the trouble he had with the man he referred to as "Red Curtains."

VI. He has always lived in the Belfast area, and for a period during his higher education he lived in student accommodation. He found this difficult and was glad to move home when he left in his second year. He has moved three times in as many years and asserts that this is due to trouble from neighbors. This history appears to reflect that these house moves are, at least in some part, associated with a deterioration in his mental health.

VII. Premorbid personality: Adam reports himself as positive in outlook with hopes to secure employment for the near future. Although he describes "moderately close friends," as noted earlier these appear to be close family members and he actually appears to have limited contact with them. Therefore, although he describes moderately close friends with whom he is in regular contact, he is in actuality quite socially isolated.

11. Mental State Examination

Guidance: The intention of this section is to examine the client's mental state on the date you are recording it. It is a clinical "snapshot" that describes the person sitting with you in your office. The following structure is a standard one.

Notes for Adam are as follows

I. This is the mental state examination of Mr. Adam [LAST NAME] completed during his new patient assessment on [DATE AND TIME].

II. *Appearance and Behavior:* Adam was a young man with short cut hair and an athletic build. He was assessed in Mirabilis Health and was unaccompanied by choice. He did consent to my contacting and speaking with his father. He was socially appropriate throughout the course of the interview and polite throughout. There was some evidence of verbal/nonverbal suspiciousness/guardedness on examination. He did, however, settle and engaged comfortably in interview. He appeared to understand the questions well, and it was my opinion that he tried hard during the interview. He was warm emotionally and generally presented himself in a friendly manner. Eye contact was normal and hygiene had been normally attended to.

Consider the following:
This first section is a "word picture" of the person in front of you. Imagine that you are describing the person over the phone to someone who cannot see him or her.

III. *Speech:* Was spontaneous and normal in tone, quantity, quality, and prosody (the melody of speech).

Consider the following:
This section comments on the flow of speech, its melody. We are not focusing on the content of the speech here.

IV. *Affect:* Subjectively and objectively he presented a reactive mood with some evidence of anxiety and distress when discussing the content of his recent thoughts. He denied any major aberrations of mood, and the affective disturbance failed to meet threshold for caseness. There was possible, subtle muting of his affective range that was likely to be secondary to his medication, but this was mild. There was no evidence of any inappropriate affect. His affect was stable and well modulated. Sleep was normal, with a healthy routine. There was no initial insomnia; he sleeps the whole night through and awakes with an alarm after 8 hours of sleep. He feels refreshed by the sleep attained. Appetite and weight are unchanged. There are no thoughts that life was not worth living and no thoughts of self-harming. Preventative factors to completion of suicide exist in the form of his belief in God and his being a practicing Christian, and he was also very aware of the effect it could have on his family.

Consider the following:
This section focuses on mood. I recommend starting with a subjective description of how the person is feeling—listen to how the client describes his or her feelings and only then seek to describe them qualitatively. As in the previous section, this section also looks at sleep, appetite, and weight, as well as suicidal or self-harming thoughts and actions, including preventative factors to completion of suicide.

V. *Thought form:* There was no evidence of any formal thought disorder on examination. Speech was goal directed, with tight and easy-to-follow associations. Global organization of speech and thought was good.

Consider the following:
This section looks at the flow of thoughts and how they link together. This is a proxy for examining the person's thought processes. The formal thought disorders present disorganized thinking, evidenced by disorganized speech. Formal thought disorders include the following:

A. *Overinclusion* is where the boundaries of concepts are extended so that elements of thought that are not normally closely associated become grouped together.

B. *Loosening of associations* refers to the loss of the normal organization of thinking. When this is present in a person's speech, the therapist will often experience difficulty in following and understanding what is being said. Three kinds of loosening of association have been described:

    1. *Knight's move thinking* or *derailment*, in which the flow of thoughts suddenly takes an unexpected direction. The term "knight's move" refers to the way the knight piece in chess moves.

    2. *Talking past the point* (aka vorbeireden), in which a person fails to get to the point; his or her speech appears to be aiming for a point but goes past it. Answers are not given and speech is elliptical.

    3. *Word salad* (aka verbigeration), in which speech is unintelligible, a jumble of words, word fragments, and phrases.

  C. *Concrete thinking* is a very literal interpretation of concepts characterized by failed abstraction. Asking the person to explain the meaning of a familiar proverb, such as "people in glass houses shouldn't throw stones," can examine for this.

  D. *Thought block* is a sudden cessation in the flow of thoughts. If you believe you are observing this phenomenon, it is important to ask the person what is occurring, as a similar appearance can be given by mere distraction.

VI. *Thought content:* He asserted that previous beliefs about "Red Curtains," including those of a persecutory nature, had decreased considerably, but they were still present. He did state that previous "dirty things" had come back up and were distressing him. He was currently unsure if he had anything inserted in his body, but could not be certain that no one wished him harm. He freely admitted that he previously had believed so and thought that this had definitely been the case at the time. He explained this change in thinking as being related to the medication and having had some time to rest and let his system recover.

Consider the following:
This section is a summary of the information garnered from your discussion with the client and will detail delusions, overvalued ideas, and the themes or ruminations and intrusions.

VII. *Perception:* Was normal on examination, with no evidence of any active psychotic phenomena.

Consider the following:
Here you will be looking for evidence of hallucinations, illusions, and eidetic imagery (flashbacks). I also usually include posttraumatic nightmare content here too, as these and flashbacks are related closely, with the former being the way flashback material manifests during dreaming.

VIII. *Cognition:* He was orientated in time, place, and person. He was able to understand and receive information, reflect upon it, and use it to come to a reasoned decision.

Consider the following:
If there is felt to be a cognitive impairment, an appropriate referral is recommended. Those who are appropriately trained will commonly complete a Mini-Mental State Examination (MMSE).

IX. *Insight:* He rationalized his past behavior as all being secondary to stress and now denied any definite persecutory beliefs. He acknowledged the benefit of his current medication.

Consider the following:
This section comments on the client's capacity to reflect on his or her situation.

12. Formulation

Notes for Adam for this section are as follows

I. Adam is a 28-year-old businessman who presents with paranoid/persecutory delusional thoughts. He gives a positive family psychiatric history in an aunt, but the specific mental disorder is not known. He has received anger management treatment with a psychologist and no previous psychiatric treatment apart from a brief psychiatric admission following acute intoxication following his 21st birthday celebrations. There is a description of heavy cannabis use in his past. Although there is a history given of a head injury as a child, no definite diagnosis was made. There was no "T" trauma but the change of circumstances at 13 years of age was a form of "t" trauma. To date he has been treated by his general practitioner. Traumatology considers a big "T" trauma as one that meets Criterion A of the *DSM*'s diagnosis of posttraumatic stress disorder. A small "t" trauma is a more common life event that is emotionally disturbing.

At this stage, as a psychiatrist I would now be forming a diagnosis, but this is not necessary for progressing to psychotherapy. Often a diagnosis is mere "shorthand," and, ultimately, as psychotherapists we want to see the individual who is before us and not merely behold a diagnostic label. After all: labels are for jars, not people. Our formulation will gather the information from the previous sections and draw it together to create a cohesive picture. Now that we are beginning to see the person in front of us, we can begin to relate at a deeper level. Through listening and dialogue, we listen to the voice that the person's suffering has chosen (Seikkula & Olson, 2003) and therapy can begin in earnest.

REFERENCES

Addington, J., Heinssen, R. K., Robinson, D. G., Schooler, N. R., Marcy, P., Brunette, M. F., . . . Kane, J. M. (2015). Duration of untreated psychosis in community treatment settings in the United States. *Psychiatric Services, 66*(7), 753–756. doi:10.1176/appi.ps.201400124

Gurland, B. (1976). Aims, organization, and initial studies of the Cross-National Project. *International Journal of Aging and Human Development, 7*(4), 283–293.

Harrison, P. J., & Lewis, D. A. (2003). Neuropathology of schizophrenia. In S. R. Hirsch & D. Weinberger (Eds.), *Schizophrenia (part two) biological aspects* (Vol. 2, pp. 310–325). Oxford, England: Blackwell.

Johnstone, E., Owens, D., Bydder, G., Colter, N., Crow, T., & Frith, C. (1989). The spectrum of structural brain changes in schizophrenia: Age of onset as a predictor of cognitive and clinical impairments and their cerebral correlation. *Psychological Medicine, 19*, 91–103.

Kendler, K., Spitzer, R., & Williams, J. (1989). Psychotic disorders in *DSM-III-R. American Journal of Psychiatry, 146*, 953–962.

Kendler, K. S., Maguire, M., Gruenberg, A. M., & O'Hare, E. A. (1993, July). The Roscommon Family Study I. Methods, diagnosis of probands, and risk of schizophrenia in relatives. *Archives of General Psychiatry, 50,* 527–539.

Lyne, J., Joober, R., Schmitz, N., Lepage, M., & Malla, A. (2015). Duration of active psychosis and first-episode psychosis negative symptoms. *Early Intervention Psychiatry.* doi:10.1111/eip.12217

McGuffin, P., Owen, M. J., & Gottesman, I. I. (Eds.). (2002). *Psychiatric genetics and genomics.* Oxford, England: Oxford University Press.

Owen, M., Cardno, A., & O'Donovan, M. (2000). Psychiatric genetics: Back to the future. *Molecular Psychiatry, 5,* 22–31.

Ross, C. A. (2004). *Schizophrenia: Innovations in diagnosis and treatment.* Binghamton, NY: Haworth Maltreatment and Trauma.

Seikkula, J., & Olson, M. E. (2003). The open dialogue approach to acute psychosis: Its poetics and micropolitics. *Family Process, 42*(3), 403–418.

Siegel, D., & Buczynski, R. (2014). *The neurobiology of trauma treatment: How brain science can lead to more targeted interventions for patients healing from trauma.* Retrieved from http://www.nicabm.com/treatingtrauma2014/a1-transcript-sample/?del=11.14.1 4LTsampleemailunreg

Srihari, V. H., Tek, C., Pollard, J., Zimmet, S., Keat, J., Cahill, J. D., . . . Woods, S. W. (2014). Reducing the duration of untreated psychosis and its impact in the U.S.: The STEP-ED study. *BMC Psychiatry, 14*(1), 335. doi:10.1186/s12888-014-0335-3

Straub, R. E., Jiang, Y., MacLean, C. J., Ma, Y., Webb, B. T., Myakishev, M. V., . . . Kendler, K. S. (2002). Genetic variation in the 6p22.3 gene DTNBP1, the human ortholog of the mouse dysbindin gene, is associated with schizophrenia. *American Journal of Human Genetics, 71*(2), 337–348. doi:S0002-9297(07)60479-0 [pii] 10.1086/34175

Ucok, A., & Ergul, C. (2014). Persistent negative symptoms after first episode schizophrenia: A 2-year follow-up study. *Schizophrenia Research, 158*(1–3), 241–246. doi:10.1016/j.schres.2014.07.021

Wing, J., & Nixon, J. (1975). Discriminating symptoms in schizophrenia: A report from the International Pilot Study of Schizophrenia. *Archives of General Psychiatry, 32*(7), 853–859.

Wing, J. K. (1976). A technique for studying psychiatric morbidity in in-patient and out-patient series and in general population samples. *Psychological Medicine, 6*(4), 665–671.

Zubin, J., & Gurland, B. J. (1977). The United States–United Kingdom project on diagnosis of the mental disorders. *Annals of the New York Academy of Sciences, 285,* 676–686.

FOUR

Psychotherapy for Psychosis and Schizophrenia: The "Wizard of Oz Fallacy"

"Knowledge is of two kinds. We know a subject ourselves, or
we know where we can find information upon it."
—*Samuel Johnson*

Intention: *To equip the reader with an awareness of key aspects of the other
psychotherapies being used in schizophrenia and the other psychoses.*

In discussing the care of people with severe mental illness, Andrew Powell,
founding chair of the Psychotherapy and Spirituality Special Interest Group of
the Royal College of Psychiatrists (United Kingdom [UK]), wrote: "[T]he thrust
of biological psychiatry in the UK has been extraordinarily denying, and sometimes downright intolerant of the psychodynamic contribution, which in many
other countries has been taken for granted" (Mace & Margison, 1997, p. x). On
the other side of the pond, in the United States, Steven Sharfstein, 2005 president
of the American Psychiatric Association (APA), has said: "As we address these
Big Pharma issues, we must examine the fact that as a profession we have allowed the bio-psycho-social model become the bio-bio-bio model. In a time of
economic constraint, a 'pill and an appointment' has dominated treatment. We
must work hard to end this situation and get involved in advocacy to reform our
health care system from the bottom up" (Sharfstein, 2005, p. 3). Let us see how
the talking therapies can assist us in doing better.

A CHANGE OF PLAN

When planning the content of this book, I initially thought to give an overview of
the psychotherapies, other than eye movement desensitization and reprocessing

(EMDR) therapy, that are currently being used in schizophrenia and psychosis. However, as I gathered up and read through the vast amount of material currently in existence, I was struck by the following realization. In a book focusing on EMDR therapy for psychosis and schizophrenia, any attempt to condense the other psychotherapies down into an overview contained within one chapter risked ending up with one of two extremes: Either it would amount to a huge endeavor that would warrant a book in itself, or it would condense to a such a degree that it would have the density of a small black hole, where not even light could escape. I hope to shed some light on the area and not generate too much heat. Having talked this through with a friend who is not working in the mental health field (*thanks, Neil M.*), he suggested that a comparison would be helpful in understanding the unique selling point (USP) of EMDR therapy for psychosis and also the similarities between the different methods. Those specialists who are expert in these other psychotherapeutic modalities will eventually shed light on my reflections regarding their areas of expertise. At least I hope they will, and this is why I believe we must collaborate and share our theories and findings: for the benefit of all who seek our help. My treatment of them here is not intended to be in any sense summative or exhaustive. I believe that when we share our perspectives and expertise, we will ultimately find that we have much more in common than we perhaps imagined. This is my intention for this chapter: to generate a general awareness of other paradigms that an interested person may then explore further.

THE WIZARD OF OZ FALLACY

I have already introduced this fallacy to you, but I hope to unpack it here. It attempts to encapsulate the most vital and important thesis that EMDR therapy brings through the adaptive information processing (AIP) model. The presenting problem is not the core pathology; it is an icon of the core pathology. In other words, "psychotic" material need not be seen as pathology to be remedied. The person's presenting problems result from what is taking place as the person is attempting to adapt to this core pathology (Romme & Escher, 1993), which belongs to the dysfunctional memory network (DMN), and the DMN is the *real* problem, stemming from what has happened to the person.

The Primary Target Is the DMN

In the Indicating Cognitions of Negative Networks (ICoNN) model, psychotic phenomena can lead us to the real pathological material of the DMN that requires *psychological metabolism* through the use of EMDR therapy. The psychotic material that is being manifested by the person seeking help is a bridge that connects to the DMN. Remember that if we formulate the person's case within the AIP model, at all times the primary target for our therapeutic endeavors is the DMN. The other phenomena, such as the delusions and hallucinations of schizophrenia, are driven by the DMN, which is the primary problem. Remember that there will also be times when, as in the quote at the start of the book, like Menninger's fish on a line, the adaptive experiences that we know as psychosis may achieve their aim: Not all people with these experiences will seek or need treatment.

The Wizard of Oz and The Hero's Journey

When presenting a meaningful metaphor to people who present with a disorder of function, as a result of their experiences, I use the analogy of talking to "the man behind the curtain." This comes from the point in the story (Baum, 2006) where Dorothy goes to meet the Wizard of Oz, having returned to the Emerald City after killing the Wicked Witch. The necessary focus for EMDR reprocessing is "the man behind the curtain," or, in AIP terms, the DMN. We will never fully solve the presenting problems by "talking to the big scary green face of the wizard"; that will only send us off on false quests to do battle with wicked witches and flying monkeys, and we will not reach home that way. It is misspent time in therapy, as getting "home to Kansas" is what we really need to do, and that requires looking behind the curtain. This reparative endeavor within the therapeutic dynamic is reminiscent of the stage in *The Hero's Journey* that Campbell (2004) calls the "Rescue from Without." The hero at this point has had help to begin the quest, and, having responded to the call to adventure, has received supernatural help/assistance to get past the "threshold guardians" and crosses the threshold: the threshold between the known and unknown. This is the beginning of transformation in the monomyth (Campbell, 2004): the journey from the territory of that which is "known" to that which is "unknown." People seeking help with their "psychotic" experiences have failed to adapt in a functional manner and thus require "thinking at a different level of thinking," as Einstein states, to solve the conundrum. In other words, they need more resources.

Toto and the Man Behind the Curtain—Assistance From Without

During the subsequent stages in the archetypal journey of the monomyth (Campbell, 2004), our hero descends, completes a series of challenges/tasks (sometimes with the aid of helpers or a mentor), and then, following the *revelation* and *transformation*, begins to ascend once again, cross the threshold, and return to the "'known" world. Just as a hero may require help to begin the expedition, the *mythopoeia* allows powerful guides and rescuers to return individuals to their everyday lives (Freer, 2015; Lyons, Lloyd, West, & Goodwin, 1997; Tolkien & Tolkien, 1988). In *The Wizard of Oz* (Baum, 2006) we see this "assistance from without" coming in the form of Dorothy's little dog Toto, which leads her ultimately to look behind the curtain. In the treatment of psychosis within EMDR therapy, our "little dog" is the methodology of the ICoNN model. It takes us to where we need to go to allow us to engage therapeutically with the DMN. The psychosis is an adaptation to the DMN, and just as Dorothy could have ended up remaining in Oz as a consequence of her negative cognition (NC) of "I am a failure," people may continue to be overwhelmed, and as a consequence they remain in their psychosis. Dorothy cannot "get home to Kansas" by meeting the demands of the "big scary green face of the wizard," for his power is only an illusion. Only once the curtain is pulled back and the flesh-and-blood "wizard" is engaged with face to face does the opportunity to get home actually present itself (the hot-air balloon). Even this proves to be inadequate and fails to get her home. Eventually Dorothy is directed to look at the solution that she has had all along: the ruby slippers and her "heart's desire."

I believe that the *mythopoeia* of the Wizard of Oz story has a powerful *mythos* that resonates with the ICoNN methodology. If we help to ground the individuals seeking help, assist them in examining their heart's desires, and connect them with the resources already available in the community, we can help them to "get back to Kansas." We must attend to the source of "real power" if we are to get back to the "real world." In respect to psychosis, this means seeing beyond the thing that appears to hold all the power, psychotic phenomena (the wizard), and attending instead to the real source of pathology that is driving the presenting problem, the DMN (the man behind the curtain). In other words, we ask the question that Eleanor Longden invites us to ask, "Tell me what happened to you?" instead of "What's wrong with you?" (Eleanor Longden, 2013). One expert-through-lived-experience spoke of the power that drives psychosis as being "threat and betrayal . . . [that] feed psychosis" (Boevink, 2006), and these are intimately related to the trauma that the person has experienced.

The Crossing of the Return Threshold

This next stage of the hero's journey (Campbell, 2004) is the crossing of the return threshold, and here our hero preserves the wisdom gained on the quest and integrates it into his or her life and that of the community. In our experience as a whole person, "you can't not know what you know," and that is what we do by reprocessing the DMN through ICoNN methodology: We know the same thing in a new way. In EMDR therapy terms, the NC associated with the DMN has been metabolized and no longer exists; the positive cognition (PC) has now replaced it, and should Dorothy ever find herself in Oz again, she knows how to get home.

So, in summary, as we now proceed to look in cameo at the other psychotherapies for psychosis, let us keep in mind that we hypothesise that EMDR therapy utilizes the innate information processing system of the human mind/brain complex to target the DMN. This is done within a vital and dynamic intersubjective intimacy, which is generated between the people "making therapy," as one German friend once described it to me. The DMN is a state-dependent memory system that has failed to be *psychologically metabolized*, which relates intimately to unprocessed data that pertain to what has happened to the person. It is proposed that the dual attention stimulation/bilateral stimulation (DAS /BLS) element of the EMDR therapy method engages a wider association and neural exploration in the brain to facilitate problem solving, a characteristic of memory processing that occurs during rapid eye movement (REM) sleep. This is not seen in exposure therapy, which focuses on the trauma memory.

OTHER PSYCHOTHERAPIES FOR PSYCHOSIS AND SCHIZOPHRENIA

The best evidence base for psychotherapy for psychosis and schizophrenia exists for cognitive behavioral therapy (CBT). It is important to remember that this is not the same thing as saying that other modalities do not work; the CBT community has merely been the best at gathering and publishing its research (Read, 2013). This also does not mean that we all ought to rush out and become

CBT therapists; however, it can encourage us to become better EMDR therapists through reflective practice, research, and the scrutiny of peer-reviewed publications. We must avoid the so-called *argument-from-ignorance fallacy* (*argumentum ad ignorantiam*); in other words, *the absence of evidence is not evidence of absence.* Dr. Francine Shapiro always reminds the gathered therapists that we need to do more than just have a reflective practice; we also need to publish.

Jerome Frank describes four fundamental components of an efficacious psychotherapy paradigm (Frank, 1961):

1. An emotionally charged relationship
2. A therapeutic environment
3. A rationale or myth that provides a plausible explanation for the symptoms
4. A procedure to resolve them

We can all recognize these as core tenets of any good psychotherapy. However, it has been stated that the best predictive factor of a positive outcome remains the quality of the therapeutic relationship (Read, 2013). Interestingly, when the same factor was examined in relation to the efficacy of medication, this relationship was still found to be true (Read, 2013). In other words, how effective your antidepressant is strongly correlates with the therapeutic rapport that you have with your psychiatrist.

This picture, where the therapeutic relationship is given essential, foundational status, stands in stark contrast to the experiences in our health systems of far too many people, which are all too similar to that described by Wilma Boevink:

If you enter the psychiatric business as a patient, then you have a high chance of being reduced to a *disturbed object* or *to the disorder itself.* Only that which is significant to the diagnostic examination is seen and heard. We are examined but not really seen; we are listened to but not really heard. Psychiatry does not regard us as serious discussion partners: after all, with a disorder you cannot speak [emphasis added]. (Boevink, 2006, p. 17)

Wilma, when asked to comment upon the thing that she thought rendered her vulnerable to psychosis, describes a dissociative dynamic, one where, as a child, she was "forced" to accept a distortion of reality in order to maintain attachment. The importance of attachment has already been explored from the phenomenological standpoint in Chapter 2; however, it is worth quoting Boevink again:

The betrayal of the family that says, "you must have asked for it," instead of standing up for you. That excuses the offender and accuses the victim. And forces the child to accept the reality of the adults . . . That is a distortion of reality that is very hard to deal with when you're a child. You are forced to betray yourself. That is what causes the twilight zone. What makes you vulnerable for psychosis." (Boevink, 2006, p. 18)

The EMDR therapy paradigm understands Wilma Boevink's experiences through the lens of the AIP model. We see from her statement a failure in the normal operation of the information processing system, and in order to maintain attachment there is dissociation. The dissociation maintains attachment at the cost of a true account and gains in its place a distorted NC, which is attached to the DMN. It may be that a person is well aware of the event that led to this happening, so Read invites us as clinicians to ask clients, "What happened to you?" This is the same request that we hear from experts-through-lived-experience, such as Eleanor Longden (2013) or Elyn Saks (2012). The description of the creation of a *dysfunctional psychological pathogen* as a result of a traumatic/touchstone event is referred to by different terminology across the various psychotherapeutic paradigms, but to my mind they all belong to the same *pedigree* of concepts, as follows:

1. Janet—*fixed ideas* (Janet, 1889/2015, 1907)
2. Jung—*complexes* (Jung, McGuire, Shamdasani, & Jung, 2012)
3. Bowlby—*internal working models* (Bretherton & Munholland, 1999)
4. Baldwin—*core relational schemas* (Waldinger et al., 2003)
5. Briere—*deep cognitive structures* (Briere, 2002)
6. Shapiro—*dysfunctional memory network* (Solomon & Shapiro, 2008)

I believe all of these represent a view of a psychological *pathogen*, which has been generated in the psyche as a result of trauma (remember to ask, "What happened to you?"). This subsequently drives a psychopathology or pattern of behavior that the person presents with because of dysfunction. I will not look further at those therapies that acknowledge and therefore utilize a dissociation paradigm for psychosis and schizophrenia. They will be explored later in the book.

In the 1920s, Birnbaum's attempt to explain how a psychosis formed became hugely influential in European psychiatry (Birnbaum, 1923). Psychosis was recognized by Birnbaum as a group of heterogeneous disorders and not a single nosological entity, "a highly intricate, discrete, animate, functional complex" (quoted in Mace & Margison, 1997, p. 4); sounds familiar, doesn't it?—yet another member of the pedigree listed previously, in my opinion. Birnbaum explained that this entity had biological factors that determined why it was "psychosis" and not another mental illness, as well as pathoplastic factors that "shape the disorder in that they give content, coloring and contour to individual illnesses whose basic form and character have already been established" (Mace & Margison, 1997, p. 4). The problem here was that the stage was then set for the pathoplastic factors to take a backseat and for the biological factors to be seen as the principal ones. This resulted in the biological factors becoming the main target for therapeutic attention. From the perspective of Locke, the English philosopher and physician, people are malleable and "madness" can be thought of as a consequence of life events, rather than due to some constitutional diathesis:

> For they [madmen] do not appear to me to have lost the faculty of reasoning; but, having joined together some ideas very wrongly, they mistake them for truths, and they err as men do that argue right from wrong principles. For by the violence of their imaginations having taken them their fancies for realities, they make right deductions from them . . . madmen put wrong ideas together, and

so make wrong propositions, but argue and reason right from them. (Locke, 1894, pp. 94–95)

This led the "mad doctors," as they were then known in the 18th century, who were basing their therapeutic endeavors upon these premises, to see the most important and efficacious element of treatment as "direct engagement between the will of the physician and that of the patient" (Mace & Margison, 1997, p. 5). So we can see that from the earliest days of psychiatric treatments, therapeutic rapport has always been acknowledged as being of primary importance (Read, 2013), and we forget that at our peril. People like Jerome Frank and Mark Dworkin are resonant iterations of this golden rule; there is, as Dworkin puts it, a *relational imperative* in therapy (Dworkin, 2005). This relational imperative is as true for EMDR therapy as it is for any of the psychotherapies.

Increasingly as the era of materialism came center stage, psychotherapeutic endeavors were thought to hold less potential to bring about a cure for the psychoses. Whereas Freud had only secondhand experience of treating psychosis, Bleuler had influenced Jung during his time at the Burghölzli Hospital, and he retained a lifelong interest in schizophrenia. Jung summed up, at the end of his career, that he believed there was a much greater number of people with "latent schizophrenia"; those hospitalized with schizophrenia were only the tip of an iceberg (Jung, 1934/1960). He believed that people with schizophrenia had a much greater *autonomy of complexes*, and for me this draws on the Janetian, dissociative roots of "the schizophrenias" (Moskowitz, 2006). Rather than hold the therapeutically nihilistic view built into *dementia praecox* by Kraepelin, Jung held the view that substantial clinical improvement and sometimes "cure" was possible for these individuals through analytic psychology (Jung, 1962, 1974). However, he also stated that after "psychological elimination" through his method, the person with schizophrenia was left with a remaining core organic factor (Jung, 1957). Here we see that in the reflections of a lifetime of practice, it is more often seen to be a case of *both/and* rather than *either/or*.

In the United States, Harry Stack Sullivan, a neo-Freudian psychiatrist and psychoanalyst, focused on the importance of cultural and interpersonal factors in mental disorder. He held that the personality formed and existed in the intersubjective space, a complex interplay of interpersonal relations (Mace & Margison, 1997). He also placed great importance upon early intervention when treating these disorders (Sullivan, 1953). Once the focus had been broadened beyond the intrapersonal to the interpersonal, the way was opened for people like Gregory Bateson, the first husband of Margaret Mead, to formulate theories of causation that had an environmental focus—in his case the *double bind* theory (Bateson, 1956). Bateson revisited the double bind later in his career and emphasized that the dynamic was most properly understood by examining the system the person exists within (Bateson, 1962):

> The most useful way to phrase double bind description is not in terms of binder and a victim but in terms of people caught up in an ongoing system which produces conflicting definitions of the relationship and consequent subjective distress. (p. 42)

This is a foundational principle of the open dialogue approach developed in Finland (Holmesland, Seikkula, & Hopfenbeck, 2014; Holmesland, Seikkula, Nilsen, Hopfenbeck, & Erik Arnkil, 2010; Olson, Laitila, Rober, & Seikkula, 2012; Seikkula & Alakare, 2004; Seikkula, Karvonen, Kykyri, Kaartinen, & Penttonen, 2015; Seikkula & Olson, 2003).

Behavioral psychotherapy, which had its origins in learning theory, attributed mental disorder to faulty learning. From a pragmatic perspective this led practitioners to focus their therapeutic efforts on intervening with the psychotic symptoms, in addition to education of the family/carers, and seeking to enhance already present coping skills (Mace & Margison, 1997). Aaron Beck did not fall foul of Jaspers, which is very important, and he states: "the fact that people diagnosed as schizophrenic have a circumscribed set of irrational beliefs does not mean that they are irrational individuals" (Kingdon & Turkington, 1994, foreword).

One important connecting thread among these disparate therapies is that the analytic/dynamic and the behavioral/cognitive approaches all emphasize a continuum between individuals experiencing psychosis and those who do not. The psychodynamic interest in schizophrenia was greater in the United States than in the UK, largely through the influence of Sullivan (Mace & Margison, 1997). However, many psychiatrists returning from the war who had found some measure of success in treating *shell shock* with Freudian principles also enthusiastically brought Freudian psychoanalysis to the United States. Freud viewed the person with psychosis as being incapable of forming the necessary transference with the analyst, whereas Jung believed that the disorder resulted from a fragmented ego that was being overwhelmed by the imagery from the collective unconscious (Jung, 1928). Again we see Jung's Janetian influence and the prominence of dissociation. If, as therapists, we keep the person grounded and present with us in the "therapeutic window" (Briere, 2002), effective processing can take place in therapy and a healing, intersubjective dynamic may form. Freud saw the pathology of the person with schizophrenia as a regression to a dreamlike state; Klein saw it as a regression to the paranoid-schizoid position of the infant, with the attendant defense mechanisms such as splitting, projective identification, and others (Mace & Margison, 1997). Sullivan believed it only made sense when viewed as a complex interpersonal dynamic, and Winnicott saw psychosis as a deficiency state resulting from an environmental failure in the mother–child milieu and a lack of secure holding—that is to say, in this context, "good enough" mothering. Winnicott's concepts of *unintegration* as the starting point of development and *disintegration* as pathology form the basis for understanding that he saw schizophrenia as a regression to a state of *unintegration*. Bion's idea of "the container and the contained" (Bion, 1962) also helps us to gather together the thinking that has been occurring within and around these various paradigms and schools of thought. He believed that encouraging the analysand to "seek after truth" helped the person, through analysis, to understand and manage the powerful interactions within the psychotic transference, thus rendering the unmanageable experiences manageable—"the successfully treated patient as one who has introjected the holding/containing function of the therapist, translating ideas familiar from Bion, Balint, Winnicott to a contemporary Jungian framework" (Reilly, 1997, p. 19). This again emphasizes that the therapeutic relationship is king in the treatment of psychosis. Once this safe container is constructed, there exists a space that is strong enough and capable enough to explore the dynamics at play in the person's presentation. Cox refers to the iconography of the psychotic phenomena as "passwords to the psychotic's inner world" (Cox, 1997, p. 31). He emphasizes that this rich iconography will never be shared if the person fails to develop a trusting relationship with the patient. This is where we will see "therapeutic neutrality" come into its own (Ross, 2004). It is also important that this container be strong, as it may at times need to be able to contain the risk of suicide, which leads one commentator to remind us that therapy ought to be supportive and create safe boundaries that protect the person in therapy, and not be overambitious (Cotton, Drake, & Gates, 1985; Drake, Gates, Whitaker, & Cotton, 1985).

Within a therapeutic container characterized by connection, affirmation, and empowerment, which is constructed by listening, loving, and learning—or CAEL (see Chapter 5 for full explanation)—a place of compassion, acceptance, and respect is built, giving the therapist and the person seeking help a space in which to work through what has happened to the individual. As a consequence, the capacity to manage the related phenomena is developed and grown. This takes place largely in the intersubjective space. The therapist, by providing a cultural and clinical context for the person's experiences, helps the individual to avoid getting trapped within his or her disturbing phenomena; rather, the therapist mentors and guides the person, within a milieu of hope, to heal himself or herself. Here we once again observe the central tenets of good therapy (Frank, 1961). As we will see later when we examine the ICoNN methodology, there is an ethno-biopsychosocial archetype that these tenets resonate with. In many ways Frank's four factors are the same as those revealed by Phil Borges, which he refers to as the "shaman's advantage" (Borges & Amnesty International, 1998):

1. There is a cultural connection between the shaman and the person experiencing these terrifying phenomena.
2. The community buys into the paradigm offered by the shaman and therefore the experiences of the person are not stigmatized; they are a recognized part of a necessary journey the person must take toward wholeness. The community honors the person's uniqueness.
3. The shaman provides a positive cultural context for the person's experiences and asserts that the person will come through the shaman and that he or she will have gained from doing so. It is commonly also stated that if the person does not respond to this "call," it will lead to illness.
4. The shaman is an expert-through-lived-experience of these phenomena, and the shaman mentors the person through the experiences, as it is "home ground" for the shaman.

For further exploration of Phil Borges, please go to http://philborges.com/crazywise.

"The gift of fantasy has meant more to me than my talent for absorbing positive knowledge."
—*Albert Einstein*

For me the common threads here are striking. We need to make meaning of our journey in life, and myth is one way that helps us to do that. Joseph Campbell is quoted as having defined myth as "other people's religion" (Campbell & Kennedy, 2001). He spoke of how myth helps us travel more successfully through life, by providing a map that helps us get to our destination, which he called "bliss." As he compared and studied mythology across different cultures, he saw how mythos facilitated the hero's journey we ought to all make (Campbell, 2004). Eleanor Longden, made famous by her TED Talk, helps us to see that one key to finding wholeness is asking about what has happened, and this opens a door to the journey of healing (Corstens, Longden, McCarthy-Jones, Waddingham, & Thomas, 2014; Johns et al., 2014; Longden & Proctor, 2012; Longden, Madill, & Waterman, 2012; Thomas & Longden, 2013). She states that on her journey she realized that, "These people empowered me to save myself" (Longden, 2013).

So perhaps the effective and efficacious aspects of these therapeutic paradigms are not as different as we think. Let us focus on what works and apply this to our therapeutic endeavors.

REFERENCES

Bateson, G. (1956). Communication in occupational therapy. *American Journal of Occupational Therapy, 10*(4, Pt. 2), 188.

Bateson, G. (1962). A note on the double bind. In C. E. Sluzki & D. C. Ransom (Eds.), *Double bind: The foundation of the communicational approach to the family* (pp. 39–42). New York, NY: Grune and Stratton.

Baum, L. F. (2006). *The wizard of Oz* (Updated ed.). London, England: Ladybird.

Bion, W. R. (1962). The psycho-analytic study of thinking. A theory of thinking. *International Journal of Psychoanalysis, 43*, 306–310.

Birnbaum, C. O. (1923). *Der Aufbau der Psychose: Grundzüge der Psychiatrischen Strukturanalyse* [The structure of psychosis: Broad psychiatric structural analysis]. Berlin, Germany: Springer.

Boevink, W. A. (2006). From being a disorder to dealing with life: An experiential exploration of the association between trauma and psychosis. *Schizophrenia Bulletin, 32*(1), 17–19. doi:10.1093/schbul/sbi068

Borges, P., & Amnesty International. (1998). *Enduring spirit*. New York, NY: Rizzoli.

Bretherton, I., & Munholland, K. A. (1999). Internal working models in attachment relationships: A construct revisited. In J. Cassidy & P. R. Shaver (Eds.), *Handbook of attachment: Theory, research, and clinical applications* (pp. 89–114). New York, NY: Guilford Press.

Briere, J. (2002). Treating adult survivors of severe childhood abuse and neglect: Further development of an integrative model. In J. E. B. Myers (Ed.), *The APSAC handbook on child maltreatment* (2nd ed., pp. 174–204). Thousand Oaks, CA: Sage.

Campbell, J. (2004). *The hero with a thousand faces* (Commemorative ed.). Princeton, NJ: Princeton University Press.

Campbell, J., & Kennedy, E. C. (2001). *Thou art that: Transforming religious metaphor*. Novato, CA: New World Library.

Corstens, D., Longden, E., McCarthy-Jones, S., Waddingham, R., & Thomas, N. (2014). Emerging perspectives from the hearing voices movement: Implications for research and practice. *Schizophrenia Bulletin, 40*(Suppl. 4), S285–S294. doi:10.1093/schbul/sbu007

Cotton, P. G., Drake, R. E., & Gates, C. (1985). Critical treatment issues in suicide among schizophrenics. *Hospital and Community Psychiatry, 36*(5), 534–536.

Cox, M. (1997). The great feast of languages: Passwords to the psychotic's inner world. In C. Mace & F. Margison (Eds.), *Psychotherapy of psychosis* (pp. 31–48). London, England: Gaskell.

Drake, R. E., Gates, C., Whitaker, A., & Cotton, P. G. (1985). Suicide among schizophrenics: A review. *Comprehensive Psychiatry, 26*(1), 90–100.

Dworkin, M. (2005). *EMDR and the relational imperative: The therapeutic relationship in EMDR treatment*. New York, NY: Routledge.

Frank, J. D. (1961). *Persuasion and healing: A comparative study of psychotherapy*. Baltimore, MD: Johns Hopkins Press.

Freer, S. A. (2015). *Modernist mythopoeia: The twilight of the gods*. Basingstoke, England: Palgrave Macmillan.

Holmesland, A. L., Seikkula, J., & Hopfenbeck, M. (2014). Inter-agency work in open dialogue: The significance of listening and authenticity. *Journal of Interprofessional Care, 28*(5), 433–439. doi:10.3109/13561820.2014.901939

Holmesland, A. L., Seikkula, J., Nilsen, O., Hopfenbeck, M., & Erik Arnkil, T. (2010). Open dialogues in social networks: Professional identity and transdisciplinary collaboration. *International Journal of Integrated Care, 10*, 1–14.

Janet, P. (1907). *The major symptons of hysteria: Fifteen lectures given in the Medical School of Harvard University*. New York, NY: Macmillan.

Janet, P. M. F. (2015). *L'automatisme psychologique: Essai de psychologie expérimentale sur les formes inférieures de l'activité humaine* [The psychological automatism: Experimental psychology test on lower forms of human activity]: *Paris, 1889*. London, England: Forgotten Books. (Original work published 1889)

Johns, L. C., Kompus, K., Connell, M., Humpston, C., Lincoln, T. M., Longden, E., . . . Laroi, F. (2014). Auditory verbal hallucinations in persons with and without a need for care. *Schizophrenia Bulletin, 40*(Suppl. 4), S255–S264. doi:10.1093/schbul/sbu005

Jung, C. G. (1928). *Two essays on analytical psychology*. (n.p.): Bailliére, Tindall and Cox.

Jung, C. G. (1957). *The collected works of C. G. Jung. Vol. 1. Psychiatric studies*. (n.p.).

Jung, C. G. (1960). *Experimental researches on the doctrine of complexes* (R. F. C. Hull, Trans., pp. 598–604). London, England: Routledge & Kegan Paul. (Original work published 1934)

Jung, C. G. (1962). *Symbols of transformation: An analysis of the prelude to a case of schizophrenia*. New York, NY: Harper.

Jung, C. G. (1974). *The psychology of dementia praecox*. Princeton, NJ: Princeton University Press.

Jung, C. G., McGuire, W., Shamdasani, S., & Jung, C. G. (2012). *Introduction to Jungian psychology: Notes of the seminar on analytical psychology given in 1925* (Rev. ed.). Princeton, NJ: Princeton University Press.

Kingdon, D. G., & Turkington, D. (1994). *Cognitive-behavioral therapy of schizophrenia*. Hove, England: Erlbaum.

Locke, J. (1894). *An essay concerning human understanding: With the notes and illustrations of the author, and an analysis of his doctrine of ideas, also, questions on Locke's essay, by A. M.* London, England: Ward, Lock & Bowden.

Longden, E. (2013). The voices in my head. *TED Talks*. Retrieved from http://www.ted.com/talks/eleanor_longden_the_voices_in_my_head?language=en

Longden, E., Madill, A., & Waterman, M. G. (2012). Dissociation, trauma, and the role of lived experience: Toward a new conceptualization of voice hearing. *Psychological Bulletin, 138*(1), 28–76. doi:10.1037/a0025995

Longden, E., & Proctor, G. (2012). A rationale for service responses to self-injury. *Journal of Mental Health, 21*(1), 15–22. doi:10.3109/09638237.2011.608744

Lyons, J., Lloyd, E., West, S., & Goodwin, S. (1997). *Mythopoeia: A process of being.* Wrexham, England: Wrexham County Borough Council, Education & Leisure Directorate.

Mace, C., & Margison, F. (1997). *Psychotherapy of psychosis.* London, England: Gaskell.

Moskowitz, A. (2006, February). *Pierre Janet's influence on Bleuler's concept of schizophrenia.* Paper presented at the Trauma, Dissoziation, Persönlichkeit, Pierre Janets Beiträge zur modernen Psychiatrie, Psychologie und Psychotherapie, Lengerich.

Olson, M. E., Laitila, A., Rober, P., & Seikkula, J. (2012). The shift from monologue to dialogue in a couple therapy session: Dialogical investigation of change from the therapists' point of view. *Family Process, 51*(3), 420–435. doi:10.1111/j.1545-5300. 2012.01406.x

Read, J. (2013). *Childhood adversity and psychosis.* Retrieved from https://www.youtube .com/watch?v=Y6do5bkUEys

Reilly, S. P. (1997). Psychoanalytic and psychodynamic approaches to psychosis: An overview. In C. Mace & F. Margison (Eds.), *Psychotherapy of psychosis* (pp. 13–30). London, England: Gaskell.

Romme, M., & Escher, S. (1993). *Accepting voices.* London, England: MIND Publications.

Ross, C. A. (2004). *Schizophrenia: Innovations in diagnosis and treatment.* Binghamton, NY: Haworth Maltreatment and Trauma.

Saks, E. (2012). Elyn Saks: A tale of mental illness—from the inside. *TEDGlobal.* Retrieved from http://www.ted.com/talks/elyn_saks_seeing_mental_illness?language=en

Seikkula, J., & Alakare, B. (2004). [Open dialog: alternative point of view in psychiatric patient care]. *Duodecim, 120*(3), 289–296.

Seikkula, J., Karvonen, A., Kykyri, V. L., Kaartinen, J., & Penttonen, M. (2015). The embodied attunement of therapists and a couple within dialogical psychotherapy: An introduction to the Relational Mind Research Project. *Family Process.* doi:10.1111/ famp.12152

Seikkula, J., & Olson, M. E. (2003). The open dialogue approach to acute psychosis: Its poetics and micropolitics. *Family Process, 42*(3), 403–418.

Sharfstein, S. S. (2005, August 19). Big Pharma and American psychiatry: The good, the bad, and the ugly. *Psychiatric News, 3.* Retrieved from http://psychnews.psychiatryonline .org/doi/full/10.1176/pn.40.16.00400003

Solomon, R. M., & Shapiro, F. (2008). EMDR and the adaptive information processing model. *Journal of EMDR Practice and Research, 2*(4), 315–325.

Sullivan, H. S. (1953). *The interpersonal theory of psychiatry* (1st ed.). New York, NY: Norton.

Thomas, P., & Longden, E. (2013). Madness, childhood adversity and narrative psychiatry: Caring and the moral imagination. *Medical Humanities, 39*(2), 119–125. doi:10.1136/ medhum-2012-010268

Tolkien, J. R. R., & Tolkien, J. R. R. M. (1988). *Tree and leaf: Including the poem Mythopoeia.* London, England: Unwin Hyman.

Waldinger, R. J., Seidman, E. L., Gerber, A. J., Liem, J. H., Allen, J. P., & Hauser, S. T. (2003). Attachment and core relationship themes: Wishes for autonomy and closeness in the narratives of securely and insecurely attached adults. *Psychotherapy Research, 13*(1), 77–98. doi:10.1093/ptr/kpg008

FIVE

Eye Movement Desensitization and Reprocessing (EMDR) Therapy

Paul William Miller and Derek Farrell

Intention: *To equip the reader with a comprehensive overview of how to understand presenting issues within an AIP model and to describe the standard eight-phase, three-pronged protocol of the standard model.*

Our journey together is now well advanced. We have looked at the link between trauma, schizophrenia, and psychosis; explored dissociation and psychosis phenomenologically; and formulated a method for gathering the relevant history and completing an appropriate examination of mental state in this client group. Having set the context for applying psychotherapy in psychosis, we then explored the psychotherapies apart from EMDR therapy. Now we will proceed to specifically study EMDR therapy.

A REVIEW OF THE STANDARD MODEL

If interconnectedness characterizes health and mental well-being, then disconnection characterizes disorder and mental illness. Sadly, we can see this inner disconnection reflected in the outer reality of mental health professions. One such example is the schism between psychiatry and neurology, which can result in an unbalanced view of our patients and ourselves. I invite us to be mindful of all that we are, by reuniting body and mind. The other divide that we ought to bear in mind is the one between the patient and the therapist. In my experience this divide is even more pronounced within the treatment of psychosis, as compared with the treatment of neuroses or affective disorders. For me, this is in part due to the legacy of Jaspers's belief that psychosis is unintelligible, where psychotic phenomena are believed to be meaningless (Jaspers, 1963). The presentation of a mind "degenerated" into meaningless babble is frightening for most of us to behold, and humanity seeks to distance itself from such a situation, stating, "I am not like that and never could be." However, I believe that we are all capable of such a state as much as we are all capable of dreaming. Humanity and the human mind at its most functional are fundamentally about connection and our interconnectivity with the people and places around us. Disconnection is more often than not a pathological state for humans, and solitary confinement is universally recognized as the severest of all punishments. Incoming neural traffic is initially a jumble of unconnected pieces. The raw perceptual data that enter the nervous system as "noise" are normally processed into a connected and meaningful signal. "Humans are creatures of meaning, and finding meaning in our experiences is not just another name for spirituality [it] is also the very shape of human happiness" (Rohr, 2011). We need connection, and connecting allows us to find happiness.

In the field of psychotherapy, eye movement desensitization and reprocessing (EMDR) therapy is an important and integrated psychotherapeutic method that utilizes our innate biology to facilitate healing (Shapiro, 2001). Allan J. Hobson, a Harvard psychiatrist and dream researcher, when writing with the medical journalist Jonathan Leonard, coined the term *neurodynamic*. In doing so, they hoped to encourage a "third way" for mental health in general and psychiatry in particular—one that integrates the psychodynamics of the psychotherapists' formulation with the neurobiology of the neurologist (Hobson & Leonard, 2001). For me their book did achieve the aim of articulating a third way for mental health professionals, and this helped bring me a sense of opportunity and hope for my area of clinical practice. Perhaps, as mental health professionals, we can choose to step outside the conventional "trench warfare" of body, mind, and soul and instead focus on our unity. I believe that we learn from the environment we are in.

"Myths are public dreams, dreams are private myths."
—*Joseph Campbell (1993)*

The Greeks spoke of the learning models of logos and mythos. In modernity people have generally come to think of the learning through logos as superior to learning through mythos. However, we can learn much through a mythopoetic approach to life and the world in which we live and breathe and have our being. I think that this mythosophical approach can teach us much through songs and stories and ought not to be considered mere fairy tales for children. I believe that mythos is also the milieu of dreams and perhaps also of psychosis.

One of my favorite Jewish traditional songs is "Hine Ma Tov." Its lyrics are the first verse of Psalm 133, which reads, "Behold, how good and how pleasant it is for people to dwell together in unity!" When we as mental health professionals and healers choose to "dwell together in unity," we can achieve great things. In my opinion, EMDR therapy is neurodynamic in the true sense of Hobson and Leonard's term, and this positions it powerfully as an effective, integrative psychotherapy. It is my firm belief that we will come to apply EMDR therapy to a widening range of mental illnesses. EMDR therapy researchers are working hard to examine and publish their findings on its efficacy in areas such as addictions, self-harming behaviors, and depression. More research is needed.

If we are to be capable of treating the whole person who presents in our clinics, our understanding of mental illness and its treatments must be similarly holistic. EMDR therapy utilizes an information processing model, which is proposed to be innate: the adaptive information processing (AIP) model. An EMDR therapist needs to have a detailed knowledge of the AIP model, as this is the foundation upon which we build an understanding of the patient's presenting problems. This solid foundation is the bedrock of AIP and it also shapes our treatment plan. We also know that AIP is predictive of outcome. The AIP model proposes the normal mechanism by which information processing takes place, resulting in a functional and integrated memory network. If the AIP system is blocked or the process derailed, it is proposed that this results in the formation of a dysfunctional memory network (DMN). This is why identifying the DMN and reprocessing it results in the presenting problems ameliorating or resolving entirely.

The AIP model refers to a postulated innate information processing system that metabolizes all of the data entering the mind through our senses. It takes these data and converts them into a meaningful neural signal: a functional memory network. We do not need to learn how to do this. I believe that every healthy child born into the world has the AIP system encoded in his or her DNA, which ultimately gives us the potential to generate narrative. This system brings meaning to the chaos of the world of data that surrounds us, which is the journey from "noise" to "signal" by integrating the building blocks of consciousness: beliefs, images, feelings, and sensations (Bergmann, 2012). I believe that we all have this drive to seek meaning for our lives. However, the AIP system is more than merely a system that generates narrative and meaning. It is an intrinsic information processing system that is fundamental to how the brain operates and functions. Our brains are constantly digesting and processing material and information all of the time. When the body is exposed to stress responses (including stress hormones), this can affect the natural information processing system, resulting in the brain not being able to digest and assimilate experiences. The AIP model is consistent with the understanding of information processing postulated by Freud and Pavlov stating, "there appears to be a neurological balance in a distinct physiological system that allows information to be processed to an 'adaptive resolution'" (Shapiro, 2001, p. 30).

Our life's journey will invariably contain experiences of suffering, and we all struggle to find meaning in the midst of our pain and discomfort. Being able to find meaning for our life's journey is the thing that gives birth to that most human of attributes: hope. We all need hope if we are to have any sense of peace and contentment in our life's journey. I believe that this is fundamentally what we, as EMDR therapists, help our clients to find: meaning, hope, and contentment. One man who must surely have made such a journey said the following:

"Hope is not the conviction that something will turn out
well but the certainty that something makes sense, regardless
of how it turns out."
—*Vaclav Havel (First democratically elected president
of Czechoslovakia [1989–1993],
first president of the Czech Republic
[1993–2003] after the Czech–Slovak split)*

THE STANDARD THREE-PRONGED EMDR THERAPY PROTOCOL

In a moment we will outline the standard eight phases of EMDR therapy. This sits within the standard three-pronged EMDR protocol, which guides the overall treatment plan. Targets are categorized into three prongs: past experiences that have generated the psychological "pathogen," the DMN; the present-day triggers that evoke the traumatic material; and the future templates that are "necessary for appropriate future action" (Shapiro, 2001, p. 76). In this way a treatment plan may target, for example, the road traffic collision (past) and red cars (present-day trigger of traumatic material), and then build a future template focusing on how to cope with driving the same route that the collision occurred on.

THE STANDARD EIGHT-PHASE EMDR THERAPY PROTOCOL

The standard EMDR therapy protocol is divided into eight phases, with a three-pronged protocol that processes material considering the past, present, and future (Shapiro, 2001). The eight phases are:

1. History and treatment planning
2. Preparation
3. Assessment
4. Desensitization
5. Installation
6. Body scan
7. Closure
8. Re-evaluation

We will look at all of the phases in detail and explore the intention behind each. There is a logical reason for the sequence, which fits with our current knowledge of neurobiology and the AIP model. In regard to EMDR therapy as a psychotherapy paradigm, although phases 1 and 2 can be considered generic for all models of psychotherapy, we will look at them specifically through the lens of the AIP model at all times. This book deals with a modification of the standard protocol, so it is essential that we begin with a complete understanding of the standard protocol. This allows us to be clear on what elements of EMDR therapy we are modifying. We need also be able to give a reasoned answer as to why we are doing so.

History and Treatment Planning (Phase 1)

Intention for this treatment phase: *To gather information from the client that will inform an AIP-based understanding and formulation of the presenting issues. This AIP-based formulation will then facilitate treatment planning by identifying and sequencing targets for reprocessing that correlate with DMNs. By viewing the history through the three-pronged aspect of the model we focus on: (a) past history related to the formation of the DMN, (b) present-day triggers, and (c) future templates that target future "predicted" dysfunction.*

The AIP model views the negative behaviors and mental state of the client as being the result of dysfunctionally held information, which we refer to as the

DMN. This DMN is proposed to result from a failure in the processing of information that relates to the perceptions occurring at the time it was generated; we refer to this as state-specific form. Distinct from the cognitive behavioral model, a negative self-belief in the AIP model is not seen as the cause of the client's present dysfunction; rather, it is understood to be a symptom of the unprocessed data of earlier life experiences. The DMN is like a time capsule buried in the psyche; it contains the affect and perspective of the period of time at which it was created. Therefore, in the EMDR therapy model of understanding, attitudes, emotions, and sensations are not considered to be merely simple reactions to a past event; they are seen as manifestations of the physiologically accumulated perceptions stored in memory and the mind's reaction to them. This is not entirely a new way to consider information stored in the psyche, and Moskowitz reminds us that the "complex" of Jung and the "fixed ideas" of Janet are very similar constructs (Moskowitz, 2005). In my opinion, the DMN of Shapiro is merely another iteration of this same concept. As quoted by van der Kolk and van der Hart (1989, p. 1532), Janet reminds us that dysfunctionally stored material consists of

> new spheres of consciousness around memories of intensely arousing experiences, which . . . organise cognitive, affective and visceral elements of the trauma while simultaneously keeping them out of conscious awareness.

Jung adds that it is an active and dynamic system, stating, "It is the image of a certain psychic situation which is strongly accentuated emotionally. . . . This image has a powerful inner coherence, it has its own wholeness, and in addition, a relatively high degree of autonomy . . . and therefore behaves like an animated foreign body in the sphere of consciousness" (Jung, 1934/1960, p. 96). These characteristics are at the very core of what a DMN is: a fractured and separate part of the psyche, stored in state-specific form that is not functionally interdependent with healthy memories. A DMN has cognitions, affect, and somatosensory elements that can direct the choices, feelings, and behaviors of a person in the present. These are, more often than not, what the patient presents with. If you recall our metaphor of a polluted river, we are seeking to identify the pollutant at the point it enters the river; in other words, we are seeking to identify the point where the AIP fails, processing halts, and a dysfunctional memory network is created; this point will then be targeted within phases 3 to 7.

It has—now famously—been stated that "the body keeps the score" in regard to trauma:

> If we look beyond the list of specific symptoms that entail formal psychiatric diagnoses, we find that almost all mental suffering involves either trouble in creating workable and satisfying relationships or difficulties in regulating arousal (as in the case of habitually becoming enraged, shut down, overexcited, or disorganized). Usually it's a combination of both. (van der Kolk, 1994, pp. 78–79)

The effects of trauma are biopsychosocial, and the emotional ramifications are experienced in our bodies. DMN, acting as a time capsule, contains the snapshot of the psychophysiological state that the person was in at the time of the trauma. This explains why some people experience somatic, gustatory, and olfactory phenomena as flashbacks. The body really does keep the score. When we take a holistic approach to our clients, our history taking is not simply guided by a semistructured interview, but also involves us paying attention to what the client feels in his or her body as well as what is perceived in the client's mind. In the initial phases of EMDR therapy we are connecting with the client in the intersubjective. This is not just an information-gathering exercise through question and answer. It ought to be a genuine connection that helps clients to connect to their emotions as well as their thoughts. The importance of this somatosensory aspect of DMNs will be further developed, as it is important in the approach we take to the treatment of psychosis with EMDR therapy. It is also important to keep in mind that EMDR therapy is a two-person dynamic, and so, as therapists, we must also pay attention to what is taking place in our own bodies and minds.

Therapeutic Alliance

As we are starting out the therapeutic journey, the client is choosing a person whom he or she can trust to guide the client through difficult emotional terrain. In my experience, there are two extremes of a spectrum along which people sit in respect to their attitude toward therapy. The first group is passive and present in a manner that essentially states, "Here I am; fix me." The other, more active end of the spectrum states, "Here I am; now what do I need to do to get resolution?" Before we can move forward with clients, we need them to trust us. They need to have a sense that we know where we are going and also that we are capable of guiding them. For me, the most important task in phases 1 and 2 is the building of therapeutic alliance strong enough to support healing.

Be the Therapist You Would Want to See

It is helpful to keep in mind that the process at this point is as much about the client interviewing you for the job of becoming his or therapist as it is about you interviewing him or her for the post of client. If clients feel that your questioning is too aggressive or challenging, or if they feel you are not fully present with them in the therapy space because you are not listening attentively, then they will often choose not to enter into therapy with you. Therapeutic attunement is very important at this point, and within the therapy space the client and therapist ought to create and enter a "golden bubble of therapy" (Shapiro, 2001). In other words, the client and therapist should be feeling a sense of "we" rather than "me." We can think of attunement as "a kinesthetic and emotional sensing of others, knowing their rhythm, affect and experience by metaphorically being in their skin, and going beyond empathy to create a two-person experience of unbroken feeling connectedness" (Erskine, 2015, p. 45). In other words, we choose to be fully present and intentionally focused on the person in front of us, actively listening to the client and connecting nonverbally with him or her in an energetic exchange that creates the feeling of "we" (Siegel & Buczynski, 2014). This attunement is integral to generating a strong therapeutic rapport. It is like the foundation of a house; you cannot simply omit it. The Leaning Tower of Pisa may be a famous landmark because of the problems with its foundation;

however, few therapists and even fewer clients would wish to participate in therapy built upon unsecure foundations. Attunement is an essential item, and not an optional extra, in an environment where a person is being invited to choose to be very vulnerable. From this place of connection—vulnerability—the sharing and experiencing of painful material can take place in a cathartic way. This healing potential is in part due to the fact that vulnerability creates the potential for healthy and reparative intimacy in the therapy space (Brown, 2012). This is a dynamic that ought to be at the heart of all psychotherapeutic relationships, and attunement and good therapeutic rapport are just as vital in EMDR therapy as they are in any of the schools of psychotherapy.

Relational EMDR Therapy

An advocate for this relational aspect of EMDR therapy is Mark Dworkin, who emphasizes the power of the relational dynamic in EMDR and developed the relational interweave concept (Dworkin, 2005). If a client is defended and closed off emotionally from the therapist, the client will not be capable of getting to a place of vulnerability, and as a consequence the psychotherapeutic bond will be weak and superficial. However, when we are fully present with the client in the therapy space we will be best placed to learn why this person is sitting here on this day, in this therapy space; so listen. Listen fully and empathically; listen with heart, mind, and soul. As St. Benedict said, "Listen . . . and attend with the ear of your heart" (Fry, 1981, p. 15). This will empower the client to guide you where you both need to go in this therapeutic journey. In looking at the process of history taking through the lens of AIP, listen attentively and keep in mind that we are like farmers being given seeds of clients' life stories that we, as EMDR therapists, sow in the soil of the AIP model. For EMDR therapists, AIP must be the seedbed for our formulations and the resulting treatment plans for our patients.

The Big Four of Effective Psychotherapy

As far back as 1961, Jerome D. Frank wrote an influential book that helped a whole generation of psychiatrists and psychologists to think more deeply about psychotherapy (Frank, 1961). In his book, *Persuasion and Healing*, he identified four features shared by all psychotherapies that accounted for most of their effectiveness: an emotionally charged relationship, a therapeutic environment, a rationale or myth that provides a plausible explanation for the client's symptoms, and a procedure to resolve the symptoms. Unsurprisingly, EMDR therapy has all of these four features.

I will examine phase 1 in two parts, history taking (phase 1a) and treatment planning (phase 1b), to help with clarity when we come to discuss the modifications of the Indicating Cognitions of Negative Networks (ICoNN) approach in the later chapters.

History Taking (Phase 1a)

I recommend using a standard structure for history taking that can be used flexibly and allow a client to tell his or her story. This approach is sensitive to identifying the phenomena described in Chapter 3. This semistructured approach will ensure, as much as is reasonably possible, that we do not miss something important. However, that does not mean that the client will recall all pertinent details at this point in the therapeutic journey. Please remember that omissions by the client at this stage may often prove to be of great significance later on. We must also be mindful that a semistructured approach to history taking ought not to be applied too rigidly. Consider that by the time clients have arrived in your office, some will have spent many hours thinking about what they are going to say and will have been, most likely, rehearsing it. Their stories at this point often come tumbling out in a disjointed manner. This fragmentation reflects the noncontiguous way that trauma memories are laid down, when storage changes to a more flashbulb fashion, where there is no complete and flowing narrative. Some clients present at this point like a bottle of champagne; when the cork is popped, the story gushes forward all at once. I invite you to allow clients to tell their stories by using open questions that will generate a narrative answer, rather than simple yes/no questions, known as closed questions. At this point, avoid trying to engage clients in a detailed question-and-answer session, as allowing them to tell their stories is vital and much therapy time is wasted if we attempt to make them fit within an overly rigid assessment protocol. The aim at this point is twofold: to succeed in helping clients to feel that they have told their stories and that you have heard them. Success in this makes for a good prognosis. It is of vital importance that the examination of psychosis be completed with the attitude that Colin Ross refers to as active neutrality (Ross, 2004). This stance means that rather than immediately questioning the veracity of delusional material, we take a keener interest in the client's attendant emotions and behavioral responses. In the case of a young man who presented with a delusional belief that he had female breasts, my questioning explored how that made him feel, rather than challenging the belief through confrontation with facts.

Please note that for some clients, history taking doesn't happen all at once. People may tell their stories in a variety of different ways. Some experiences may involve shame responses in which the person may be apprehensive about disclosure of certain aspects of the experiences, which may unfold only after some reprocessing has occurred.

Miller's CAEL

One of the authors (Paul William Miller) developed the following model to assist therapists in respect to how they relate interpersonally with patients; it is summarized by the acronym CAEL. The Gaelic term *cael* can be translated as "victorious people," and that is exactly what we are aiming for through our therapeutic collaboration with the client. We want people to live a life full of victory and find a way through their challenges. CAEL consists of two blocks of three elements: the letters C, A, and E represent the character of the therapeutic relationship, and the L, of which there are three, represents how we build that. The first block is further explained as follows:

   C is for CONNECT: At its simplest level the therapeutic relationship is a connection. This connection ought to be created in such a way as to allow clients to be vulnerable in a safe way, enabling them to do the therapeutic work that they need to do.

A is for AFFIRM: The connection between the therapist and the client is to be one that affirms the client. To affirm someone can be defined as declaring our support for the client: upholding or defending him or her. Or we can think of it as offering the client emotional support or encouragement.

E is for EMPOWER: The connection is also one that empowers clients to achieve their therapeutic journeys. Albert Einstein stated that you couldn't solve a problem by thinking at the same level of thinking at which the problem was created. The facilitation and input of the therapist allows clients to think on a different level, empowering them to find the solutions they seek. This often involves the empowered individuals developing confidence in their own newly found capabilities.

One of the powerful distinctions of EMDR from other psychotherapies is that we, as therapists, facilitate clients in utilizing their own information processing systems rather than formulating a pattern of thinking that we then encourage them to adopt. Ultimately, the EMDR therapy process is one that helps clients re-engage their information processing systems to functionally integrate a trauma experience.

The three Ls of CAEL represent how we aim to bring about such a therapeutic dynamic, as follows:

LISTEN: This is the most important task of the therapist, and we have already underlined its importance in the history-taking section. I remind supervisees that we have two ears and one mouth, so a good rule of thumb is to listen twice as much as we speak. Here we see the whole CAEL model in action: By listening we connect, we affirm, and we empower.

LOVE: This is about the unconditional positive regard that we, as therapists, offer our clients. It is the glue that creates the therapeutic bond. We demonstrate this through a nonjudgmental and open attitude within which the person allows himself or herself to be vulnerable. The Quantum Brain model (Eccles, 1994) states that the three brains of the Triune Brain model (MacLean, 1990) are driven energetically by fear, and that ultimately the self is slowly converting the brain to function on the universal energy of love. It is proposed that it is love that is the energy that unites all things; it certainly ought to characterize the therapeutic relationship.

LEARN: This characteristic of the therapeutic relationship is a commitment to the attitude of being a lifelong learner. We are constantly learning from the client and from the world around us. Because EMDR therapy is about helping facilitate clients' reprocessing of DMNs within their own AIP systems, we are guided in many ways by the client. This makes learning what works, and what doesn't, a very important skill.

> "Learning is not a product of schooling but the lifelong attempt to acquire it."
> —*Albert Einstein*

I invite you to make the assessment format presented in Chapter 3 fit the client, and not the other way around. The method I propose to create this healing dynamic is CAEL: connection that is affirming and empowering, by listening, loving, and learning. Assessment and history taking is one time where one size does not fit all—to make for good therapy, your approach needs to be tailored to the person with whom you are working collaboratively. The fruit of your collaboration with the client will allow you to judge the effectiveness of your performance in this phase of EMDR therapy. The information gained from a properly completed AIP-informed assessment will result in the identification of targets for reprocessing in the later phases. Please remember that a full and detailed history will garner lots of positive information for the therapist's store of resources. This resource material will contain important functional memory networks and positive cognitions. This information is important for the therapist and vital for the client's recovery. If you are not familiar with this approach, reread Chapter 3 now and revisit it before you see a new client. Apply this method consistently, as "practice makes perfect."

Treatment Planning (Phase 1b)

After history taking we move to treatment planning. In other words, we set the route for therapy. After careful history taking, we have acquired one or more targets that relate to DMNs. These DMNs are triggered for the patient by internal and/or external stimuli, and when triggered they result in unfortunate emotional, cognitive, and behavioral reactions. These reactions are essentially the phenomena that have brought the person into therapy at this point in time. Now the task for the therapist is to plan the sequencing of the treatment. By taking a history in the form suggested, we effectively gain a timeline that allows us to place the trauma events in the order in which they occurred along the person's lifeline, up to the present day. A "first, worst, or last" approach may be taken in respect to the order of the targets for reprocessing, or the therapist may also choose to formulate "clusters" of trauma. Clusters can be linked by various common elements, such as episodes, perpetrators, domains of the negative cognitions (NCs), and involved emotions (van der Hart, Groenendijk, Gonzalez, Mosquera, & Solomon, 2014). More information on treatment planning within the standard protocol is available in the seminal text (Shapiro, 2001). I will explore this aspect of the ICoNN approach's methodology for psychosis in more detail in Chapters 6 and 7.

As therapists, we ought to keep in mind that we often take a full, detailed clinical history and mental state examination, only to later be brought face to face, within EMDR reprocessing, with a past event that the person has not mentioned. Indeed, a person will often say something along the lines of, "I haven't thought of that in years." Once we acknowledge such a target and reprocess it, there is nearly always a sense of astonishment. A previously hidden DMN is metabolized mentally, and the result is very often a resolution of the presenting problem. As we have already acknowledged, the AIP model explains mental health pathology, is indicative of targets that are suitable for reprocessing, and is predictive of outcome (Shapiro & Maxfield, 2002), and that is why we must always view our clients through the lens of the AIP model.

Preparation (Phase 2)

Intention for this treatment phase: *To ready the client for engaging in the EMDR therapy.*

> "Ostensibly preparation sets the stage for all that is to follow."
> *(Bergmann, 2012, p. 177)*

This phase involves helping the client with remaining grounded enough to allow the processing of information and assists the client with emotional containment in between sessions. The preparation phase is about readying clients for processing through the building of resources and the teaching of affect-building strategies and other psychoeducational content that brings meaning to clients' experiences.

Preparation may consist of as little as one session of 60 to 90 minutes for a single incident of type I trauma resulting in posttraumatic stress disorder (PTSD). However, for complex PTSD, neuroses, or personality disorder, preparation will be an always-present element in the treatment, with the therapist pendulating the intention of the treatment phase from it to phases 3 through 7 and back again many times. This is also true in psychosis. The AIP system provides a foundation for building an understanding of how the mental disorder has arisen and allows the proposal of a plan as to how it may be resolved within the EMDR psychotherapeutic method.

Therapeutic Alliance

We have already been looking at how building a strong therapeutic alliance begins right from the start of our clinical engagement with the patient. A strong therapeutic alliance is a very important element for successful therapy (Dworkin, 2005; Frank, 1961). Some clients form this alliance readily, as the therapist facilitates them in the telling of their stories. For this group the seemingly strange dual attention stimulation/bilateral stimulation (DAS/BLS) element of the EMDR therapy method is not usually a significant issue. DAS, which refers to when the client is paying attention to both internal and external stimuli during processing, is not unique to EMDR. The BLS aspect of EMDR therapy is unique to the EMDR method and involves the application of stimulation in the form of eye movements (EMs), alternating pulsers (small devices that deliver a gentle vibration), or alternating auditory stimulation. In the age of readily accessible information on the World Wide Web, increasing numbers of patients desire and require substantially more work on the part of the therapist to help build a strong therapeutic alliance. There is an expectation that we will be able to answer the questions that they pose, or, at the very least, be capable of finding an answer through supervision. This group of questioners will require more of a description of the EMDR therapy method, and in my experience they want to know about the meaning and function of DAS/BLS in particular. Some people simply need to know that EMDR therapy and the DAS/BLS element of the method are scientifically purposeful, rather than just some form of "smoke and mirrors," before they can allow themselves to begin to engage. Therefore, it is important that EMDR therapists equip themselves with the knowledge that is needed to explain what the DAS/BLS element is, and this is why an increasing number of EMDR trainers include a firm foundation in the neurobiology of trauma in their training syllabi. Next I will present my proposed theory, with metaphors, to explain how the DAS/BLS element functions within the information processing system of the human mind. This rationale ought to equip us as EMDR therapists in meeting the needs of our clients, whatever their level of inquisitiveness. The psychoeducational explanations that we provide as therapists continue to build a sound therapeutic alliance and help to build trust, in the method and in us.

The Credibility Gap

I recall one client whom I was asked to see as an inpatient. He had experienced a severe trauma during which he nearly lost his life following a horrific stabbing. At this stage he was severely affected by PTSD, and I had been asked to screen him for treatment with EMDR therapy. After giving an introduction to the method and a description of what would be involved, we parted company and arranged to meet again at my clinic. Only after EMDR therapy was successfully completed did the client later reveal that when, after many years of suffering, he had heard me say that I could help him dispel his symptoms by "waving my fingers," he had thought that I should be the one admitted to the psychiatric unit. We have since spoken together at conferences and he still tells this story to audiences with amusement. For me this is also a wonderful example of how we can enter into EMDR therapy with a client who has a lot of doubt in the method. Belief that EMDR therapy will work is not essential—as long as the therapeutic rapport is strong enough and the client is willing to step into a place of being an observer who trusts the process, healing can occur. In my experience, introducing the client to EMDR therapy through the safe/calm place exercise, which I facilitate with DAS/BLS, allows the client to experience a decrease in arousal, as clients often come to the office with a great deal of anticipatory anxiety and stress in their systems. This experience that the EMDR therapy method can bring early on is very useful in building trust in the client for the psychotherapeutic method.

Psychoeducation: 1... 2... 3...

Part of the preparation of the client for processing involves the giving of information. I include three key areas of psychoeducation that assist me in the preparation phase with clients. Having a solid awareness of these is necessary, but each need not be utilized to the same depth of detail for every client. The key areas are as follows:

1. An overview of the AIP model (as described in the history-taking section)
2. A basic overview of the mind/brain interconnectedness by mapping AIP onto MacLean's Triune Brain model (MacLean, 1990)
3. An overview of how the DAS/BLS element of the EMDR therapy method facilitates information processing and the resultant resolution of presenting problems (this builds primarily on the stochastic resonance [SR] model proposed by one of the authors, Paul William Miller)

AIP and MacLean's Triune Brain Model

We have already examined the AIP model, so let us now turn our attention to mind/brain interconnectedness and the Triune Brain model of Paul MacLean (1990). For more than 20 years, this model has formed a core part of what I teach clients during the psychoeducational aspects of the preparation phase. I find that people can easily identify with it and it thus forms a structure upon which they can hang the AIP model. People need a framework to help them understand the EMDR therapy paradigm, and as therapists we ought to be able to present it in a cogent and coherent manner; this builds trust and therapeutic rapport. Keep in mind that for some a basic overview is all that is needed; nevertheless, the benefit of using the three elements of psychoeducation listed earlier is that they can be taught to different levels of detail. In this way, for those clients who want to know a detailed explanation of AIP, the currently postulated interaction of structural neurobiology relevant to EMDR therapy and the proposed neurodynamics of SR can meet their needs. For the client who wishes to know merely that EMDR has an unpinning and foundational model that is supported in a meaningful way by current research, the same building blocks can be utilized, but to a different depth. As Frank proposed in his influential 1961 book, one of the four key factors that explain most of the effectiveness of psychotherapy is a "rationale" or a "myth" that provides a plausible explanation for the client's symptoms, which the client can accept from the therapist. I hope you will feel that the information presented here is rationale rather than mythology, but as I have already stated, a mythosophical approach can be equally valid.

Common Ground

It is important that we teach clearly, in an understandable way, whatever model we choose to rely upon, so that this model becomes common ground on which we can meet with the client. However, it is also important that we keep in mind that it is still a theoretical model, which continues to develop as new advances elucidate more knowledge. In this way we can avoid becoming dogmatic in our professional stance and integrate new knowledge as it comes to us on our journey of lifelong learning and professional development. Some readers may prefer to use an alternative model such as the Quantum Brain model of Sir John Eccles, and for those who wish a more detailed look at this model I recommend his book *How the Self Controls Its Brain* (Eccles, 1994). I will not further elucidate it here, as I have personally not found it necessary for clients' preparation for EMDR therapy.

Triune Brain Theory

MacLean's Triune Brain theory teaches that the brain can be thought of as three brains in one rather than one single brain. We can think of these brains as being a building with three floors: a ground floor, first floor, and top floor. The building also has two wings: a left wing and a right wing. The floors relate to three brains: the reptilian, the limbic, and the neocortical. The wings are the left and right hemispheres.

The reptilian brain is the ground floor and is so named because we share this type of brain with all reptiles. It deals with nonconscious functions and instincts, such as breathing and digestion. This region is not a rational, reasoning part of the central nervous system (CNS). Paul Pierre Broca first described the "limbic lobe" in 1878, and the term *limbic system* was coined by Paul MacLean in 1952 to describe the parts of the brain that deal with emotion (Rajmohan & Mohandas, 2007). The neocortex is the most "human" part of the system, and thoughts here are operating in a rational fashion; it can easily understand concepts such as cause and effect.

Information in the form of data enters the neural system through the five senses. At the reptilian level it is sensed and relayed onward as long as there is no sensing of danger or threat. The part of the brain that decides on threat versus no threat is the amygdala, which acts as an area of interconnectivity. In the amygdala, information from all of the senses is connected and given an emotional value. The sensory data from the eyes, mouth, skin, and ears travel first to the thalamus and are then relayed on to the amygdala via a single synapse (Bergmann, 2012; LeDoux, 1986), whereas the sense of smell bypasses the thalamus and is relayed straight to the amygdala (LeDoux, 1986). This is why smell is so evocative of emotion. Another, second branch relays signal from the thalamus to the neocortex, where it will pass through several layers before its full perception. As well as coming up through the levels of the CNS, information also crosses the midline at the level of the thalamus and shifts from the right hemisphere to the left, where the language center lies in the majority of people. This also allows access to the language centers of the brain, and so a normally encoded, functional memory network will have a contiguous narrative with an elucidated emotional valence that can be spoken of in a contextually relevant manner for the client.

Only after a neocortical assessment of the data has been made is a conscious response able to be initiated. However, if a threat has been flagged in the amygdala, then a behavioral response can be initiated immediately by the amygdala, outside of consciousness.

Let us assume that there is no threat. In this circumstance it is proposed that the data will pass through the amygdala, which detects no threat, and the thalamus will shift it from the left to the right hemisphere. This allows the development of a narrative and progress through the layers of the neocortex that encodes it as a functional memory network. However, if a threat has been sensed by the amygdala, surges in levels of epinephrine (adrenalin) and norepinephrine (noradrenalin) course through the body as a response. A thalamic signal triggers epinephrine release from the adrenal gland, and norepinephrine comes from the brain region known as the locus coeruleus. The greater the intensity of the arousal of the amygdala, the greater is the strength of the memorial imprint (LeDoux, 1986). If the information processing system is unable to cope with the quantum of threat signal that is elicited, thalamic activity decreases; this is a consistent finding in PTSD (Bergmann, 2008; Sartory et al., 2013; Yan et al., 2013). The important role of the thalamus and of cortico-thalamic "noise" is explored in more detail in the following section. This "failure" of the AIP is modeled as occurring at the level of the thalamus, and this is suggested to result in the creation of a DMN.

DAS/BLS Element of EMDR Therapy
AIP lacks an agreed-upon neurobiological foundation, and there is a lack of consensus across EMDR therapy clinicians. This is a limitation for the method and

a point of weakness that draws criticism. The standard EMDR therapy protocol utilizes a series of guided biological actions that are directed by the therapist to facilitate the processing of the DMN being targeted. At this time, the precise mechanism of these guided biological actions—eye movements, auditory tones, and tapping—remains unclear, and a range of proposed means by which the DAS/BLS element facilitates information processing has been offered in the scientific literature (Bergmann, 2008). Just as AIP is thought of as a universal information processing system that exists in humans, it is proposed to be the case that DAS/BLS works through a process that is just as ubiquitous. I propose that the physiological mechanism of action that is responsible is stochastic resonance (SR). SR was first mentioned in the scientific literature in 1980 (McDonnell & Abbott, 2009), and its proposed role in a number of biological systems is growing. SR is linked with random input, which appears initially unhelpful and could be thought of simply as noise. In the current era, which strives to experience everything in "high definition," noise is a negative experience, and science goes to substantial lengths to clean up signals by removing it. We do not want white noise in our music or during our cell phone calls. However, some research invites us to consider that "not all noise is bad" (Kosko, 2006). As noise is all around us, it would not be surprising at all that the mind not only copes with it, but actually utilizes it to facilitate processing within the neural system. One such example of helpful noise that is proposed to be functioning in the human brain is downward cortico-thalamic feedback—in other words, a signal coming from the higher centers of the brain (the cortex) to the area that functions as an essential information crossroads (the thalamus). Because the thought of helpful noise can appear oxymoronic, it has been suggested that SR can be more usefully thought of as "helpful randomness" (McDonnell & Abbott, 2009). The concept of helpful randomness is not actually a new idea; sailors, for example, used to believe that randomly falling raindrops could bring calm to a stormy sea. A mentor of mine taught me that good therapists are good storytellers, and Jim Knipe is one such person. He was a great help when I was developing the hypothesis for how the phenomenon of SR may function within EMDR therapy. As we discussed SR, he suggested to me that we think of it in the following way:

> Many people like to go to a crowded restaurant in order to enjoy socializing with friends. The presence and the noise of other people may facilitate good conversations by being stimulating, and also by providing a constant reminder of the importance of paying close attention to what the other person is saying. (Knipe, personal communication, 2014)

This metaphor may be the only explanation of SR that some clients need. For those readers who wish a detailed review of the current work around the proposed neurobiology of DAS/BLS and SR, please refer to the Appendix.

Teaching the Stop Signal

One of the aspects of EMDR therapy's preparation phase that I especially like is that we make clients fully aware that they are in control of the pace and process. It is their brains doing the healing, and if they need a break, they are encouraged to make that clear to us. We highlight that the locus of control is with the person undergoing therapy. Clients are able to stop the process if they feel that they need to. We empower them in doing so by teaching them a clear and unambiguous stop signal. This is, by convention, usually a raised a hand with the statement, "Stop!" It is important that we ask for a physical indication as well as speech because at some times the speech centers may be offline during the re-experiencing of traumatic material and the person may be unable to speak. Similarly, a client may say "stop" as he reiterates something said at the time of the trauma, but not intend to have the processing stop. A colleague once shared that one of his clients noted that the raising of the hand proved unsuitable; the client found it too similar to the position that his father assumed as he was about to strike the client. This reminds us that we must be focused and attend to the person who is with us in the room. Triggers for traumatic material are idiosyncratic, and even something that we intend as a tool to empower the client can be unsuitable. The key principle is that together, we agree on a suitable stop signal for the client.

Teaching the Safe/Calm Place

We similarly empower clients by introducing them to the skills entailed in the safe/calm place exercise. This provides the clinician and the person undergoing EMDR therapy with a powerful tool that may be used to close down an incomplete session. It may also help clients, in these early phases of EMDR therapy, to experience a degree of feeling relaxed: a state change. In some cases it may have been some considerable time since the client has felt relaxed. If this is the case, the safe/calm place exercise can act as a very potent catalyst in the forging of a "good enough" therapeutic alliance. Safe/calm place may be taught and installed with or without DAS/BLS. My personal practice is that I teach it and utilize DAS/BLS while doing so. I believe that this is more efficient, and clients appear to find it helpful. The fact that clients intellectually understand the function of the safe/calm place exercise, and that they have also experienced it, provides a strong sense of empowerment because they are acquiring skills and practical tools to manage the challenges that lie ahead in the therapeutic journey.

A Room That Exists Outside of Time and Space

In addition to the standard safe/calm place exercise, I also, in many cases, have the person imagine a "room that exists outside of time and space." I use the following word pictures to help the client to build this space:

> Imagine a room: a room that exists outside of time and space.
>
> It has a comfortable chair, much like the chair that you are now sitting on.
>
> Beside the chair is a low-set table, much like the table that is beside you now.
>
> On the table are three keys: one marked past, one marked present, and one marked future.
>
> Please take the keys—they are yours. You cannot lose them, and no one can use them without your permission.

The keys relate to three doors, of which you now become aware; they are in the wall in front of you.

There are three doors: one marked past, one marked present, and one marked future. Take some time to examine the doors and ensure that they are good, solid, safe, and secure. There is no way over them, around them, under them, or through them—without opening them.

If you need to add any security measures to the doors, or change the material that they are made out of, please do so. You are completely in control in this space.

Now come out of that room and return to your safe/calm place . . .

This room acts as a second safe/calm place, and in some cases where the safe/calm place has become tainted or corrupted in some way, I have found this method very helpful.

Useful Metaphors

At times the person in therapy may feel that the traumatic material of the DMN is too frightening and become unable to tolerate the level of affect. This can push the client outside the window of tolerance within which it is necessary for the client to remain for effective psychotherapy to take place (Siegel, 1999). Remaining in the window of tolerance is important—that is, avoiding under- and over-arousal states—as this is where the person can focus on internal and external stimuli and work toward integration. The following are standard metaphors that can provide a degree of distance from the material being processed:

1. Imagine that you are on a train that is speeding past a scene and you are glimpsing the scene as you pass by. You are not in the scene; you are observing it from the train.
2. Imagine that you are seated in front of a large TV. You have the remote control in your hand. You are playing the scene on the TV and you have the ability to speed it up, slow it down, pause it, or even switch it off.

The intention here is that the person shifts more to the position of the observer, rather than that of the participant. This may be all that is necessary to keep the client within the window of tolerance.

An alternative is the TICES strategies: Target = Image + Cognition + Emotion + Sensation. If targeting of the entire DMN is overwhelming the person, TICES strategies that work on one aspect can be effective in keeping the person within the window of tolerance. For example, the person can picture the image as a black-and-white picture instead of color, or focus on one emotion or sensation at a time.

Summary of Phase 2

At the completion of phase 2 the client needs to have solid foundation to build his or her therapy upon. The foundation is made up of psychoeducation and practical tools. The foundation contains the AIP model, the Triune Brain and the neurobiology of DAS/BLS, plus or minus the mechanism of SR—all bound together by the mortar of a strong therapeutic alliance. With this foundation in place, the client can be fully present for desensitization and reprocessing in sessions and remain emotionally continent between sessions too. The safe/calm place and the room outside of time and space exercises help the person to safely close down incomplete sessions and decrease the reasonable fear about delving into traumatic material, only to leave it partially processed. By presenting a plausible and coherent model to people entering EMDR therapy and explaining the method by which it resolves the psychological sequelae of trauma, we meet two of the four criteria necessary for effective psychotherapy (Frank, 1961): a rationale or myth providing a plausible explanation for the client's symptoms, and a procedure to resolve them.

Lifelong learning is a vital skill for the EMDR therapist. As already stated, a good model, even a great model, is still a model, and we owe it to the people who seek our expertise to remain open and questioning, always ready to integrate new research.

Assessment (Phase 3)

Intention: *To appropriately identify and target the DMN for phase 4 (desensitization).*

At this stage, history taking and preparation are intentionally beginning to draw together the unlinked trauma data of the DMN. This process has gathered an appreciation of the resources and positive, functional memory networks of the client. Part of the function of assessment is to find a way to access the DMN. Freud referred to dreams as the "Royal Road" to the unconscious (Freud & Brill, 1915); by understanding the neurobiological and AIP rationale for the sequence of the elements of this phase, we understand that this sequence is EMDR therapy's Royal Road to the DMN. The standard model first attains a static visual image associated with the DMN and assesses all of the sensory modalities, as sometimes smells or even tastes may be highly emotionally laden. Next we assess for the predictive outcomes of information processing (Bergmann, 2012), first examining for the negative cognition (NC). NCs are the distorted or inaccurate outcomes of information processing, and they are noted to consistently lead to self-limiting or self-denigrating beliefs (Shapiro, 2001). Now we progress to assess the positive cognition (PC) associated with the identified target memory. Due to the disconnected state of PCs, they exist only in abstract or semantic form. They are a "head knowledge" that the client may be able to acknowledge at some level as being capable of existing, but they do not exist as a "heart knowledge" and therefore are not "felt" or fully owned. Essentially they are not really believed. We assess the level of belief with the Validity of Cognition (VoC) scale that stretches from 1, which means that the PC is "not at all believable," to 7, which means that the PC is "completely believable." At this point we now return to examine the NC by looking at the feeling. Feelings are the composite perceptions—what Uri Bergmann calls "cortical translations"—of what the client is emoting and perceiving in the client's state of mind at the time the DMN was generated. Our assessment

CASE EXAMPLE

> Jack remembered his father (a police officer in the Royal Ulster Constabu-
> lary) checking under the family car every time he would leave the house,
> whether going alone or traveling with the family. For Jack the worst epi-
> sode was when his father found "something" under the family car and the
> bomb disposal team came and their street was evacuated.
>
> Previously Jack had always believed the story that his father had told
> him—that he was checking to make sure that a cat wasn't asleep under the
> car. On that day he realized that his father and his family were at risk.
>
> Jack had presented with a fear of travel and had become increasingly
> unable to travel after a recent road traffic collision (RTC). This had resulted
> in nightmares and flashbacks of the incident from his childhood—the time
> when he had realized that his father was checking for under-car bombs and
> not for sleeping cats.
>
> The image that was connected to his dysfunction was seeing his fa-
> ther running in from the car shouting a warning to Jack to run to the back
> of the house.
>
> NC - I am not safe to travel by car   SUDS = 8/10
> PC - I am safe to travel by car   VoC = 3/7
> The feeling was FEAR and in his body he had a sense of twisting tension
> in his stomach.

of the quantum of feeling is through the use of the Subjective Units of Distress Scale (SUDS), where 0 is "no distress" and 10 is the "greatest level of distress imaginable." The SUDS allows us to assess what is going on in the client's body, which is essentially an assessment of emotion. Emotion largely consist of ac-tions carried out in our bodies, including facial expressions, postural stances, and physiological responses. Therefore, if we take a moment and reflect on the neurobiological import of this sequence, we are moving from a higher cortical articulation of the trauma memory toward what is felt and experienced in the body, which is fundamentally what we need to be targeting within the EMDR therapy method. This can be kept in the forefront of our minds by the adage, "you have got to feel to heal."

Because dissociation and psychosis are being explored as very closely re-lated phenomena, if not indeed the same thing, I will explore any modifications to the standard model that they warrant when we examine the ICoNN approach's methodology in Chapters 6 and 7.

Desensitization (Phase 4)

Intention: *To target the identified DMN and desensitize its overwhelming and re-experienced, trauma-based emotions through the application of DAS/BLS, aiming to reduce the SUDS score to zero.*

1. For illustrative purposes, we will consider a single-incident (type I) trauma. The seminal explanation is given in the text by Shapiro (Shapiro, 2001). This phase of the treatment is primarily the targeting of the DMN for reprocessing. It involves the client being asked to hold the visual target, NC, body sensations, and the emotions that link with the DMN while DAS/BLS are applied. As noted earlier, these DAS/BLS may be visual, auditory, or tactile (e.g., pulsers or alternating knee taps). It is important to note that the current evidence suggests that EMs are superior to other forms of BLS. At the end of each set of DAS/BLS, the therapist asks what material has come up, and this material is usually the focus of the next set. If processing becomes blocked or loops, there are a number of different methods that the therapist can apply to help the client achieve therapeutic resolution. See Shapiro, 2001, for specific details. We will later explore those tools that relate specifically to psychosis and schizophrenia. The therapist ensures that processing is occurring with repeated sets of DAS/BLS, resulting in a decrease in the SUDS score. This process is repeated as long as the SUDS scores are decreasing and ideally until the SUDS score reaches zero when the client is thinking of the target memory. Each set ought to be approximately 30 seconds in duration for the reprocessing function to be achieved. This recommendation is linked with research noting that EMs generate an increase in the vividness of episodic memory retrieval and expansion of association networks (Christman, Garvey, Propper, & Phaneuf, 2003) following 30 seconds of horizontal saccadic eye movements. Other work also supported this set length as being important to tax working memory (Andrade, Kavanagh, & Baddeley, 1997; Leer, Engelhard, & van den Hout, 2014). The pace is to be as fast as the client can tolerate and thus saccadic and not smooth pursuit, as the latter was not found to be efficacious (Christman et al., 2003). In this regard it is important to remember that there are technical skill aspects of the method that the EMDR clinician needs to develop as well as the psychotherapeutic skills. We know that the level of adherence to the protocol is related to the treatment outcomes (Maxfield & Hyer, 2002; Shapiro, 2001, 2007), and this is why it is so important to have adequate supervision and ongoing lifelong learning principles built into the mindset of every EMDR therapist.

2. **Blocked Processing:** If the person has stalled in the processing, follow the basic fundamental steps as taught in your training. Change the direction/speed/length of your EMs. Change the modality you are using to deliver the BLS (e.g., change from EMs to auditory stimuli). Focus only on what the person is experiencing in his or her body. If a client has his or her eyes closed, invite the client to open them. Remember also to be mindful of the possibility of a feeder memory that needs to be reprocessed—the affect-bridge methodology is discussed in Chapters 6 and 7, as it is very useful in psychosis.

   Additional tools can be located in the following resources:
   a. Hensley, B. J. (2009). *An EMDR primer: From practicum to practice.* New York, NY: Springer Publishing Company. (Hensley, 2009)
   b. Knipe, J. (2015). *EMDR toolbox: Theory and treatment of complex PTSD and dissociation.* New York, NY: Springer Publishing Company. (Knipe, 2015)

3. **Therapeutic Interweaves** (Hensley, 2009): These are strategies that equip a client with the information required to facilitate processing.
   a. A therapist introduces a therapeutic interweave in the following circumstances delineated by Hensley (2009): *looping safe/calm place*—the client goes through several sets of BLS without the SUDS score decreasing; *lack of information*—the client lacks the necessary information to cognitively or behaviorally process the traumatic material; *lack of generalization*—despite success in processing the target, there is a failure in this generalizing to additional related targets; *time restrictions*—the client is running out of time in an abreaction and the therapist needs to facilitate appropriate closure of the session; and *exhaustion*—the client is reaching the point of exhaustion in an abreaction.
   b. The man I have come to see as the "father of relational EMDR therapy," Mark Dworkin, developed the *relational interweave*. Dworkin's description of EMDR therapy emphasizes the practice and conceptualization of EMDR as a rich psychotherapy (Dworkin, 2005). He reminds us, as EMDR therapists, to avoid taking a mechanistic view of the EMDR therapy method; instead, he calls us to see that "the synergy of procedure, attachment and intersubjectivity has always been an intrinsic part of the [EMDR therapy] methodology" (Dworkin, 2015, p. 1).
      Resource: Dworkin, M. (2005). *EMDR and the relational imperative: The therapeutic relationship in EMDR treatment*. New York, NY: Routledge.
      Note: The *relational interweave* is also known as the *intersubjective interweave*, and this underlines why it can prove to be so valuable in the application of EMDR therapy to psychosis. It works in the intersubjective space between the therapist and the client and connects with both neural networks that are at play in the therapeutic alliance. As the therapist becomes aware of the mis-attunement, this can be acknowledged, and, in a "moment of meeting" (Stern, 2004), the therapist can restore the therapeutic alliance and attunement. On one occasion a client expressed that he felt that I was becoming frustrated with him for his lack of progress within the EMDR session. I acknowledged that I was feeling frustration at present in my body but noted that it was a small amount of emotional energy, as I was confident and pleased with the progress the client had been making. I wondered out loud with the client whether this emotion was something that we were both feeling at some level. The client was very pleased I had answered in a way that confirmed how he was feeling, as in previous sessions with another therapist he had felt that his feelings were invalidated. This acknowledgment between us was a "moment of meeting," and it confirmed that he could trust his feelings. We then installed this relational/intersubjective interweave with BLS.
      I will explore the procedure for this in more detail within the IConn approach's methodology in Chapters 6 and 7.
   c. Noncognitive Interweaves: A therapeutic interweave can also involve getting our clients to *do* something. This can borrow from therapies such as psychodrama (Moreno, 1969), and I have heard Joany Spierings from the

Netherlands give wonderful workshops about the use of such interweaves. One that I have used is as follows:

I invite clients to visualize generating the energy that they need to get beyond the block in processing. Let's imagine a client feels that she needs more confidence. I have the client imagine connecting to this energy—through visualization—and then I inflate a balloon. I ask the client to picture the inflated balloon as being full of the confidence the client wants. Wrapping it in a cloth that is the color that the client associates with the energy named, I have the client embrace it tightly. Now I invite the client to picture squeezing it into her energy system, and at the time the client squeezes most tightly, either the client pops the balloon or I help with a pin (this method will not be suitable for some clients because of the loud pop of the balloon). Usually the person gets a sense that the positive resource energy has suddenly been integrated (this is a noncognitive interweave); I then do a couple of sets of BLS.

As Spierings suggests, be creative and get your clients to *do* things.

Installation (Phase 5)

Intention: *To install the identified PC through the application of DAS/BLS, aiming to increase the VoC score to 7.*

Now that the DMN targeted in phases 3 to 4 has been desensitized, the therapist and client return to the PC defined in phase 3. On some occasions the PC is refined or redefined by the client prior to installation. Younger children may have difficulty in defining a NC and PC, and in these cases the client will often develop a spontaneous PC. The client is asked to hold the target memory in conscious thought along with the PC, and DAS/BLS are once again undertaken. In a way similar to the previous phase, the therapist monitors for change and processing—in this case progress toward installation of the PC. Now the degree of believability of the PC is measured by the VoC scale, described earlier, and the sets are continued until the VoC score is ideally a 7/7.

Body Scan (Phase 6)

Intention: *To confirm that the target memory and identified PC are fully installed and that there is no residual material that requires further targeting from that specific DMN.*

Once the PC has been installed, the therapist returns the client to attend to the client's body, the "instrument of emotion," assessing if there is any residual material to be further targeted. As we remember that "the body keeps the score" (van der Kolk, 1994), we invite the client to observe his or her body while revisiting the original target and holding the PC in conscious thought. The client is asked to "scan" his or her body, at the same time searching for anything that feels out of balance, tense, or uncomfortable. Any negative sensations are targeted with DAS/BLS until the body feels neutral. In this phase we are aiming to achieve a situation where the original target memory and the PC can be thought about and spoken of without any sense of reliving emotional or physical discomfort.

Closure (Phase 7)

Intention: *To end the session and close with the client feeling in control and grounded.*

In some cases the trauma data being targeted may not be completely desensitized or the process of installation of the PC completed fully. In such cases the therapist will ensure that the session is brought to closure safely and in a controlled manner. This is often done through bringing the client back to a grounded and present-day–oriented space through use of the safe/calm place exercise. The client is usually instructed on how to use such methods in between sessions; contact arrangements are made clear; and the client is encouraged to keep a log of any intrusions, flashbacks, or posttraumatic nightmares to assist the client with developing future targets in the next session.

Re-Evaluation (Phase 8)

Intention: *To re-evaluate the DMN targeted in the previous session and assist in appropriately targeting any residual material that requires further targeting from that specific DMN or confirming the next step in the AIP-based treatment plan.*

In the next session the therapist re-evaluates the targets from the previous session to check for any residual trauma memories. The therapist will also review with the client how the client has coped and functioned in the intervening time period. It is important for the therapist to review any feedback that the client has been asked to keep, as many clients can feel upset if they do not get to review things that they have made a note of. It is important to remember that because trauma memory is not laid down in a contiguous, joined-up manner, a client may need to use lists and notes to recall vital clues that will guide the processing of targets. Re-evaluation is an extremely important part of the method; it is the cement that links together the overall treatment plan. In this phase we are re-examining the three prongs—past, present, and future—that we have been processing. We ensure that the past targets that have been processed are clear, with no remaining emotional residue that energizes an NC; we check on *present* triggers of DMN and examine the *future* templates that have been installed. This centrality of the three-pronged protocol ensures that we keep the individual therapeutic battles, fought with the eight phases, working toward winning the therapeutic war that is guided by the three-pronged protocol.

These are the eight phases of the standard EMDR therapy model. When we deviate from this standard we ought to hold two things in mind: First, we need to actually know that we are deviating from the standard, and second, we need a clear rationale as to why we are doing so. The ICoNN model is a paradigm that is a deviation in respect to case formulation, and it guides the targeting and processing methodology. In the next chapter, we will examine the supporting evidence and outline the rationale that undergirds the use of EMDR therapy for the treatment of psychoses and schizophrenia.

REFERENCES

Andrade, J., Kavanagh, D., & Baddeley, A. (1997). Eye-movements and visual imagery: A working memory approach to the treatment of post-traumatic stress disorder. *British Journal of Clinical Psychology*, 36(2), 209–223.

Bergmann, U. (2008). The neurobiology of EMDR: Exploring the thalamus and neural integration. *Journal of EMDR Practice and Research*, 2(4), 300–314. doi:10.1891/1933-3196. 2.4.300

Bergmann, U. (2012). *Neurobiological foundations for EMDR practice.* New York, NY: Springer Publishing Company.

Brown, B. (2012). *Daring greatly: How the courage to be vulnerable transforms the way we live, love, parent, and lead.* New York, NY: Gotham.

Campbell, J. (1993). *Myths to live by.* New York, NY: Arkana.

Christman, S. D., Garvey, K. J., Propper, R. E., & Phaneuf, K. A. (2003). Bilateral eye movements enhance the retrieval of episodic memories. *Neuropsychology*, 17(2), 221–229.

Dworkin, M. (2005). *EMDR and the relational imperative: The therapeutic relationship in EMDR treatment.* New York, NY: Routledge.

Dworkin, M. (2015). *Relational EMDR: The synergy of procedure, therapeutic attachment, and intersubjectivity—implications for an expanded conceptualization of adaptive information processing and EMDR psychotherapy.* Retrieved from http://emdr-web.org/relational-emdr/

Eccles, J. C. (1994). *How the self controls its brain.* Berlin, Germany: Springer-Verlag.

Erskine, R. G. (2015). *Relational patterns, therapeutic presence: Concepts and practice of integrative psychotherapy.* London, England: Karnac.

Frank, J. D. (1961). *Persuasion and healing: A comparative study of psychotherapy.* Baltimore, MD: Johns Hopkins Press.

Freud, S., & Brill, A. A. (1915). *The interpretation of dreams* (4th ed.). London, England: G. Allen & Unwin/The Macmillan Company.

Fry, T. (Ed.). (1981). *RB 1980: The rule of St. Benedict in English.* Collegeville, MN: Liturgical Press.

Hensley, B. J. (2009). *An EMDR primer: From practicum to practice.* New York, NY: Springer Publishing Company.

Hobson, J. A., & Leonard, J. (2001). *Out of its mind: Psychiatry in crisis.* Cambridge, MA: Perseus Publishing.

Jaspers, K. (1963). *General psychopathology* (Trans. from the German 7th ed.). Manchester, England: Manchester University Press.

Jung, C. G. (1960). *Experimental researches on the doctrine of complexes* (R. F. C. Hull, Trans., pp. 598–604). London, England: Routledge & Kegan Paul. (Original work published 1934)

Kosko, B. (2006). *Noise.* New York, NY: Viking.

LeDoux, J. E. (1986). Sensory systems and emotions. *Integrative Psychiatry*, 4, 237–248.

Leer, A., Engelhard, I. M., & van den Hout, M. A. (2014). How eye movements in EMDR work: Changes in memory vividness and emotionality. *Journal of Behavior Therapy and Experimental Psychiatry*, 45(3), 396–401. doi:10.1016/j.jbtep.2014.04.004

MacLean, P. D. (1990). *The triune brain in evolution: Role in paleocerebral functions.* New York, NY: Plenum Press.

Maxfield, L., & Hyer, L. (2002). The relationship between efficacy and methodology in studies investigating EMDR treatment of PTSD. *Journal of Clinical Psychology*, 58(1), 23–41.

McDonnell, M. D., & Abbott, D. (2009). What is stochastic resonance? Definitions, misconceptions, debates, and its relevance to biology. *PLoS Computational Biology*, 5(5), e1000348. doi:10.1371/journal.pcbi.1000348

Moreno, J. L. (1969). *Psychodrama Vol. 3: Action therapy and principles of practice.* Beacon, NY: Beacon House.

Moskowitz, A. (2005). *Pierre Janet's influence on Bleuler's concept of schizophrenia.* Paper presented at the the First Symposium of the Pierre Janet Gesellschaft, Freiburg, Germany.

Rajmohan, V., & Mohandas, E. (2007). The limbic system. *Indian Journal of Psychiatry, 49*(2), 132–139. doi:10.4103/0019-5545.33264

Rohr, R. (2011). *Falling upward: A spirituality for the two halves of life* (1st ed.). San Francisco, CA: Jossey-Bass.

Ross, C. A. (2004). *Schizophrenia: Innovations in diagnosis and treatment.* Binghamton, NY: Haworth Maltreatment and Trauma.

Sartory, G., Cwik, J., Knuppertz, H., Schurholt, B., Lebens, M., Seitz, R. J., & Schulze, R. (2013). In search of the trauma memory: A meta-analysis of functional neuroimaging studies of symptom provocation in posttraumatic stress disorder (PTSD). *PLoS One, 8*(3), e58150. doi:10.1371/journal.pone.0058150

Shapiro, F. (2001). *Eye movement desensitization and reprocessing (EMDR): Basic principles, protocols, and procedures* (2nd ed.). New York, NY: Guilford Press.

Shapiro, F. (2007). EMDR, adaptive information processing, and case conceptualization. *Journal of EMDR Practice and Research, 1*(2), 68–87.

Shapiro, F., & Maxfield, L. (2002). Eye movement desensitization and reprocessing (EMDR): Information processing in the treatment of trauma. *Journal of Clinical Psychology, 58*(8), 933–946. doi:10.1002/jclp.10068

Siegel, D., & Buczynski, R. (2014). *The neurobiology of trauma treatment: How brain science can lead to more targeted interventions for patients healing from trauma.* Retrieved from http://www.nicabm.com/treatingtrauma2014/a1-transcript-sample/?del=11.14.1 4LTsampleemailunreg

Siegel, D. J. (1999). *The developing mind: Toward a neurobiology of interpersonal experience.* New York, NY: Guilford Press.

Stern, D. N. (2004). *The present moment in psychotherapy and everyday life.* New York, NY: W. W. Norton.

van der Hart, O., Groenendijk, M., Gonzalez, A., Mosquera, D., & Solomon, R. (2014). Dissociation of the personality and EMDR therapy in complex trauma-related disorders: Applications in phases 2 and 3 treatment. *Journal of EMDR Practice and Research, 8*(1), 33–48. doi:10.1891/1933-3196.8.1.33

van der Kolk, B. A. (1994). The body keeps the score: Memory and the evolving psychobiology of posttraumatic stress. *Harvard Review of Psychiatry, 1*(5), 253–265.

van der Kolk, B. A., & van der Hart, O. (1989). Pierre Janet and the breakdown of adaptation in psychological trauma. *American Journal of Psychiatry, 146*(12), 1530–1540.

Yan, X., Brown, A. D., Lazar, M., Cressman, V. L., Henn-Haase, C., Neylan, T. C., . . . Marmar, C. R. (2013). Spontaneous brain activity in combat related PTSD. *Neuroscience Letters, 547*, 1–5. doi:10.1016/j.neulet.2013.04.032

SIX

EMDR for Schizophrenia and Other Psychoses: Rationale and Research to Date

Intention: *To equip the reader with a working knowledge of the rationale for the application of EMDR therapy to psychosis and to summarize the current literature on EMDR therapy in psychosis.*

WHY USE EMDR THERAPY FOR PSYCHOSIS AND SCHIZOPHRENIA?

At this point we have presented a plausible link between trauma, dissociation, schizophrenia, and the other psychoses. I have also argued that in many instances dissociation and psychosis are the same thing phenomenologically. This agrees with the work of Colin Ross (2004, 2013). Historically, when we examine the diagnosis of schizophrenia we note that the original intention of Bleuler, in describing "the schizophrenias," was for the diagnosis to represent a group of disorders (Bleuler, 1911). It is important to keep in mind, therefore, that from its inception, schizophrenia was not conceptualized as a single disorder. At this point in the field of mental health we are seeing a return to the use of psychological therapies for schizophrenia and psychosis. However, that of course does not mean that every case will be equally responsive to such therapeutic endeavors. Most likely we are likely to find that some cases are more amenable to treatment than others. The challenge we face as clinicians in working with people who have these experiences is how to define who will most likely benefit from these therapies in general, and from eye movement desensitization and reprocessing (EMDR) therapy in particular. The return to psychological therapies for schizophrenia and other psychoses is not altogether surprising, after more than 100 years of attempting to adequately treat these individuals. Karl Jaspers, in 1913, asserted that psychoses were only understandable as a biological disorder and considered them incomprehensible as a psychological disorder, in contrast to neuroses, which he considered psychologically comprehensible (Jaspers, 1913, 1963). This assertion ended up seriously hobbling the application and study of psychotherapy for people with experiences that were labeled as psychotic. Only now are we observing a determined move to correct that situation.

History—What's in a Name?

The concept of "neuroses" was first introduced in 1784 by William Cullen; by 1840, refinements to the diagnosis that had been made by Étienne-Jean Georget, a brilliant French psychiatrist and student of Pinel, were published posthumously (Beer, 1996). Baron Ernst von Feuchtersleben then coined the term *psychosis* in 1845 (Burns, 1954). At this point Feuchtersleben thought of the psychoses as a subgroup of the neuroses (Beer, 1996). Interestingly, in the late 18th century the neuroses were believed to be organic diseases of the nerves and muscles, and the insanities were "of the mind" and thus did not have a physical origin. However, by the start of the 20th century this had been completely reversed, with neuroses being seen as functional illnesses of the mind and psychoses being incomprehensible biological processes (Beer, 1996). So where do we now sit at the start of the 21st century?

Many mental health professionals are still looking at mental illness within the psychosis/neurosis split; although *neurosis* is not often used clinically now, the dichotomy remains. The importance of the functioning of the mind and the limitations of medication have encouraged some clinicians to advance the use of psychotherapy. In the present period this is mostly in the form of cognitive behavioral therapy (CBT) for schizophrenia and psychosis, and this is strongly promoted in the British Psychological Society (BPS) publication "Understanding Psychosis and Schizophrenia: Why People Sometimes Hear Voices, Believe Things That Others Find Strange, or Appear Out of Touch With Reality, and What Can Help" (Basset et al., 2014). Although this document has not been received without criticism, it makes some very interesting reading for us as EMDR therapists and students of the Indicating Cognitions of Negative Networks (IConN) model. The meta-analyses that showed the most encouraging effect sizes were looking at two groups: (1) treatment-resistant schizophrenia (Burns, Erickson, & Brenner, 2014), and (2) forms of psychotherapy that were highly specific and tailored according to case formulation, targeting delusions and auditory hallucinations (van der Gaag, Valmaggia, & Smit, 2014). As we will see, these studies support the rationale for case selection and treatment targeting that we propose in the IConN model.

Treatment-Resistant Schizophrenia

It is possible that the first group, consisting of those labeled as having treatment-resistant schizophrenia, represents a subphenotype of schizophrenia that may be more amenable to psychotherapeutic intervention. The drugs that are being used in schizophrenia are, at this point in history, mostly working on the dopaminergic system of the brain. However, dissociative mechanisms have been described as being linked more closely with the endogenous opiate system (Frewen

& Lanius, 2006; Lanius, 2005; Lanius, Paulsen, & Corrigan, 2014). Considering the current data and proposed models, it is possible that a highly dissociative group of people within the group labeled as having a treatment-resistant form of schizophrenia may benefit little from drugs that target the dopaminergic system, but they may be amenable to psychotherapy. It has also been proposed that there is a role for drugs such as low-dose naltrexone (Lanius, 2005; Lanius et al., 2014), which blocks activity in the endogenous opiate system. This has been observed to facilitate psychotherapy in people with high levels of dissociation (Lanius, 2005; Lanius et al., 2014). Further study of this group of individuals in particular could yield a more complete understanding of the specific phenomenology that is most likely to benefit from EMDR therapy.

Psychotherapy of a Highly Specific and Tailored Form, Targeting Delusions and Auditory Hallucinations

The novel therapy termed *avatar therapy* (Basset et al., 2014; Leff, Williams, Huckvale, Arbuthnot, & Leff, 2014) yielded the largest effect size within the hal-lucination studies group. The second meta-analysis referred to focuses upon psychotherapeutic endeavors in which the client's delusions and auditory hal-lucinations are the focus of treatment. In these therapies the intervention content was directed by the specifics of the case formulation for each individual; that is, each was a highly tailored and individualized intervention. As we will see later, engaging with the specifics of the phenomena being experienced and dialoguing with auditory hallucinations is one aspect of the ICoNN model. It is difficult to view avatar therapy as merely "CBT for schizophrenia," as upon close examina-tion it has much more in common with therapies that accept a dissociative model for schizophrenia (Miller, 2014). This suggests to me that this meta-analysis is more supportive of psychotherapies for schizophrenia that are working with a dissociative understanding of the phenomenology, rather than for those with a cognitive or cognitive behavioral understanding. Additionally, it suggests that the most effective treatment endeavors may well target dissociative pathologies, and it is from this premise that I propose the ICoNN model.

Summary of the Rationale for Using EMDR Therapy in Psychosis

In summary, we know that EMDR therapy is effective in the treatment of post-traumatic stress disorder (PTSD); this is now well recognized, is supported in the literature, and has been adopted by many international guidelines that advise on the psychological treatment of PTSD. As clinicians we see and apply EMDR therapy to a much wider group of conditions that extends beyond a simple PTSD diagnosis. So if we are to be open-minded, the least we will do is consider a role for EMDR therapy in the treatment of psychosis. Growing numbers of therapists acknowledge the link between trauma, dissociation, and psychosis. Psychother-apy for psychosis has been resurrected and schizophrenia repatriated into the dis-sociative group of disorders, where it was first conceptualized. For those of us in the field of psychotraumatology, this sits instinctively well with what we observe from our everyday clinical experiences. For example, we see EMDR therapy being effectively used, in combination with ego state therapy, for the treatment of dissociative cases. It is therefore logical that EMDR therapy be examined as a treatment for psychosis and schizophrenia. This has to date been completed by several international groups, with promising results, as we have seen (Kikuchi, 2008, personal communication, 2012; Kim et al., 2010). It has also been used safely and effectively to treat symptoms of PTSD in people with diagnoses of schizophrenia and psychosis (van den Berg et al., 2015). It therefore makes sense that we formulate a model that allows us to offer a rationale and mythos for the etiology of psychosis that is in keeping with the adaptive information processing (AIP) model of EMDR therapy. I propose that the IConN model can inform and guide the application of EMDR therapy to psychosis in its many forms. It allows us to formulate a management plan that is informed by the AIP model. EMDR therapy can then be effectively delivered within a comprehensive treatment plan for psychosis. Because the IConN model helps us to target the dysfunctional memory networks (DMNs) that we believe are driving the experiences, processing them ought to result in the amelioration of these experiences, which have been understood as psychosis. This is indeed what these early studies have been showing. Although this work is still in its infancy, it lays the foundation for further research that is necessary in this area of unmet clinical need. What is now clear and becoming increasingly accepted is that rather than the "either/or" thinking of medication or psychotherapy, or CBT or EMDR therapy, we can best serve the people with lived experience of these phenomena by applying "both/and" thinking. Together we are better, and ultimately we all ought to be on the same team, with the "enemy" being the functional impairment that can accompany these phenomena.

Summary of the Literature Discussing the Use of EMDR Therapy for Schizophrenia and Psychosis

In recent years we have witnessed an increase in mental health professionals revisiting the use of psychotherapy for people with psychosis. This in itself is not surprising, given the significant risks and often substantial side effects that the drug treatments for schizophrenia and psychosis carry. It has been said by some that the risk/benefit considerations for antipsychotic drugs are characterized by less-than-impressive benefits. There are now several research groups in different regions of the world that have published and are actively researching EMDR therapy's application to psychosis in general and to schizophrenia in particular (Kikuchi, 2008; Kim et al., 2010; Laugharne, Marshall, Laugharne, & Hassard, 2014; Miller, 2010; Roques, 2008; van den Berg, van der Vleugel, Staring, de Bont, & de Jongh, 2013). In psychotherapies apart from EMDR therapy, recent work by experts in schizophrenia has utilized a trauma and dissociation model where the dissociative phenomena within the illness have been the focus of treatment (Moskowitz, Schäfer, & Dorahy, 2008). Cognitive therapy and CBT have a growing research base, and treatment protocols are well developed for patients with schizophrenia and psychosis. One group of researchers, with links in the CBT community, developed avatar therapy, which uses computer software to generate a realistic face that utilizes lip-synchronizing software to make it appear as if the avatar is capable of interacting with the patient. The therapist, speaking from a separate location, has his or her spoken words vocalized in a voice selected by the patient, which represents the persecutory "voice" that usually is heard as a part of the patient's illness; those words are then animated by the avatar. This computer avatar enables individuals to talk with their perceived "persecutors" (Leff et al., 2014). The researchers observed that once the person was able to interact with the avatar, as an external entity, this gave the person a feeling of having more control over these experiences, and as a result the person's level of distress decreased. This study actually provided the largest effect size of all the studies included in one meta-analysis of CBT for schizophrenia (van der Gaag et al., 2014), although it is argued to be far from CBT (Kinderman, McKenna, & Laws, 2015)—indeed, it is closer to ego-state work and similar therapies (Miller, 2014). Although this computerized method takes aspects of this form of intervention to a new level technologically, this interaction is a key aspect of what we recognize as the central feature of several therapies that acknowledge dissociative dynamics as being at play in psychosis (Miller, 2014). Research such as this is an excellent way of helping people to make more sense of the notion of identity and takes us away from an overly simplistic paradigm. However, colleagues have been conscious of the need to be mindful that we avoid the possibility that, in a climate of quick and inexpensive fixes, therapies such as the avatar program become misappropriated in an attempt to replace the dynamic of the therapist–client dyad. The therapist in the room with the person seeking therapy facilitates the creation of the therapeutic "we," which, like people, involves more than mere words, the voice. I agree with those who would argue that the therapeutic dynamic requires the involvement of the fabric of the whole person. This requires the inclusion of nonverbal communications and is best manifested by the relationship between two individuals in the same room. I imagine that this premise may be increasingly challenged in the years ahead as technology continues to facilitate the development of telemedicine. Often telemedicine via applications such as Skype has allowed therapy to be delivered to remote regions that would otherwise be denied access to services, and the comments of users are positive (Edirippulige, Levandovskaya, & Prishutova, 2013). My personal belief is that new communication technologies can allow for the formation of the therapeutic dyad, but we must recognize that there is much still to be learned about how to deliver therapy via such novel methods.

THE DIVIDED SELF

Psychotherapeutic methods that acknowledge the links between trauma, dissociation, and psychosis, which we alluded to earlier, all have in common some method of dialoguing with the variously named dissociated parts, voices, or ego states. The methods employed in this group of therapies have much in common. One method that I have experience with is the Jungian concept of "active imagination" (Johnson, 1986), which, along with his paradigm of dream analysis, formed a core aspect of his school of analysis. Jung's own application of these methods resulted in the writings that became known as the *Liber Novus*, now more widely known as *The Red Book* (Jung, McGuire, Shamdasani, & Jung, 2012; Jung & Shamdasani, 2009)—a record of his journaling that represents, for me, a dream-like form of processing. Another of these therapy methods is voice dialogue. Voice dialogue was developed in 1972 by Hal Stone, PhD, and Sidra Stone, PhD, and in full it is sometimes known as *voice dialogue, relationship, and the psychology of selves*; it is also known to some as the *psychology of the aware ego* (Stone & Stone, 1989). This methodology grew out of these two psychologists' aspiration to create a method of deepening relationships, and because of this origin, plus the fact that it was not created in a clinical setting, the recognition of parts and a dialoguing between these parts of the whole is not considered pathological. The voice dialogue paradigm views a person as a collective of "many selves within" that work together as subpersonalities to make up the whole self. More information on this method is freely available online at Hal and Sidra Stone's website (http://www.voicedialogueinternational.com). It is valuable to remember that not all people who experience themselves as a collective view this state of being as pathological. This is underlined by the work of researchers such as Professor Richard Bentall, Professor Tony Morrison, and Professor Daniel Freeman (Bentall, 1992, 2003, 2009; Freeman, Bentall, & Garety, 2008; Jones & Bentall, 2006; Read, Mosher, & Bentall, 2004; Slade & Bentall, 1988) and by organizations such as the Hearing Voices Network (http://www.hearing-voices.org). In the United Kingdom (UK) report "Understanding Psychosis and Schizophrenia," compiled by a working party of clinical psychologists associated with the BPS's Division of Clinical Psychology, the experience of psychosis is framed in a much wider paradigm than the mere medical model, and it is noted that for some people, and in certain cultures, experiences such as hearing voices are valued and not at all viewed as illness (Basset et al., 2014). This ought to at least invite us, as clinicians, to consider how we view these experiences.

EMDR Therapy and the Divided Self

I first came across the approach of working with "parts" of the personality at an EMDR therapy workshop given by Carol Forgash, whom I consider a champion for the integration of ego-state therapy with EMDR therapy (Forgash & Copeley, 2008). The creation of ego-state therapy is well known as the work of the late Professor John G. Watkins, PhD, and his wife Helen H. Watkins, MA, who survives him (Barabasz, Barabasz, Christensen, French, & Watkins, 2013; Watkins, 1993; Watkins & Watkins, 1984, 1990). Ego-state therapy is a psychodynamic approach that uses a variety of techniques borrowed from group therapy and family therapy. These techniques are used to resolve conflicts between the various ego states that comprise a "family of self" existing within the individual. As we see, all of these paradigms recognize that the individual is a sum of a number of parts that can be encouraged to work together to the benefit of the whole person. The aim of the approaches is not to make all of the identified parts the same; rather, it is to get the parts to collaborate and cooperate. At times this entails dialoguing with parts that are deemed negative or destructive. However, we must remain mindful that the aim of therapy is *unity* of the ego and not *uniformity* of the various ego states that may make it up. Even when a part is seemingly destructive, the therapist ought not agree to work with the person to destroy it. At such times we need to find a way to sit down and negotiate with the perceived "enemy." Remy Aquarone, a colleague of mine and past president of the European Society for Trauma and Dissociation (ESTD), likes to use the example of when the late "Iron Lady," Margaret Thatcher (former British prime minister), sat down to negotiate with Mikhail Gorbachev (last leader of the Soviet Union). They had fundamental areas of disagreement that were never going to change and yet they found a way to make their political relationship work. I agree with Remy Aquarone; that is a good analogy for this work. We can also usefully consider the principle contained within the *law of conservation of energy* stating that the total energy of an isolated system is constant; energy can be transformed from one form to another, but cannot be created or destroyed. This law was alluded to in the works of Empedocles, a Greek pre-Socratic philosopher (490–430 BCE). He spoke of matter as being comprised of four "classical elements" (earth, air, water, fire) that are the basic ingredients that nature combines and reconstitutes in differing amounts and permutations to form all matter; "nothing comes to be or perishes" (Parmenides, Empedocles, & Lombardo, 1982). We can consider that in a similar way the whole psyche is made up of these different parts of the ego (ego states) that act together in various combinations, but the energy of these ego states that we conceptualize as parts cannot be destroyed. We should never attempt to destroy a part of the self; instead, we work with the person to transform the energy into different forms that can work together in a unified system. In this way the ego state associated with an internalized abuser, for example, is negotiated with and an agreement reached rather than attempting to annihilate it. In this way, unity for the person can be achieved without the need for uniformity within the system of ego states—something that could never be achieved, in my opinion.

The utility of using an ego-state approach within an EMDR framework is that it is very flexible and potentially widely applicable across a number of clinical problems (Forgash & Copeley, 2008). I have found much success with people when using this combination of therapeutic approaches. In brief, we can summarize ego-state work as creating a workspace, such as a board room table or a forest clearing, that can function as a therapeutic space for the inner collection of ego states to dialogue with one another, assisted by the therapist. This dialogue is further facilitated by the dual attention stimulation/bilateral stimulation (DAS/BLS) element of the EMDR therapy method. Those seeking further details are directed to read Carol Forgash's book (Forgash & Copeley, 2008) or to attend one of her practical workshops. Ego-state therapy is a method that appears to be now firmly established within the EMDR therapy community.

EMDR THERAPY FOR PSYCHOSIS

Considering the resurgence in the use of psychotherapies for the treatment of psychosis, I found that a logical next step was to explore a potential role for EMDR therapy in people with these experiences. In acknowledging the link between trauma, dissociative mechanisms, and psychosis (Read & Bentall, 2012; Ross, 2004, 2013; Ross, Anderson, Heber, & Norton, 1990), EMDR therapy naturally warrants further examination, as it is a psychotherapy that is already known to be effective within psychological reactions to trauma (National Institute for Health and Care Excellence [NICE], 2005; World Health Organization [WHO], 2013) and dissociative pathological dynamics (Kim et al., 2010; Miller, 2014; Ross, 2013). Several research groups have taken this next step of examining EMDR therapy's usefulness for the group of people who report experiences that have been labeled as schizophrenia. This work has generated some promising outcomes in the area of schizophrenia in particular. Research and academic study are actively taking place in Spain, Japan, Korea, and the Netherlands and have shown potential benefits (Gonzalez, Mosquera, & Moskowitz, 2012; Kikuchi, 2008, personal communication, 2012; Kim et al., 2010; van den Berg & van der Gaag, 2012; van den Berg, van der Vleugel, & Staring, 2010; van den Berg et al., 2014). To date the Dutch group has been the most active in publishing, but further research is planned and is under way in Japan, Korea, and the UK, including Northern Ireland. The fact that this work is now being presented and published allows us to review the work completed to date and to push forward with the much-needed further research. Although this area of clinical exploration is moving forward apace, much work is still necessary. The Dutch group has also demonstrated that EMDR therapy for trauma can be safely and acceptably undertaken in people diagnosed with psychotic disorders (van den Berg et al., 2015). This is important work because many people find the experiences that are diagnosed as psychosis to be traumatic—although, as noted earlier, that is not the case for all. I believe that by sharing the research to date and by forming effective international collaborations, together we can advance our understanding of these complex experiences.

> "It is amazing what you can accomplish if you do not care who gets the credit."
>
> —*Harry S. Truman*

EMDR Therapy for Psychosis: Research Completed to Date

The Dutch team has discussed three areas where trauma, dissociation, and psychosis interface (van der Vleugel, van den Berg, & Staring, 2012). Their model suggests that the research completed to date can be categorized into the following three groups (van der Vleugel et al., 2012):

1. Patients diagnosed with psychosis who have experienced trauma that is believed to have had a role in the onset and content of their psychosis
2. Patients diagnosed with psychosis whose experiences and their associated treatment have resulted in posttraumatic symptoms
3. Patients whose PTSD symptoms and diagnosis of psychosis are comorbid and whose symptom clusters are thought to negatively reinforce each other, with comorbidity acting as a source of further traumatization

Trauma That Is Thought to Be Resulting in Psychosis

First let's consider patients with psychosis who have experienced trauma that is believed to have had a role in the onset and content of their psychosis. We have explored in detail within Chapters 1 and 2 the assertion that trauma, psychosis, and schizophrenia are linked etiologically. For me the evidence is compelling, and this link was one that many of the so-called "originators" of psychotherapy and the psychoanalytic schools accepted as a foundational truth. Andrew Moskowitz has pointed out that although the mental health field had lots of dissociation-based models for what became known as schizophrenia, it opted for an alternate model made popular by Freud. This was argued to owe more to Freud's proselytizing rather than to the scientific veracity of the model (Moskowitz, 2005; Moskowitz et al., 2008). This assertion reminds us that in the earliest days of the modern characterization of mental illness, these experiences were thought to have had dissociative roots, resulting from trauma. Research in this clinical area and examination of psychotherapy for psychosis is currently experiencing a renaissance (Anketell et al., 2010; Arseneault et al., 2011; Croes et al., 2014; Dorahy et al., 2009; Fisher et al., 2014; Gonzalez et al., 2012; Knipe, 2015; Leff et al., 2014; Moskowitz et al., 2008; Read & Bentall, 2012; Ross, 2004, 2013; van den Berg et al., 2013; van der Hart & Dorahy, 2006), and this creates a natural place for EMDR therapy in the management of these experiences.

The research into EMDR therapy for schizophrenia and psychosis is still in its infancy, but the fact that we are beginning to publicize our clinical experiences and invite the healthy scrutiny of our peers bodes well for the future. We have already gained some very useful insights into interface areas with EMDR therapy being used in people with these experiences that have come to be diagnosed as schizophrenia, or more generically as psychosis. A Japanese researcher (Kikuchi, 2008, personal communication, 2012) completed and published the earliest peer-reviewed article detailing EMDR therapy being applied to schizophrenia. This work has not yet been published in English. However, in a personal correspondence with the researcher, Kikuchi noted that the Japanese model has four key components and borrows much from the cognitive and cognitive behavioral work of Nicholas Tarrier (Lewis et al., 2002; Sellwood, Wittkowski, Tarrier, & Barrowclough, 2007; Tarrier, 2005, 2010; Tarrier et al., 1999; Tarrier et al., 1998; Wykes, Steel, Everitt, & Tarrier, 2008) and Douglas Turkington (Christodoulides, Dudley, Brown, Turkington, & Beck, 2008; Kingdon & Turkington, 1994, 2005; Naeem, Kingdon, & Turkington, 2006; Rathod, Kingdon, Smith, & Turkington, 2005; Rathod, Kingdon, Weiden, & Turkington, 2008; Velligan et al., 2014). I personally believe that there is a great potential for synergy between the CBT and EMDR therapy fields.

The Four Components of the Japanese Model

1. Psychoeducation takes place within a group format. This consists of a five-session program that covers the following topics:
   a. An overview of the diagnosis of schizophrenia
   b. The epidemiology of schizophrenia
   c. An explanation of the common symptoms experienced in schizophrenia
   d. Medications commonly used for treatment
   e. Psychosocial interventions that are available locally
2. The clinician then obtains a detailed timeline of the course of events leading up to the current psychotic experiences beginning to manifest. If a "good enough"

level of insight is present, the clinician may also discuss the concept of a prodromal period (a period when a person is beginning to manifest these experiences, which fall outside of the person's normal functioning, but where full diagnostic criteria are not yet met for recognizable psychiatric illness [psychosis or schizophrenia]) before the acute illness and explore possible early warning signs.
3. This next section borrows most from the cognitive therapy (CT) and CBT work of the authors noted earlier and includes techniques such as:
   a. Normalizing
   b. Cognitive restructuring
   c. Behavioral experimentation
4. If, by this stage, the clinician is considering EMDR therapy, a Dissociative Experiences Scales (DES) assessment (Carlson et al., 1993) is completed.

The Work in the Netherlands

As noted, research in the Netherlands has generated the largest number of publications and includes proposed case conceptualization models, case report material, and a randomized controlled trial (RCT) examining the efficacy of treatments for PTSD in comorbid psychosis (Croes et al., 2014; van den Berg et al., 2015; van den Berg & van der Gaag, 2012; van den Berg et al., 2010; van den Berg et al., 2013; van den Berg et al., 2014; van der Vleugel et al., 2012). In an open trial of 27 people with comorbid diagnoses of PTSD and psychotic disorders, the Dutch researchers were able to show that after six sessions of EMDR therapy for PTSD, participants showed significant improvements. They also noted that it was possible to use the standard protocol in such cases and that EMDR therapy need not be delayed by long periods of stabilization (van den Berg et al., 2010). These findings were then more rigorously examined in the most recent RCT. This RCT demonstrates that EMDR therapy and prolonged exposure are effective, safe, and feasible to deliver for people with PTSD and severe psychosis (van den Berg et al., 2015). Another very helpful model that van den Berg et al. have developed is in respect to targeting of therapy. As already stated, they note in particular the fact that the standard EMDR therapy protocol can be utilized for treating PTSD comorbid with schizophrenia. They have also shown that this is also the case for treating some aspects of schizophrenia itself (Croes et al., 2014; van den Berg et al., 2013).

Dutch Paradigm for Identifying Targets for EMDR Therapy

The method of identifying suitable targets for EMDR therapy that the Dutch researchers suggest are as follows:

1. Identify significant trauma events that are believed to significantly contribute to the etiology of psychosis on the person's timeline.
2. Identify dysfunctional core beliefs or immediate assumptions and then seek out the memories that underlie them. These memories can then be ranked according to how much "evidence" they are believed to provide that supports the dysfunctional core beliefs or immediate assumptions.
3. Perhaps the most novel targeting method is based upon work that builds on the growing evidence that imagery is very important in the development

and perpetuation of emotional disorders (van den Berg et al., 2013). In particular, this last method of targeting that they describe involves the imagery that a person has about feared future events, which are referred to as *flash-forwards* (Engelhard, van den Hout, Dek, et al., 2011; Engelhard, van den Hout, & Smeets, 2011; Leer, Engelhard, Altink, & van den Hout, 2013; van den Hout, Bartelski, & Engelhard, 2013; van den Hout et al., 2011). This methodology is noted to be a deviation from the standard EMDR therapy model, as paradigmatically the standard model targets images associated with past events. It is believed to open up the possibility of EMDR therapy being more widely applicable in other clinical areas (Engelhard, van den Hout, Dek, et al., 2011).

Korean Research

So far we have largely been examining studies that target PTSD within people with a comorbid diagnosis of psychosis. If we now look specifically at EMDR therapy for schizophrenia, one of the most important studies in this area is the Korean research (Kim et al., 2010) in which 45 people diagnosed with acute-stage schizophrenia were recruited into one of three study arms. The first group received three sessions of EMDR in addition to treatment as usual (TAU), the second group received progressive muscular relaxation (PMR) plus TAU, and the last group received only TAU. The TAU group received psychotropic medication, individual supportive psychotherapy, and ward-based group activities. Of the study group, 89% completed the posttreatment evaluations. All three of the groups showed improvements for symptoms of schizophrenia, anxiety, and depression, but statistical analysis showed no significant difference for the TAU-alone group. Of note is that the effect size for negative symptoms was large (0.60) in the EMDR group (Kim et al., 2010). Further research is clearly needed, but I do believe that these results ought to encourage us to continue to develop further studies examining EMDR therapy for schizophrenia and psychosis.

Developing Targets for EMDR Therapy

Although some people are aware of traumatic events in their timelines or become aware of them during therapy, it is important to note that many people are unaware of specific trauma that may be causing the presenting experiences that are diagnosed as psychosis. The Dutch team, as noted earlier, has suggested that we may also work backward from dysfunctional core beliefs or immediate assumptions to identify target memory networks. This approach stands squarely on the shoulders of CT and CBT for schizophrenia. However, in my experience, it can be difficult for people to cognitively identify dysfunctional core beliefs or the immediate assumptions. If we consider the neurobiology theories that sit alongside the AIP model of EMDR, we are invited to pay attention to what is going on in the body of the individual while he or she is experiencing the psychotic phenomena. By doing so we will see that the ICoNN model of targeting allows us to connect to the felt emotion, which we can then track back to identify the DMN.

We will outline the methodology of the IConN model in detail later in the book. Although it is not necessarily always the case that a person is unaware of the trauma that has resulted in the diagnosis of psychosis, the causative experiences are, more often than not, uncertain upon examination. The IConN model provides a paradigm that enables targeting of these experiences within the EMDR therapy method. The IConN method guides the therapist to the DMN without needing the person to present with a clear awareness of the touchstone event that is resulting in, or significantly contributing to, the experiences being diagnosed as psychotic.

Phenomena as Trauma

It is not hard for any of us working in the area of mental health to understand why many people experience a diagnosis of a psychotic disorder as something deeply troubling. However, for some it is the experiences themselves that are, in the true sense of the word, traumatic. As Japanese researcher Akiko Kikuchi noted, some patients only become traumatized after they regain stability and become capable of looking back on their actions that occurred while psychotic phenomena affected their behavior (Kikuchi, personal communication, 2012). I witnessed this phenomenon as a junior psychiatrist when I was caring for patients with diagnoses of schizophrenia who were very unwell and who had previously failed to respond to treatment until they were started on the then-novel antipsychotic clozapine. For some of these patients it was as if someone had just switched the light on. They suddenly, over a period of weeks, came to life and became capable of interacting with others in a manner that was vastly different from how they had been able to interact for years. Clinicians observed that the renewed activity and improved cognitive and metacognitive functioning allowed them to begin to evaluate themselves and reflect upon how they functioned in the world. These people, who were now recovering or substantially improved, began to feel that they had made very little progress in terms of achievement. They assessed their own lives as being relatively empty compared to those of their peers. Many judged that their peers had far surpassed them by going on to pursue successful careers and building families. All of this, they believed, stood in stark contrast to their lives, which had been marred by psychosis. Often their life journeys to date had been associated with long periods of hospitalization, and treatment entailed heavy doses of sedating medications, at times given against their will by injection. For some people this realization was too much to bear, and they ended their lives by suicide. Psychiatric illness in and of itself can be traumatizing, and so too can the realization of the impact that illness has had, once recovery has been attained. As clinicians we must be mindful of the consequences of our interventions, as even getting better can have unintended consequences. During a period of active psychosis the experiences, such as delusional beliefs and hallucinations, are often extremely emotionally charged. These phenomena are, in and of themselves, capable in some cases of overwhelming the pathways and neural systems that assess and monitor fear and threat. Considering this dynamic, it is not at all surprising that these experiences can be equivalent in emotional valence to the *Diagnostic and Statistical*

Manual of Mental Disorders, fifth edition (*DSM-5*) Criterion A positive events of the PTSD diagnosis (American Psychiatric Association [APA], 2013). In his seminal book that explored the psychology of human evil, psychiatrist M. Scott Peck (1992) discussed the case of a man who presented to his office stating that he had sold his soul to the devil. In the book, Peck noted that it was not necessary for him as a therapist to acknowledge or believe in a "personal devil" in order to treat this person effectively. Rather, what was required of him was that he be willing to consider what such an act said about the man who believed he had done such a thing. This could best be considered within the context of the man's belief system. This for me was a lovely example of therapeutic neutrality advocated by Colin Ross (2004). We can reasonably appreciate that his delusional belief that he had sold his soul to the devil, and the associated fears around what that meant for him, was traumatizing. Indeed, we could consider it to be a PTSD Criterion A positive event, per the *DSM-5* (APA, 2013). If this man had come to me, as a clinician I would certainly have considered treating the psychological impact of his perceived deal with the devil by using EMDR therapy. If we acknowledge that psychotic phenomena can be traumatic and are therefore capable of resulting in the generation of a DMN—which in EMDR therapy we see as the physiological equivalent of the nidus of an infection—we can formulate the presenting problems within an AIP model. This allows us to understand the causation and target our treatment accordingly within the standard EMDR therapy. The benefits of an AIP formulation have been described in the EMDR therapy literature. An AIP model allows us to generate a rationale that explains why symptoms are manifesting, it guides treatment planning, and it predicts outcome (Shapiro & Maxfield, 2002). When we correctly identify a DMN, target it within EMDR therapy, and reprocess it, there is a predictable and observable clinical improvement. This is no less true for trauma caused by the experience of psychosis than for general trauma cases; both may be understood within an AIP formulation.

The Standard Protocol Can Be Used in Psychosis

For many cases where a trauma can be identified and a traditional target developed in the assessment phase, the standard eight-phase, three-pronged protocol can be used. As noted by the work in the Netherlands, some cases of psychosis require little or no modification to the standard model (van den Berg et al., 2014). It is important that we do not rush past that last statement. Let me reiterate it: In some cases of psychosis, little to no modification to the standard model is necessary. However, we must note that this is not the same thing as saying that therapists who are unfamiliar with treating this group of people can consider themselves fully equipped to work with them just because the therapists are trained in EMDR therapy. We must be competent in the client group that we are working with and not stray outside our area of expertise; supervision is helpful in this regard.

> "...there is nothing either good or bad, but thinking makes it so."
> —*Hamlet, Act 2, Scene 2, 249–251*

Treatment as Trauma

Another area suitable for the application of EMDR therapy in this group of people is treatment for the trauma related to the treatment they have received. We can think of this as pertaining to several aspects of treatment:

1. How the treatment is delivered
2. The effects of the treatment itself
3. Side effects of the treatment

How the Treatment Is Delivered

In cases of psychosis, the observation that the person does not see himself or herself as ill means that there is often a disagreement between the treating clinicians and the person himself or herself. Why agree to therapy in any form if you are not ill? In cases where obvious harm is occurring to the person or to others, or where there is judged to be a significant and substantial risk of harm to self or others, there is often the sanction in most jurisdictions to treat the person against his or her will. In most developed countries this is now generally enshrined within legislation that protects the rights of the person. However, even when therapeutic actions are undertaken with the best of intentions, there can be unintended consequences. I have treated one person who, when admitted for treatment against his will following a diagnosis of a psychotic disorder, found the act of being physically restrained and transferred from one ward to another very traumatizing. I have heard Professor Elyn Saks, a chaired professor of law, psychology, and psychiatry at the USC Gould School of Law, who has been given a diagnosis of chronic schizophrenia, speak in a similar way of her own experiences of being restrained (Saks, 2012). It is a distressing thing to listen to, and it is yet another reason that we need to listen to those who share these experiences that we characterize as psychosis or schizophrenia. Think of how you would feel being physically restrained and forcibly treated. I recall another person who spoke to me of the extreme pain he experienced when having had a drug injected into his deep muscle tissue. Both of these actions—restraint and forced medication—were judged as necessary at the time by the clinical teams responsible for the clients' care, but in neither case did that intention mitigate the traumatic impact that those actions later had upon the individuals receiving them. In people who have had experiences such as these, it is possible to target the associated DMN with the standard eight-phase, three-pronged protocol of EMDR therapy; no adaptation to the protocol is necessary. The important issue to remember is that it is not about the intention of the treatment; it is about the associated narrative that the people receiving it tell themselves. Too many therapists get distracted by attempting to assess and test the veracity of the experiences that the person reports, but this is not about truth—it is about "story," as so very often the story the person tells himself or herself is what causes the psychological pain. It is the abused child who believes it was her fault who is so badly wounded in life; it is the scoutmaster who, after having been robbed at gunpoint, can no longer believe that people are essentially good and stops volunteering; and it is the man who believes that his body has been taken over by a persecuting entity who believes he will never be at peace again. Tell me, is it more important to discuss and settle the issue of veracity for these people, or ought we to really listen and hear the stories they are telling? In EMDR therapy we call these narratives negative cognitions (NCs). NCs and positive cognitions (PCs) are the predictive outcomes of information processing (Bergmann, 2012). Therefore, we can understand NCs as evidence of faulty information processing. They focus on our environment, those around us, and, in the case of humans, ourselves (e.g., good, capable, powerless). The predictive function of the brain is adaptive and protective; its role and function is to prepare us for operating effectively in the future. PCs may be available in abstract or semantic form, but, we imagine, due to poor neural linkage, they are felt not to be truly believable: there is a "head knowledge" but not a "heart knowledge." It is proposed that EMDR therapy facilitates healing through the person's own AIP system. Because we are not imposing or seeking to offer a compelling alternative memory network, this allows us to avoid the possibility of derailing processing if the alternate model we propose doesn't fit for the person being treated. By trusting the innate process of AIP as the therapist, it is this process, which the person utilizes every moment of every day, that brings resolution. In facilitating the person's own information processing system, we help people to come to a place where they can begin to trust themselves again.

The Effects of the Treatment Itself

In some cases the treatment can result in an improvement in functioning, and we have already examined the fact that an unintentional consequence of this increased awareness can be traumatic realizations for the person. However, we must note that, more often than not, treatment often fails to provide the outcome desired by the person who is suffering under the weight of illness. People may go through a plethora of medications, and with each change in medication or dose their hope of cure and wellness diminishes. Eventually many submit to settling for a life of disablement and illness: their own personal "slough of despond." My late sister used to have a little statue on her desk with this quote: "Happiness is not being clever enough to know what to worry about." However, it is not so much *cleverness* as *insight* that is the important matter here. Becoming increasingly aware of your place in the world and becoming capable of measuring your level of functioning against that of others carries with it a burden. EMDR therapy in people who have dealt with psychosis can help them to reframe this aspect of their experience. I believe that understanding the traumatic and dissociative origins of these experiences that are diagnosed as psychosis can be of great assistance to those who have suffered under them. Framing these experiences as an understandable disorder of mind and body, occurring as a consequence of what they have been experiencing biologically, psychologically, and socially, is preferable to framing the person as suffering from a broken mind and body. I believe that the trauma and dissociation model for these experiences can empower a person, and it avoids the potential promotion of victimhood and therapeutic paternalism. When individuals are able to know that their suffering is understandable, they appear to be more able to bear up under it. In my work I have found that those who have suffered for a known reason coped better than those who were random victims—tortured at the whim of a terrorist, having been merely "in the wrong place at the wrong time." I now routinely have my clients complete the Post-Traumatic Growth Inventory (PTGI) at the completion of their therapy (Tedeschi, 2011; Tedeschi & Calhoun, 1996). I do this so that they can see that there are aspects of their experience that, once processed and integrated within their life's journey, can result in the enrichment of their lives going forward. Not all of these experiences warrant consideration as illness, and where it may be argued that they do, we ought to keep in mind that not all illness destroys irreparably and not all mental illness leaves a lifelong disability. Sometimes there is great learning and growth on the journey through an individual's own personal "vale of tears." The fictional teacher Mr. Chipping reminds us of this when he reflects on the terrible loss, in the First World War, of so many of the young men that he taught. He quotes Virgil in his fictional retirement speech in the film *Goodbye, Mr. Chips*: "Forsan et haec olim, meminisse juvabit" (Book I, line 203 of Virgil's *Aeneid*: "Perhaps at some time we will look back on even these times fondly").

Side Effects of the Treatment

Neurobiologists observe how trauma alters the structure and function of the brain and nervous system. Psychoanalysts observe the subjective impact of trauma: how traumatic stress alters and even shatters one's experience of meaning and of self (e.g., scoutmaster and gunman example presented earlier). Sometimes the medication being used in treatment can result in unwanted effects, so-called side effects. These include abnormalities of motor functioning with the first-generation antipsychotic medications, disorders such as tardive dyskinesia (Miller, 2007), and, in the case of the newer antipsychotic medications, the potential for metabolic syndrome and excessive weight gain. These disorders further set apart the people with these experiences from the so-called "normal" majority. The side effects of these medications and their associated stigma can add greatly to the suffering of the people in receipt of them.

SUMMATION

In summary, we see that the research completed specifically around EMDR therapy for schizophrenia and psychosis is sparse. There is much that yet needs to be critically examined and peer reviewed. However, some clinicians have presented case reports where EMDR therapy has been successfully used for the treatment of these conditions, formally and informally. At this stage the case-report evidence appears in line with what we have already discussed. Past trauma, when identified as being etiologically contributory to psychosis, can be treated with EMDR therapy and results in its amelioration or resolution. PTSD can be safely and effectively treated in people with comorbid psychotic experiences, without destabilizing the psychotic condition. Phenomena such as "dysfunctional core beliefs" can be tracked back to identify suitable targets for reprocessing. We will see from the ICoNN method that the modifications described are, first of all, largely in respect to the identification of targets, remembering the links between trauma, dissociation, and psychosis. Last, the model will delineate methods for the stabilization and reunification of dissociated material, which, it is argued, results in the amelioration and resolution of psychotic phenomena. This AIP-informed understanding of psychosis is very helpful, and we see that here too, in respect to psychosis, the AIP formulation explains pathology, guides therapeutic endeavors, and is predictive of outcome.

REFERENCES

American Psychiatric Association. (2013). *Diagnostic and statistical manual of mental disorders* (5th ed.). Washington, DC: Author.

Anketell, C., Dorahy, M. J., Shannon, M., Elder, R., Hamilton, G., Corry, M., . . . O'Rawe, B. (2010). An exploratory analysis of voice hearing in chronic PTSD: Potential associated mechanisms. *Journal of Trauma and Dissociation: The Official Journal of the International Society for the Study of Dissociation (ISSD)*, 11(1), 93–107.

Arseneault, L., Cannon, M., Fisher, H. L., Polancyk, G., Moffitt, T. E., & Caspi, A. (2011). Childhood trauma and children's emerging psychotic symptoms: A genetically sensitive longitudinal cohort study. *American Journal of Psychiatry, 168*, 65–72.

Barabasz, A., Barabasz, M., Christensen, C., French, B., & Watkins, J. G. (2013). Efficacy of single-session abreactive ego state therapy for combat stress injury, PTSD, and ASD. *International Journal of Clinical and Experimental Hypnosis, 61*(1), 1–19. doi:10.1080/00207144.2013.729377

Basset, T., Bentall, R., Boyle, M., Cooke, A., Cupitt, C., Dillon, J., . . . Weaver, Y. (2014). In A. Cooke (Ed.), *Understanding psychosis and schizophrenia: Why people sometimes hear voices, believe things that others find strange, or appear out of touch with reality, and what can help*. A report by the Division of Clinical Psychology. Leicester, England: British Psychological Society, Division of Clinical Psychology.

Beer, M. D. (1996). The dichotomies: Psychosis/neurosis and functional/organic: A historical perspective. *History of Psychiatry, 7*(26, Pt. 2), 231–255.

Bentall, R. P. (1992). *Reconstructing schizophrenia*. London, England: Routledge.

Bentall, R. P. (2003). *Madness explained: Psychosis and human nature*. London, England: Allen Lane.

Bentall, R. P. (2009). *Doctoring the mind: Is our current treatment of mental illness really any good?* New York, NY: New York University Press.

Bergmann, U. (2012). *Neurobiological foundations for EMDR practice*. New York, NY: Springer Publishing Company.

Bleuler, E. (1911). *Dementia praecox, oder Gruppe der Schizophrenien* [Dementia praecox, or the group of schizophrenias]. Leipzig, Germany: Deuticke.

Burns, A. M., Erickson, D. H., & Brenner, C. A. (2014). Cognitive-behavioral therapy for medication-resistant psychosis: A meta-analytic review. *Psychiatric Services, 65*(7), 874–880. doi:10.1176/appi.ps.201300213

Burns, L. C. (1954). A forgotten psychiatrist—Baron Ernst von Feuchtersleben. *Proceedings of the Royal Society of Medicine, 47*(3), 190–194.

Carlson, E. B., Putnam, F. W., Ross, C. A., Torem, M., Coons, P., Dill, D. L., . . . Braun, B. G. (1993). Validity of the Dissociative Experiences Scale in screening for multiple personality disorder: A multicenter study. *American Journal of Psychiatry, 150*(7), 1030–1036. doi:10.1176/ajp.150.7.1030

Christodoulides, T., Dudley, R., Brown, S., Turkington, D., & Beck, A. T. (2008). Cognitive behaviour therapy in patients with schizophrenia who are not prescribed antipsychotic medication: A case series. *Psychology and Psychotherapy, 81*(Pt. 2), 199–207. doi:10.1348/147608308X278295

Croes, C. F., van Grunsven, R., Staring, A. B., van den Berg, D. P., de Jongh, A., & van der Gaag, M. (2014). [Imagery in psychosis: EMDR as a new intervention in the treatment of delusions and auditory hallucinations]. *[Journal of Psychiatry]*, *56*(9), 568–576.

Dorahy, M. J., Shannon, C., Seagar, L., Corr, M., Stewart, K., Hanna, D., . . . Middleton, W. (2009). Auditory hallucinations in dissociative identity disorder and schizophrenia with and without a childhood trauma history: Similarities and differences. *Journal of Nervous and Mental Disease*, *197*(12), 892–898. doi:10.1097/NMD.0b013e3181c299ea 00005053-200912000-00004 [pii]

Edirippulige, S., Levandovskaya, M., & Prishutova, A. (2013). A qualitative study of the use of Skype for psychotherapy consultations in the Ukraine. *Journal of Telemedicine and Telecare*, *19*(7), 376–378. doi:10.1177/1357633x13506523

Engelhard, I. M., van den Hout, M. A., Dek, E. C., Giele, C. L., van der Wielen, J. W., Reijnen, M. J., & van Roij, B. (2011). Reducing vividness and emotional intensity of recurrent "flashforwards" by taxing working memory: An analogue study. *Journal of Anxiety Disorders*, *25*(4), 599–603. doi:10.1016/j.janxdis.2011.01.009

Engelhard, I. M., van den Hout, M. A., & Smeets, M. A. (2011). Taxing working memory reduces vividness and emotional intensity of images about the Queen's Day tragedy. *Journal of Behavior Therapy and Experimental Psychiatry*, *42*(1), 32–37. doi:10.1016/ j.jbtep.2010.09.004

Fisher, H. L., McGuffin, P., Boydell, J., Fearon, P., Craig, T. K., Dazzan, P., . . . Morgan, C. (2014). Interplay between childhood physical abuse and familial risk in the onset of psychotic disorders. *Schizophrenia Bulletin*. doi:10.1093/schbul/sbt201

Forgash, C., & Copeley, M. (2008). *Healing the heart of trauma and dissociation with EMDR and ego state therapy*. New York, NY: Springer Publishing Company.

Freeman, D., Bentall, R. P., & Garety, P. A. (2008). *Persecutory delusions: Assessment, theory, and treatment*. Oxford, England: Oxford University Press.

Frewen, P. A., & Lanius, R. A. (2006). Neurobiology of dissociation: Unity and disunity in mind-body-brain. *Psychiatric Clinics of North America*, *29*(1), 113–128, ix. doi: S0193-953X(05)00099-7 [pii] 10.1016/j.psc.2005.10.016

Gonzalez, A., Mosquera, D., & Moskowitz, A. (2012). *[EMDR in psychosis and severe mental disorders]*. Paper presented at the annual meeting of EMDR Europe Association, Madrid, Spain.

Jaspers, K. (1913). *Allgemeine psychopathologie* [General psychopathology]. Berlin, Germany: Springer.

Jaspers, K. (1963). *General psychopathology* (Trans. from the German 7th ed.). Manchester, England: Manchester University Press.

Johnson, R. A. (1986). *Inner work: Using dreams and active imagination for personal growth* (1st ed.). San Francisco, CA: Harper & Row.

Jones, S., & Bentall, R. P. (2006). *The psychology of bipolar disorder: New developments and research strategies*. Oxford, England: Oxford University Press.

Jung, C. G., McGuire, W., Shamdasani, S., & Jung, C. G. (2012). *Introduction to Jungian psychology: Notes of the seminar on analytical psychology given in 1925* (Rev. ed.). Princeton, NJ: Princeton University Press.

Jung, C. G., & Shamdasani, S. (2009). *The red book = Liber novus* (1st ed.). New York, NY: W. W. Norton.

Kikuchi, A. (2008). [Application of EMDR for schizophrenia]. *Clinical Psychology: Various Aspects*, *27*(2), 317–324.

Kim, D. C., Choi, J., Kim, S. H., Oh, D. H., Park, S.-C., & Lee, S. H. (2010). A pilot study of brief eye movement desensitization and reprocessing (EMDR) for treatment of acute phase schizophrenia. *Korean Journal of Biological Psychiatry*, *17*(2), 93–101.

Kinderman, P., McKenna, P., & Laws, K. R. (2015). Are psychological therapies effective in treating schizophrenia and psychosis? *Progress in Neurology and Psychiatry, 19*(1), 17–20.

Kingdon, D. G., & Turkington, D. (1994). *Cognitive-behavioral therapy of schizophrenia.* Hove, England: Erlbaum.

Kingdon, D. G., & Turkington, D. (2005). *Cognitive therapy of schizophrenia.* New York, NY: Guilford.

Knipe, J. (2015). *EMDR toolbox: Theory and treatment of complex PTSD and dissociation.* New York, NY: Springer Publishing Company.

Lanius, U. F. (2005). EMDR processing with dissociative clients: Adjunctive use of opioid antagonists. In R. Shapiro (Ed.), *EMDR solutions—pathways to healing* (pp. 121–146). New York, NY: W. W. Norton.

Lanius, U. F., Paulsen, S. L., & Corrigan, F. M. (Eds.). (2014). *Neurobiology and treatment of traumatic dissociation: Towards an embodied self.* New York, NY: Springer Publishing Company.

Laugharne, R., Marshall, D., Laugharne, J., & Hassard, A. (2014). A role for EMDR in the treatment of trauma in patients suffering from a psychosis: Four vignettes. *Journal of EMDR Practice and Research, 8*(1), 19–24. doi:10.1891/1933-3196.8.1.19

Leer, A., Engelhard, I. M., Altink, A., & van den Hout, M. A. (2013). Eye movements during recall of aversive memory decreases conditioned fear. *Behavioral Research and Therapy, 51*(10), 633–640. doi:10.1016/j.brat.2013.07.004

Leff, J., Williams, G., Huckvale, M. A., Arbuthnot, M., & Leff, A. P. (2014). Computer-assisted therapy for medication-resistant auditory hallucinations: Proof-of-concept study. *British Journal of Psychiatry, 202,* 428–433. doi:10.1192/bjp.bp.112.124883

Lewis, S., Tarrier, N., Haddock, G., Bentall, R., Kinderman, P., Kingdon, D., . . . Dunn, G. (2002). Randomised controlled trial of cognitive-behavioural therapy in early schizophrenia: Acute-phase outcomes. *British Journal of Psychiatry, 43*(Suppl.), s91–s97.

Miller, P. W. (2007). *The genetic epidemiology of tardive dyskinesia in Northern Ireland.* Doctoral dissertation, Queen's University Belfast, Belfast, Ireland.

Miller, P. W. (2010). *EMDR in psychosis—2 year follow-up of a case series of severe depression, with psychosis; delusional dysmorphophobia and schizophrenia, treated with EMDR.* Paper presented at the EMDR UK and Ireland meeting, Dublin, Ireland.

Miller, P. W. (2014). Psychosis / dissociation—a rose by any other name [eLetter]. Retrieved from http://bjp.rcpsych.org/content/202/6/428.e-letters#psychosis—dissociation—a-rose-by-any-other-name

Moskowitz, A. (2005). *Pierre Janet's influence on Bleuler's concept of schizophrenia.* Paper presented at the the First Symposium of the Pierre Janet Gesellschaft, Freiburg, Germany.

Moskowitz, A., Schäfer, I., & Dorahy, M. J. (2008). *Psychosis, trauma, and dissociation: Emerging perspectives on severe psychopathology.* Chichester, England: Wiley-Blackwell.

Naeem, F., Kingdon, D., & Turkington, D. (2006). Cognitive behaviour therapy for schizophrenia: Relationship between anxiety symptoms and therapy. *Psychology and Psychotherapy, 79*(Pt. 2), 153–164. doi:10.1348/147608305X91538

National Institute for Health and Care Excellence. (2005). *Post-traumatic stress disorder (PTSD): The management of PTSD in adults and children in primary and secondary care. Clinical Guideline 26.* London, England: Author.

Parmenides, Empedocles, & Lombardo, S. (1982). *Parmenides and Empedocles: The fragments in verse translation.* San Francisco, CA: Grey Fox Press.

Peck, M. S. (1992). *People of the lie.* New York, NY: Simon & Schuster.

Rathod, S., Kingdon, D., Smith, P., & Turkington, D. (2005). Insight into schizophrenia: The effects of cognitive behavioural therapy on the components of insight and association with sociodemographics—data on a previously published randomised controlled trial. *Schizophrenia Research, 74*(2–3), 211-219. doi:10.1016/j.schres.2004.07.003

Rathod, S., Kingdon, D., Weiden, P., & Turkington, D. (2008). Cognitive-behavioral therapy for medication-resistant schizophrenia: A review. *Journal of Psychiatric Practice, 14*(1), 22–33. doi:10.1097/01.pra.0000308492.93003.db

Read, J., & Bentall, R. P. (2012). Negative childhood experiences and mental health: Theoretical, clinical and primary prevention implications. *British Journal of Psychiatry, 200,* 89–91. doi:10.1192/bjp.bp.111.096727

Read, J., Mosher, L. R., & Bentall, R. P. (2004). *Models of madness: Psychological, social and biological approaches to schizophrenia.* Hove, England: Brunner-Routledge.

Roques, J. (2008). *[EMDR—A therapeutic revolution and paradigm shift].* Paper presented at the EMDR Canada Annual Conference, Montreal, Canada.

Ross, C. (2013). *Psychosis, trauma, dissociation, and EMDR.* Paper presented at the 18th EMDR International Association Conference, Austin, TX.

Ross, C. A. (2004). *Schizophrenia: Innovations in diagnosis and treatment.* Binghamton, NY: Haworth Maltreatment and Trauma.

Ross, C. A., Anderson, G., Heber, S., & Norton, G. R. (1990). Dissociation and abuse among multiple-personality patients, prostitutes, and exotic dancers. *Hospital and Community Psychiatry, 41*(3), 328–330.

Saks, E. (2012). Elyn Saks: A tale of mental illness—from the inside. *TEDGlobal.* Retrieved from http://www.ted.com/talks/elyn_saks_seeing_mental_illness?language=en

Sellwood, W., Wittkowski, A., Tarrier, N., & Barrowclough, C. (2007). Needs-based cognitive-behavioural family intervention for patients suffering from schizophrenia: 5-year follow-up of a randomized controlled effectiveness trial. *Acta Psychiatrica Scandinavica, 116*(6), 447—452. doi:10.1111/j.1600-0447.2007.01097.x

Shapiro, F., & Maxfield, L. (2002). Eye movement desensitization and reprocessing (EMDR): Information processing in the treatment of trauma. *Journal of Clinical Psychology, 58*(8), 933–946. doi:10.1002/jclp.10068

Slade, P. D., & Bentall, R. P. (1988). *Sensory deception: A scientific analysis of hallucination.* Baltimore, MD: Johns Hopkins University Press.

Stone, H., & Stone, S. (1989). *Embracing our selves: The voice dialogue manual.* San Rafael, CA: New World Library.

Tarrier, N. (2005). Cognitive behaviour therapy for schizophrenia—a review of development, evidence and implementation. *Psychotherapy and Psychosomatics, 74*(3), 136–144. doi:10.1159/000083998

Tarrier, N. (2010). Cognitive behavior therapy for schizophrenia and psychosis: Current status and future directions. *Clinical Schizophrenia and Related Psychoses, 4*(3), 176–184. doi:10.3371/CSRP.4.3.4

Tarrier, N., Wittkowski, A., Kinney, C., McCarthy, E., Morris, J., & Humphreys, L. (1999). Durability of the effects of cognitive-behavioural therapy in the treatment of chronic schizophrenia: 12-month follow-up. *British Journal of Psychiatry, 174,* 500–504.

Tarrier, N., Yusupoff, L., Kinney, C., McCarthy, E., Gledhill, A., Haddock, G., & Morris, J. (1998). Randomised controlled trial of intensive cognitive behaviour therapy for patients with chronic schizophrenia. *British Medical Journal, 317*(7154), 303–307.

Tedeschi, R. G. (2011). Posttraumatic growth in combat veterans. *Journal of Clinical Psychology in Medical Settings, 18*(2), 137–144. doi:10.1007/s10880-011-9255-2

Tedeschi, R. G., & Calhoun, L. G. (1996). The Posttraumatic Growth Inventory: Measuring the positive legacy of trauma. *Journal of Traumatic Stress, 9*(3), 455–471.

van den Berg, D. P., de Bont, P. A., van der Vleugel, B. M., de Roos, C., de Jongh, A., Van Minnen, A., & van der Gaag, M. (2015). Prolonged exposure vs eye movement desensitization and reprocessing vs waiting list for posttraumatic stress disorder in patients with a psychotic disorder: A randomized clinical trial. *JAMA Psychiatry.* doi:10.1001/jamapsychiatry.2014.2637

van den Berg, D. P., & van der Gaag, M. (2012). Treating trauma in psychosis with EMDR: A pilot study. *Journal of Behavior Therapy and Experimental Psychiatry, 43*(1), 664–671. doi:10.1016/j.jbtep.2011.09.011

van den Berg, D. P. G., van der Vleugel, B. M., & Staring, A. (2010). [Trauma, psychosis, PTSD and the use of EMDR]. *Directieve Therapie, 30*(4), 303–328. doi:10.1007/s12433-010-0242-9

van den Berg, D. P. G., van der Vleugel, B. M., Staring, A. B. P., de Bont, P. A. J., & de Jongh, A. (2013). EMDR in psychosis: Guidelines for conceptualization and treatment. *Journal of EMDR Practice and Research, 7*(4), 208–224.

van den Berg, D. P. G., van der Vleugel, B. M., Staring, A. B. P., de Bont, P. A. J., & de Jongh, A. (2014). [EMDR in psychosis: Guidelines for conceptualization and treatment]. *Journal of EMDR Practice and Research, 8*(3), E67–E84. doi:10.1891/1933-3196.8.3.E67

van den Hout, M. A., Bartelski, N., & Engelhard, I. M. (2013). On EMDR: Eye movements during retrieval reduce subjective vividness and objective memory accessibility during future recall. *Cognition and Emotion, 27*(1), 177–183. doi:10.1080/02699931.2012.691087

van den Hout, M. A., Engelhard, I. M., Rijkeboer, M. M., Koekebakker, J., Hornsveld, H., Leer, A., . . . Akse, N. (2011). EMDR: Eye movements superior to beeps in taxing working memory and reducing vividness of recollections. *Behaviour Research and Therapy, 49*(2), 92–98. doi:10.1016/j.brat.2010.11.003

van der Gaag, M., Valmaggia, L. R., & Smit, F. (2014). The effects of individually tailored formulation-based cognitive behavioural therapy in auditory hallucinations and delusions: A meta-analysis. *Schizophrenia Research, 156*(1), 30–37. doi:10.1016/j.schres.2014.03.016

van der Hart, O., & Dorahy, M. (2006). Pierre Janet and the concept of dissociation. *American Journal of Psychiatry, 163*(9), 1646; author reply 1646.

van der Vleugel, B. M., van den Berg, D. P., & Staring, A. B. P. (2012). Trauma, psychosis, post-traumatic stress disorder and the application of EMDR. *Rivista di Psichiatria, 47*(2, Suppl. 1), 33S–38S. doi:10.1708/1071.11737

Velligan, D. I., Tai, S., Roberts, D. L., Maples-Aguilar, N., Brown, M., Mintz, J., & Turkington, D. (2014). A randomized controlled trial comparing cognitive behavior therapy, cognitive adaptation training, their combination and treatment as usual in chronic schizophrenia. *Schizophrenia Bulletin.* doi:10.1093/schbul/sbu127

Watkins, H. H. (1993). Ego-state therapy: An overview. *American Journal of Clinical Hypnosis, 35*(4), 232-240.

Watkins, J. G., & Watkins, H. H. (1984). Hazards to the therapist in the treatment of multiple personalities. *Psychiatric Clinics of North America, 7*(1), 111–119.

Watkins, J. G., & Watkins, H. H. (1990). Dissociation and displacement: Where goes the "ouch?" *American Journal of Clinical Hypnosis, 33*(1), 1–10; discussion 11–21.

World Health Organization. (2013). *WHO guidelines on conditions specifically related to stress.* Geneva, Switzerland: WHO Press.

Wykes, T., Steel, C., Everitt, B., & Tarrier, N. (2008). Cognitive behavior therapy for schizophrenia: Effect sizes, clinical models, and methodological rigor. *Schizophrenia Bulletin, 34*(3), 523–537. doi:10.1093/schbul/sbm114

SEVEN

An End to Therapeutic Nihilism

Intention: *To help the reader in understanding the justifiable optimism when applying EMDR therapy to psychosis and to equip clinicians with the skills to identify those people experiencing psychosis who are most suitable for EMDR therapy.*

COGNITIVE BEHAVIORAL THERAPY FOR PSYCHOSIS

The majority of people who are not trained in eye movement desensitization and reprocessing (EMDR) therapy know of EMDR therapy only as a treatment for posttraumatic stress disorder (PTSD), if they know of it at all. Therefore, the application of EMDR therapy for the treatment of psychosis and schizophrenia will be new to many. It is unfortunately still considered by some clinicians to be controversial. Readers, however, will be aware of the path forged by cognitive behavioral therapy (CBT) for psychosis, which is now well developed (Christodoulides, Dudley, Brown, Turkington, & Beck, 2008; Habib, Dawood, Kingdon, & Naeem, 2015; Hepworth, Ashcroft, & Kingdon, 2013; Lewis et al., 2002; Mitford, Reay, McCabe, Paxton, & Turkington, 2010; Moorhead & Turkington, 2001; Morrison et al., 2012; Naeem et al., 2014; Naeem, Kingdon, & Turkington, 2006; Rathod, Kingdon, Phiri, & Gobbi, 2010; Rathod, Kingdon, Smith, & Turkington, 2005; Rathod, Kingdon, Weiden, & Turkington, 2008; Rathod et al., 2013; Turkington et al., 2014; Velligan et al., 2009; Velligan et al., 2014). I had first come across the use of CBT for psychosis through the work of a colleague whom I was working with in a community mental health team (CMHT). This person was a community psychiatric nurse (CPN) who had a trained with Douglas Turkington and David G. Kingdon. These men are champions in the application of CBT for schizophrenia and they have contributed much to this clinical area; they continue to do so. They have assisted us in advancing toward the goal they have set: the removal of the psychological nihilism in psychosis to replace it with therapeutic optimism. Surely this is a goal around which we can all unite as clinicians, carers, and people with lived experience. Sometimes people with these experiences need us to carry their hopes for a time. How can we do so if we don't have any hope of healing for psychosis? The Declaration of Melbourne made by the Hearing Voices Network on November 21, 2013, states, "We believe everyone can recover and the systemic holding of this hope is central to people's recovery." CBT for psychosis/schizophrenia endeavors to offer optimism to clinicians through the dissemination of research and treatment paradigms (Kingdon & Turkington, 1994, 2005). Interestingly, Aaron T. Beck, the "father of cognitive behavioral therapy," began to develop CBT by exploring the clinical area of psychosis (Beck, 1952; Beck & Valin, 1953). He abandoned the area only to return to it many years later (Morrison, 2002; Rector & Beck, 2002), and we are all the richer for his work. When therapists are openhearted and open-minded, we, as a community of therapists, stop seeing each other as a threat. A great many EMDR therapists are also trained as CBT therapists and have respect for the method. I hope there can be mutual respect and professional unity (*not uniformity*) that respects diversity, which can enable us to benefit from all the work done to date in the area of psychotherapy for psychosis. My experience of EMDR therapy has been one that is characterized by a very integrative and diverse clinical practice, and I hope that the CBT community can recognize the value that EMDR therapy brings to this clinical area. This invites us to be open to the potential wisdom and knowledge that is being uncovered within all of the psychotherapies being utilized in the treatment of psychosis.

EMDR therapy has been utilized by its proponents in many clinical areas beyond PTSD (Forgash & Copeley, 2008; Knipe, 2015; MacCulloch, 2006; Manfield, 1998; Shapiro & Forrest, 1997; Shapiro, Kaslow, & Maxfield, 2007; van den Berg, van der Vleugel, Staring, de Bont, & de Jongh, 2013; Zengin, 2009). Although clinicians see and describe these benefits, observed in everyday clinical practice, there is much need for good research to be completed with respect to EMDR therapy. In this regard it lags behind CBT. At present for EMDR therapy practitioners, our clinical experiences are not fully represented in, or backed up by, the available research literature. The adaptive information processing (AIP) model and the dysfunctional memory network (DMN) are paradigms that have validity beyond PTSD; they are just as valid for addictions, obsessive-compulsive disorder, depression, and, as I argue in this book, psychosis. This is why Dr. Francine Shapiro is constantly calling for us to publish what we are seeing in our everyday clinical practice.

Why Listen?

As we move further into the 21st century, mental health professionals have increasingly been revisiting paradigms that acknowledge that psychotic phenomena have meaning within them, albeit highly abstract and symbolic meaning most of the time. I believe that this has begun to happen at the same time as we have shifted how we think about those people who have these experiences. In particular, I believe that seeing them as experts with lived experience greatly improves our therapeutic approach. It is not so much that amazing individuals, such as Professor Elyn Saks, who have been given the diagnosis of chronic schizophrenia have found a voice, for they always had that; it is more that these individuals have now found a group of mental health professionals who are willing to listen. As mental health professionals we need to first adhere to the foundational principle of *primum non nocere*—"first, do no harm." If we are to achieve this, then we must, above all else, listen. This provides us with the best chance of coming to understand why an individual is having the experiences that he or she is presenting with. In my opinion, we made a grave error when we began to fail to listen to the detailed content of our patients in whom we diagnosed psychosis and/or schizophrenia. When I worked as a part of the Genetic Epidemiology of Mental Illness in Northern Ireland (GEMINI) research team, part of our job was to review the clinical notes and case records of those people whom we believed to have a diagnosis of schizophrenia. This was one of the things that allowed us to decide whether they were suitable for inclusion in the genetic epidemiological analysis. One thing that I observed in the process of examining case files was that the more recent the notes were, the less detailed the descriptions of the phenomenology. Often, there would be a categorical record of, for example, persecutory delusions, grandiose delusions, and so forth, but the actual phenomenological detail was, more often than not, missing. This reflects mental health professionals', and in particular psychiatrists', approach to mental disorder and in particular psychosis, where the specific content is presumed to be meaningless jibber-jabber. This is a serious error in my opinion, and I believe that it continues to take us further down the incorrect path established by Jaspers. We ought to listen and attend to the psychotic phenomena in detail. If we do not, then we are effectively saying to the people who present to us asking for help, "Come in, and sit down. Tell me what troubles you." At first we listen, but on hearing of the voices and the bizarre visual experiences, we collate our findings, formulate the case, diagnose psychosis, and then adopt the position that the content is mere nonsense flowing from a broken biological mechanism. Why try to understand it or engage with it? Surely that will only encourage such nonsense. I hope that when you finish reading this book, if nothing else, you will at least commit to listen more to what these people, who are seeking our help, are saying.

As time and resource pressures are increasing within many clinical practices, the Jaspersian lie that the content of psychosis is meaningless is tempting. If we believe Karl Jaspers, then we need not listen in detail to the content, as that would only encourage the psychosis. Medication is the answer to this biological disorder. However, we have had more than 100 years of such an approach, and if anything we have gone far beyond the position that Jaspers took, by almost entirely having squeezed psychotherapy out of our treatment models. It is therefore by looking back that clinicians and researchers have returned to hypotheses posited in the past that link trauma, psychosis, and dissociation. Like the ancient symbol of the Ouroboros, we are coming full circle. If we have learned something valuable over the past 100 years or so, it ought to be that it is not the therapist or psychiatrist "making" people better; it is people getting better in partnership. Our role as mental health professionals ought to demand that we work in partnership with those who are experts through the lived experience of what we call psychosis and schizophrenia.

At times we can look at the present paradigms that we have for psychosis, and we may feel that there is little we can do other than medicate. However, as Margaret Mead (the famous American cultural anthropologist) is purported to have said,

> "Never doubt that a thoughtful group of committed citizens
> can change the world, for indeed it is the only thing that
> ever has."
> —*(quoted in Lutkehaus, 2008)*

The Same Old News From the Trenches

Following the release of the report of the British Psychological Society (BPS), "Understanding Psychosis and Schizophrenia: Why People Sometimes Hear Voices, Believe Things That Others Find Strange, or Appear Out of Touch With Reality and What Can Help" (Basset et al., 2014), there resulted much debate. I believe that debate can be good, if it breaks the soil of academia and finds the hidden gold of clinical application. Unfortunately there was much of the predictable "trench warfare." Opposing sides continued "digging in" to their respective trenches, in preparation for battle. Boom: "the effect sizes for CBT in psychosis shrinks to ineffectiveness when the CBT trials are blinded" (Kinderman, McKenna, & Laws, 2015), it is argued from one trench—dash, down, crawl, observe, set sights, return fire. Bang, the other trench opens fire: "psychopharmacology poisons people with little effectiveness. Neuroleptics increase the risk to metabolic syndrome" (Kinderman et al., 2015). Who are the casualties? These are the people in no man's land, whose heads we shoot above: the experts through lived experience. Sadly, they all too often also experience our war making, getting caught in the crossfire and lost in the process. Do we really want another century of trench warfare? In my opinion, we ought to be fighting for the people who are currently caught in the crossfire. So instead of shooting at each other, over the heads of the experts with lived experience of these frightening manifestations, we can choose to lay down our weapons and climb out of our trenches. The "enemy" is not CBT, nor EMDR, nor pharmacotherapy; the "enemy" ought to be the experiences that distress and diminish the quality of life for these people. There is no health without mental health, after all.

"CBT Is as Beneficial as Medication"

Controversy has been stirred up by the BPS report's assertion that people benefit as much from CBT for psychosis as from antipsychotics. As I have noted, it has been argued that this potentially paradigm-shifting claim, which the BPS report makes, appears to be built largely upon two meta-analyses: one that examined people with treatment-resistant schizophrenia (Burns, Erickson, & Brenner, 2014) and a second that looked at "individually tailored formulation-based CBT in auditory hallucinations and delusions" (van der Gaag, Valmaggia, & Smit, 2014). Considering the first of the two, the meta-analysis states that these people experience benefits above and beyond those conferred by medication (Burns et al., 2014). However, the report's authors go further, suggesting that there exists a "general consensus" that people with psychosis derive as much benefit from CBT as they do from medication. Although this is something that may be felt to be true based upon naturalistic clinical experience, the published data do not yet appear to allow such a statement to be made so strongly (Kinderman et al., 2015). Therefore, unsurprisingly, this has been a target for criticisms of the report, and it has received a predictably mixed reception from opposing sides in the debate. Although the BPS report relies upon a large number of references, members of one group whose meta-analysis was included (Jauhar et al., 2014) have been highly critical of the final interpretations by the BPS report authors. They go as far as stating, "Why should anyone take them seriously?" (Kinderman et al., 2015, p. 20). This group's very comprehensive meta-analysis found that the effect size for CBT in psychosis was consistently in the small range: 0.33 for overall symptoms, 0.25 for positive symptoms (e.g., delusions and hallucinations), and 0.13 for negative symptoms (e.g., social constriction and amotivation) (Jauhar et al., 2014). They also stated that a weakness in the studies that were examined was a particular bias related to whether the study was blinded or not. They reported that for the 20 clinical trials that were blinded (i.e., where the individuals in receipt of therapy are unaware if they are in the active arm of the study or in a control group, such as receiving treatment as usual), there was a reduction in effect sizes to 0.15 for overall symptoms (a small effect) and 0.08 (a nonsignificant finding) for positive symptoms (Jauhar et al., 2014). The issue of blinding in psychological studies is important but complex, and I do not intend to explore it at length here. Suffice it to say that if we are to publish in this area, we need to be able to construct suitably robust study models to answer these criticisms. This effort will benefit from collaboration between clinicians and academics.

Two of the meta-analyses that are cited by the BPS report authors are criticized for being old and out of date, as they are from 2006 and 2008 (Kinderman et al., 2015). Notably, a more recent meta-analysis (Turner, van der Gaag, Karyotaki, & Cuijpers, 2014) reports an effect size of 0.16 in studies of CBT in psychosis, which is in line with the effect size (0.15) in the 20 blind trials referred to earlier (Jauhar et al., 2014). Considering those meta-analyses that give the most positive results for CBT in schizophrenia, the first one cited, which examined treatment-resistant schizophrenia (Burns et al., 2014), used an idiosyncratic method to determine effect size. This meant it was unable to be compared with the studies applying the standard method. In the second meta-analysis that looked at CBT, which was highly specific and tailored according to case formulation, targeting delusions or auditory hallucinations (van der Gaag et al., 2014), the 11 studies that targeted delusions had an effect size of 0.36. This was reduced in blind studies to 0.24, and the nine studies that targeted hallucinations gave an effect size of 0.44. It is interesting to note that the largest effect size in the hallucination studies was found in the study looking at the novel avatar therapy (Basset et al., 2014; Leff, Williams, Huckvale, Arbuthnot, & Leff, 2014). I have noted elsewhere that the avatar method appears to acknowledge the dissociative nature of schizophrenia (Miller, 2014). For me, if anything can be taken from this result, it encourages further exploration of therapeutic models for schizophrenia that build on the links between trauma, dissociation, and psychosis. EMDR therapy in psychosis is too young in its development to attract even a mention in the BPS report at this time; however, we need to work to build a literature that can be scrutinized critically.

"If you are irritated by every rub, how will you be polished?"
—Rumi (quoted in Jalāl al-Dīn, Barks, & Green, 1997)

The Good Old Days?

I am reminded of the earliest days of my psychiatric training when my trainer and mentor shared with me his experiences of the evolution of the understanding of schizophrenia. In his career he had watched a shift away from a "gloomy" prognosis, this move being heralded by the 5-year outcome study in early schizophrenia (Wing, 1966) and contributed to by the later work around expressed emotion, or EE (Leff & Vaughn, 1985). EE is a measure of the family environment that focuses on the type of interaction between the person who is presenting as ill and a key caregiver. There has been lots of research into this dynamic, and it continues to be recognized as an important factor in understanding relapse in people diagnosed with schizophrenia (Amaresha & Venkatasubramanian, 2012; Butzlaff & Hooley, 1998). The concept was first described in the work of George Brown in the 1950s (Leff, 2000; Leff & Vaughn, 1985). At the time, the new antipsychotic medication chlorpromazine was the standard treatment for schizophrenia, and it was allowing people who had been long-stay patients to leave the asylums and have the hope of a positive prognosis (Wing, 1966). However, relapses were observed, and Brown was tasked with the job to study these patients and gain a better understanding as to why some were at a higher risk of relapse than others (Brown & Harris, 2000). There was seen to be a higher rate of relapse in those discharged to family or spouse as compared with those who were living in lodgings or with a sibling (Brown, Birley, & Wing, 1972). This research led to the construct of EE, which comprises three factors/behavioral patterns: criticism, hostility, and emotional over involvement (Brown & Harris, 2000). The studies looking at the relapse risk for patients discharged to high- or low-EE environments consistently showed a higher risk of relapse for those in high-EE environments. This finding is characterized by a well-known study that showed the median relapse rates in a high-EE environment as compared with a low-EE environment, which were 48% and 21%, respectively (Kavanagh, 1992). These findings had obvious relevance to discharge policy in the long-term management of these people and led to a number of interventions, including family therapy to decrease EE. Further work showed three key areas where the relapse rate could be affected (Vaughn & Leff, 1976): a high-EE environment as compared with a low-EE environment, the time spent in a high-EE environment, and with or without medication. In particular I recall one summary chart. On this chart, the figure of 15% relapse rate in 9 months stood out for me, as it was the same for two groups: one group consisting of those in a low-EE environment who were drug-free and the other group consisting of people in a high-EE environment who spent less than 35 hours per week there and took medication (Vaughn & Leff, 1976). This 15% is what comes to mind when I now see the debate around the BPS report and the arguments around CBT for psychosis and schizophrenia. I am reminded that the best outcome can be achieved from a biopsychosocial approach, and that influencing how individuals engage with the world around them can be a powerful treatment in itself. Perhaps through psychotherapy we are acting to lower people's levels of distress as they attempt to make sense of the world around them. This may be doing something similar to creating a low-EE environment. I argue for inclusion of the biological aspects of treatment because in the same study, those who had schizophrenia within a low-EE environment and took medication had a 9-month relapse rate of 0% (Vaughn & Leff, 1976). In the light of this early work, I feel that the BPS report is now revisiting related territory and we ought to remain open-minded toward it; more research is needed. I believe that the research on expressed emotion demonstrates that both psychopharmacology and psychosocial interventions work, and are of potential benefit within the individuals who describe these experiences. By embracing a more fully neurodynamic model, as proposed by Hobson and Leonard (2001), we choose to climb out of our trenches and can begin effective collaboration. Just as the people who have these experiences are able, with assistance, to unite the dissociation within, we as clinicians have the opportunity to work toward creating unity without, and that neither requires nor insists upon uniformity within or without. It is in embracing our diversity and recognizing the rich skills mix that is potentially available that we can be at our strongest. It is from our own unique position and perspective that we can hope to bring the different level of thinking that will take us beyond the level of thinking that generated the problem in the first place. For us, as mental health professionals, this may in part mean that we stop seeing as pathological those things that experts through lived experience do not feel are disordered. Humble, honest hearing and listening from a therapeutically neutral stance will, in my opinion, allow us to fully appreciate the landscape before us, and perhaps then together we may map the way ahead. Perhaps when we climb up out of our trenches and stop the barrage, when the smoke of battle clears, we may see an entirely unexpected way ahead; perhaps we may see that we are headed in the wrong direction. I do not know for certain, but what is sure is that if we remain in the fog of war we will see nothing. The future of therapy for psychosis and schizophrenia has and will remain unclear as long as we battle each other. Instead, let us commit to working with one another and find a way to cut this Gordian knot.

DESCRIBING THE PEOPLE WITH PSYCHOSIS WHO ARE MOST SUITABLE FOR EMDR THERAPY

The first principle we must remind ourselves of is that, as with all EMDR therapy, clinicians ought not to be working with a population that they are unfamiliar with. It is dangerous for both the clinician and the person undergoing the procedure. The intention of this book is not to encourage clinicians who are unfamiliar in working with people who have these experiences to do so; rather, it is to equip and encourage a more coherent and informed approach by those who are already working with this population. I hope that it will also promote further research in the EMDR therapy community. It has been the members of this experienced group of clinicians who have approached me after I have given presentations on using EMDR therapy for psychosis. They share their experiences of seeing resolution, marked phenomenological shifts, and modest, yet significant changes in phenomena following EMDR therapy. These changes that they observe include reductions in the levels of distress reported by the clients. I am convinced that EMDR therapy can be effectively offered to some of this group of clients with good outcome. As a colleague and expert through lived experience reminded me, small changes are not trivial.

The Indicating Cognitions of Negative Networks Model

The Indicating Cognitions of Negative Networks (IConN) model assists the clinician, in a safe and loving therapeutic environment, to provide an explanation as to why the client's experiences are present. This leads naturally to the AIP model's explanation of the EMDR therapeutic intervention to resolve them. When we formulate and target the experiences within the IConN model's methodology, I have observed that EMDR reprocessing can remove or significantly ameliorate the psychological toxicity of the DMN. This removes the primary problem and so the phenomena resolve or decrease accordingly. As the person with these experiences sees them decrease or abate, this further strengthens the therapeutic bond and catalyzes efficacy. These, we recognize, are Jerome D. Frank's four factors, which he believed were present in all efficacious psychotherapies (Frank, 1961). So, we have a healthy therapeutic rapport, a therapeutic environment, a rationale or mythos providing a plausible explanation for the symptoms, and a procedure to resolve the distressing symptoms. In this case the procedure is EMDR therapy, which is being applied with the guidance and targeting of the IConN model. However, none of this is of any benefit if we cannot first identify those people who are most capable of benefiting from these therapeutic endeavors.

We will consider those people who are suitable for EMDR therapy for psychosis, using the IConN model, in two groups: first, those people with psychosis who have a clear trauma history or comorbid PTSD; and second, those who meet the current criteria for schizophrenia within the *Diagnostic and Statistical Manual of Mental Disorders* (*DSM*) and *International Classification of Diseases* (*ICD*) classification systems in addition to the proposed criteria for dissociative schizophrenia (Ross, 2004).

As noted in the summary of the current literature discussing EMDR therapy for schizophrenia and psychosis, it may be applied safely in people with psychosis who have a comorbid PTSD (van den Berg et al., 2015; van den Berg & van der Gaag, 2012). Previously, people who had diagnoses of psychoses were routinely excluded from studies examining the treatment of PTSD. In considering this group we can use the suggested Dutch model in which the researchers categorize the research completed to date (van der Vleugel, van den Berg, & Staring, 2012) into three groups: people with psychosis who have an identifiable trauma that appears etiologically linked; people with psychosis who experience the psychotic phenomena, or their treatment, as traumatic; and people with comorbid PTSD and psychosis, with the comorbidity acting as a perpetuating factor in their presentation. These categories can act as an appropriate guide for generating a case formulation that informs the treatment plan. We have looked at this in more detail in Chapter 5, so it is sufficient for now to stress that we look for a traumatic event (or series of events) that informs a meaningful case formulation within the AIP model. This is why it is of first importance that we listen and attend to the detailed content of the phenomenology of the psychotic and dissociated material.

Psychosis With a Clear Trauma History or Comorbid PTSD

The formulation of the client's experiences is of vital importance, as it must resonate enough with the client that he or she and you can unite around it. It is not enough that you as the clinician see a connection between the traumas and the current presenting problems; the client must also accept this as valid, or at least potentially valid. The proposed EMDR therapy target ought to be meaningful within a well-defined formulation, as the guiding principle is a central tenet of the AIP model; that is, the phenomena are not the problem, they are a symptom of the problem. The problem is the DMN and the symptoms are how to identify and get to the material needing targeting (Shapiro & Maxfield, 2002). The AIP model theorizes that by reprocessing the DMN into a functionally interconnected energy system (a *healthy memory system*), there is nothing left to generate the distressing symptoms. So the client must have the capacity to register the rationale/mythos being given to him or her, accept it, and store it for at least long enough to be capable of utilizing the information to come to an informed decision. This is not the same as the person "believing" that EMDR therapy will work, for EMDR therapy is not a matter of faith. I have experienced many times the situation where the client and I choose to travel a therapeutic journey characterized by doubt and skepticism. Even in this context the EMDR therapy undertaken still facilitates improvement, and as a consequence, rapport and trust grow and significant gains are possible. In this category of people who are presenting with experiences characterized as psychosis or schizophrenia, we are able to target the trauma with the standard eight-phase, three-pronged protocol of EMDR therapy. There is often little or no adaptation required for phases 3 to 7 (de Bont et al., 2013; van den Berg, van der Vleugel, & Staring, 2010; van den Berg et al., 2013; van den Berg et al., 2014; van den Berg et al., 2015; van der Vleugel et al., 2012). Gonzalez and Mosquera suggest that we view this as targeting the "traumatic layer" of the phenomena, and after doing so we are able to observe the psychotic symptomatology change (Gonzalez, Mosquera, & Moskowitz, 2012; van der Hart, Groenendijk, Gonzalez, Mosquera, & Solomon, 2014). This is what I have experienced clinically in the cases I discuss in the later chapters looking at case formulation and the ICoNN model.

People Diagnosed With Schizophrenia Who Meet the Criteria for Dissociative Schizophrenia

Given that the original diagnosis conceptualized a group of disorders, "the schizophrenias" (Bleuler, 1911), I am proposing that there is likely to be one or several subphenotypes within the group currently diagnosed as schizophrenia that are more amenable to psychotherapy in general and EMDR therapy in particular. This is in keeping with Colin Ross's concept of dissociative schizophrenia (Ross, 2004). I owe him a great deal nosologically, as his work inspired much of my thinking in this area. We have discussed the nosology and phenomenology of schizophrenia earlier, in Chapter 2. If you are not a diagnostician you may wish to reread it at this time. However, the most important issues to consider at this point are the proposed criteria for dissociative schizophrenia, as this is foundational to selecting those people who may most benefit from the EMDR therapeutic approach within the IConN model of targeting. In the cognitive therapy of schizophrenia it is noted that schizophrenia may be viewed from three perspectives: the disorder itself, subtypes, and symptoms (Kingdon & Turkington, 2005). In the IConN model we are most interested in the perspective that looks at symptoms/phenomena; we are less focused on the categorization of the disorder of schizophrenia itself and its subtypes. We can understand the position that the IConN model assumes when we keep in mind the key principle that at all times we are examining the disorder through the lens of the AIP model (Shapiro & Maxfield, 2002). Therefore, phenomena are symptoms of the problem and not the problem itself, which is the DMN that we are trying to identify for EMDR reprocessing. For this reason we will not explore the current diagnostic systems of the *ICD* or the *DSM* in detail with regard to schizophrenia. It is sufficient to say that both systems make the diagnosis based on the inclusion and exclusion of a number of factors. I've summarized some general points in the following sections. More detail on the phenomenology utilized in these diagnostic systems is contained in Chapter 2.

ICD-10

(*Note: Readers are encouraged to examine the full details criteria within the original diagnostic classification.*)

Schizophrenia is characterized as a severe and enduring mental illness. Diagnostic criteria include descriptions of characteristic disturbances of thinking and perceptions associated with abnormalities of affect. There should be no clouding of consciousness, and cognitive functioning ought to be normal, with the preservation of intellectual functioning. Some abnormalities of cognitive functioning do appear as the illness progresses; these are thought of as negative symptoms (Crow, 1981). Affective symptoms, such as depression and mania, should not be the foremost phenomena, or if they are substantial the schizophrenic phenomena should have preceded them. Another criterion specifically excludes overt brain disease or abnormal brain states resulting from withdrawal or intoxication by substances. The general criteria required by the *ICD-10* is one phenomenon from a list of syndromes, symptoms, and signs that are considered to be clearly indicative of schizophrenia, or two from a list of lesser symptoms and signs. The phenomena need to have been present during an episode of psychotic illness for a least a 1-month period or for a part of each day over a 1-month period. The current iteration of the *ICD* classifies schizophrenia into the following subtypes: paranoid, hebephrenic, catatonic, undifferentiated, residual, simple, and other (World Health Organization [WHO], 1992, 1993).

DSM-5

(Note: Readers are encouraged to examine the full details criteria within the original diagnostic classification.)

In the most recent iteration of the *DSM*, the fifth edition (*DSM-5*; American Psychiatric Association [APA], 2013), the criteria required to make a diagnosis of schizophrenia have seen the bar being raised. It now requires there to be two of the specified symptoms that have been present for at least 6 months, with active psychotic illness having manifested for at least 1 month. At this point the most notable deviation from the *ICD* is that there is no longer a division into subtypes. The authors of the *DSM-5* have stated that the subtypes are no longer felt to be valid, as people often move from one category to the other during the course of their illness. As such, attempting to diagnose subtypes of schizophrenia results in a weakening of the validity of the diagnosis (APA, 2013).

Dissociative Schizophrenia

The overlap between the core features of dissociative identity disorder (DID) & schizophrenia cannot be reduced to a problem of comorbidity because the two are not discrete & separate categories. They
cannot be comorbid with each other as they are too often and too
much the same thing. (Ross, 2004)

We examined the phenomenology of dissociation and psychosis in Chapter 2, and we looked at how to obtain the relevant history and mental state examination of a person presenting with these experiences in Chapter 3. For a diagnostician, the usefulness of the diagnosis of dissociative schizophrenia, although not recognized by either the *ICD* or *DSM* at this point, is that it invites a treating clinician to consider the use of psychotherapy for patients with a diagnosis of schizophrenia. The therapeutic model that Ross articulates leans very heavily upon the recognition of a connection between trauma, dissociation, and psychosis (Ross, 2004), and this will come as no surprise to the reader. He conveys that by formulating the person's experiences as dissociative schizophrenia we can overcome the bias against the provision of psychological service for those diagnosed with psychosis or schizophrenia. The attitudes of many toward the use of talking therapies for these experiences is changing, and we are seeing a growing acceptance that psychological therapy is of benefit to many people who are placed in these diagnostic categories (Basset et al., 2014). Indeed, many do not receive psychotherapy because of a lack of support or demand for it, but because of a lack of resources to provide it. As clinicians and researchers we need to continually fight against the dissociation of our clinical systems and show that if we deliver a unified treatment approach, which includes the talking therapies, there can be substantial savings (Lloyd, 2011). Work completed by a colleague (Lloyd, 2011) from the European Society for Trauma and Dissociation (ESTD) demonstrated an annual savings in the cost of mental health treatment of £18,797 ($30,075) per year for a woman with previously undiagnosed dissociative identity disorder (DID) who was being treated in the United Kingdom (UK). This was a decrease from £29,492 ($47,187) to £10,695 ($17,112), which was seen after she was given a diagnosis of DID and received treatment, including talking therapy. Ross states that 25% to 40% of people who have currently been given a diagnosis of schizophrenia would meet his criteria for dissociative schizophrenia, and two thirds of people with DID meet structured interview criteria for schizoaffective disorder or schizophrenia. We see here the close relationship between these disorders. This reflects the nosological challenges and has led to the BPS in the UK suggesting that we move away from our current diagnostic categories entirely: "There is no scientific evidence that psychiatric diagnoses such as schizophrenia and bipolar disorder are valid or useful" (Doward, 2013). Ross notes that the cases that do meet criteria for dissociative schizophrenia can often achieve integration. If this is achieved, he states that their psychoses go into long-term remission (Ross, 2004). This is also what I have experienced clinically.

Criteria for Dissociative Schizophrenia

Dissociative schizophrenia is a type of schizophrenia in which the clinical picture is dominated by *at least three* of the following:

1. Dissociative amnesia
2. Depersonalization
3. The presence of two or more distinct identities or personality states
4. Auditory hallucinations
5. Extensive comorbidity
6. Severe childhood trauma

These are the criteria that Ross (2004) has suggested for dissociative schizophrenia. I have not found it necessary for the person to be experiencing distinct identities or personality states to benefit from EMDR therapy, but certainly these people do benefit. By using these criteria we can begin to delineate a group of people who may be most likely to benefit from EMDR for psychoses. We have already emphasized the importance of obtaining a clear and detailed clinical history, so hopefully by this point we will already have identified any history consistent with severe childhood trauma. The clinical picture will also readily demonstrate the presence or absence of extensive comorbidity. If we now turn our attention to the recognized dissociative phenomena listed as criteria 1 to 4 in the previous list, the first three have been clearly described in Chapter 2. It is helpful to consider whether there is anything distinctive about the type of auditory hallucinations that occur in dissociative schizophrenia. I concur with the comments made by Akiko Kikuchi, a clinical psychologist who has published work in respect to this population in Japan:

> My impression is that the hallucinations of the high-DES [Dissociative Experiences Scale] patients are more understandable. I don't hear devils and gods as common interpretations of their voices. The origins of voices are thought by the patients to be someone from the past, such as the bully. (Kikuchi, personal communication, 2012)

When looking to identify clients who may be suitable for EMDR therapy for psychosis, we should look for people diagnosed with psychoses whose psychotic material is less bizarre, or that has a clear link with past traumatic events. We should ask the individuals whether they are able to enter into dialogue with their voices/parts/auditory hallucinations, and if so, to what degree. As we will see, those more able to engage in dialogue with their parts/auditory hallucinations may prove more suitable for EMDR therapy for psychosis.

It is my opinion that for those more dissociative subtypes of schizophrenia, the abnormal mental state is more closely linked, in biological terms, with the endogenous opiate system, rather than the dopaminergic system (Frewen & Lanius, 2006a, 2006b; Hopper, Frewen, van der Kolk, & Lanius, 2007; Lanius, Paulsen, & Corrigan, 2014). I tend to find that the people who are most suitable for treatment with EMDR therapy for psychosis are among those individuals who are prescribed clozapine. This, I suspect, is in part due to the fact that individuals are require to have failed to respond to two standard antipsychotic medications, which operate on the dopaminergic system, before being deemed suitable to commence clozapine, with all of its necessary blood monitoring.

Summary

So, in summary, those people most likely to benefit from EMDR for schizophrenia/psychosis, using the ICoNN methodology, will be able to be understood within an AIP formulation or have clear dissociative phenomena (such as criteria 1 to 3 of Ross's dissociative schizophrenia criteria), or have less bizarre psychotic material and auditory hallucinations that the person can interact with. At this point, this is the phenomenology that ought to raise the possibility of using EMDR therapy; more study is clearly needed.

> "Within reach, close and not lost, there remained, in the midst
> of losses, this one thing: language."
> —*Cellan (poet, quoted in Felman, 1995)*

PSYCHOSIS AS AN ADAPTATION

By considering psychosis to be an adaptive and meaningful response to disorder within the person's mind and by accepting that the phenomenology of psychosis has meaning and purpose, we offer people the opportunity to move from being passive victims to instead becoming victors in their arena of illness. We offer the person empowerment when we accept that the phenomenology of these experiences, which we label as psychosis and schizophrenia, has meaning. We assist them in becoming an active agent in the struggle toward health and well-being— a struggle we must all make. The mental health community has come full circle from the earliest days of Janet and Bleuler and is once again acknowledging that these experiences can be adaptations to trauma. In acknowledging this link it is not at all difficult to then sociologically and anthropologically revisit people and societies where such experiences are celebrated. In a group where the person who hears voices and sees inexplicable things that others do not see is the

shaman or the prophet, we meet archetypal figures that invite right-brain thinking. This is the territory of symbols and archetypes: the land of dreams and of
the Greek and Roman gods. When we stop attempting to numb or invalidate
these phenomena and instead attend to them, we see and hear some very interesting things. The research we read about earlier that allows people to engage
in dialogue with their persecutory voices via a computer avatar found a significant reduction in the levels of distress in the participants (van der Gaag et al.,
2014). In our earlier discussions we noted the similarities of this paradigm with
the various other modalities that therapeutically involve talking to parts of the
psyche. For me in particular, this is very reminiscent of working with the shadows—the things we deny, repress, or hide. By acknowledging our shadows we
can turn and face them, explore them, and hopefully eventually confront them;
some refer to this as "shadow work." It has been said that shadow work is the
work of a lifetime; it is our journey through life. To attempt to flee from shadow
work is folly, and I feel that to ignore the relationship of trauma, psychosis, and
dissociation is equally foolish. In Ursula Le Guin's book *A Wizard of Earthsea*, we
see the central character fleeing from a monster that he has conjured up from the
shadows. Late in the book, when the protagonist makes his stand and confronts
this shadow, he discovers that it is a part of himself. This, of course, is the theme
of many an ancient myth, and we see that it is only by confronting the shadow
and embracing it that a person is restored to healing and wholeness (Campbell,
2004). This reunification allows a person to move from a place of fear to one with
some measure of peace. It is important that we note that reintegration in this
sense represents unity of the parts of the psyche and is not a forceful imposition
of uniformity, which would ultimately diminish the person.

Dysfunctional Memory Networks

In my opinion, when we consider trauma, dissociation, and psychosis alongside
the AIP model of EMDR therapy, we can logically propose that it is the DMN
that distorts thinking. I believe that we facilitate a return to an untainted schema,
representative of a premorbid state, through EMDR therapy. This untainted state
is described, in my opinion, by a number of different authors. Owen Barfield,
British philosopher and poet, who incidentally was a close friend of C. S. Lewis
and called him, "The best and wisest of my unofficial teachers" (Lewis, 1936), referred to this untainted state as our *original participation* (Barfield, 1965), a state in
which, he proposed, perception and thinking are not separated, as they are for us
now. Karl Jaspers, the famous German psychiatrist and philosopher, introduced
the concept of the *axial age* (German: Achsenzeit, "axis time") and called this untainted state of being the *preaxial* (Jaspers, 1951). Last, Ken Wilber, an American
writer and philosopher, refers to this simpler way of being as *prerational*, an undifferentiated unconscious universalism (Wilber, 1980). I agree with the conclusion
of writer and thinker Richard Rohr when he states that these three philosophers
are referring to the same state (Rohr, 2015). This perhaps is the collective unconscious that Jung speaks of too. Wilber states that Jung's thinking falls foul of what
he calls the pre/trans fallacy, which he notes he fell prey to himself in his earlier
writing. He is critical of Jung and describes his thinking of our return to more

primitive strata of consciousness as the confusion between the prerational state and the transrational—this is the pre/trans fallacy. This, he opines, takes place because both are nonrational and are therefore liable to be confused, something he accuses Freud of as well (Wilber, 2000). It is beyond the scope of this book to consider in detail whether we are returning to the "original participation" of perfect, absolute unity or whether we are ascending to a higher state. I know which I hold to; the reader must make his or her own journey there. What I believe is clear is that ultimately there is growth and development through trauma—posttraumatic growth—I have both seen it and experienced it.

WHAT DOES IT ALL MEAN?

Our struggle in this life is not about the pursuit of happiness, and neither is it a battle for temporal power; it is, as Viktor Frankl asserted, a "search for meaning" (Frankl, 1988, 1992). Sadly, in the face of trauma we experience a disruption of our innate mechanisms of processing information. The result of this disruption is the inability to perceive meaning in our experiences. This dynamic was recognized by the authors of the third edition of the *DSM* (*DSM-III*) when they ushered in the diagnosis of posttraumatic stress disorder. The *DSM-III* diagnostic criteria for PTSD were revised in the *DSM-III-R* (1987), *DSM-IV* (1994), and *DSM-IV-TR* (2000), and in its most recent iteration, the *DSM-5* (APA, 2013). An alternative iteration of the syndrome is described in the *ICD-10* (the *ICD-10 Classification of Mental and Behavioural Disorders: Clinical Descriptions and Diagnostic Guidelines*; WHO, 1993). Looking briefly at the nosological development of the PTSD diagnosis (Friedman, 2007) we see, as noted earlier, that when the APA added PTSD to the *DSM-III* in 1980, there was a paradigm shift in the diagnostic concept. This shift was the inclusion of an essential qualifying criterion which stated that the etiological agent was outside the individual (i.e., a traumatic event) rather than something intrinsic (i.e., a "lack of moral fibre" [McCarthy, 1984]). In the initial *DSM-III* PTSD formulation, a traumatic event was thought of as a catastrophic stressor that was "outside the range of usual human experience" (Friedman, 2007). The people who formulated the original PTSD diagnosis considered experiences such as war, torture, rape, the Nazi Holocaust, the atomic bombings of Hiroshima and Nagasaki, natural disasters (such as earthquakes, hurricanes, and volcano eruptions), and human-made disasters (such as factory explosions, airplane crashes, and automobile accidents) (Friedman, 2007). This characterization of traumatic stressors was based on a belief that although most individuals have the ability to cope with the ordinary vagaries of life, a person's adaptive abilities are likely to fail in the face of a traumatic stressor. This description of trauma became what many now refer to as the "gatekeeper criterion": Criterion A of the PTSD diagnosis.

According to EMDR therapy's current theory, traumatic events generate a DMN, and I propose that it is this DMN that taints and distorts individuals' perceptions and self-conceptualizations. The distortions of the DMN are the psychotic phenomena that take individuals away from their premorbid state of being. This is a central tenet of EMDR therapy's AIP model: Psychotic phenomena are not the problem; they are a symptom of the problem, which is the DMN.

As we model psychosis within the AIP model, we hypothesize that by processing the DMN we remove the distortion that results in dysfunction, and this ought to restore wellness (Shapiro & Maxfield, 2002), and this is what we do see. Some would continue to insist that psychosis is purely a biological disease, generating meaningless jibber-jabber that necessitates drug therapy. Others believe psychotherapy holds the key. I believe that both are correct. It is most likely that what we currently diagnose as schizophrenia is, as Bleuler intended us to understand, actually a group of disorders: "the schizophrenias" (*plural*) (Bleuler, 1911). In my opinion, medication does have a role some of the time, in some cases, and so also do psychotherapy and family therapy. These are the tools at hand, and the job of the clinician, the healer, and the expert through lived experience is to endeavor to work out together how best to use all of these tools in collaboration. Cognitive behavioral therapy (CBT) for psychosis is better established at this point in time, but EMDR for psychosis is building momentum, with research and exploration taking place in numerous parts of the world. Dogma and arrogance-based medicine have no place in the healthy critical examination of a therapeutic method. We must measure what we can and ask what we must. Lifelong learning requires us to observe and examine what we witness with open and inquiring minds. This is the only state of mind that will provide an opportunity for growth in the light of new knowledge and experience.

When I first began to use EMDR therapy in PTSD treatment, several colleagues sought me out to tell me that this therapy did not work and that there was no evidence base for it. However, I could not deny my own experiences; I was witnessing people getting better through EMDR therapy. This encouraged me to continue to deploy and develop my skills within the method, and now EMDR therapy has a very strong and robust evidence base for PTSD (NICE, 2005; Watts et al., 2014; WHO, 2013). It does currently lag behind CBT with respect to evidence of efficacy in other therapeutic areas, and I hope that this encourages us to actively explore, research, and document our findings, because that is the only way that we will map the landscape of the unknown terrain ahead.

> "Never, for the sake of peace and quiet, deny your own experience or convictions."
> —*Dag Hammarskjöld*
> *(Swedish diplomat and the second*
> *secretary-general of the United Nations, 1966)*

The ICoNN model offers a way to understand psychosis: a mythos/rationale around which the therapist and the person experiencing these phenomena can unite. This paradigm of understanding through mythos is one that was familiar to the ancients. Mythos is the land of dreaming, and this is where we must form the therapeutic bond because that is where the person experiencing psychosis is journeying. Now together we can battle against the troubling experiences we characterize as psychosis. If therapist and sufferer have achieved therapeutic interconnectedness in the milieu of mythos, then we have all of Jerome Frank's four elements for successful psychotherapy (Frank, 1961): the emotionally charged relationship, a therapeutic environment, a rationale or myth that provides a plausible explanation for the symptoms, and a procedure to resolve the symptoms. I firmly believe that by utilizing the modifications within the IConN model, EMDR therapy for psychosis has all of these four features. Remember that we formulate an understanding of the person with us in the therapy space within the AIP model of EMDR and deliver EMDR therapy within the IConN model for psychosis. This means that we apply the standard eight-phase, three-pronged protocol where possible and use the IConN modifications when necessary.

REFERENCES

Amaresha, A. C., & Venkatasubramanian, G. (2012). Expressed emotion in schizophrenia: An overview. *Indian Journal of Psychological Medicine, 34*(1), 12–20. doi:10.4103/0253-7176.96149

American Psychiatric Association. (2013). *Diagnostic and statistical manual of mental disorders* (5th ed.). Washington, DC: Author.

Barfield, O. (1965). *Saving the appearances: A study in idolatry*. New York, NY: Harcourt.

Basset, T., Bentall, R., Boyle, M., Cooke, A., Cupitt, C., Dillon, J., . . . Weaver, Y. (2014). In A. Cooke (Ed.), *Understanding psychosis and schizophrenia: Why people sometimes hear voices, believe things that others find strange, or appear out of touch with reality, and what can help.* A report by the Division of Clinical Psychology. Leicester, England: British Psychological Society, Division of Clinical Psychology.

Beck, A. T. (1952). Successful outpatient psychotherapy of a chronic schizophrenic with a delusion based on borrowed guilt. *Psychiatry, 15*(3), 305–312.

Beck, A. T., & Valin, S. (1953). Psychotic depressive reactions in soldiers who accidentally killed their buddies. *American Journal of Psychiatry, 110*(5), 347–353.

Bleuler, E. (1911). *Dementia praecox, oder Gruppe der Schizophrenien* [Dementia praecox, or the group of schizophrenias]. Leipzig, Germany: Deuticke.

Brown, G. W., Birley, J. L., & Wing, J. K. (1972). Influence of family life on the course of schizophrenic disorders: A replication. *British Journal of Psychiatry, 121*(562), 241–258.

Brown, G. W., & Harris, T. (2000). *Where inner and outer worlds meet: Psychosocial research in the tradition of George W. Brown.* London, England: Routlege.

Burns, A. M., Erickson, D. H., & Brenner, C. A. (2014). Cognitive-behavioral therapy for medication-resistant psychosis: A meta-analytic review. *Psychiatric Services.* doi:10.1176/appi.ps.201300213

Butzlaff, R. L., & Hooley, J. M. (1998). Expressed emotion and psychiatric relapse: A meta-analysis. *Archives of General Psychiatry, 55*(6), 547–552.

Campbell, J. (2004). *The hero with a thousand faces* (Commemorative ed.). Princeton, NJ: Princeton University Press.

Christodoulides, T., Dudley, R., Brown, S., Turkington, D., & Beck, A. T. (2008). Cognitive behaviour therapy in patients with schizophrenia who are not prescribed antipsychotic medication: A case series. *Psychology and Psychotherapy, 81*(Pt. 2), 199–207. doi:10.1348/147608308X278295

Crow, T. J. (1981). Positive and negative schizophrenia symptoms and the role of dopamine. *British Journal of Psychiatry, 139*, 251–254.

de Bont, P. A., van den Berg, D. P., van der Vleugel, B. M., de Roos, C., Mulder, C. L., Becker, E. S., . . . van Minnen, A. (2013). A multi-site single blind clinical study to compare the effects of prolonged exposure, eye movement desensitization and reprocessing and waiting list on patients with a current diagnosis of psychosis and co morbid post traumatic stress disorder: Study protocol for the randomized controlled trial Treating Trauma in Psychosis. *Trials, 14*, 151. doi:10.1186/1745-6215-14-151

Doward, J. (2013). Psychiatrists under fire in mental health battle. *Mental Health*. Retrieved from http://www.theguardian.com/society/2013/may/12/psychiatrists-under-fire-mental-health

Felman, S. (1995). Education and crisis, or the vicissitudes of teaching. In C. Caruth (Ed.), *Trauma: Explorations in memory* (pp. 13–60). Baltimore, MD: Johns Hopkins University Press.

Forgash, C., & Copeley, M. (2008). *Healing the heart of trauma and dissociation with EMDR and ego state therapy*. New York, NY: Springer Publishing Company.

Frank, J. D. (1961). *Persuasion and healing: A comparative study of psychotherapy*. Baltimore, MD: Johns Hopkins Press.

Frankl, V. E. (1988). *The will to meaning: Foundations and applications of logotherapy* (Expanded ed.). New York, NY: New American Library.

Frankl, V. E. (1992). *Man's search for meaning: An introduction to logotherapy* (4th ed.). Boston, MA: Beacon Press.

Frewen, P. A., & Lanius, R. A. (2006a). Neurobiology of dissociation: Unity and disunity in mind-body-brain. *Psychiatric Clinics of North America, 29*(1), 113–128, ix. doi: S0193-953X(05)00099-7 [pii] 10.1016/j.psc.2005.10.016

Frewen, P. A., & Lanius, R. A. (2006b). Toward a psychobiology of posttraumatic self-dysregulation: Reexperiencing, hyperarousal, dissociation, and emotional numbing. *Annals of the New York Academy of Sciences, 1071*, 110–124.

Friedman, M. J. (2007). *PTSD history and overview*. Retrieved from http://www.ptsd.va.gov/professional/pages/ptsd-overview.asp

Gonzalez, A., Mosquera, D., & Moskowitz, A. (2012). *[EMDR in psychosis and severe mental disorders]*. Paper presented at the annual meeting of EMDR Europe Association, Madrid, Spain.

Habib, N., Dawood, S., Kingdon, D., & Naeem, F. (2015). Preliminary evaluation of culturally adapted CBT for psychosis (CA-CBTp): Findings from Developing Culturally-Sensitive CBT Project (DCCP). *Behavioural and Cognitive Psychotherapy, 43*(2), 200–208. doi:10.1017/S1352465813000829

Hammarskjöld, D. (1966). *Markings*. London, England: Faber and Faber.

Hepworth, C. R., Ashcroft, K., & Kingdon, D. (2013). Auditory hallucinations: A comparison of beliefs about voices in individuals with schizophrenia and borderline personality disorder. *Clinical Psychology and Psychotherapy, 20*(3), 239–245. doi:10.1002/cpp.791

Hobson, J. A., & Leonard, J. (2001). *Out of its mind: Psychiatry in crisis*. Cambridge, MA: Perseus Publishing.

Hopper, J. W., Frewen, P. A., van der Kolk, B. A., & Lanius, R. A. (2007). Neural correlates of reexperiencing, avoidance, and dissociation in PTSD: Symptom dimensions and emotion dysregulation in responses to script-driven trauma imagery. *Journal of Trauma and Stress, 20*(5), 713–725. doi:10.1002/jts.20284

Jalāl al-Dīn, R., Barks, C., & Green, M. (1997). *The illuminated Rumi* (1st ed.). New York, NY: Broadway Books.

Jaspers, K. (1951). *Way to wisdom: An introduction to philosophy*. New Haven, CT: Yale University Press.

Jauhar, S., McKenna, P. J., Radua, J., Fung, E., Salvador, R., & Laws, K. R. (2014). Cognitive-behavioural therapy for the symptoms of schizophrenia: Systematic review and meta-analysis with examination of potential bias. *British Journal of Psychiatry, 204*(1), 20–29. doi:10.1192/bjp.bp.112.116285

Kavanagh, D. J. (1992). Recent developments in expressed emotion and schizophrenia. *British Journal of Psychiatry, 160*, 601–620.

Kinderman, P., McKenna, P., & Laws, K. R. (2015). Are psychological therapies effective in treating schizophrenia and psychosis? *Progress in Neurology and Psychiatry, 19*(1), 17–20.

Kingdon, D. G., & Turkington, D. (1994). *Cognitive-behavioral therapy of schizophrenia.* Hove, England: Erlbaum.

Kingdon, D. G., & Turkington, D. (2005). *Cognitive therapy of schizophrenia.* New York, NY: Guilford.

Knipe, J. (2015). *EMDR toolbox: Theory and treatment of complex PTSD and dissociation.* New York, NY: Springer Publishing Company.

Lanius, U. F., Paulsen, S. L., & Corrigan, F. M. (Eds.). (2014). *Neurobiology and treatment of traumatic dissociation: Towards an embodied self.* New York, NY: Springer Publishing Company.

Leff, J. (2000). Expressed emotion: Measuring relationships. In G. W. Brown & T. Harris (Eds.), *Where inner and outer worlds meet: Psychosocial research in the tradition of George W. Brown* (pp. 97–100). London, England: Routlege.

Leff, J., Williams, G., Huckvale, M. A., Arbuthnot, M., & Leff, A. P. (2014). Computer-assisted therapy for medication-resistant auditory hallucinations: Proof-of-concept study. *British Journal of Psychiatry, 202,* 428–433. doi:10.1192/bjp.bp.112.124883

Leff, J. P., & Vaughn, C. (1985). *Expressed emotion in families: Its significance for mental illness.* New York, NY: Guilford Press.

Lewis, C. S. (1936). *The allegory of love: A study in medieval tradition.* Oxford, England: Clarendon Press.

Lewis, S., Tarrier, N., Haddock, G., Bentall, R., Kinderman, P., Kingdon, D., . . . Dunn, G. (2002). Randomised controlled trial of cognitive-behavioural therapy in early schizophrenia: Acute-phase outcomes. *British Journal of Psychiatry, 43*(Suppl.), s91–s97.

Lloyd, M. (2011). How investing in therapeutic services provides a clinical cost saving in the long term. *Health Service Journal.* Retrieved from http://www.hsj.co.uk/resource-centre/best-practice/care-pathway-resources/how-investing-in-therapeutic-services-provides-a-clinical-cost-saving-in-the-long-term/5033382.article#.VeOE3XtBDkA

Lutkehaus, N. (2008). *Margaret Mead: The making of an American icon.* Princeton, NJ: Princeton University Press.

MacCulloch, M. (2006). Effects of EMDR on previously abused child molesters: Theoretical reviews and preliminary findings from Ricci, Clayton, and Shapiro. *Journal of Forensic Psychiatry and Psychology, 17*(4), 531–537. doi:10.1080/14789940601075760

Manfield, P. (Ed.). (1998). *Extending EMDR: A casebook of innovative applications.* New York, NY: W. W. Norton.

McCarthy, J. (1984). Aircrew and "lack of moral fibre" in the Second World War. *War and Society, 2*(2), 87–101.

Miller, P. W. (2014). *Psychosis/dissociation—a rose by any other name* [eLetter]. Retrieved from http://bjp.rcpsych.org/content/202/6/428.e-letters#psychosis—dissociation—a-rose-by-any-other-name

Mitford, E., Reay, R., McCabe, K., Paxton, R., & Turkington, D. (2010). Ageism in first episode psychosis. *International Journal of Geriatric Psychiatry, 25*(11), 1112–1118. doi:10.1002/gps.2437

Moorhead, S., & Turkington, D. (2001). The CBT of delusional disorder: The relationship between schema vulnerability and psychotic content. *British Journal of Medical Psychology, 74*(Pt. 4), 419–430.

Morrison, A. P. (2002). *A casebook of cognitive therapy for psychosis.* East Sussex, England: Taylor & Francis.

Morrison, A. P., Turkington, D., Wardle, M., Spencer, H., Barratt, S., Dudley, R., . . . Hutton, P. (2012). A preliminary exploration of predictors of outcome and cognitive mechanisms of change in cognitive behaviour therapy for psychosis in people not taking antipsychotic medication. *Behavioral Research and Therapy, 50*(2), 163–167. doi:10.1016/j.brat.2011.12.001

Naeem, F., Habib, N., Gul, M., Khalid, M., Saeed, S., Farooq, S., . . . Kingdon, D. (2014). A qualitative study to explore patients', carers' and health professionals' views to culturally adapt CBT for psychosis (CBTp) in Pakistan. *Behavioral and Cognitive Psychotherapy,* 1–13. doi:10.1017/S1352465814000332

Naeem, F., Kingdon, D., & Turkington, D. (2006). Cognitive behaviour therapy for schizophrenia: Relationship between anxiety symptoms and therapy. *Psychology and Psychotherapy, 79*(Pt. 2), 153–164. doi:10.1348/147608305X91538

National Institute for Health and Care Excellence. (2005). *Post-traumatic stress disorder (PTSD): The management of PTSD in adults and children in primary and secondary care. Clinical Guideline 26.* London, England: Author.

Rathod, S., Kingdon, D., Phiri, P., & Gobbi, M. (2010). Developing culturally sensitive cognitive behaviour therapy for psychosis for ethnic minority patients by exploration and incorporation of service users' and health professionals' views and opinions. *Behavioral and Cognitive Psychotherapy, 38*(5), 511–533. doi:10.1017/S1352465810000378

Rathod, S., Kingdon, D., Smith, P., & Turkington, D. (2005). Insight into schizophrenia: The effects of cognitive behavioural therapy on the components of insight and association with sociodemographics—data on a previously published randomised controlled trial. *Schizophrenia Research, 74*(2–3), 211–219. doi:10.1016/j.schres.2004.07.003

Rathod, S., Kingdon, D., Weiden, P., & Turkington, D. (2008). Cognitive-behavioral therapy for medication-resistant schizophrenia: A review. *Journal of Psychiatric Practice, 14*(1), 22–33. doi:10.1097/01.pra.0000308492.93003.db

Rathod, S., Phiri, P., Harris, S., Underwood, C., Thagadur, M., Padmanabi, U., & Kingdon, D. (2013). Cognitive behaviour therapy for psychosis can be adapted for minority ethnic groups: A randomised controlled trial. *Schizophrenia Research, 143*(2–3), 319–326. doi:10.1016/j.schres.2012.11.007

Rector, N. A., & Beck, A. T. (2002). Cognitive therapy for schizophrenia: From conceptualization to intervention. *Canadian Journal of Psychiatry, 47*(1), 39–48.

Rohr, R. (2015, January 23). *Nature as the first Bible. Reality trumps words.* Richard Rohr's Daily Meditation. Retrieved from http://campaign.r20.constantcontact.com/render?ca=b6692502-fba6-4ce4-9572-91f8648c75ea&c=67029b80-eef1-11e3-b66c-d4ae526edc76&ch=67849cc0-eef1-11e3-b6de-d4ae526edc76

Ross, C. A. (2004). *Schizophrenia: Innovations in diagnosis and treatment.* Binghamton, NY: Haworth Maltreatment and Trauma.

Shapiro, F., & Forrest, M. S. (1997). *EMDR: The breakthrough therapy for overcoming anxiety, stress, and trauma* (1st ed.). New York, NY: Basic Books.

Shapiro, F., Kaslow, F. W., & Maxfield, L. (2007). *Handbook of EMDR and family therapy processes.* Hoboken, NJ: John Wiley & Sons.

Shapiro, F., & Maxfield, L. (2002). Eye movement desensitization and reprocessing (EMDR): Information processing in the treatment of trauma. *Journal of Clinical Psychology, 58*(8), 933–946. doi:10.1002/jclp.10068

Turkington, D., Munetz, M., Pelton, J., Montesano, V., Sivec, H., Nausheen, B., & Kingdon, D. (2014). High-yield cognitive behavioral techniques for psychosis delivered by case managers to their clients with persistent psychotic symptoms: An exploratory trial. *Journal of Nervous and Mental Disorders, 202*(1), 30–34. doi:10.1097/ NMD.0000000000000070

Turner, D. T., van der Gaag, M., Karyotaki, E., & Cuijpers, P. (2014). Psychological interventions for psychosis: A meta-analysis of comparative outcome studies. *American Journal of Psychiatry, 171*(5), 523–538. doi:10.1176/appi.ajp.2013.13081159

van den Berg, D. P., de Bont, P. A., van der Vleugel, B. M., de Roos, C., de Jongh, A., Van Minnen, A., & van der Gaag, M. (2015). Prolonged exposure vs eye movement desensitization and reprocessing vs waiting list for posttraumatic stress disorder in patients with a psychotic disorder: A randomized clinical trial. *JAMA Psychiatry*. doi:10.1001/jamapsychiatry.2014.2637

van den Berg, D. P., & van der Gaag, M. (2012). Treating trauma in psychosis with EMDR: A pilot study. *Journal of Behavior Therapy and Experimental Psychiatry, 43*(1), 664–671. doi:10.1016/j.jbtep.2011.09.011

van den Berg, D. P. G., van der Vleugel, B., & Staring, A. (2010). [Trauma, psychosis, PTSD and the use of EMDR]. *Directieve Therapie, 30*(4), 303–328. doi:10.1007/ s12433-010-0242-9

van den Berg, D. P. G., van der Vleugel, B. M., Staring, A. B. P., de Bont, P. A. J., & de Jongh, A. (2013). EMDR in psychosis: Guidelines for conceptualization and treatment. *Journal of EMDR Practice and Research, 7*(4), 208–224.

van den Berg, D. P. G., van der Vleugel, B. M., Staring, A. B. P., de Bont, P. A. J., & de Jongh, A. (2014). [EMDR in psychosis: Guidelines for conceptualization and treatment]. *Journal of EMDR Practice and Research, 8*(3), E67–E84. doi:10.1891/1933-3196.8.3.E67

van der Gaag, M., Valmaggia, L. R., & Smit, F. (2014). The effects of individually tailored formulation-based cognitive behavioural therapy in auditory hallucinations and delusions: A meta-analysis. *Schizophrenia Research, 156*(1), 30–37. doi:10.1016/ j.schres.2014.03.016

van der Hart, O., Groenendijk, M., Gonzalez, A., Mosquera, D., & Solomon, R. (2014). Dissociation of the personality and EMDR therapy in complex trauma-related disorders: Applications in phases 2 and 3 treatment. *Journal of EMDR Practice and Research, 8*(1), 33–48. doi:10.1891/1933-3196.8.1.33

van der Vleugel, B. M., van den Berg, D. P., & Staring, A. B. P. (2012). Trauma, psychosis, post-traumatic stress disorder and the application of EMDR. *Rivista di Psichiatria, 47*(2, Suppl. 1), 33S–38S. doi:10.1708/1071.11737

Vaughn, C. E., & Leff, J. P. (1976). The influence of family and social factors on the course of psychiatric illness: A comparison of schizophrenic and depressed neurotic patients. *British Journal of Psychiatry, 129*, 125–137.

Velligan, D. I., Draper, M., Stutes, D., Maples, N., Mintz, J., Tai, S., & Turkington, D. (2009). Multimodal cognitive therapy: Combining treatments that bypass cognitive deficits and deal with reasoning and appraisal biases. *Schizophrenia Bulletin, 35*(5), 884–893. doi:10.1093/schbul/sbp075

Velligan, D. I., Tai, S., Roberts, D. L., Maples-Aguilar, N., Brown, M., Mintz, J., & Turkington, D. (2014). A randomized controlled trial comparing cognitive behavior therapy, cognitive adaptation training, their combination and treatment as usual in chronic schizophrenia. *Schizophrenia Bulletin*. doi:10.1093/schbul/sbu127

Watts, B. V., Shiner, B., Zubkoff, L., Carpenter-Song, E., Ronconi, J. M., & Coldwell, C. M. (2014). Implementation of evidence-based psychotherapies for posttraumatic stress disorder in VA specialty clinics. *Psychiatric Services, 65*(5), 648–653. doi:10.1176/appi .ps.201300176

Wilber, K. (1980). *The Atman Project: A transpersonal view of human development.* Wheaton, IL: Theosophical Publishing House.

Wilber, K. (2000). *Sex, ecology, spirituality: The spirit of evolution* (2nd ed.). Boston, MD: Shambhala.

Wing, J. K. (1966). Five-year outcome in early schizophrenia. *Proceedings of the Royal Society of Medicine, 59*(1), 17–18.

World Health Organization. (1992). *The ICD-10 classification of mental and behavioural disorders: Clinical descriptions and diagnostic guidelines.* Geneva, Switzerland: Author.

World Health Organization. (1993). *The ICD-10 classification of mental and behavioural disorders: Diagnostic criteria for research.* Geneva, Switzerland: Author.

World Health Organization. (2013). *WHO guidelines on conditions specifically related to stress.* Geneva, Switzerland: WHO Press.

Zengin, F. (2009). [Treatment of hearing loss and tinnitus with EMDR therapy]. In R. Plassmann (Ed.), *Im eigenen rhythmus, die EMDR-behandlung von essstörungen, bindungsstörungen, allergien, schmerz, angststörungen, tinnitus und süchten* [At their own pace, the EMDR treatment of eating disorders, attachment disorders, allergies, pain, anxiety disorders, tinnitus and addictions] (pp. 155–164). Giessen, Germany: Psychosozial-Verlag.

EIGHT

Case Formulation and Treatment Planning: EMDR Therapy + IConN Model

Intention: *To equip the reader to understand the person presenting in the office, by viewing the individual through the lens of the AIP model of EMDR therapy. To give the reader a method for formulating a case using both the AIP and IConN models. Readers will gain a working knowledge of the IConN model to target and be capable of using it in people diagnosed with schizophrenia or other psychoses.*

> "I see the solution to each problem as being detectable in the pattern and web of the whole. The connections between causes and effects are often much more subtle and complex than we with our rough and ready understanding of the physical world might naturally suppose."
> —*Douglas Adams speaking in the voice of his character Dirk Gently (Adams, 1987)*

EMDR THERAPY AND THE IConN MODEL: THE 18TH CAMEL

Let me tell you a story…

Once upon a time there were three sons whose father had died, leaving them all that he had. In his will, he left instructions for his eldest son to have half of his camels, to his middle son one-third of his camels, and to the youngest son one-ninth of his camels. The sons were quite happy with this arrangement for they loved their father and trusted him in death as they had in life. Well, they were happy until they counted the camels, for there were 17. Now the brothers could not divide 17 by 2, or 3, or 9 and still come up with a whole number, and no brother was prepared to take more or less than he believed his father wanted him to have. This disagreement began to grow and soon developed into an argument, which was very out of character for the brothers. Soon all three brothers were brawling in the middle of the street. This was the scene that the wise woman of the village came upon as she walked to the well with her old camel. When she spoke to the brothers they stopped arguing at once, out of respect and in order to give her their proper attention. She asked them what was going on, for the brothers were normally known to be friends and reasonable men, not given to brawling. The youngest boy explained their predicament. After thinking for a time she placed the rope that she was leading her camel by into the hands of the youngest brother, "Here, take my camel. Now you have 18 camels and can divide up the caravan of camels as your father intended." And so the eldest brother took his half: 9 camels. The middle boy took his third: 6 camels and the youngest took one-ninth: 2 camels. (*Just to make it easy for you:* 9 + 6 + 2 = 17) The wise woman then, having had her camel returned to her, went on her way. The brothers went on their way too, content that they had each honored their father's wishes.

Think

On too many occasions people get caught up with the thought that they can only gain because of another's loss. I want to invite you to think that, like the old woman in the story, we can bring an 18th camel to the challenge of psychosis, and, after all is said and done, we can still leave again with our camel. Psychosis and schizophrenia can result in serious functional impairment and suffering in the lives of people who are unable to adapt to these experiences. In these people the experiences trigger a descent into distress and dysfunction. We have, in the case of psychosis and the schizophrenias, to remember that we are dealing conceptually with a group of disorders. Some cases may be linked with profound biological changes that stem from the epigenetic effects of the person's journey through life plus his or her genetic inheritance. Treatment can never be a one-size-fits-all affair; it ought to be crafted and tailored to an individual's desires, needs, and presentation. I want us to consider that the biopsychosocial elements of good treatment are like the three sons in the chapter-opening story. The father's wishes, expressed in his will, represent psychosis that a person presents with: the challenge. Each treatment element needs a differing level of priority within the treatment plans of the individuals who present with psychosis, but all three will be included in some form. The problem remains how to divide up the camels (*the treatment*)—as eye movement desensitization and reprocessing (EMDR) therapists we can bring an 18th camel that facilitates an acceptable solution. We do not need to insist that we favor one of the biopsychosocial elements over another; all are needed to some degree. By applying the adaptive information processing (AIP) and the ICoNN models, we bring an 18th camel and facilitate a more complete solution. I do not believe that EMDR therapy is a stand-alone therapy for psychosis and schizophrenia.

I do, however, believe that it is most appropriately placed within a biopsycho-social package of care, where no one aspect warrants more attention. There will be some individuals who can receive EMDR therapy in a safe and supportive community and require little or no medication. For others, medication may have to take a higher priority. The one thing that is likely is that all three elements will have to be present in one form or another in the majority of cases. Professor Kenneth Kendler refers to this approach as *compassionate pluralistic psychiatry* (Lieberman, 2015), and for me this represents a united biopsychosocial approach that benefits the person seeking help. By avoiding the limitations of a binary choice between biological versus psychological therapy and opting instead for a multidisciplinary biopsychosocial treatment approach, we use the rich skill mix available within a multidisciplinary approach. We must also be mindful that, having experienced a biological bias in the treatment elements for psychosis, we must not merely shift the bias elsewhere.

The Journey So Far...

At this stage in our journey we have examined the connections between trauma, psychosis, and schizophrenia (Arseneault et al., 2011). We have explored the phenomenology of dissociation, psychosis, and schizophrenia and how to observe and recognize them. As we look at psychotherapy for psychosis and schizophrenia, we can appreciate how similar they are, in respect to their most efficacious elements. These observations accord with the remarks of Jerome Frank in his book *Persuasion and Healing* (Frank, 1961), where he introduces the four features that he feels are shared by all good psychotherapies. He believes that these four features account for most of a psychotherapy's effectiveness: *an emotionally charged relationship, a therapeutic environment, a rationale or myth that provides a plausible explanation for the client's symptoms*, and *a procedure to resolve the symptoms*. We have already noted that, unsurprisingly, EMDR therapy has all four of these features; so too does the Indicating Cognitions of Negative Networks (ICoNN) model, which helps us to understand and treat psychosis and schizophrenia. EMDR therapy offers an efficient method to digest the toxic psychological pathogen, which we hypothesize to be the dysfunctional memory network (DMN). This, in turn, according to the AIP model (Shapiro & Maxfield, 2002), ought to result in a diminution or resolution of psychosis, and that is what we will see described in the cases explored in the following chapter.

> "It doesn't make sense to attempt to cure signals of problems, and it's not an approach that is particularly successful either because the traumatic background is not recognised and the emotions involved not coped with."
>
> *(Romme, 2009, p. 9)*

ICoNN AS IT RELATES TO THE STANDARD EIGHT-PHASE, THREE-PRONGED EMDR THERAPY MODEL

The first two of Frank's factors are *an emotionally charged relationship* and *a therapeutic environment*. In ICoNN we must be actively present and work to build both of these elements. They are a vital part of the standard model; however, there are some characterological differences within the IConN methodology. IConN stands for *Indicating Cognitions of Negative Networks*; the "Negative Networks" of the acronym are the DMN of the AIP model. An icon in modern terms is a graphic that represents, and links to, an underlying program that operates with a function and purpose. The icon is something that represents the program symbolically, facilitates recognition, and can link the user to it, but it is not the actual program. In the IConN model we will see that psychotic phenomena, which I propose are dissociative, act as icons that can be focused upon and, in some cases, followed back to the source program: the DMN. In other cases we can use the IConN as a proxy, to access the program (DMN) and facilitate processing, somewhat like a user interface. This is the case when working with voices using a voice dialogue or ego-state methodology. Because IConN builds on the standard model, I will outline the customary intention of the treatment phase in the standard model before noting the relevant IConN modifications.

THE STANDARD EIGHT PHASES OF EMDR THERAPY AND THEIR IConN MODIFICATIONS

Phase 1 is history and treatment planning. I will divide this into 1a—history, and 1b—treatment planning, for ease of discussion of the IConN modifications.

History (Phase 1a)

Standard intention for this phase: To gather information from the client that will inform an AIP-based understanding and formulation of the presenting problems. This AIP-based formulation will then facilitate treatment planning by identifying and sequencing targets for reprocessing that correlate with DMNs. When viewing the history through the three-pronged aspect of the model we focus on: (a) past history related to the formation of the DMN, (b) present-day triggers, and (c) future templates that target future "predicted" dysfunction.

IConN Modifications to History (Phase 1a)

It is stated that in psychosis the person presents with emotional distress consequent to the delusional beliefs, but the individual views the upset and disorder as the consequence of a real experience. At this stage in the assessment, the first impulse we feel, as clinicians, is a need to point out the erroneous nature of the psychotic material. We must be conscious not do this. The risk is that the person being confronted may feel rejected and judged, or merely form the opinion that you are the one who has gotten it wrong. Listen and be actively neutral (Ross, 2004, 2013); that is to say, consciously choose to adopt a neutral stance, neither confirming nor dismissing the material that your client is presenting to you. Remember the risk that the client is choosing to take in sharing it with you: Honor that risk taking. Your primary role at this point is to create a container within which the person can feel safe enough to share his or her psychotic material with you. I have already outlined a schema for testing and forming the sort of attuned relationship that is needed for working with psychosis (see Chapter 5's discussion of CAEL). By applying the CAEL model, or Caelian principles—connect, affirm, empower, listen, love, learn—you will build a therapeutic container that is capable of holding the psychotic dynamic and allows work to be undertaken on it. Jung often used the symbol of the alchemist when discussing therapy, and I find it a helpful metaphor. Therapy is a hazardous endeavor that ought to take place in a safe and appropriate container. As a junior psychiatrist, just starting out in my career, I remember colleagues speaking about giving paraldehyde injections to induce rapid tranquilization in distressed people. Paraldehyde must be given in a glass syringe because it dissolves plastic. This recollection reminds me that not every container for treatment is a safe one, so we must choose wisely.

Treatment Planning (Phase 1b)

Standard intention for this phase: Treatment planning sets the route for the therapeutic journey. In a standard case, careful history taking acquires one or more targets that relate to DMNs. These DMNs are triggered for the person by internal and/or external stimuli, and when triggered they result in unfortunate emotional, cognitive, and behavioral reactions. These reactions are essentially the phenomena that have brought the person into therapy at this point in his or her life.

IConN Modifications to Treatment Planning (Phase 1b)

In this phase, when working with psychosis the intention is still to set a direction for the therapeutic journey. Gather a clear sense of what goals the person has come into therapy with. Listen carefully. By utilizing the available information gathered from the history and initial presentation, you are already beginning to attune and unite with the client in achieving the client's treatment goals. By maintaining active neutrality you will avoid being drawn into scrutinizing the truthfulness of the psychotic material. We should make our primary focus the emotional reaction that the psychotic phenomena elicit. The importance of doing this will be demonstrated when we explore together the case of a young man with *body dysmorphophobia*, who believed that he had female breasts. When we work with psychosis, the emotional experiences that are connected to the psychotic material are the key phenomena. The "organ of emotion" where we experience emotion (*emote*) is the body. We therefore invite clients to pay close attention to what they are experiencing in their bodies and do likewise with regard to our own bodies, for both ought to be involved in the therapeutic dynamic.

Preparation (Phase 2)

"Ostensibly preparation sets the stage for all that is to follow."
(Bergmann, 2012, p. 177)

Standard intention for this treatment phase: To ready the client for engaging in the EMDR therapy.

This involves helping the client to remain grounded enough to allow the processing of information and assists the client with emotional containment between sessions. The preparation phase may consist of as little as one session of 60 to 90 minutes when treating a single-incident, type I trauma resulting in posttraumatic stress disorder (PTSD). However in complex PTSD, neuroses, or personality disorder, preparation will be an *always-present element* in therapy. The therapist will focus the intention of the therapeutic endeavors from preparation (phase 2) to processing (phases 3–7), and back again many times.

IConN Modifications to Preparation (Phase 2)

Effective Connection Through Focusing on the Caelian Principles

As with the complex presentations noted previously, in psychosis and schizophrenia, a movement between phase 2 and the treatment phases 3–7 may occur many times. Holding the person in a safe, contained, and grounded intersubjective-focused relationship enables phases 3–7 to proceed. A return to phase 2 is taken when needed. The therapist engages the person presenting with psychosis through the Caelian principles we have already noted: The *connection* is *affirming* and *empowering*. This allows the therapist to facilitate the shift to a different level of thinking than the level at which the problem was created. In so doing the therapist is acting as an 18th camel that allows the problem to be solved. The therapist is an essential catalyst in finding a solution, but does not expend energy in doing so.

The Realm of the Intersubjective

> "The illnesses that have shaped psychiatry do, however,
> have a clear thread running through them. They exist
> between people."
> —*Professor Tom Burns (2013, p. xiii)*

Together the therapist and client elevate the processing to a different level of thinking and interaction, where reprocessing is possible. This does not mean that the therapist need conspire with the person seeking help—for example, we need not confirm that the Central Intelligence Agency (CIA) is spying on a person. However, we can engage the client by connecting through the emotion that the client feels, which is connected to the client's *belief* that the CIA is spying on him or her. So, without confirming or denying the person's assertion about the CIA, I can understand and acknowledge the strong emotion elicited. This is where *attunement* (Erskine, 1998; Schore, 2012; Siegel & Buczynski, 2014) and the *relational imperative* of EMDR therapy are essential (Dworkin, 2005). As therapists, when we are preparing for the assessment and processing of the DMN that is driving psychotic phenomena, we need to be connecting effectively with the person. This is the realm of the intersubjective. We referred to Parnas when we looked at the phenomenology of psychosis in Chapter 2. He observes that psychosis is understood most fully in the intersubjective dynamic. Professor Tom Burns is making the same point in the quote used at the start of this paragraph. Good therapy has to involve two people who are actively engaging in an emotionally charged, relational dynamic.

AIP, IConN, and the DMN

As EMDR therapists applying the AIP and IConN models, we hypothesize that the DMN is dissociated material that represents what Parnas described as "a trait alteration of the very structure of consciousness" (Parnas, 2012, p. 68). The DMN is a lens through which individuals with psychosis experience an altered consciousness of the world around them, including their dynamic with the therapist. These psychotic and dissociated phenomena are the *state* experiences that clients are generally distressed by and from which they are seeking relief. As they seek to bring meaning to this altered state of consciousness, their narratives are dreamlike and fractured, yet rich in symbolism and iconography, a product of the mind seeking meaning (Frankl, 2014). In such a place the therapist may find it difficult to equip some clients in respect to the third of Frank's criteria—that is, presenting a rationale or myth that provides a plausible explanation for their symptoms (Frank, 1961).

Importance of Family and Community

Mental illness is a family disease. For the person presenting with psychosis or schizophrenia, it is vitally important that the preparation phase extend to consider the family/community that the person lives within. Giving clients a mythos/rationale that explains their phenomena is very important, and Frank lists it in his key elements of an effective psychotherapy for good reason (Frank, 1961). However, we must equip clients in such a way that they understand the mythos well enough to explain it to their family members/community. As a medical student I was advised to "see one… do one… teach one." Although it is easy to criticize this pedagogical method, it does emphasize the importance of teaching something clearly enough so that it can be practiced and taught. Consider our partners in this journey with psychosis: the clients. Do we show them clearly how to approach their psychosis, so that they can understand it and be capable of teaching their family members and close community the same paradigm? I encourage each client to consider inviting a key person in his or her life to join with us in a therapy session. This allows the family to learn the model that the person has come to understand as explaining his or her experiences. After all, the client may have benefited from many hours of input, and the next-of-kin received next to none. I believe that history has already noted the importance of family/community interactions between those experiencing mental illness and psychosis and key persons. The work on expressed emotion (EE) is a very good example of such research (Amaresha & Venkatasubramanian, 2012; Butzlaff & Hooley, 1998; Greenley, 1986; Kavanagh, 1992; Leff & Vaughn, 1985; Santos et al., 2001). Labels such as psychosis and schizophrenia often mean very little to people and their families. Or, if they are familiar with these terms, they have negative associations and are misunderstood. For example, many think that people with schizophrenia are more likely to be violent and cannot be expected to live a fulfilling life. These folklores are simply untrue and add to the stigma around mental illness in general and psychosis in particular. They allow an environment of fear and therapeutic nihilism to persist. When educating individuals who present with these experiences, we are seeking to bring meaning to their experiences. In equipping clients with a rationale for these experiences, we engender hope and offer it by proxy to their families and communities. Hope grows in the intersubjective dynamic involving therapist, professional team members, the client, and the client's family system. No one exists in complete isolation.

Psychoeducation

"Myths are neither true nor false but symbolic stories that give
us meaning and teach us how to act."
—*Joseph Campbell (2004)*

Psychoeducation involves the second two of Frank's principles: a rationale or myth that provides a plausible explanation for the client's symptoms, and a procedure to resolve the symptoms (Frank, 1961). At this stage we need to meet clients where they are. On initial consultation they are often very distressed. Any endeavor to uncover the "truth" at this time will prove to be futile. Primarily this difficulty arises because many people, although distressed and disordered as a consequence of the psychotic material, do not see themselves as ill. They believe that how they feel is an understandable reaction to what is happening to them. For example, a client is upset because members of the CIA never leave him alone, they invade his privacy and they write down everything that he thinks about and share it widely. Therefore, in the ICoNN model we must often modify the "1 . . . 2 . . . 3. . ." psychoeducation paradigm that we outlined in Chapter 5. We do so according to the person's capacity to engage with the models. Remember that we are presenting a new conscious awareness to the person: We have listened to and heard the client's concerns, and we acknowledge that these result in *real* emotions. The emotion that the person is experiencing is indisputably experienced in the client's body. This is a genuine phenomenon, and we must work to help the person trust these experiences and the process of EMDR therapy that works with it to bring about resolution. More than that, we must present a model that explains how and why these experiences are occurring: Meaning brings hope. This is then further developed to explain the methodology that we use to resolve the symptoms. In psychosis, if there is some awareness that a degree of misperception is occurring, and the client is able to accept and follow the rationale offered to him or her, we can begin to build the client's understanding. This library of *mythos* that we draw upon contains the AIP model, the Tribrain model, and the dual attention stimulation/bilateral stimulation (DAS/BLS) element of the EMDR therapy method. Although these are not ironclad demonstrable facts, they are a valuable rationale around which the therapist and client can unite. I have found that many people who experience psychotic phenomena are capable of participating in exactly the same psychoeducation as people with nonpsychotic presentations. However, when clients are very distressed by active psychosis, they are best prepared by generally focusing on an understanding of how emotional distress affects the body/mind system, and medication may be needed. If the person is capable of understanding an overview of the normal alert and arousal systems in the brain, this is useful to include at this point. I do not always fully develop the psychoeducational concepts of negative cognitions (NCs) and positive cognitions (PCs), as this can lead to a sense that you, as the therapist, are saying that the psychotic material is "not real." It may also result in clients feeling that you either disbelieve them, or are simply not taking them seriously. By focusing on clients' emotions, you are connecting to the "organ of emotion" (*the body*), and by grounding clients in their bodily experiences you achieve several things at the same time: Clients feel you are attuned to their distress—that is to say, you "get it," and they sense that you are present with them as they work to resolve their difficulties. In other words, you are playing on their team. In the *Caelian* method we are *listening to, loving with,* and *learning from* the person. This creates a strong feeling of connection and prepares us to work intersubjectively. We will examine how this looks in practice using the case material in the next chapter.

The Hearing Voices Network

Society experiences a Gestalt around psychotic phenomena such as voice-hearing: They are not a "good" thing to experience. We observe this in our modern literature:

> "No. Hearing voices no one else can hear isn't a good sign,
> even in the wizarding world."
> (*J. K. Rowling speaking through her*
> *character Ron; Rowling, 1999, p. 110*)

The materials and resources provided by the Hearing Voices Network, consisting of work by Professor Romme and Sandra Escher from Maastricht University, and a Dutch self-help group, Foundation Resonance (Romme, 2009; Romme & Escher, 1993), can help a person to understand that many people hear voices, which others do not hear, at some point in their lives. This is quite a shift in understanding for many people, including some professionals, I'm sad to say. The Maastricht approach and the original work that it borrows from, the voice dialogue approach, are very helpful tools in working with psychosis and voice hearers.

Check out the information and resources available at the following sites:

http://www.hearing-voices.org
http://www.hearingvoicesusa.org
http://www.hearingvoicesusa.org/resources#videos
http://www.voicedialogue.org.uk/home
http://www.voicedialogueinternational.com/index.htm

The Hearing Voices Network states that, at some point in their lives, between 3% and 10% of people hear voices that others cannot hear. If we include one-off experiences, such as hearing someone shout your name when no one is there, or feeling your phone vibrate when it has not, then that figure rises to 75%. These figures usually come as a great surprise to people, as society wants us to think of them as rare and unusual—experiences that mark out the psychiatrically ill among us. Discussing this sort of information with the person experiencing voices allows us to introduce the concept of a *healthy* voice-hearer. It is important to clarify that not all experiences of hearing voices, or other hallucinatory experiences (sensation, visual, smell, and taste), need to be characterized as illness that should be cured. Brain-scanning technology has been able to demonstrate that brain activity is the same for *disordered* voice-hearers as it is in *healthy* voice-hearers. In other words, this demonstrates that the level of disorder relates to how well the person adapts to the voice-hearing experience and is not due to the hearing of voices per se (Romme, 2009).

Voice Dialogue and the Maastricht Approach

The Maastricht approach (Corstens, Escher, & Romme, 2008) has been developed by the Hearing Voices Network as a way to conceptualize and work with voices. It is a modification of the voice dialogue approach (Stone & Stone, 1989) developed by Hal and Sidra Stone. This paradigm is referred to in the Executive Summary of the most recent publication of the British Psychological Society's Division of Clinical Psychology (United Kingdom) that is encouraging psychotherapy for psychosis: "This report describes a psychological approach to experiences that are commonly thought of as psychosis, or sometimes schizophrenia" (Basset et al., 2014, p. 6). I like the voice dialogue methodology for a number of reasons. People can read up on it and engage with it easily, without the need to see themselves as ill. They need not see their experiences as the consequences of a broken or diseased mind. Hal and Sidra Stone frame the model as "an exploration of consciousness." The voices are viewed as "selves" that represent "energy systems" in a person and are not viewed as pathology. The emphasis of the voice dialogue method is to develop and grow the *aware ego*. I believe that this is a very accessible approach for people who hear voices.

The Bus and Bus Drivers Metaphor

We can helpfully think of the voices a person hears as being a "peopled wound" (McCarthy-Jones, 2012), as this gives people a useful rationale for this phenomenon. I have used the following metaphor for many years to explain ego-states/voices/energy systems and find it a helpful one that most clients can follow and understand:

Imagine that you are a bus, a bus that is traveling on your life's journey. On the bus are many different people. All of the people are bus drivers, but, naturally, only one person can drive the bus at any given time. Other drivers may offer support, or opinions, but only one is in ultimate control. Each of the drivers has a detailed knowledge of a route and uses a particular style of driving best fitted for a certain route and terrain. Ideally, when the system is working and everyone is cooperating, the drivers swap as and when required to do so, allowing the bus to continue traveling in the best way possible. However, sometimes a driver ends up continuing to drive when he ought not, or a new driver takes control when another would be a better choice. This results in the bus journey running into problems, and old patterns of behavior may be used inappropriately to adapt to the situation. At these times the other drivers may begin to heckle the person driving, and we can think of this as representing what the "voices" are doing.

Some of the drivers are very healthy and adaptive in a helpful way, whereas others represent energy systems that are formed in times of trauma and are not fully integrated with the other drivers. These dysfunctional drivers are connected to the DMN of trauma. The aim of therapy is to achieve a healthy, united team of drivers who cooperate in a functional way to allow the bus to travel the route safely. Some people with an aware ego are conscious of the drivers changing and even notice the comments of the other drivers, whereas others remain blissfully unaware of all the activity.

Assessment (Phase 3)

Standard intention for this treatment phase: To appropriately identify and target the DMN for phase 4 (desensitization).

IConN Modifications to Assessment (Phase 3)

I want us to consider the person with psychosis, including schizophrenia, as falling within one of the following four IConN categories of case presentation:

1. **IConN 1:** In this first category, psychotic phenomena are present on examination and distress the person, causing a functional impairment. The psychological pathogen (DMN) can be identified and is acknowledged by the person as a memory system that holds strong emotion with a negative valence, which is etiologically felt to be connected to the psychosis. This DMN may be targeted with the standard model and reprocessed.

2. **IConN 2:** In the second category, the psychotic phenomena are evident upon examination and distress the person, causing a functional impairment. However, the psychological pathogen (DMN) cannot be identified in the standard way. As a consequence, the DMN cannot be understood and acknowledged by the person as the memory system that is driving the psychotic material causing distress and dysfunction. In this group, strong emotions, which can be felt, are tracked back across an *affect bridge*, allowing identification of the DMN. This is then reprocessed in the standard way.

3. **IConN 3:** In the third category of presentations, the psychotic phenomena are evident upon examination and distress the person, causing a functional impairment. However, the psychological pathogen (DMN) cannot be identified in the standard way. In this group, the strong emotions *cannot* be tracked back across an affect bridge, but there are "heard voices" that can be engaged with. As noted earlier, the voices can be thought of as a "peopled wound" (McCarthy-Jones, 2012). As such, these voices act as a proxy for engaging with the DMN, which is ultimately reprocessed using an ego-state approach (Watkins, 1993, 2005)/voice dialogue approach (Stone & Stone, 1989) with the facilitation of the DAS/BLS elements within the EMDR therapy method.

4. **IConN 4:** In the fourth and final category of presentations, the psychotic phenomena are causing distress and a functional impairment to the person, but the psychological pathogen (DMN) cannot be identified in the standard way. Strong emotions *cannot* be tracked back across an affect bridge, and there are no "heard voices" capable of being engaged. What *can* be identified is a Gestalt that relates to psychotic material being presented, which possesses strong, and negatively valenced, emotion. It is this Gestalt with its emotional system that is targeted in reprocessing of IConN 4 cases. We will see precisely how this is done in the case of Janus in a later chapter.

• **FIGURE 8.1 Flowchart Used by Clinician to Ascertain Which IConN Section the Patient Lies Within**

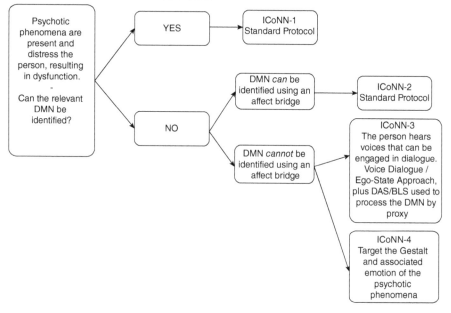

These four groups can be helpfully understood using the diagram in Figure 8.1.

"You've Got to Feel to Heal"

One important principle that must be kept in mind as we deliver therapy, which is especially true when working with psychosis, is that "you've got to feel to heal." This reminds us to maintain the person within the therapeutic window (Briere, 2002): neither too aroused nor too dissociated. From this place of healthy connection the attuned therapist (Schore, 2012) links to the negatively valenced emotion, which ensures that "we" (Siegel & Buczynski, 2014) are connecting with the DMN; this allows processing to proceed (Shapiro & Maxfield, 2002).

The AIP/IConN Formulation

As we have already acknowledged, the power of the AIP model is its capacity to explain mental health pathology, be indicative of targets for reprocessing (DMN), and predict outcome (Shapiro & Maxfield, 2002). Please remember that the IConN model augments the AIP model and does not stand separate from it. Even in psychosis we must always view the person seeking our assistance through the lens of the AIP model. In doing this we hypothesize that there is a DMN driving the pathology. In **IConN 1** presentations the trauma and corresponding DMN are identified in the standard way. In **IConN 2** presentations the DMN may not be immediately accessible, but strong emotion can be identified and used as an *affect bridge* that takes the therapist back to the DMN. In **IConN 3** presentations, strong emotions cannot be tracked back across an affect bridge, but "heard voices," which can be engaged in dialogue, act as a proxy for the DMN. IConN 4 presentations are the most nebulous, with no clear DMN to target; however, the therapist can identify a Gestalt that relates to the psychotic material being presented. This Gestalt possesses strong, and negatively valenced, emotion, which acts as a proxy for the cryptic DMN. In these IConN 4 presentations the crucial methodology that facilitates processing is the ability to keep the person grounded, connected to the therapist with the strong emotion being felt. The therapist's attention is on the intersubjective. Knowledge of Dworkin's relational imperative (Dworkin, 2005) is an essential addition to an EMDR therapist's toolbox to work effectively with psychosis and schizophrenia. The therapist invites the client to focus on the strong emotion that he or she feels, which characterizes the Gestalt of the psychosis. The therapist must also be aware of what is going on within himself or herself, and that is the *praecox feeling* (*praecox gefühl*) (Rümke, 1958). This dual attention greatly enhances a conscious awareness of the resonance between client and therapist in the intersubjective, where the therapeutic work will ultimately occur. The therapist models an *aware ego* to clients, as described in the voice dialogue approach (Stone & Stone, 1989), and coaches clients in developing the skills that they will utilize to manage their experiences.

Desensitization (Phase 4)

Standard intention for this treatment phase: To target the identified DMN and desensitize its overwhelming, re-experienced, trauma-based emotions through the application of DAS/BLS, aiming to reduce the Subjective Units of Distress Scale (SUDS) score to zero.

IConN Modifications to Desensitization (Phase 4)

IConN 1 and IConN 2

Considering the four IConN presentations described earlier, in scenarios 1 and 2 we are able to identify a DMN that can then be targeted *in the standard way*, working with an NC and the SUDS to guide the desensitization.

IConN 3

In IConN 3 presentations the voices become a proxy for accessing and desensitizing the DMN. If we consider again the symbolism of *The Wizard of Oz*, we are gaining access to the "man behind the curtain" (DMN) by talking to the projected face of the wizard that Dorothy and her companions see—in other words, the voices. Although we could think of talking to the projected "big green scary face" as merely a sham, and consider it unlikely to be effective, doing so allows us to access and influence the DMN indirectly. We will examine how this is done when we describe the case of a young man who experiences hearing the voices of his abusers, which goad and distress him. The Maastricht approach, voice dialogue approach, and ego-state approach all inform the therapeutic endeavors utilized within this category of presentation.

ICoNN 4

In an ICoNN 4 presentation, as illustrated by the case of Janus, which we will see later in full, the Gestalt of psychotic phenomena can be targeted, providing another method of accessing the DMN. In the case of Janus, we see a complex experience that included a visual hallucination of his thoughts being extracted from his head, floating in the air around him in speech bubbles, which were connected to his brain by strings. He described a delusional system of beliefs associated with this experience. He believed that others could read these thoughts, and he had a number of behaviors to deal with this. Rather than beginning to deconstruct this cluster of phenomena, the Gestalt of the experiences was connected to by directing Janus to recall the phenomena. At this stage the therapist asks the client to notice and connect to what is going on in his or her body (*the organ of emotion*), and this is used as a target for reprocessing. Bergmann (2012) helpfully defines for us that *emotions* are phenomena that are largely actions occurring in the body—for example, facial expressions, posture, and muscular tone. Feelings, in contrast, are composite perceptions, which he also refers to as *cortical translations*, of what we experience in our bodies (*emoting*), plus our perception of our state of mind (Bergmann, 2012). The scripted session for this process will be outlined in the following chapter.

Installation (Phase 5)

Standard intention for this treatment phase: To install the identified PC through the application of DAS/BLS, aiming to increase the Validity of Cognition (VoC) score to 7.

ICoNN Modifications to Installation (Phase 5)

Now that the DMN has been targeted and desensitized—either directly in ICoNN 1 and ICoNN 2 or indirectly in ICoNN 3, and ICoNN 4—the therapist and client work toward the installation of a PC.

ICoNN 1 and ICoNN 2

In the ICoNN 1 and ICoNN 2 cases, the therapist will generally have been capable of defining a PC in phase 3, and the standard model is followed accordingly.

ICoNN 3

In the ICoNN 3 cases we can think of "installation of a positive cognition" being achieved by working with the voices to create a sense of unity among the dissociated system. Here we work therapeutically to coordinate an agreed-upon system of cooperation between the disparate energy systems/voices/ego states. This is much more realistic than attempting to achieve complete reintegration, which may not be a normal state for some. It is vitally important that the therapist and the person experiencing the voices understand that this is *not* the same as making all the voices perform the same function—that is, uniformity—as each has its own adaptive role, which was functional at least at one point and may prove so again in the future. Equally, do not agree to work toward annihilating a voice or part. Remember the first law of thermodynamics; we are seeking to convert an energy system into something positive and interconnected: a united whole. If NCs have been identified as relating to particular voices/DMNs, then the appropriate PC is installed for that voice/DMN.

ICoNN 4

In ICoNN 4 cases the key phenomena lie in the organ of emotion; in other words, the body. We attend to what the client tells us is going on in his or her body and we similarly attend to what is going on in our bodies. As the shift from negative valence to positive occurs, we expect the client and therapist to *feel* a shift occurring in what is *being experienced in the body*. This experience is the emotional tone of the Gestalt, which is being targeted and digested through the action of the DAS/BLS. Sometimes at this point the person will experience a spontaneous PC arising. If this does occur, it is very important to acknowledge it and install this per the standard protocol. If no PC arises, focus your attention and the client's on what is going on in the body. Invite the client to be an observer; there is no right/wrong at this level and we are in a nonrational form of processing. Do not attempt to offer clever insights or analyses at this stage, as that pulls a person out of nonrational processing and into a state of blocked rational thinking. For ICoNN 4 cases it is very important to attend fully to phase 6.

Body Scan (Phase 6)

Standard intention for this treatment phase: To confirm that the target memory and identified PC are fully installed and that there is no residual material that requires further targeting from that specific DMN. In this phase we aim to achieve an outcome where the original target memory and the PC are brought into conscious thought and can be spoken about without any sense of reliving or emotional/physical discomfort.

ICoNN Modifications to Body Scan (Phase 6)

The therapist keeps in mind that the primary instrument of emotion is the body. The treatment phase is used to look for any residual material requiring further targeting. Because "the body keeps the score" (van der Kolk, 1994), we invite the client to assess his or her body while revisiting the original target and holding the PC in conscious thought.

ICoNN 1 and ICoNN 2

For ICoNN 1 and ICoNN 2, the standard model is followed until the body feels neutral, which indicates that processing is complete.

ICoNN 3

In ICoNN 3 cases, the therapist checks that there is unity and accord within the system of voices. At this point some voices may cease to manifest, whereas others may merely change in character and behavior but remain present. It is very important to acknowledge the statement made by Professor Marius Romme: As therapists we need to accept that there is such a thing as a "healthy voice-hearer" (Romme, 2009; Romme & Escher, 1993). This is a huge paradigm shift for many, so let us give one another the time and space to respectfully explore these concepts.

IConN 4

In IConN 4 scenarios, our guide is the negatively valenced emotion associated with the Gestalt that the client feels, and the therapist is also paying attention to the *praecox feeling*. Therefore, in phase 6, it is both instruments of emotion that must be attended to: the client's and the therapist's, with both instruments being of equal importance. In psychosis cases the attuned therapist is not merely judging successful desensitization by the subjective report of the client; the therapist is also noticing what is present within himself or herself.

Closure (Phase 7)

Standard intention for this treatment phase: To end the session and close with the client feeling in control and grounded. In cases where the DMN being targeted is not completely desensitized or where the process of installation of the PC is not fully completed, the therapist ensures that the session is brought to closure safely and in a controlled manner. This is often done through bringing the client back to a grounded and present-day–oriented space through the use of the safe/calm place exercise. The client is usually instructed on how to use such methods in between sessions; contact arrangements are made clear; and the client is encouraged to keep a log of any intrusions, flashbacks, or post-traumatic nightmares to assist the client with developing future targets in the next session.

IConN Modifications to Closure (Phase 7)

In **IConN 1, IConN 2, and IConN 4** the therapist follows the standard model.

In **IConN 3** the therapist works to achieve cooperation among the system of voices, if possible, before moving to safe/calm place.

Re-Evaluation (Phase 8)

Standard intention for this treatment phase: To re-evaluate the DMN targeted in the previous session and assist in appropriately targeting any residual material from that specific DMN or confirming the next step in the AIP-based treatment plan. In the next session the therapist re-evaluates previous targets, checking for any residual trauma memories. The therapist reviews how the client has coped and functioned in between sessions. The therapist must review any logs that the client has been asked to keep. Clients can feel upset if they do not have an opportunity to review things that they have made a note of.

ICoNN Modifications to Re-Evaluation (Phase 8)

The therapist follows the modifications detailed in phase 3 in addition to the standard intention just noted.

CONCLUDING NOTES

By starting with a solid foundation in the standard model, we hope that therapists can be clear regarding when and why they are applying the ICoNN modifications. Therapists must understand this fully because they are facilitating the therapeutic work that the client is doing. Therapists should be able to explain the rationale if asked to do so by the client (or a supervisor). In the following chapter, we will walk through the ICoNN modifications using clinical examples.

REFERENCES

Adams, D. (1987). *Dirk Gently's holistic detective agency*. London, England: Heinemann.

Amaresha, A. C., & Venkatasubramanian, G. (2012). Expressed emotion in schizophrenia: An overview. *Indian Journal of Psychological Medicine, 34*(1), 12–20. doi:10.4103/0253-7176 .96149

Arseneault, L., Cannon, M., Fisher, H. L., Polancyk, G., Moffitt, T. E., & Caspi, A. (2011). Childhood trauma and children's emerging psychotic symptoms: A genetically sensitive longitudinal cohort study. *American Journal of Psychiatry, 168,* 65–72.

Basset, T., Bentall, R., Boyle, M., Cooke, A., Cupitt, C., Dillon, J., . . . Weaver, Y. (2014). In A. Cooke (Ed.), *Understanding psychosis and schizophrenia: Why people sometimes hear voices, believe things that others find strange, or appear out of touch with reality, and what can help.* A report by the Division of Clinical Psychology. Leicester, England: British Psychological Society, Division of Clinical Psychology.

Bergmann, U. (2012). *Neurobiological foundations for EMDR practice.* New York, NY: Springer Publishing Company.

Briere, J. (2002). Treating adult survivors of severe childhood abuse and neglect: Further development of an integrative model. In J. E. B. Myers (Ed.), *The APSAC handbook on child maltreatment* (2nd ed., pp. 1–26). Thousand Oaks, CA: Sage.

Burns, T. (2013). *Our necessary shadow. The nature and meaning of psychiatry.* London, England: Allen Lane.

Butzlaff, R. L., & Hooley, J. M. (1998). Expressed emotion and psychiatric relapse: A meta-analysis. *Archives of General Psychiatry, 55*(6), 547–552.

Campbell, J. (2004). *The hero with a thousand faces* (Commemorative ed.). Princeton, NJ: Princeton University Press.

Corstens, D., Escher, S., & Romme, M. (2008). Accepting and working with voices: The Maastricht approach. In A. Moskowitz, I. Schäfer, & M. J. Dorahy (Eds.), *Psychosis, trauma, and dissociation: Emerging perspectives on severe psychopathology* (pp. 319–332). Chichester, England: Wiley-Blackwell.

Dworkin, M. (2005). *EMDR and the relational imperative: The therapeutic relationship in EMDR treatment.* New York, NY: Routledge.

Erskine, R. G. (1998). Attunement and involvement: Therapeutic responses to relational needs. *International Journal of Psychotherapy, 3*(3), 235–244.

Frank, J. D. (1961). *Persuasion and healing: A comparative study of psychotherapy.* Baltimore, MD: Johns Hopkins Press.

Frankl, V. E. (2014). *Man's search for meaning.* Boston, MA: Beacon Press.

Greenley, J. R. (1986). Social control and expressed emotion. *Journal of Nervous and Mental Disorders, 174*(1), 24–30.

Kavanagh, D. J. (1992). Recent developments in expressed emotion and schizophrenia. *British Journal of Psychiatry, 160*, 601–620.

Leff, J. P., & Vaughn, C. (1985). *Expressed emotion in families: Its significance for mental illness.* New York, NY: Guilford Press.

Lieberman, J. (2015). *Shrinks: The untold story of psychiatry* (1st ed.). New York, NY: Little, Brown.

McCarthy-Jones, S. (2012). *Hearing voices: The histories, causes, and meanings of auditory verbal hallucinations.* Cambridge, England: Cambridge University Press.

Parnas, J. (2012). The core Gestalt of schizophrenia. *World Psychiatry, 11*(2), 67–69.

Romme, M. (2009). *Living with voices: 50 stories of recovery.* Ross-on-Wye, England: PCCS Books in association with Birmingham City University.

Romme, M., & Escher, S. (1993). *Accepting voices.* London, England: MIND Publications.

Ross, C. (2013). *Psychosis, trauma, dissociation, and EMDR.* Paper presented at the 18th EMDR International Association Conference, Austin, TX.

Ross, C. A. (2004). *Schizophrenia: Innovations in diagnosis and treatment.* Binghamton, NY: Haworth Maltreatment and Trauma.

Rowling, J. K. (1999). *Harry Potter and the chamber of secrets.* London, England: Bloomsbury.

Rümke, H. C. (1958). [Clinical differentiation within the group of schizophrenias]. *Nervenarzt, 29*(2), 49–53.

Santos, A., Espina, A., Pumar, B., Gonzalez, P., Ayerbe, A., & Garcia, E. (2001). Longitudinal study of the stability of expressed emotion in families of schizophrenic patients: A 9-month follow-up. *Spanish Journal of Psychology, 4*(1), 65–71.

Schore, A. N. (2012). *The science of the art of psychotherapy* (1st ed.). New York, NY: W. W. Norton.

Shapiro, F., & Maxfield, L. (2002). Eye movement desensitization and reprocessing (EMDR): Information processing in the treatment of trauma. *Journal of Clinical Psychology, 58*(8), 933–946. doi:10.1002/jclp.1006

Siegel, D., & Buczynski, R. (2014). *The neurobiology of trauma treatment: How brain science can lead to more targeted interventions for patients healing from trauma.* Retrieved from http://www.nicabm.com/treatingtrauma2014/a1-transcript-sample/?del=11.14.1 4LTsampleemailunreg

Stone, H., & Stone, S. (1989). *Embracing our selves: The voice dialogue manual.* San Rafael, CA: New World Library.

van der Kolk, B. A. (1994). The body keeps the score: Memory and the evolving psychobiology of posttraumatic stress. *Harvard Review of Psychiatry, 1*(5), 253–265.

Watkins, H. H. (1993). Ego-state therapy: An overview. *American Journal of Clinical Hypnosis, 35*(4), 232–240.

Watkins, J. G. (2005). Over-resonance, the emaciation and destruction of Judy's self: Modifications to ego state theory. *Journal of Trauma Dissociation, 6*(3), 1–9. doi:10.1300/J229v06n03_01

NINE

EMDR Therapy + IConN 1 Category Case Examples

Intention: *To demonstrate to the reader, with clinical case material, the methodology for formulating cases using the AIP and IConN models in conjunction. To equip clinicians with the knowledge of how to target EMDR therapeutic endeavors for the treatment of people diagnosed with schizophrenia or other psychoses.*

"It takes courage to experience the full measure of our feelings and emotions, without reacting to them or cutting them off. Yet here is where our freedom lies. As Albert Camus tells us, 'We all carry within us our places of exile, our crimes, our ravages. Our task is not to unleash them on the world, it is to transform them in ourselves and others.'"
—*Jack Kornfield, Buddhist teacher* (2008, p. 134)

IConN CASE MATERIAL

The case examples in this chapter and the next three chapters are based on actual case studies of people whom I have treated in my clinic in Holywood, County Down. Some of the details have been changed to maintain confidentiality, and in some cases they represent a composite of several similar cases.

"We are not just an illness, we are a person."
—*Voice-hearer speaking at the launch of the Hearing Voices Network in Ireland, 2015*

Any therapist seeking to work with psychosis must remain conscious that this is no easy path to take, neither for the therapist nor the client. Being fully present and modeling an *aware ego process* (Stone & Stone, 1989) for the person you are facilitating is energetically demanding, yet it is what is necessary. Categories

1 and 2 of the Indicating Cognitions of Negative Networks (ICoNN) model are normally more straightforward cases to treat than those belonging to categories 3 and 4. Therefore, I recommend that when starting to use eye movement desensitization and reprocessing (EMDR) therapy in this area, treat people in categories 1 and 2 to begin with. This will allow your experience in using EMDR therapy with psychosis to grow in a steady and safe manner. However, I want us to remember that EMDR therapy can take us on unexpected twists and turns, even in cases that, on the surface, appear straightforward. If processing becomes blocked, you may begin to feel the influence of a feeder-memory, and that dysfunctional memory network (DMN) could have disowned selves/ego states associated with it that may make a bid to seize control when triggered. The therapist, as a facilitator of the healing journey, must be aware enough to observe and sense the arrival of these disowned selves. In doing so the therapist remains connected to the DMN while still safely containing the associated emotion. In working with psychosis, do not become distracted by the symbolism of the phenomena. Remember that just as Joseph Campbell (2004) tells us, myth is neither true nor false; its function is to teach and bring meaning to our experiences. In ICoNN terms, this means that we focus on the meaning given to the psychotic experience and sense the associated emotion experienced in the body. In doing this, do not become distracted in assessing the veracity of the psychotic material. As processing occurs, there is a shift in emotion felt by the client within his or her body. If the therapist is appropriately attuned, he or she should also experience this shift in his or her own body. Engaging and holding a client with psychosis in this safe intersubjective dynamic requires a biopsychosocial container to be generated within a robust therapeutic alliance. Ideally, the future of mental health provision will involve a functionally interdependent team that can produce this biopsychosocial container. This team must also include input from people with lived experience, as well as people from the person's family and social networks. This is one of the key learning points from the ground-breaking work of the open dialogue approach developed in Finland (Holmesland, Seikkula, & Hopfenbeck, 2014; Holmesland, Seikkula, Nilsen, Hopfenbeck, & Erik Arnkil, 2010; Seikkula, 2002; Seikkula, Karvonen, Kykyri, Kaartinen, & Penttonen, 2015). Such a team approach brings the necessary skill mix to the person living within these challenges and works *together* with the person. The system ought to work together (*unity*) to bring the different areas of expertise together, rather than everyone having generic skills and a one-size-fits-all mindset (*uniformity*). In the book *Shrinks*, one past president of the American Psychological Association speaks of the need for "a compassionate and pluralistic psychiatric physician" (Lieberman, 2015, p. 300). The fifth edition of the *Diagnostic and Statistical Manual of Mental Disorders* (*DSM-5*) was launched during his tenure, and he sees it as "an unbridled triumph of pluralism" (Lieberman, 2015, p. 290). The man who taught me the importance of a full and skillful examination of phenomenology in psychiatry, Professor Ken Kendler, coined the phrase "pluralistic psychiatric practice." He taught me that normal people also hear voices and can experience other psychotic phenomena. I remain grateful and indebted to him for his teaching. In the ICoNN model, a safe container is constructed using a biopsychosocial paradigm. In recommending that ICoNN be embedded in this pluralistic approach, I hope

to avoid dogmatism, something Kendler is quoted as referring to as "epistemic hubris" (Lieberman, 2015). In other words, Kendler cautions us against saying, "this approach is the only way." The psychotic group of illnesses, some of which we have come to label as schizophrenia, are heterogeneous. There can be no one-size-fits-all approach to treatment, and so, like an *aware ego process* (Stone & Stone, 1989), the therapeutic team recognizes all the skills available to it, gives value to all, and unites all, for the good of all. In this book I propose a trauma-focused etiology for schizophrenia and psychosis. However, I am not saying that all cases of schizophrenia and psychosis are caused by trauma. "The schizophrenias" are, and always have been from their first elucidation (Bleuler, 1911), a multifarious group of illnesses that are likely to have a complex origin and etiology. It is my belief that the phenomenology that we characterize as schizophrenia most likely constitutes a "final common pathway" for these diverse etiologies. The adaptive information processing (AIP) model of EMDR therapy invites us to acknowledge that psychosis has meaning that is driven by the DMN, which is the core pathogen. So, as Steinman (2009, p. xviii) states, "As in Fitzgerald's *Rubaiyat of Omar Khayyam*, I came out 'by the same door where in I went.'" If, as healers, we once again focus our therapeutic endeavors on helping people pay attention to what has happened, recognizing that psychosis is adaptive, we can help complete the process of adaptation with them. We have had more than 100 years of experience of treating these disorders, but our "report card" justifiably states: "tries hard, but could do better." Steinman, who uses intensive psychotherapy for schizophrenia, delusional states, and dissociative identity disorder, challenges us, in his excellent book *Treating the "Untreatable"—Healing in the Realms of Madness*, to consider the question of why: Why do these people not get appropriate treatment? His answer warrants quotation:

> [T]he field of psychiatry itself tends to abandon schizophrenics and delusional people, treating them (if at all) with reality testing, anti-psychotic medication, socio-therapies and supportive psychotherapy without dealing with the underlying thought disorder and its emotional and psychological origin. (Steinman, 2009, p. 184)

This echoes the comments of Romme, Escher, Read, Bentall, and many others in the field. We must ask the question that stares us in the face when we see our clients: "What has happened to you?" Why ask? We ask because, as John Read and Richard Bentall have repeated many times, "Bad things happen and can drive you crazy!" As EMDR therapists who utilize the AIP model, the "bad things" that happen result in a failure of the normal information processing system and generate a DMN. So we must ask, and that means we must also *listen*.

ICoNN 1

In ICoNN 1, psychotic phenomena are present on examination and distress the person, causing a functional impairment. The psychological pathogen (DMN) is identified and is acknowledged by the person as holding strong emotion with a negative valence, which is etiologically connected to the psychosis. This DMN may be targeted with the standard EMDR therapy model and reprocessed.

ICoNN 1 CASE: PAUL

Synopsis of Paul's History

This is the case of a young man, age 17, whom we will call Paul. He presented to the outpatient clinic following a referral from my colleague who had seen and assessed him and his family. They had been held hostage while their father was forced to steal from his own company. On the night in question, they had been at home relaxing when the doorbell rang. Naturally, the son had answered the door as usual, but upon doing so a masked paramilitary group burst in with guns. They took the family hostage and only released them after the robbery of the father's firm had taken place. Counseling was offered to the family per standard company policy, and after four sessions of counseling Paul was referred for a psychiatric assessment, as the therapist was concerned that he was becoming actively suicidal.

Presenting Issues at the Time of Paul's Psychiatric Assessment

• Depressive symptoms of low mood with associated suicidal ideation—no active plans.
• Self-blame and guilt about having opened the door to the terrorists, unwittingly giving them entry to the family home.
• Significant sleep disturbance with initial insomnia and early-morning wakening.
• Poor concentration, decreased attention, and poor motivation.
• Poor appetite with associated weight loss.
• Cotard's phenomena, described as "my insides are all messed up," with an accompanying conviction that something serious was happening to his internal organs "like they are rotting."
• Posttraumatic symptoms of hypervigilance and increased fear and anxiety; intrusive memories, posttraumatic nightmares, and avoidance. As some of the depression became less pronounced, it became clear that a diagnosis of posttraumatic stress disorder (PTSD) was also warranted within the diagnostic formulation.
• Dissociative symptoms were present, including derealization that he described as, "it feels like I'm in a film."
• Delusions of reference: he believed that the television was telling him that he wasn't normal and that he could get "addicted to food." The television also had the power to control health professionals involved in his care.

History of Presenting Issues and Treatment

Three months after being taken hostage with his entire family, his father's employee assistance program referred Paul for counseling. After four counseling sessions he was referred to me for a psychiatric assessment because of suicidal ideation.

On psychiatric assessment, his mood was found to be low with suicidal ideation present. However, there was no active suicidal intent or plans. His depressive phenomena resulted in a significant and substantial functional impact and he met the diagnostic criteria for a *severe* depressive episode. He described delusions of reference that involved the television (noted previously) and reported Cotard's syndrome, stating that all of his internal organs were "rotting away." He described a general feeling of derealization throughout the day, reporting this as feeling "as though I'm in a film." There was no history of drug or alcohol abuse and no past psychiatric illness, and prior to the trauma he was a normally functioning, well-adjusted young man who was making plans to enter tertiary-level education.

Case Formulation

Paul's formulation proposed that psychiatric disorder had occurred in a premorbidly healthy and well-adjusted 17-year-old following a traumatic event involving him and his entire family. In particular, there were several touchstone moments within the chain of events that led to generation of the psychosis. These were indicators of the associated DMN and NCs. Initially the main priority was successful engagement and the commencement of constructing a safe container for treatment.

Diagnosis

A full psychiatric assessment, which included history taking and mental state examination, was completed. Following this it was apparent that he was not actively suicidal and did not wish to die; rather, he believed that his internal organs were already dead and rotting, and that he was walking around as a living shell with a dead interior. These phenomena are consistent with *Cotard's syndrome*: His beliefs were held with delusional intensity. In Paul's case this was comorbid with severe depressive episode with psychotic symptoms, F32.3 in the *International Classification of Diseases (ICD-10)* classification (World Health Organization [WHO], 1993). As noted, it was later decided to add PTSD disorder to the formulation, 309.81 in the *DSM-IV* (American Psychiatric Association [APA] & American Psychiatric Association Task Force on *DSM-IV*, 2000). His symptoms also met criteria for PTSD contained in the *DSM-5* (309.81; APA, 2013) and the *ICD-10* (F43.1; WHO, 1993).

Cotard's Syndrome—A Brief Description

Cotard's syndrome is described as a psychotic disorder that is traditionally characterized by a nihilistic delusion that part of the body is either rotting or no longer exists. Jules Cotard first described this eponymous syndrome in 1880 (Berrios & Luque, 1999; Debruyne, Portzky, Van den Eynde, & Audenaert, 2009) and he called it *délire des negations*—"the delirium of negation." He described a woman, Mademoiselle X, who was convinced that parts of her body had ceased to exist. She also reasoned that she did not need to eat because she been condemned to eternal damnation and cursed to live forever. She eventually died as a result of starvation. The *ICD-10* typically classifies Cotard's syndrome as a delusional disorder (F22.0; WHO, 1993), although it is not specifically named within the nosological system. The *ICD-10* defines *delusional disorder* (F22.0) as "A disorder characterized by the development either of a single delusion or of a set of related delusions that are usually persistent and sometimes lifelong. The content of the delusion or delusions is very variable" (WHO, 1993, p. 97). Similarly, the most recent iteration of the *DSM* does not specifically include Cotard's syndrome among its nomenclature, but codifies it as a delusional disorder (297.1; APA, 2013). Some authors have suggested that subtypes for Cotard's syndrome should be delineated (Berrios & Luque, 1999), the relevant one in Paul's case being "Cotard's as part of a severe depressive episode with psychotic symptoms" (F32.3; WHO, 1993). In one review of 100 people with Cotard's syndrome, 89% had a diagnosis of depression (Berrios & Luque, 1995).

Neuropsychological Considerations

Neuropsychologically, Cotard's syndrome and Capgras syndrome are viewed as related disorders. They both involve abnormal affect being applied to familiar visual objects (Gerrans, 2000). In Cotard's syndrome the focus of the process is the patient, whereas in Capgras syndrome it involves others. Physically the person appears normal; however, the individual experiences a depressed affect that he or she is unable to accept, own, and assimilate. Being unable to integrate the familiar visual stimulus with the experience of an unfamiliar affect, the patient experiences dissonance, which has to be resolved. The mind adapts to this by creating an explanation for the apparent conflict—in AIP terms, this explanation is the NC. The NC concludes that something abnormal must be occurring within parts of the person's body (*the organ of emotion*) in order for the person to feel so miserable. In its most extreme form, the NC becomes the thought that the part of the body experiencing the emotion no longer exists. Because the person is unable to accept or understand this emotional state, the person attempts to disengage his or her physical experience from it. This is not possible, and the process of dissociation remains incomplete. Cotard's syndrome that develops as a consequence of this dynamic remains mood congruent and retains the patient's emotional affect. In most people this belief would then undergo *belief revision* and subsequently be disregarded. However, it is proposed that the deficit in reasoning, rigidity of thinking, and cognitive distortions associated with depressive illness allow the belief to persist (Gerrans, 2000). This is the state that Paul presented in at his initial assessment.

Treatment

Phases 1 and 2 were completed as per standard protocol. Following his initial psychiatric assessment, given the level of distress and the counselor's assessment of him as "high risk for completion of suicide," it was decided to proceed with medication immediately. As it was in Paul's case, medication can be a useful part of the treatment plan. I describe my intention in using medication as being a way to help prepare the person for other aspects of the treatment plan. He was commenced on the selective serotonin reuptake inhibitor (SSRI) escitalopram, 10 mg daily, and the second-generation antipsychotic (SGA) quetiapine, 25 mg at night.

Progress

One week later, the belief that his internal organs were rotting was less intense and he no longer held it with delusional intensity; it was now at the level of an overvalued idea. However, his mood remained low, with feelings of guilt; he blamed himself for being taken hostage and especially for having given the terrorists access to the family home. He was also experiencing posttraumatic symptoms of intrusive memories, anxiety, hypervigilance, flashbacks, and posttraumatic nightmares. At this point the escitalopram was increased to 20 mg daily and quetiapine increased to 50 mg at night.

Two months after his initial appointment, his mood had much improved and he no longer described delusional beliefs regarding his internal organs. He stated that what I formulated as Cotard's syndrome was his way of expressing his feelings at that time. This insight developed following psychoeducation and with the commencement of medication. He continued to have significant posttraumatic symptoms in the form of flashbacks, hypervigilance, avoidance, poor concentration, and poor sleep. At this stage it was decided that he would benefit from EMDR therapy for the PTSD, and his dose of quetiapine was decreased to 25 mg daily in anticipation of this.

EMDR Treatment

Paul underwent three sessions of EMDR reprocessing. The targets were developed per the standard protocol, and these were all connected directly to some aspect of the traumatic event noted earlier. No deviation from the standard protocol was necessary. The NCs for each session were, respectively: "I am not in control," "I am going to die," and "I am a bad person." Each NC was desensitized to a SUDS score of 0, and the respective PC installed to a VoC score of 7. It is important to emphasize the fidelity to the standard paradigm. In many cases of psychosis we may be able to apply the standard eight-phase, three-pronged protocol of EMDR therapy; this has been demonstrated by the work in the Netherlands (van den Berg, van der Vleugel, Staring, de Bont, & de Jongh, 2013; van den Berg & van der Gaag, 2012).

After EMDR reprocessing sessions were completed, there were two occasions (lasting 2 weeks and 3 weeks, respectively) when he was nonconcordant with his medication and stopped both the escitalopram and quetiapine. During these periods he experienced a relapse in depression without a recurrence of Cotard's syndrome. On both occasions his antidepressant medication was reinstated and there was prompt improvement in his depressive symptoms.

Five months following his initial presentation, he had no intrusive memories and no nightmares, and his depressive symptoms had largely resolved. His treatment had included quetiapine, to a maximum level of 50 mg at night. This had been completely discontinued by his review at 5 months. Escitalopram 20 mg daily was continued for 6 months, and he had received a total of three EMDR reprocessing sessions. This case accords with the findings of the Dutch research demonstrating that EMDR therapy for trauma can be safely and acceptably undertaken in people with psychotic disorders (van den Berg et al., 2015).

Note Regarding Medication

Although medication, including an antipsychotic, was used in the treatment of this case, it is notable that the dose was low—no higher than 50 mg daily. Epocrates® (2015) notes the following guidance for prescribing quetiapine (Seroquel):

> *Schizophrenia [150–750 mg/day PO divided bid-tid]. Start: 25 mg PO bid, then incr. by 50–150 mg/day up to 300–400 mg/day PO divided bid-tid by day 4, then may adjust dose by 50–100 mg/day no more frequently than q2 days prn; Max: 800 mg/day*

A dose of 25 to 50 mg of quetiapine would normally be considered sub-therapeutic when treating psychotic phenomena. In one review of the treatment of delusional disorder, one patient treated with quetiapine was on 150 mg and another had doses between 200 mg and 700 mg, which both patients failed to respond to (Fear, 2013). In this case the psychotic symptoms received pharmacological treatment within approximately 3 to 4 months of their development. Paul required a maximum of 50 mg quetiapine per day rather than larger doses of 300 to 600 mg per day. It has been suggested in the literature that early treatment of psychotic symptoms may allow much lower doses of antipsychotics to be effective, and this may be due to a reduction of the toxic effects resulting from untreated psychosis (Clarke et al., 2006). It is generally accepted that a longer duration of untreated psychosis is associated with a significantly poorer prognosis.

TAKE-HOME FOR ICoNN 1 CASES

The initial phases 1 and 2 were completed according to the guidance described in a previous chapter. A robust therapeutic rapport developed, which provided a suitable container for working with the psychosis. It is important that the initial contact not be rushed, as it is difficult completing a new-patient psychiatric assessment within a routine new-patient slot. Those who have researched delusional disorders (Fear, 2013; Fear, McMonagle, & Healy, 1998; Fear, Sharp, & Healy, 1996) note how challenging it can be to gain the trust of these individuals. If the guidance for the initial phases is followed, clients ought to feel safe enough to allow themselves to be vulnerable enough to share their beliefs.

In people presenting in the ICoNN 1 category, we are able to target the known trauma (DMN) with the standard eight-phase, three-pronged protocol of EMDR therapy; in the case of Paul, no adaptation was required for phases 3 to 7 (de Bont et al., 2013; van den Berg et al., 2013, 2015; van den Berg, van der Vleugel, & Staring, 2010; van den Berg et al., 2014; van der Vleugel, van den Berg, & Staring, 2012). As I have stated, the ICoNN model hypothesizes a relationship between trauma, dissociation, and psychosis. By targeting the "traumatic layer" of the person's presentation, we observe the psychotic symptoms resolve, and it remains thus in the long term, as is predicted in the literature (Gonzalez, Mosquera, & Moskowitz, 2012; van der Hart, Groenendijk, Gonzalez, Mosquera, & Solomon, 2014). In this manner the ICoNN model is comparable to the AIP model (Shapiro & Maxfield, 2002): It explains mental health pathology (*psychotic phenomena*), is indicative of targets that are suitable for reprocessing (*ICoNN 1, 2, 3, and 4*), and is predictive of outcome.

Key Points for IConN 1

1. Build a safe container for treatment using Caelian principles.
2. Listen and allow the person to tell his or her story.
3. Be actively neutral.
4. Facilitate the person's connection with his or her feelings.
5. Pay attention to the emotions you are experiencing in your body as the therapist.
6. Adhere to the standard eight-phase, three-pronged protocol.

REFERENCES

American Psychiatric Association. (2013). *Diagnostic and statistical manual of mental disorders* (5th ed.). Washington, DC: Author.

American Psychiatric Association & American Psychiatric Association Task Force on *DSM-IV*. (2000). *Diagnostic and statistical manual of mental disorders: DSM-IV-TR* (4th ed.). Washington, DC: American Psychiatric Association.

Berrios, G., & Luque, R. (1995). Cotard's syndrome: Analysis of 100 cases. *Acta Psychiatrica Scandinavica, 91*(3), 185–188.

Berrios, G. E., & Luque, R. (1999). Cotard's "On hypochondriacal delusions in a severe form of anxious melancholia." *History of Psychiatry, 10*(38, Pt. 2), 269–278.

Bleuler, E. (1911). *Dementia praecox, oder Gruppe der Schizophrenien* [Dementia praecox, or the group of schizophrenias]. Leipzig, Germany: Deuticke.

Campbell, J. (2004). *The hero with a thousand faces* (Commemorative ed.). Princeton, NJ: Princeton University Press.

Clarke, M., Whitty, P., Browne, S., McTigue, O., Kamali, M., Gervin, M., . . . O'Callaghan, E. (2006). Untreated illness and outcome of psychosis. *British Journal of Psychiatry, 189*, 235–240. doi:10.1192/bjp.bp.105.014068

de Bont, P. A., van den Berg, D. P., van der Vleugel, B. M., de Roos, C., Mulder, C. L., Becker, E. S., . . . van Minnen, A. (2013). A multi-site single blind clinical study to compare the effects of prolonged exposure, eye movement desensitization and reprocessing and waiting list on patients with a current diagnosis of psychosis and comorbid posttraumatic stress disorder: Study protocol for the randomized controlled trial Treating Trauma in Psychosis. *Trials, 14*, 151. doi:10.1186/1745-6215-14-151

Debruyne, H., Portzky, M., Van den Eynde, F., & Audenaert, K. (2009). Cotard's syndrome: A review. *Current Psychiatry Reports, 11*(3), 197–202.

Epocrates. (2015). *Seroquel (quetiapine)*. Retrieved from https://online.epocrates.com/drugs/1230/Seroquel

Fear, C. (2013). Recent developments in the management of delusional disorders. *Advances in Psychiatric Treatment, 19*, 212–220.

Fear, C., Sharp, H., & Healy, D. (1996). Cognitive processes in delusional disorders. *British Journal of Psychiatry, 168*(1), 61–67.

Fear, C. F., McMonagle, T., & Healy, D. (1998). Delusional disorders: Boundaries of a concept. *European Psychiatry, 13*(4), 210–218. doi:10.1016/S0924-9338(98)80006-0

Gerrans, P. (2000). Refining the explanation of Cotard's delusion. *Mind & Language, 15*(1), 111–122. doi:10.1111/1468-0017.00125

Gonzalez, A., Mosquera, D., & Moskowitz, A. (2012). *[EMDR in psychosis and severe mental disorders]*. Paper presented at the annual meeting of EMDR Europe Association, Madrid, Spain.

Holmesland, A. L., Seikkula, J., & Hopfenbeck, M. (2014). Inter-agency work in open dialogue: The significance of listening and authenticity. *Journal of Interprofessional Care, 28*(5), 433–439. doi:10.3109/13561820.2014.901939

Holmesland, A. L., Seikkula, J., Nilsen, O., Hopfenbeck, M., & Erik Arnkil, T. (2010). Open dialogues in social networks: Professional identity and transdisciplinary collaboration. *International Journal of Integrated Care, 10,* 1–14.

Kornfield, J. (2008). *The wise heart: Buddhist psychology for the West.* London, England: Rider.

Lieberman, J. (2015). *Shrinks: The untold story of psychiatry* (1st ed.). New York, NY: Little, Brown.

Seikkula, J. (2002). Open dialogues with good and poor outcomes for psychotic crises: Examples from families with violence. *Journal of Marital and Family Therapy, 28*(3), 263–274.

Seikkula, J., Karvonen, A., Kykyri, V. L., Kaartinen, J., & Penttonen, M. (2015). The embodied attunement of therapists and a couple within dialogical psychotherapy: An introduction to the Relational Mind Research Project. *Family Process.* doi:10.1111/famp.12152

Shapiro, F., & Maxfield, L. (2002). Eye movement desensitization and reprocessing (EMDR): Information processing in the treatment of trauma. *Journal of Clinical Psychology, 58*(8), 933–946. doi:10.1002/jclp.10068

Steinman, I. (2009). *Treating the "untreatable": Healing in the realms of madness.* London, England: Karnac Books.

Stone, H., & Stone, S. (1989). *Embracing our selves: The voice dialogue manual.* San Rafael, CA: New World Library.

van den Berg, D. P., de Bont, P. A., van der Vleugel, B. M., de Roos, C., de Jongh, A., Van Minnen, A., & van der Gaag, M. (2015). Prolonged exposure vs eye movement desensitization and reprocessing vs waiting list for posttraumatic stress disorder in patients with a psychotic disorder: A randomized clinical trial. *JAMA Psychiatry.* doi:10.1001/jamapsychiatry.2014.2637

van den Berg, D. P., & van der Gaag, M. (2012). Treating trauma in psychosis with EMDR: A pilot study. *Journal of Behavior Therapy and Experimental Psychiatry, 43*(1), 664–671. doi:10.1016/j.jbtep.2011.09.011

van den Berg, D. P. G., van der Vleugel, B. M., & Staring, A. (2010). [Trauma, psychosis, PTSD and the use of EMDR]. *Directieve Therapie, 30*(4), 303–328. doi:10.1007/s12433-010-0242-9

van den Berg, D. P. G., van der Vleugel, B. M., Staring, A. B. P., de Bont, P. A. J., & de Jongh, A. (2013). EMDR in psychosis: Guidelines for conceptualization and treatment. *Journal of EMDR Practice and Research, 7*(4), 208–224.

van den Berg, D. P. G., van der Vleugel, B. M., Staring, A. B. P., de Bont, P. A. J., & de Jongh, A. (2014). [EMDR in psychosis: Guidelines for conceptualization and treatment]. *Journal of EMDR Practice and Research, 8*(3), E67–E84. doi:10.1891/1933-3196.8.3.E67

van der Hart, O., Groenendijk, M., Gonzalez, A., Mosquera, D., & Solomon, R. (2014). Dissociation of the personality and EMDR therapy in complex trauma-related disorders: Applications in phases 2 and 3 treatment. *Journal of EMDR Practice and Research, 8*(1), 33–48. doi:10.1891/1933-3196.8.1.33

van der Vleugel, B. M., van den Berg, D. P., & Staring, A. B. P. (2012). Trauma, psychosis, post-traumatic stress disorder and the application of EMDR. *Rivista di Psichiatria, 47*(2, Suppl. 1), 33S–38S. doi:10.1708/1071.11737

World Health Organization. (1993). *The ICD-10 classification of mental and behavioural disorders: Diagnostic criteria for research.* Geneva, Switzerland: Author.

TEN

EMDR Therapy + ICoNN 2 Category Case Examples

Intention: *To demonstrate to the reader, with clinical case material, the methodology for formulating cases using the AIP and ICoNN models in conjunction. To equip clinicians with the knowledge of how to target EMDR therapeutic endeavors with people diagnosed with schizophrenia or other psychoses.*

ICoNN 2

In the second category of presentations in the Indicating Cognitions of Negative Networks (ICoNN) approach, the psychotic phenomena are evident upon examination and cause distress resulting in a functional impairment. However, the psychological pathogen (dysfunctional memory network, DMN) cannot be identified in the standard way. As a consequence, the DMN cannot be understood and acknowledged by the person as the memory system that is driving the psychosis. However, strong emotions, which can be felt, are tracked back across an *affect bridge*, which allows identification of the DMN. This is then reprocessed in the standard way.

> "Certain emotions bridge the years and link unlikely places.
> Sometimes by this linking the sense of place is destroyed, and
> we are ourselves alone: the young man, the boy, the child."
> —V. S. Naipaul in The Mimic Men *(2011, p. 154)*

Case Material for ICoNN 2

Both of the people discussed in this chapter have cases of *body dysmorphophobia.* In one person, the beliefs were felt to be held with the intensity of an overvalued idea (Jude) and therefore nondelusional; in the other, the beliefs were thought to be held with delusional intensity (William).

Body Dysmorphophobia (Body Dysmorphic Disorder)—A Brief Description

Body dysmorphic disorder is described in the *International Classification of Diseases* (*ICD-10*) as follows:

> The essential feature is a persistent preoccupation with the possibility of having one or more serious and progressive physical disorders. Patients manifest persistent somatic complaints or a persistent preoccupation with their physical appearance. Normal or commonplace sensations and appearances are often interpreted by patients as abnormal and distressing, and attention is usually focused upon only one or two organs or systems of the body. Marked depression and anxiety are often present, and may justify additional diagnoses. (World Health Organization [WHO], 1993, p. 164)

Individuals with this condition are described as having pervasive and intrusive thoughts, which both Jude and William described. Both men spent a huge amount of time dwelling on their perceived problems. Neither was convinced that they had a mental illness and were hoping that the ultimate solution lay in the hands of a surgeon. William had already been turned down for plastic surgery, and Jude was hopeful he would persuade his general practitioner (GP) to make the referral. In both men, although they attended for a psychiatric assessment, they thought it perfunctory and had little expectation of receiving any real benefit. In Jude's case his presentation is coded in the *ICD-10* as *hypochondriacal disorder* (F45.2; WHO, 1993) and the fifth edition of the *Diagnostic and Statistical Manual of Mental Disorders* (*DSM-5*) codes it as *body dysmorphic disorder* (300.7; APA, 2013). The *DSM-5* also further specifies the level of insight into the disorder: The level of insight is assessed as ranging from good to poor, where present, and where insight is absent the delusional force of the beliefs can be noted. Jude had a poor level of insight, but was not delusional. Please note that it is often very difficult to assess the level of insight in these cases, especially given that the person is often extremely reluctant to discuss the topic (Phillips, Hart, Simpson, & Stein, 2014). In the case of Jude, he had come to "keep the psychiatrist happy," who wanted him assessed because he was unwilling to agree to take medication. In William's case, he was hoping to get a letter stating that he was "sane," so that he could take it to his plastic surgeon to persuade him to proceed with the requested surgery. These people often view plastic surgery as the "silver bullet" for their problem. As such, it is a common goal for people presenting with this group of disorders (Collins, Gonzalez, Gaudilliere, Shrestha, & Girod, 2014; de Brito et al., 2015; McConnell, Lee, Black, & Shriver, 2015; Tadisina, Chopra, & Singh, 2013; Woolley & Perry, 2015). Indeed, some plastic surgeons have proposed a role for surgery in the treatment of these cases: so-called eumorphic plastic surgery (de Brito, Nahas, & Ferreira, 2012; Morselli & Boriani, 2012). William's case is classified as *other persistent delusional disorders* (F22.8) in the *ICD-10* (WHO, 1993) and as *body dysmorphic disorder with absent insight/delusional beliefs* (300.7) in *DSM-5* (APA, 2013). Although body dysmorphic disorder is cited as having a point prevalence of 2%, which is higher than that for schizophrenia (1%), it remains relatively poorly researched and poorly understood (Phillips, 2014). People who present with this condition are typically reported to be difficult to engage, drop out readily from treatment, and are frequently nonconcordant with medications (Rashid, Khan, & Fineberg, 2014), and yet they experience substantial and significant suffering (Fang & Wilhelm, 2015; Gonzalez-Rodriguez, Molina-Andreu, Imaz Gurrutxaga, Catalan Campos, & Arroyo, 2014; Phillips et al., 2014; Rashid et al., 2014).

IConN 2 CASE: JUDE

Synopsis of Jude's History

This is the case of Jude, age 22. He presented to my new-patient clinic following his referral from my colleague who had seen and assessed him for medication in the National Health Service (NHS). Because Jude believed that there was nothing wrong with him—"I genuinely feel that there isn't a psychiatric problem!"—he had refused to take medication when he attended the NHS psychiatrist. Given that there was a delay in him making an appointment to see me (6 months from his NHS assessment), he had been persuaded to start fluoxetine by his GP. He had been taking this for 1 month when I did finally see him. His rationale for agreeing to the medication was that the GP had told him that it might "break the cycle of my thinking." He denied any trauma history and gave an unremarkable personal history that culminated in a successful education and his managing to secure a job in his chosen profession. There was a mild decrease in mood, evident upon examination, but nothing that reached diagnostic criteria for a comorbid affective disorder.

Presenting Issues at the Time of Jude's Psychiatric Assessment

- He believed that he has "big fat nipples"—he expanded upon this at assessment, explaining that they were like women's breasts.
- This belief was held at the intensity of an overvalued idea (i.e., *not reaching the intensity of belief of a delusion*).
- He believed that he would ultimately need surgery and stated that he saw his assessment with me as a step toward that goal.

History of Presenting Issues and Treatment

Jude gave a history of having presented to his GP with two conditions: phimosis (tight foreskin) and gynecomastia (hypertrophy of the breast tissue in a male). He attended the GP requesting circumcision for the phimosis and treatment, which might also be surgical, for the gynecomastia. Given that there was no abnormality of his chest, the GP felt that he was "having undue concern regarding the size of his nipples and this is causing a significant degree of anxiety and distress" and referred him to a NHS psychiatrist. The NHS colleague had given him a diagnosis of body dysmorphic disorder, which Jude was not at all comfortable with, and he was "unwilling" to consider medication for the condition. He obtained a private referral letter from his GP to my service but waited 6 months to arrange an appointment. As noted earlier, he had been on fluoxetine 20 mg daily for 1 month when I first saw him. He agreed to my completing a routine new-client psychiatric assessment and almost immediately informed me that he was there to keep his parents "quiet," as they were complaining that they found him "grumpy . . . unhelpful, and self-centered" (his report). He also hoped it would allow him to make progress toward his ultimate goal of surgery. His assessment was unremarkable apart from the symptoms already noted. He denied any history of trauma of any kind (i.e., "T" and "t" trauma), describing a happy childhood with his two sisters and birth parents. Big "T" trauma meets Criterion A of the DSM diagnostic criteria for posttraumatic stress disorder. Small "t" traumas are those that are not Criterion A positive events, but which nonetheless cause a substantial and significant emotional impact.

Case Formulation

Jude's formulation proposed that psychiatric disorder had occurred in a premorbidly healthy 22-year-old with no clear history of trauma and no touchstone events. As such, there was no clear access to a DMN and associated negative cognitions (NCs). Initially the main priority was successful engagement and the commencement of constructing a safe container for treatment.

Diagnosis

A full psychiatric assessment, which included history taking and mental state examination, was completed. Following this it was apparent that he believed that he had female breast tissue; he held his beliefs at the intensity of an overvalued idea when I assessed him. He was not reassured that he had a normal male chest anatomy despite having seen several doctors by the time he attended me. These phenomena are consistent with a diagnosis of body dysmorphophobia (nondelusional). In Jude's case this is coded in the ICD-10 as hypochondriacal disorder (F45.2, WHO, 1993), and in the DSM-5 as body dysmorphic disorder with poor insight (300.7; APA, 2013).

Treatment

Phases 1 and 2 were completed per standard protocol. In Jude's case the assessment went very quickly, as he essentially denied any relevant past history on open questioning. He was very upfront with his opinions and he was aware that I knew the diagnosis he had been given and also that he disagreed with it. Given the level of information to hand, from both the GP and his NHS psychiatrist, I chose not to attempt reality orientation or a detailed examination of his level of insight. I instead chose to connect with him around how such a belief must affect him emotionally. I acknowledged that he had worked extremely hard to get as far as here and reflected to him that he must feel very strong emotions connected with such a journey. He acknowledged that he did and shared that he felt embattled, given the attitude of medical professionals and his family. Still having time available in his 1-hour new-client slot, I asked him if anyone had ever talked him through an explanation of how we believe information and emotions are processed. He said no, and expressed a willingness to hear more. At this point I took him through the psychoeducation detailing the adaptive information processing (AIP) model. This completed our initial appointment and he agreed to a review appointment to explore how he could manage the emotions related to his current experiences.

Progress

When he returned for review, he said that following the last appointment he felt "a sense of hope" and now believed that he might be able to change how he felt about his body. Note that he was *not* saying that he no longer believed he had female breast tissue. He reported that he continued to spend excessive time looking at himself in the mirror. When asked if he could have three wishes, he stated he would ask for a "normal" chest, get rid of his "sticky-out thighs," and have a less pasty complexion. After reviewing the psychoeducation about eye movement desensitization and reprocessing (EMDR) therapy and AIP model with him, he requested that we work on how he felt about the appearance of his chest. The target here, according to the IConN model, is guided by the strong emotion that is being experienced in the client's body. I asked him to summon up in his mind the internal image that he had of his chest—what he perceived he saw when he looked in the mirror, or when others saw him. I next invited him to *notice* what he was experiencing in his body. He reported *anger*, and when I asked him where in his body he noticed it, I was not entirely surprised to hear him say his chest. At this stage, it may sometimes be possible to identify a negative and a positive cognition. If you do so, I recommend that you confirm that they are a good fit, once the DMN is ultimately identified.

Θεράπων—Therapón

As long as the person and the therapist are present intersubjectively and stay connected with the strongly experienced emotion, they have the potential to work on the DMN, albeit indirectly at first. Keep in mind that the word *therapist* has the same origins as the Greek word Θεράπων (*therapón*); this is the term used for the king's personal guard, who fought beside him in battle and during peacetime; these men were among his most trusted advisors. I think this a very appropriate icon for a therapist. We protect individuals in the intersubjective, allow them to do battle in relative safety, and at other times act as trustworthy advisors.

EMDR Therapy Treatment

Affect Bridge

In Jude's case he was able to develop an NC and a PC when he connected to the strong emotion he felt in his body:

> NC: "I am not good enough"; Subjective Units of Distress Scale (SUDS) score = 4/10
> PC: "I am acceptable"; Validity of Cognition (VoC) score = 4/7

Using the standard method of an affect bridge, I invited Jude to do the following:

> Connect to and notice the feeling in your body. Breathe into it.
> Now, allow yourself to float back in time; go to a time in your
> life when you felt this same feeling. Whatever comes up comes
> up. There is no right or wrong. Trust your mind where to go.
> Trust the process.

This is carried out with dual attention stimulation/bilateral stimulation (DAS/BLS).

PWM: What comes up for you now?
Jude: *I'm in the car with my sisters [one older and one younger]. I'm sitting between them in the back seat of the family car. It is sometime in the mid-1980s.*
PWM: Go with that. [DAS/BLS] What are you experiencing emotionally right now?
Jude: *I feel ashamed.*
PWM: What is happening that is bringing up this emotion?
Jude: *My father has the window rolled down and is talking to a man through the window.*
PWM: Go with that. [DAS/BLS] What comes up for you now?
Jude: *It's school; the last day of term. I'm 18 and I feel good.*

This felt like dissociation and an attempt to escape from the negatively valenced affect of what he had been looking at, so I invited him to return to the target of the car and his father.

PWM: If it's OK I would like you to return to the experience of shame and the image of your father.
Jude: *Got it.*
PWM: Go with that. [DAS/BLS]
Jude: *My father is joking with a man through the open car window. They're talking about me and saying how difficult it must be to have me, a boy, in the car. The girls are very good and well behaved in contrast to me. They are joking at my expense.*
PWM: Go with that. [DAS/BLS]

After a few more sets we had to finish due to time constraints. This was an incomplete session. I used the safe/calm place, which he had selected and installed with DAS/BLS earlier, his bedroom. The standard protocol was followed.

Next Session

At review Jude reported that he had experienced quite vivid dreams for the week following the session. He noticed that he was more comfortable with his body and appearance. His time spent in front of the mirror was reduced by 50%, and he wanted to work on getting to a point where he was not doing so at all. The progress he experienced acted as a great encouragement for Jude, strengthened the therapeutic rapport, and helped motivate him to continue EMDR therapy. When clients report active dreaming, which is not the stereotypical, recurrent dreaming seen in posttraumatic nightmares, I inform them that this is a good sign; normal information processing occurs during dreaming. There is no health without mental health, there is no mental health without healthy sleep, and there is no healthy sleep without healthy dreaming.

The standard protocol was followed and we returned to the target of the car:

Image: Being in the back of the car
Emotion: "It feels difficult."
Body: "The pit of my stomach"
NC: "I am a bad boy."[1]
PC: "I am a good boy."[1]

When distilling the NC/PC, I became aware of a sense that there was a shift in the Gestalt of Jude. He felt, to me, like a much younger person. At this stage I usually ask the following; here is an extract of the session:

PWM: How old do you *feel*, right now?
Jude: 6.
PWM: Is it OK if we do some more of the eye movements and see if things change?
Jude: Yes.
PWM: Go with that. [DAS/BLS] What comes up for you now?

At this point the desensitization was progressing well and the SUDS scores were coming down. Then he got a strong uncomfortable feeling in the pit of his stomach. He became very evasive of my questions and would not talk about what his mind had settled upon. So I once again closed the session, in keeping with the standard protocol, as we were running out of session time. There were a couple of weeks of break between this and his next session because of a seasonal holiday.

Next Session

He reported that the last session was "progressive" for him. He knew that he had experienced some nightmares during the intervening period, but had no recollection of the themes. The event that he was reluctant to discuss at the last session had been on his mind. At this point I spoke with him about my role as his therapist. I explained that this was a safe, nonjudgmental container for working through the DMN and reflected with him on his progress to date. A useful aspect of the EMDR therapy method is that clients can be made aware that the locus of control lies with them. I reminded him that he need not tell me anything that he did not want to. I wondered out loud with him whether maybe there was a part of him that wanted to deal with this event. He agreed and we proceeded to further EMDR reprocessing.

---

[1] SUDS and VoC were not ascertained on this occasion, as the younger "self"/ego state had great difficulty in completing these. This is not at all unusual. When working in this area with young "parts," allow yourself to be guided by the emotion that is experienced in the body; don't get hung up on getting a SUDS rating or a VoC score.

Jude shared the following event as being the one that had been on his mind since the last session:

Jude: *I'm 6 or 7 years old. I feel terrible—ashamed. I have been playing "doctors and nurses" with my younger sister and she is taken for her bath. I hear my mother shriek and my father rushes into my room. He is angry and tells me, "You can't be my son!" and puts me in the car. I am cowering in the front passenger footwell and he tells me he is taking me to the police. He drives for what seems a long time. He doesn't actually take me to the police, although I am expecting him to. Suddenly we are back at home. We go inside the house and the matter is never spoken of again.*

PWM: Thank you for sharing that—it is very brave of you. I could sense that you were experiencing strong emotions as you spoke. Am I correct?

Jude: *Yes. It was scary. It is good to talk about it . . . finally.*

Acknowledging how you are experiencing the intersubjective provides the opportunity to correct any mis-attunement. This is what Dworkin describes in the relational/intersubjective interweave (Dworkin, 2005, 2015). We agreed to work on this new target in the next session, as it had taken the majority of the current session to articulate the fragmentary story of the incident. It is very important to acknowledge the exhaustion and strong affect that the client experiences when connecting to and working on a DMN. This helps to maintain a strong enough therapeutic alliance that allows the client and therapist to remain present in and work within the intersubjective space.

Next Session

He felt that therapy was positive and that he was experiencing a shift. The thought about having breasts was much less intrusive, and his checking himself in the mirror had continued to decrease in frequency and intensity. Jude was very pleased with the progress and felt hopeful.

Target: He wanted to target the image where he saw his younger "self," cowering in the front footwell of the car.
Emotion: Fear
NC: "I am bad"; SUDS = 7 ½/10
PC: "I am good"; VoC = 3/7

This target was processed with the standard protocol. Jude then felt that the younger self in the car needed more support. At this point, as Jude was sensing and talking about being aware of himself at different ages, I explored with him whether there was another part of him that wanted to help out. He was conscious that his 22-year-old adult self now wanted to talk with the child in the car.

PWM: Picture "yourself as you are now" going to the "child part of you who is in the car." Follow your impulse to talk with him and tell him what you know he needs to know. Go with that. [DAS/BLS] What comes up for you now?

Jude: *He's feeling better now.*

In the psychoeducation about parts/selves/ego states, I also use the metaphor of a "Russian doll"—*a matryoshka doll*—and I have one in my office. We had previously spoken about this model after he had noticed that he was experiencing himself at different ages.

PWM: Remember the Russian doll that I showed you? It represents the different parts of ourselves that make up our whole self.
Jude: *Yes.*
PWM: If these dolls represent you, who is within whom? Is the child within the adult or the other way around?
Jude: *The child is within me.*
PWM: Go with that. [DAS/BLS] What comes up for you now?
Jude: *It's just me now and the room feels lighter.*
PWM: Go with that. [DAS/BLS] What comes up for you now?
Jude: *The image of the car is not as clear. [SUDS 5/10]*
PWM: Go with that. [DAS/BLS] What comes up for you now?
Jude: *The image has gone. [SUDS 5/10]*
PWM: Go with that. [DAS/BLS] What comes up for you now?
Jude: *Looking at the experience from very far away. [SUDS 4/10]*
PWM: Go with that. [DAS/BLS] What comes up for you now?
Jude: *I'm above the car looking in. [SUDS 3/10]*
PWM: Go with that. [DAS/BLS] What comes up for you now?
Jude: *It's just a dot. [SUDS 0/10]*
PWM: Go with that. [DAS/BLS] What comes up for you now?
Jude: *Nothing.*

The PC was installed per standard protocol to a VoC of 6/7. Jude believed this was appropriate and it got no higher after several sets. The session closed.

Jude then went travelling in South America shortly after this, and I reviewed his case about 1 year later. After his last session with me, before he took his road trip, he had reduced and stopped his fluoxetine on his own initiative, as he wanted to be medication-free when he was traveling. He was now back and had secured a new job. He had no concerns about his body image and reflected that, prior to therapy with me, the thought had been on his mind all the time.

Note Regarding Medication

Although medication was used in the treatment of this case, had I seen Jude sooner he would probably not have commenced medication. He was able to stop it easily without any difficulties. Fluoxetine leaves the body very gradually, and in my clinical experience it does not usually result in any major discontinuation problems.

Think

When I presented this case to colleagues from a psychodynamic perspective, the following points were raised. Jude identified with the feminine as "good" and his maleness as "bad." Interestingly, at the same time he presented to his GP with gynecomastia, he also presented with phimosis—there is no further information available on this, but I wonder if this may have been related to his desire to decrease his sense of maleness at a subconscious level. The key distressing aspect of the traumatic experience for him was his father's rejection of him as his son. He dissociated from this memory network to maintain attachment with his father, and this appears to have led to a degree of detachment from both his father and his own inherent maleness. A desire to identify with the females in the family, whom he saw as good, manifested as an experience of feeling he had begun to develop female breasts. However, this was in conflict with his core sense of self and therefore the psychological dissonance was experienced as distress, resulting in the body dysmorphic disorder. Once the original trauma was fully processed and the attachment with the father maintained without the need for dissociation, the psychotic adaptation and narrative was no longer necessary. This is similar to the cases that Steinman (2009) presents in his book *Treating the "Untreatable."* Jude's case illustrates how the framing of the case within the AIP model with the application of the ICoNN approach allows the identification of the DMN that needs to be reprocessed. Once the DMN is metabolized, the presenting issues abate, as expected, because there is no longer a need for the adaptive response. This psychodynamic understanding of the case, although interesting, is not necessary for application of the ICoNN approach.

ICoNN 2 CASE: WILLIAM

Synopsis of William's History

This is the case of William, age 31. He presented to the outpatient clinic following a referral from a colleague who had spoken with him briefly when he attended his wife's psychiatric assessment. He gave a 10-year history of preoccupations about his appearance. He had undergone corrective cosmetic dental work for antibiotic staining of his teeth. He was currently preoccupied with the appearance of his ears, which he thought were ugly. These thoughts had worsened over the past 2 years after noticing what he assessed as significant hair loss. He had been treated for low mood by his GP with fluoxetine. When this was increased recently to 60 mg he had experienced suicidal ideation and it was reduced again. Strong comorbid preventative factors to completion of suicide were present. The suicidal thoughts abated when the fluoxetine was decreased to 40 mg, but with no change to the preoccupations and ruminations about his appearance.

Presenting Issues at the Time of William's Psychiatric Assessment

- Preoccupation about losing his hair (*GP letter noted only minor male pattern baldness and family attempts to reassure him that it is barely noticeable*)
- He is convinced that he has "ugly" prominent ears that have become even more obvious since he has begun to lose his hair
- Mood reactive and stable—no evidence of major depressive or anxiety disorder

History of Presenting Issues and Treatment

William's concerns about his appearance have been present with him for more than 10 years. He had worries about his teeth, which had become stained after he needed a tetracycline antibiotic as a child. He had corrective cosmetic dental surgery and is pleased with the outcome. He has always been conscious of having "ugly" ears, and this became a preoccupation for him after he saw photographs of himself at a social event. He frequently uses products to attempt to reverse hair loss and was dissatisfied, at the time of his initial presentation, with the appearance of his hairline. Previous referral to NHS psychiatry took place when he began pulling his hair out in distress following the death of his father 7 years ago. He did not feel there was any connection to the death of his father and saw it as a "red herring." He attended an NHS psychiatrist and cognitive behavioral (CBT) therapist, who, he reports, both told him there was nothing they could do; his GP continued fluoxetine. He subsequently attended several plastic surgeons, requesting that his ears be pinned back, as he believed that this would make his hair loss less obvious. He had recently found a surgeon in London willing to do the work, but he had been seen without a GP referral letter. When I asked about this, he was evasive about whether he had given a full account of his mental health. He felt positive about the possibility of surgery going ahead, and his main goal in attending me was to obtain a letter to give to the plastic surgeon stating that he did not have body dysmorphophobia.

Case Formulation

William's formulation proposed that psychiatric disorder had occurred in a premorbidly healthy 31-year-old with no clear history of trauma and no touchstone events. As such, there was no clear access to a DMN and associated NCs. Initially the main priority was successful engagement and the commencement of constructing a safe container for treatment.

Diagnosis

A full psychiatric assessment, which included history taking and mental state examination, was completed. Following this it was apparent that he believed that he had abnormally prominent ears; his beliefs appeared to be held at the intensity of a delusion. He was not reassured by the surgical opinion of several plastic surgeons, his GP, or by comments from his family, including his wife. Despite having seen several surgeons, he had continued to search for one willing to perform the desired surgery (*ear pinning*). He believed he had identified one by the time he attended me. These phenomena are consistent with the diagnosis of *body dysmorphophobia* (*delusional*). In William's case this is coded in the *ICD-10* as *delusional disorder* (F22.0; WHO, 1993) and in the *DSM-5* as *body dysmorphic disorder with absent insight/delusional beliefs* (300.7; APA, 2013).

Treatment

Phases 1 and 2 were completed per standard protocol. Similar to Jude, William was treated with a selective serotonin reuptake inhibitor (SSRI). He was on fluoxetine, 40 mg daily, but remained symptomatic. The initial assessment went very quickly, as he essentially denied any relevant past history on open questioning. He was supported by his wife and requested her input. She provided essential collateral history and I was able to see, in vivo, how her attempts to reassure him held no comfort for him. He was aware that I knew the diagnosis he had been given previously and also that he disagreed with it. As with Jude, I chose not to attempt reality orientation or a detailed examination of his level of insight, instead choosing to connect with him through the emotional impact his beliefs were having upon him. I acknowledged that he must feel ambivalent about attending, given his past experience. He acknowledged that his main goal was to get the "all clear" for surgery to proceed. I reflected to him that we could work with his very strong emotions connected to his "embattled position," given the approach medical professionals were taking to his requests for intervention. At this point I outlined how we might work together to help him process the strong emotions related to his current experiences. He agreed.

Next Session

He returned for review and started the session by adding the details about the tetracycline staining of his teeth and the subsequent cosmetic dental work. I thanked him for the additional information and saw this as demonstrative of his willingness to share information that could have been considered, by some, as evidence of preoccupations about his appearance. The importance of building a container that is perceived by the client as nonjudgmental and safe is a *need* and not a mere *want*. Remember, needs are nonnegotiable. Good therapy cannot take place in an unsafe or inappropriate container. The *therapóntes* (θεράποντες) did not keep the king out of the battle; they kept him safe *in* the midst of battle and were trusted advisors who supported the king as he sought to make good choices. They did not make the choices for him. This is the embodiment of the good therapist.

In William's case I now proceeded through the standard psychoeducation with him. He had no difficulty in following and understanding it. A safe/calm place was chosen and installed with DAS/BLS; he had a good response. I gave him the feedback that this is usually indicative that a person can utilize the EMDR therapy method effectively, and he felt positive about that. As a secondary safe/calm place I installed the past–present–future room, in accordance with the script outlined previously.

In respect to our target for therapy, William wished to work on his male pattern baldness. I outlined to him that the current concerns about his hair might have a number of specific DMNs related to the Gestalt of his baldness. The targeting, according to the ICoNN model, is guided by the strong emotion being experienced in the client's body. I asked him to summon up in his mind the internal image that he had of his appearance—what he perceived he saw when he looked in the mirror, or when others saw him. I next invited him to *notice* what he was experiencing in his body—he reported *anger* (SUDS = 6/10), and when I asked him where in his body he noticed it, he stated that it was a generalized experience. At this stage, he was unable to identify a negative cognition.

Affect Bridge

In William's case he was able to float back across several affect bridges connected to the strong emotion of anger that he felt in his body. Using the standard methodology for an affect bridge process, I invited William to do the following:

> Connect to and notice the feeling in your body. Breathe into it.
> Now, allow yourself to float back in time; go to a time in your
> life when you felt this same feeling. Whatever comes up comes
> up. There is no right or wrong. Trust your mind where to go.
> Trust the process.

This is carried out with DAS/BLS.

PWM: What comes up for you now?
W^{m}: *It's 4 years ago. I'm studying for exams and pulling my hair out in anger.*
PWM: Go with that. [DAS/BLS] What comes up for you right now?
W^{m}: *I'm playing sports and realize in the changing room that I am losing my hair. I'm 21 and I'm thinking it's a nightmare.*
PWM: Go with that. [DAS/BLS] What comes up for you right now?
W^{m}: *I'm at a family wedding and someone mentions my hair—that I am losing it—I feel embarrassed. I'm 24.*
PWM: Go with that. [DAS/BLS] What comes up for you right now?
W^{m}: *I'm 16 and at a BBQ with friends. I overhear two girls talking about me. They say that it is a pity I'm "so ugly," as I am a nice person.*
PWM: Go with that. [DAS/BLS] What comes up for you right now?
W^{m}: *I'm walking home from school. I'm 11. An older boy shouts out, "You going to my school now, big ears?" I'm thinking, "Do I have big ears?"*
PWM: What emotion are you experiencing now?
W^{m}: *I'm feeling fear.*

This series of affect bridges has indicated a number of possible targets for reprocessing, and all were noted at the time. At this point I asked him to connect to his body and pay attention to which of the targets had the strongest emotion attached to it now. It was the following: *I'm 16 and at a BBQ with friends. I overhear two girls talking about me. They say that it is a pity I'm "so ugly," as I am a nice person.* Rather than start with this most intense DMN, it is best to start with the earliest if the person is not averse to doing so. In some cases you may find that the person needs to strengthen the therapeutic alliance and experience success by reprocessing a target with a lower SUDS score.

> Event: *I'm walking home from school. I'm 11. An older boy shouts out, "You going to my school now, big ears?" I'm thinking, "Do I have big ears?"*
> Target: The key aspect of this is the tone of the older boy's voice.
> Body: "Throughout my body"
> Emotion: Fear
> NC: "I am in danger"; SUDS = 7/10
> PC: "I am safe"; VoC = 3/10

This target was processed according to the standard protocol. There was a strong sense that his "adult self" wanted to stand up for the "child self." This came up in reprocessing when he pictured his adult self "coaching" the child self. He achieved SUDS to 0 and VoC to 7.

As there was sufficient time, we moved on to the next event identified on the journey across the series of affect bridges: *I'm 16 and at a BBQ with friends. I overhear two girls talking about me. They say that it is a pity I'm "so ugly," as I am a nice person.*

Target: The words being said by the two girls
Body: Stomach
Emotion: Shame
NC: "I am not good enough"; SUDS = 10/10
PC: He was unable to articulate one.[2]

Next Session

On review of his work in the last session, William felt "calmed" and both he and his wife noted that his behavior around his hair had improved; of note is that there had been a decrease in the time he spent grooming. He had no negatively valenced affect attached to either of the targets that were reprocessed, even the incomplete session. This provided a good opportunity to emphasize that EMDR therapy engages the innate information processing system of the person, and so metabolism of the DMN will often continue in between sessions. This, he opined, helped him feel "very hopeful." He reported that he remained "annoyed" if he perceived that other people did not feel he was looking good/attractive. The general Gestalt of his baldness generated an SUDS score of 6/10.

We now reviewed the other touchstone events that he had uncovered in the affect bridge process. The following touchstone incident that took place when he was 24 was now neutral: *I'm at a family wedding and someone mentions my hair—that I am losing it—I feel embarrassed.* When he thought of this he offered that he now thought of a current issue in work with two colleagues who would banter with him and make jokes about his hair, at his expense. Although he reported a good relationship with both men and didn't think that they were bullying or being malicious, he was conscious of laughing it off, only to subsequently ruminate on what had been said.

At this stage when we attempted to delineate the standard target for reprocessing, he was unable to do so and could only access the Gestalt of the event. In such a case we are dealing with a categorical shift to an ICoNN 4 type of target.

---

[2]This may occur at this stage. Do not waste time trying to get a PC, as the primary element that you are focusing on is the *emotional valence* being experienced in the person's body. If a PC is not spontaneously generated, after desensitization you can usually develop one much more easily at that point with the person. Do not "give" the person a PC, as the ability to articulate one is important, in my opinion, and you may cause a rupture in the therapeutic alliance (Safran, Muran, & Eubanks-Carter, 2011). The target was processed according to the standard protocol. On this occasion the session was incomplete and his SUDS score decreased only as far as 6/10. The standard protocol for closing an incomplete session was applied successfully.

We will discuss this session in the ICoNN 4 section that follows. This DMN was processed over two sessions and there was a subsequent improvement in behavior and a decrease in his preoccupation with his hair. He had a number of other sessions of reprocessing that adhered to the standard protocol and one that generated a future template to look at the experience of having his hair cut. This was successfully installed and he was able to do this without distress in vivo. At the end of therapy he had experienced a diminution in his feelings about losing his hair and was no longer preoccupied about the appearance of his ears. He was aware that, given his familial genetics, it was likely that he would lose his hair eventually, but his wife confirmed that there was a substantial improvement in his attitude toward this thought and that he was much more balanced. Here we observe how the three-pronged aspect of the protocol guides the treatment planning. We processed *past* events that generated the DMN; we processed *present* triggers and installed effective and adaptive *future* templates to enable appropriate behavioral choices and functioning.

Note Regarding Medication

After the last session his fluoxetine was reduced to 20 mg and he had stopped this himself by 1 month later.

Take-Home for ICoNN 2 Cases

The initial phases 1 and 2 were completed according to the guidance described in a previous chapter. A robust therapeutic alliance developed, which provided a suitable container for working with the men described in the cases in this chapter. It is vitally important that the initial contact not be rushed. As noted for the ICoNN 1 cases, it may be neither feasible nor appropriate to complete a full new-patient psychiatric assessment within a routine new-patient slot. In my experience, once such individuals discover a safe, compassionate, and nonjudgmental space, they begin to share their experiences more freely. For many this will be the first time that they have found such a place, and their stories may come jetting out. Clinicians who try to "get it all down" at this stage will feel like they are trying to drink water from a fire hydrant. Slow and steady is the course to be set. Those who have researched delusional disorders (Fear, 2013; Fear, McMonagle, & Healy, 1998; Fear, Sharp, & Healy, 1996) note how challenging it can be to gain the trust of these individuals. If the ICoNN guidance for the initial phases is followed, clients ought to feel safe enough to be vulnerable enough to share their beliefs. This is a very brave step for clients, as they usually experience a lot of shame around their beliefs. Shame is a huge block to creating the intimacy needed to do good therapy because clients become reluctant to share the "shameful" content of their minds, seeing this as leaving them too vulnerable to rejection or judgment (Brown, 2012). Keep in mind that the processing of the DMN is embedded in the three-pronged protocol—past, present, and future. By working on the past events, the present triggers, and the future templates, we enable the person to manage the past, be grounded in the present, and connect to positive and adaptive future templates, resulting in healthy function.

Key Points for ICoNN 2

1. Build a safe container for treatment using Caelian principles.
2. Listen and allow clients to tell their stories, and affirm them by acknowledging that these experiences are real.
3. Be actively neutral—seek neither to confirm nor deny the person's experiences; that is not your role.
4. Ensure that you give enough time to each client session.
5. Facilitate clients' connection with their emotions and understand how they feel about the reported experiences that they are having. Use this strongly charged emotion to travel back across an *affect bridge* to identify the cryptic DMN.
6. Pay attention to the emotions you are experiencing in your body as the therapist.
7. Adhere to the standard eight-phase, three-pronged protocol for processing the DMN, once it is identified.
8. Standard methodologies for blocked processing can be utilized.

REFERENCES

American Psychiatric Association. (2013). *Diagnostic and statistical manual of mental disorders* (5th ed.). Washington, DC: Author.

Brown, B. (2012). *Daring greatly: How the courage to be vulnerable transforms the way we live, love, parent, and lead* (1st ed.). New York, NY: Gotham.

Collins, B., Gonzalez, D., Gaudilliere, D. K., Shrestha, P., & Girod, S. (2014). Body dysmorphic disorder and psychological distress in orthognathic surgery patients. *Journal of Oral and Maxillofacial Surgery, 72*(8), 1553-1558. doi:10.1016/j.joms.2014.01.011

de Brito, M. J., de Almeida Arruda Felix, G., Nahas, F. X., Tavares, H., Cordas, T. A., Dini, G. M., & Ferreira, L. M. (2015). Body dysmorphic disorder should not be considered an exclusion criterion for cosmetic surgery. *Journal of Plastic, Reconstructive, and Aesthetic Surgery, 68*(2), 270–272. doi:10.1016/j.bjps.2014.09.046

de Brito, M. J., Nahas, F. X., & Ferreira, L. M. (2012). Should plastic surgeons operate on patients diagnosed with body dysmorphic disorder? *Plastic and Reconstructive Surgery, 129*(2), 406e–407e. doi:10.1097/PRS.0b013e31823aeee7

Dworkin, M. (2005). *EMDR and the relational imperative: The therapeutic relationship in EMDR treatment*. New York, NY: Routledge.

Dworkin, M. (2015). *Relational EMDR: The synergy of procedure, therapeutic attachment, and intersubjectivity—implications for an expanded conceptualization of adaptive information processing and EMDR psychotherapy*. Retrieved from http://emdr-web.org/relational-emdr/

Fang, A., & Wilhelm, S. (2015). Clinical features, cognitive biases, and treatment of body dysmorphic disorder. *Annual Review of Clininical Psychology, 11*, 187–212. doi:10.1146/annurev-clinpsy-032814-112849

Fear, C. (2013). Recent developments in the management of delusional disorders. *Advances in Psychiatric Treatment, 19*, 212–220.

Fear, C., Sharp, H., & Healy, D. (1996). Cognitive processes in delusional disorders. *British Journal of Psychiatry, 168*(1), 61–67.

Fear, C. F., McMonagle, T., & Healy, D. (1998). Delusional disorders: Boundaries of a concept. *European Psychiatry, 13*(4), 210–218. doi:10.1016/S0924-9338(98)80006-0

Gonzalez-Rodriguez, A., Molina-Andreu, O., Imaz Gurrutxaga, M. L., Catalan Campos, R., & Arroyo, M. B. (2014). A descriptive retrospective study of the treatment and outpatient service use in a clinical group of delusional disorder patients. *Revista de Psiquiatría y Salud Mental, 7*(2), 64–71. doi:10.1016/j.rpsm.2013.01.004

McConnell, L. K., Lee, W. W., Black, D. W., & Shriver, E. M. (2015). Beauty is in the eye of the beholder: Body dysmorphic disorder in ophthalmic plastic and reconstructive surgery. *Ophthalmic Plastic and Reconstructive Surgery, 31*(1), e3–e6. doi:10.1097/IOP.0000000000000019

Morselli, P. G., & Boriani, F. (2012). Should plastic surgeons operate on patients diagnosed with body dysmorphic disorders? *Plastic and Reconstructive Surgery, 130*(4), 620e–622e; author reply 622e. doi:10.1097/PRS.0b013e318262f65b

Naipaul, V. S. (2011). *The mimic men.* London, England: Picador.

Phillips, K. A. (2014). Body dysmorphic disorder: Common, severe and in need of treatment research. *Psychotherapy and Psychosomatics, 83*(6), 325–329. doi:10.1159/000366035

Phillips, K. A., Hart, A. S., Simpson, H. B., & Stein, D. J. (2014). Delusional versus nondelusional body dysmorphic disorder: Recommendations for *DSM-5. CNS Spectrums, 19*(1), 10–20. doi:10.1017/S1092852913000266

Rashid, H., Khan, A. A., & Fineberg, N. A. (2014). Adjunctive antipsychotic in the treatment of body dysmorphic disorder: A retrospective naturalistic case note study. *International Journal of Psychiatry in Clinical Practice,* 1–6. doi:10.3109/13651501.2014.981546

Safran, J. D., Muran, J. C., & Eubanks-Carter, C. (2011). Repairing alliance ruptures. *Psychotherapy, 48,* 80–87.

Steinman, I. (2009). *Treating the "untreatable": Healing in the realms of madness.* London, England: Karnac Books.

Tadisina, K. K., Chopra, K., & Singh, D. P. (2013). Body dysmorphic disorder in plastic surgery. *Eplasty, 13,* ic48.

Woolley, A. J., & Perry, J. D. (2015). Body dysmorphic disorder: Prevalence and outcomes in an oculofacial plastic surgery practice. *American Journal of Ophthalmology.* doi:10.1016/j.ajo.2015.02.014

World Health Organization. (1993). *The ICD-10 classification of mental and behavioural disorders: Diagnostic criteria for research.* Geneva, Switzerland: Author.

ELEVEN

EMDR Therapy + IConn 3 Category Case Examples

Intention: *To demonstrate to the reader, with clinical case material, the methodology for formulating cases using the AIP and IConn models in conjunction. To equip clinicians with the knowledge of how to target EMDR therapeutic endeavors with people diagnosed with schizophrenia or other psychoses.*

IConn 3

"The best thing is to see you as people."
—*Prof. Marius Romme, speaking at the launch*
of the Hearing Voices Network in Dublin, Ireland, 2015

In this third category of presentations in the Indicating Cognitions of Negative Networks (IConn) model, the psychotic phenomena are evident, causing distress and a functional impairment. However, the psychological pathogen (dysfunctional memory network, DMN) cannot be identified in the standard way and strong emotions *cannot* be tracked back across an *affect bridge*. The main phenomena that characterize this category of IConn cases are "heard voices" that can be spoken with. The voices have been described as a "peopled wound" (McCarthy-Jones, 2012). They act as a proxy for the DMN. Reprocessing is ultimately accomplished using an ego-state approach (Watkins, 1993, 2005)/voice dialogue approach (Stone & Stone, 1989) with the facilitation of the dual attention stimulation/bilateral stimulation (DAS/BLS) elements of the eye movement desensitization and reprocessing (EMDR) therapy method.

"We need to reclaim this ordinary human experience."
—*Jacqui Dillon, Hearing Voices Network,*
national chair, England, Ireland, 2015

Case Material for ICoNN 3

In this category the person may present with some ICoNN 1 and 2 targets. If this is the case, it is important to seek agreement from the system of parts/selves/ego states before proceeding to process the DMN. This will build the best foundation for successful work with the people whom we group under the ICoNN 3 banner. People who present hearing voices will have already internalized many stigmatizing self-beliefs. It is vitally important that the therapist work to develop the first three features of effective psychotherapy: an emotionally charged relationship, a therapeutic environment, and a rationale/myth that provides a plausible explanation for the symptoms (Frank, 1961). In the ICoNN 3 category, in regard to psychoeducation, experience gathered by Romme and his colleagues from the Hearing Voices Networks around the globe notes that voice-hearers prefer the term *normalization* in regard to working with their voice-hearing, rather than *acceptance*. This is especially relevant to those voice-hearers who are survivors of childhood abuse (CA), as they often experience voices with the characteristics of their abusers (Romme, 2009). Here it is understandably better to talk of normalization rather than acceptance of their voices, as the latter can be perceived as asking clients to accept their abusers. The case that we will discuss next is a case in point; we will refer to him as Oscar. Oscar experienced abuse in the form of sexual abuse by three separate and unconnected abusers. Some of his voices have the characteristics of these abusers.

It is important that we tell voice-hearers that their voices are real and have meaning. Sadly, people are still being told that it is dangerous to talk to or acknowledge the voices. People understandably find it difficult to trust us to act as their therapists if we deny their experiences by taking such a stance. The international community of voice-hearers has been growing and developing its resources. This diverse group is emboldened by the work of the visionary psychiatrist Professor Marius Romme and his wife Dr. Sandra Escher, both of whom call for voice-hearers to be emancipated. The Declaration of Melbourne—made November 21, 2013—has acted as a lightning rod for this constituency of people and the professionals who support them. Currently it is attracting like-minded organizations and mental health advocates. Please take the time to read it at the following link: https://www.mindaustralia.org.au/assets/docs/Resources/Hearing%20voices%20declaration.pdf

The concept of using an *ego-state approach* (Watkins, 1993, 2005) with the facilitation of the DAS/BLS elements of the EMDR therapy method was first introduced to me when I heard Carol Forgash teach on the topic. John Watkins acknowledges the common pedigree that ego-state work shares with Jungian principles such as active imagination (Watkins, 1998). I later discovered the *voice dialogue approach* (Stone & Stone, 1989) and could see many similarities between these methods, and was not at all surprised to discover that Hal Stone had trained as a Jungian psychoanalyst. Indeed, I understand that he met C. G. Jung himself.

Constant attention to maintaining a safe container for therapy is vital. In these cases it is useful to think of yourself as more of a facilitator working within a group dynamic. If the voices do indeed represent, iconically, "a peopled wound"/DMN, they must all be engaged in the therapeutic process at some point; otherwise, the wound will be incompletely treated. Because these people have been traumatized and that trauma represents a threat to attachment, a significant and substantial level of dissociation results. Remember that the function of dissociation in trauma is to maintain attachment (Freyd & Birrell, 2013). In the case of Oscar, the initial work in phases 1 and 2 was protracted and psychoeducation very limited initially, until he felt safe. By paying attention to how I felt with Oscar, I became aware of a very young "self" being present. This "self" insisted on certain things: sitting close to me by pulling his chair near to mine; biting his nails and speaking in a less assertive, high-toned voice that was child-like. As I began to engage with this younger disowned self, Oscar reported beginning to see and hear the abusers manifesting in the room. Initially this was only apparent by seeing Oscar flinch and begin to respond to the voices—telling them to "shut up" and not to be "rude." Once it was clear that Oscar was hearing voices and seeing visual hallucinations in the room, I worked to share the ICoNN rationale with him. This was done in a very gradual way and great care was taken not to suggest to Oscar that the experiences were not real. Throughout this he remained on high doses of antipsychotic and antidepressant medications. In the first instance it is important to manage your own emotions in this dynamic—pay attention to them. Colleagues who work in this area have described that when they have sought to suppress or deny their own feelings while in the therapy space, the voice-hearer has reported that parts that were manifesting have "left" because they felt "unsafe" or didn't trust the therapist. They stated that this was because the parts experienced the therapist as inauthentic. Obviously I am not suggesting that you do your own work in the session with the person, but it means that if something comes up for you that pulls you out of the intersubjective, you will experience a rupture in the therapeutic alliance. Appropriate, skilled supervision is very important when working with this constituency of people. I was able to complete phase 2 with Oscar and eventually he was able to cope with items 1 and 2 of the "1. . . 2. . . 3. . . " psychoeducation model described earlier in the book. As is typical of such cases, we returned to stabilization and resourcing many times. Oscar continues to find normalization of the voices of his abusers challenging, but he has experienced that behind each of these abuser's voices is a traumatized part of himself. At this stage I taught him about the adaptive information processing (AIP) model and the psychobiological response to threat. We worked on the normalization of his felt emotion, which was connected to the experience of voice-hearing and visual hallucinations. Oscar found this very affirming and empowering. He noted that he experienced this as someone really hearing what he was saying. He at last felt understood. This point of feeling heard and listened to was reached in therapy with me, but only after he had spent several years in a psychiatric system that he experienced as disregarding him. These professionals ignored the content of what he was telling them and failed to deal with the cause of the psychosis: part of the legacy of Jaspers. At this juncture I want to emphasize that doing the basics well is vital to making progress, and the first basic skill is to listen well.

Caelian Foundations

I have attempted to construct an easy-to-follow paradigm—*CAEL*—that guides the initial work in therapy. There are other models, and you will no doubt already use one of them. Let the clients be your guide. Ask them if they feel that you understand them. "Listen and talk and listen and talk and listen and talk," as one voice-hearer told a conference audience in Dublin. Keep in mind that, like a *therapón* (Greek term meaning "trusted advisor") to a king, we are not actually fighting the person's fight or making decisions for him or her; we have a role to play, but it ought to be one of empowerment, not paternalism. Another voice-hearer, John, said, "The way ahead is winding… together we can make it through." For many mental health professionals this will require us to do what Rory Doody, a voice-hearer and advocate, called "looking through a new pair of eyes." The open dialogue approach developed in Western Lapland has demonstrated that 75% of people describing these experiences, typically characterized by psychiatry as psychosis, have been capable of returning to work or academia within 2 years, with around 20% being on antipsychotic medication at 2-year follow-up (Holmesland, Seikkula, & Hopfenbeck, 2014; Holmesland, Seikkula, Nilsen, Hopfenbeck, & Erik Arnkil, 2010; Seikkula & Alakare, 2004; Seikkula & Olson, 2003). These statistics are laden with hope. When we show people that we accept that their experiences are real, we help to restore human dignity and void the distinction of "them and us." The open dialogue approach articulates this in a powerful phrase, "be with, not do to." By being with Oscar I was able to help him to understand that his experiences were common to humanity and that they had meaning. This gave him hope. This is why voice-hearing needs to be reclaimed as an ordinary human experience. Oscar's experience of finding a place of understanding warrants my repeating a quote that I used earlier in the book:

> "Hope is not the conviction that something will turn out
> well but the certainty that something makes sense, regardless
> of how it turns out."
> —*Vaclav Havel*

It has been my experience, both personally and in my clinical practice, that people can endure incredible things once they understand that the things they are experiencing have meaning.

> "The voices took the place of my pain."
> —*Eleanor Longden (2013)*

ICoNN 3 CASE: OSCAR

Synopsis of Oscar's History

This is the case of Oscar, age 55. He was referred to the outpatient clinic by his general practitioner (GP) after he was discharged from a local psychiatric unit. There had been a significant rupture of the therapeutic alliance with his National Health Service (NHS) psychiatrist. Oscar gave a 10-year history of hearing voices and seeing things. He had been treated with high doses of antidepressants and second-generation antipsychotics, without any marked benefit. He was compelled to retire from work on medical grounds because of a physical injury that made him unfit to carry out his usual duties. He was preoccupied with the voices he heard and believed that nothing could be done to ameliorate them. He felt "tortured" by them. During his most recent admission to a psychiatric unit he became despondent because of further molestation by a convicted pedophile, a patient on the same ward. He had subsequently self-harmed—cutting himself—following this experience. This was one of the major contributory factors to the rupture in the therapeutic alliance with his NHS team, whom he believed should have protected him. On initially seeing me he was understandably very reticent and guarded in session. It is important to make space for such an initial reaction.

Presenting Issues at the Time of Oscar's Psychiatric Assessment

• Preoccupation about past episodes of childhood sexual abuse and one episode of molestation while an inpatient as an adult
• Reports hearing voices that he identifies as his abusers (three of them) and visual hallucinations of the abusers
• Mood—depressed and anxious; instability of mood evident on examination
• Poor response to heavy doses of medication to date: antidepressant and antipsychotic
• Poor engagement with local mental health agencies; Oscar reported feeling "neglected and rejected"

History of Presenting Issues and Treatment

Oscar was a man in his mid-50s who had failed to fulfill his potential. In his mid-teens he had become rebellious and difficult—"going off the rails." His parents had been puzzled by this change in behavior at the time, as no obvious cause was evident. By his own report he stated that he had associated with "the wrong people" and used illicit drugs for a period of years, before meeting a girl and settling down together. He held down a manual job with low pay for several years and they started a family together. This was how his life continued until 5 years before his contact with my service, when he reported becoming emotionally distressed at his grandfather's funeral. This resulted in the first of a string of psychiatric admissions. He was placed on antipsychotic and antidepressant medications, but continued to report auditory and visual hallucinations, even at high doses, with which he was concordant. The relationship within the family unit became strained, as he was self-harming (*cutting*) and acting in a manner that his close family thought of as "bizarre." He eventually disclosed to the family and mental health professionals that the trigger was not the grandfather's death. He had been confronted by one of his abusers at the funeral. In the following days he had experienced flashbacks and nightmares, and increasingly heard the voices of his abusers goading him. He also occasionally saw them. When he came to my clinic he had lost hope in his clinical team, which he believed saw him as an "incurable" case; there had been an almost complete rupture in the therapeutic alliance.

Case Formulation and Treatment Plan

Oscar, a 55-year-old man, presented with psychiatric disorder resulting in a significant and substantial functional impairment. He had a history of affective disorder and a past history of heavy drinking and illicit drug use in his late teens and early 20s, which continued until he got married, settled down, and started a family. Following a confrontation with one of his abusers at a family funeral, he had been admitted to the local psychiatric unit and disclosed episodes of childhood sexual abuse. Although he described clear DMNs and associated NCs, initially he was very chaotic and difficult to engage in therapy. Initially, the main priority was successful engagement and the construction of a safe container for treatment. He had complex hallucinations that included auditory (voices), visual, and somatic modalities. He was able to interact with the voices, and although they told him what to do, he was able to resist them.

Diagnosis

A full psychiatric assessment, which included history taking and mental state examination, was completed over a period of weeks. Following this it was apparent that Oscar was suffering from recognizable psychiatric illness in the form of posttraumatic stress disorder (PTSD), meeting diagnostic criteria in the fifth edition of the *Diagnostic and Statistical Manual of Mental Disorders* (DSM-5; American Psychiatric Association [APA], 2013) and Criterion F43.1 in the *International Classification of Diseases* (ICD-10; World Health Organization [WHO], 1993).

Treatment

The child part that manifested felt very vulnerable, so I used Dr. Shapiro's metaphor for therapy: *We conduct therapy in a safe container. It's like being inside a force field: a golden bubble* (Shapiro, 2001). Initially we then used some light stream relaxation and visualization of the "golden bubble," which he found helpful. After resource installation and helping Oscar to feel that safe boundaries had been put in place, the younger self shared that he was now experiencing a time when, following the abuse, he would lock himself in the porch between the outer and inner front doors of the family home and wait until his mother returned. He felt safe in that place. I was able to sense that Oscar was allowing himself to feel vulnerable as the therapeutic alliance grew and strengthened. The young, disowned part of Oscar came to experience the same sense of safety in the "golden bubble" of therapy as he had in the front porch while waiting for his mother to come home. Subsequently, he demonstrated a capacity to manage stressors in his environment in a much more adult way.

Mythopoetics—Use Your Environment

In my office I have lots of different curios, art, and sculptures. Borrowing from the mythopoetic tradition, I asked Oscar if anything in the office felt protective for him. He pointed to my bronze sculpture of two wolves' heads. He was invited to focus on how they might be protecting him now. On doing this, he described that he could picture them guarding the "golden bubble," while we were inside doing therapy. Sometimes at the end of a session he would walk over and pat their heads before leaving the office. He even gave them names. As the rapport built and he could remain more grounded in psychotherapy, he began to bring his chair less and less close to mine, until one day when he left it where I would normally keep it for adult EMDR therapy. He also carried himself with a much more adult energy and presented as being less in his disowned child self. This shift was reflected in the collateral information from his family.

What Does That Look Like to You?

On other occasions with other clients I have made use of a large abstract painting that hangs on my wall, beside where I sit with the client when doing therapy. I will ask clients to look at the painting and tell me if they can see anything in it. What emotions do they experience the painting conveying to them? These tasks help ground people, and I have found this to be a universal experience for my dissociated clients.

The Parts/Selves/Ego States

When working with these dissociated energy systems, which I propose are associated with dysfunctional memory networks, it is very useful to help the person understand the AIP model and be clear as to where DMNs sit within the paradigm. I routinely use the bus/bus driver metaphor and the Wizard of Oz analogy, which I have outlined earlier in the book, and I discussed these with Oscar. These models were clearly understood by Oscar and he could explain them to me in his own words. Although I attempted initially to build an ego-state workspace, called the "boardroom table," he was unable to tolerate this, even with modifications. Largely this was because the voices he heard were those of his abusers. At times a strong younger (disowned) self took executive control when the abusers appeared. The difficulty here became that this part wanted to protect and defend *me*. In this scenario we see that the beliefs, cognitions, and emotional architecture of the younger (disowned) self are what we would expect the young self to contain. He had a binary view of adults: Some were abusers and others needed *him* to protect *them*. Therefore, seeing that I wasn't an abuser and feeling safe with me, he concluded that I must be in the latter category and therefore I was in need of his protection.

At this stage the opportunity now presented itself for me to demonstrate that the voices did not have power to harm me. So, we listened to the voices threaten me; we checked in the following week: I was still here and no harm had befallen me. This began to help Oscar challenge the core cognitions he held in respect to the voices (and other phenomena). In time he became able to allow me to manage my own safety and well-being. He witnessed that he did not need to protect me and therefore could focus his endeavors on protecting himself. As I spoke with the younger disowned part, this part was able to articulate his beliefs about adults: They were untrustworthy abusers, or they needed his protection. The first belief came from his experience of abuse at the hands of three separate abusers. In his mind, the fact that these three men were unconnected to each other increased the "supporting evidence" for this conclusion. The latter conclusion was stemming from the DMN linked with his first episode of sexual abuse. The abuser had told the young Oscar that if he told anyone, he could expect that his father, who he knew had access to firearms, would find out and kill the abuser. This, Oscar was told, would ultimately result in his father going to jail and he would never see him again. Therefore, Oscar had logically presumed that his father needed to be protected, and this took the form of not telling anybody about the abuse. His silence was to keep his father safe. Here we see in action how the function of dissociation, within trauma, is to maintain attachment (DePrince & Freyd, 2014; Freyd & Birrell, 2013). Further dialogue with the younger disowned part facilitated his more adult parts in sharing their thoughts to the benefit of the whole system: You can't "not know" what you "know." In Oscar's case, after the parts spoke with one another, he was able to give a police statement resulting in the successful conviction of his most recent abuser. This was an extremely reparative and empowering experience for Oscar. His younger child part, which was linked with the early abuse, began to have confidence in the belief that adults were safe and did not need his protection; in fact, he was able to accept that they could act to protect him.

Extract from therapy session:

Therapist: *I want us to talk with the adult part I spoke to recently; you spoke about your abuser to the police. Is it OK for us to talk about that?*
VH: Yes, I'd like that.
Therapist: *"Big Oscar," can you introduce yourself to "young Oscar"?*
VH: [The adult part shares a brief history of his life's journey to date. He shares that he is a 55-year-old adult energy system that is part of the collective energy that makes up "Oscar." Little Oscar replies:] *I'm amazed that I have a family.*
Therapist: *Are you open to hearing other amazing things Big Oscar has done? You can stop any time you want. You are in control.*
VH: [Big Oscar shares how they reported the abuser to the police. The abuser confessed to the abuse and is now currently serving a prison sentence. The abuser has been placed on the sex offenders list. Little Oscar responds:] *That's amazing! But if I did that daddy would kill the man and go to jail and I wouldn't see daddy.*
Therapist: *Well, let's ask Big Oscar about that and whether daddy knows about his abuser. I wonder what would happen. You can ask him now, if you want to know.* [A facilitated discussion between the two parts continues, and Big Oscar discloses that his father knew and didn't kill the person or go to jail. His father did not need Oscar to protect him in that way.]

    The entire dialogue takes place while using BLS in the form of pulsers—small devices that deliver a gentle vibration as a form of BLS. Again, it is important to note at this stage that I believe that DAS/BLS is an *essential* element that facilitates the processing of information within the EMDR therapy model. BLS has been found to be effective across a number of modalities, as discussed in more detail in Chapter 5. Please note, however, that the strongest evidence for the facilitation of processing using BLS is for eye movements (EMs). In the case of Oscar, he found EMs difficult to tolerate, and this fits clinically with what I have experienced within this group of people. I have found the use of pulsers to be a more gentle form of BLS, which has a lower risk of abreaction than the use of EMs. Some individuals struggle to use EMs while two or more selves "dialogue." For these reasons, when working with an ego-state/voice dialogue approach within an EMDR therapy treatment plan, I may initially use pulsers and later switch to EMs.

The DAS/BLS and the proxy manner of working on the DMN, via the ego-state/voice dialogue approaches, use the methodology of the respective models (Stone & Stone, 1989; Watkins, 1993, 1998). For complete exploration of the methodology of these augmentations the reader is directed to the work of their originators. The Maastricht approach borrows from the voice dialogue approach and is readily available online (see http://www.dirkcorstens .com/maastrichtapproach). It is also found in Romme's (2009) book *Living with Voices.*

The Intersubjective

The ICoNN approach, especially in regard to ICoNN 3, can be described in the same way as Lynn Hoffmann described the open dialogue approach: "Less like a set of procedures than a 'learning to learn' model" (Boscolo, 1987, p. 28).

Bear in mind that mental disorder exists in the intersubjective, the space between people (Burns, 2013). Therapy must therefore take place in the same locus. By applying the Caelian principles for interpersonal relationships (connect, affirm, empower, listen, love, learn) to intrapersonal ones, we can work to connect the parts of the person in an affirming and empowering way. The connection is characterized by unity, not uniformity, and diversity with respect is valued. Intrapersonal connectedness is established through listening actively, loving fiercely, and learning continuously. This Caelian process is very dynamic and cannot be conceptualized as merely a set of procedural steps to be slavishly followed. This intrapersonal exemplar parallels the crucial paradigmatic shift that the team in Finland made, the team that developed the open dialogue approach (Seikkula & Olson, 2003). They saw the importance of seeing everyone involved with the person as a necessary part of a working partnership. This is the stance that we assume in the ICoNN approach, but we are working with an intrapsychic "peopled wound." We work to involve all parts and the therapist in partnership, just as the open dialogue approach does with a system of people.

> "Therapy is conceived as a process created jointly, with deliberate emphasis placed on the spoken exchange and the circles of dialogue."
> —(*Seikkula & Olson, 2003, p. 408*)

The open dialogue approach has three foundational principles: *tolerance of uncertainty, dialogism, and polyphony*. **Tolerance of uncertainty** is the antithesis of a hypothesis. It describes what the IConN approach and AIP model provide us with when working with psychosis. When utilizing the IConN approach and its modifications for EMDR therapy, the therapist need not have a fully delineated formulation detailing cause and effect. By watching affect and focusing on what is experienced in the body (the *instrument of emotion*), we are guided to the DMN, the cause of the problem. To be able to journey into painful emotion requires a degree of therapeutic intimacy, which can only come about when the person allows himself or herself to be vulnerable. Such a journey needs two things: a strong therapeutic alliance and a high level of attunement between the therapist and the client. As we allow ourselves to tolerate uncertainty, the person becomes able to work with all parts. This is because none of the parts is excluded by settling upon one hypothesis: All parts are welcome. This models a quantum reality with multiple pathways existing, even in paradox. It is out of this milieu that the solution can appear, just as the increased interconnectedness of dreaming facilitates problem solving (Walker, Liston, Hobson, & Stickgold, 2002). Establishing this system, where the therapist is on an equal footing with the client, is very affirming and empowering. The client's voice is as vital and important as any other contributing to the partnership. The open dialogue approach describes a way of being within the partnership that echoes the words of Rilke, which they quote: "Live your way into the answer" (Seikkula & Olson, 2003, p. 408).

Dialogism

The dialogism of the open dialogue approach is the equivalent of the Caelian principles of the IConN approach. At the heart of therapy we are joining the client in war and peace as the client's *therapón*—a companion of the heart. This is an essential antidote to the intense and fearful alienation that is psychosis. In Caelian terms, we connect, affirm, and empower by listening, loving, and learning. As the open dialogue approach emphasizes: "The idea of listening is more important in Open Dialogue than the process of interviewing" (Seikkula & Olson, 2003, p. 409). All too often we can rush through an interview, trying to tick all the boxes. Yet, in doing so, we fail to listen. Seikkula and Olson (2003) present to us the position we need to assume as therapists, in quoting the French philosopher François Lyotard: "One speaks as a listener." In other words, meaning in psychosis ultimately arises from a place of listening and connecting.

> "Within the dialogical borderland where the person,
> the important others and the professionals meet,
> a language for suffering may be born that can give
> suffering a voice."
> *(Seikkula & Olson, 2003, p. 409)*

Polyphony

This aspect of the open dialogue approach is one that allows for many voices to speak at once.

"The conversation itself constructs the reality."
(Seikkula & Olson, 2003, p. 410)

In the ICoNN 3 category we see the importance of conversation as we seek to be present with all the voices in the peopled wound. We observe that different parts "speak" with different phenomena. The important thing is not to try to "get to the truth"; rather, we seek to hear all of the voices of the wound. All need to be present, as they all need to be a part of the solution.

In the open dialogue approach these three principles create a milieu that allows us to find a path out of the psychosis through language. I propose that the ICoNN approach is doing the same thing through the psychophysiological mechanisms of the innate AIP system, which works to give meaning and language to the "psychotic" experiences. The open dialogue approach grew out of the work of Bateson. He was to revisit his concept of the double bind and moved away from the model of a binder and a victim. He later emphasized the larger relational systems that generate a double bind, which is, in essence, the failure of community (Seikkula & Olson, 2003). By restoring connection and effective community, we bring meaning to the psychotic experiences and hope to the individual experiencing them. Those who are wounded in the community must be healed in the community.

The Wizard of Oz and Stockholm Syndrome

I have already outlined the "Wizard of Oz fallacy" and noted how the presenting problem, such as voice-hearing, is not the core problem. The core pathology is the DMN: "the man behind the curtain." In viewing voices as a "peopled wound," we need to acknowledge that they are a system of interrelating memory networks. This system of interaction may be complex and cryptic, taking many clinical contact hours to understand. In some cases, as it was in Oscar's, there are disowned child parts that hide behind the voice of an abuser. This was explained to me, in supervision, as being helpfully thought of as a phenomenon akin to Stockholm syndrome. In Stockholm syndrome, hostages become attached to their captors and have been known to defend them when rescue is attempted. There is frequently a disowned child part attached to the internalized abuser part. In Oscar's case, our secure therapeutic alliance allowed a child part to communicate with me when the abuser appeared. Remember that these disowned parts represent a DMN, and facilitating dialogue is a proxy way of communicating with and influencing the DMN. It may also be the case that, in dialogue, the therapist may be able to identify a trauma and associated DMN that can be reprocessed using the standard EMDR therapy protocol. In this way the therapist may be moving between all of the ICoNN categories in the full course of treatment for any given individual.

Note Regarding Medication

In Oscar's case I am not going to detail his medications beyond stating that, when referred to me, he was on a combination of a high-dose selective serotonin reuptake inhibitor (SSRI) and a second-generation antipsychotic (SGA). He was also taking high doses of analgesia, both bought and prescribed. The voices and visual hallucinations did not significantly respond to this medication, and within the NHS system Oscar experienced a culture of "change" or "increase." I have heard the system that many people like Oscar find themselves caught up in referred to as "the SHO-roundabout." In other words, they experience a junior doctor reviewing them every 3 to 6 months and medication is endlessly adjusted. Medication is used exclusively in the absence of other psychosocial interventions. This is a reiteration of what Stephen S. Sharfstein (2005 APA president) referred to as the profession's slip into the bio-bio-bio model (Sharfstein, 2005). This situation is not good for clients, who receive the implicit message that nothing is working and that their lack of positive response is an indication that they are biologically broken. We communicate, by our action (or lack of it), that they should just accept that they are chronically ill and get on with it. We even refer to it as "severe and enduring mental illness." Neither is it any better for the psychiatrist who moves away from a holistic and integrated bio-psycho-social model. One retired colleague referred to this journey occurring as he progressed throughout his professional career. He had started out with a passion to see and treat the "whole person," and, as time went on, because he was the only member of the multidisciplinary team who could prescribe, he dutifully assumed the role of "professional pill-pusher." This echoes the words of Sharfstein: "If we are seen as mere pill pushers and employees of the pharmaceutical industry, our credibility as a profession is compromised" (Sharfstein, 2005). Part of the challenge for Oscar at this stage in his recovery is learning to trust another psychiatrist enough to agree to safely adjust the medication. This is now happening in parallel with his psychotherapy. The journey continues.

Take-Home for ICoNN 3 Cases

The initial phases 1 and 2 were completed according to the guidance described in a previous chapter. A robust therapeutic alliance developed, which provided a suitable container for working with Oscar. It is vitally important that the initial contact not be rushed; this is also true for all subsequent sessions. As noted for the other ICoNN categories, it may not be feasible to complete a full new-patient psychiatric assessment within a routine new-patient slot. History may unfold across many sessions with ongoing therapy. Think of the person as being like a rose that is opening. You don't want to start peeling the petals open; with the right time and conditions the rose will open up naturally. Gaining Oscar's trust was initially challenging, given his previous experiences of the mental health system and other psychiatrists. This is a well-reported area of difficulty (Fear, 2013; Fear, Sharp, & Healy, 1996; Fear, McMonagle, & Healy, 1998). If the ICoNN guidance for the initial phases is followed, clients ought to feel safe enough to be vulnerable enough to share their beliefs. As well as dealing with issues of shame and guilt (Brown, 2012), clients are also dealing with a system of disowned parts/ego states that may not be in agreement. Some may be resistant to working with you in any form. Therefore, some form of agreement has to be reached to allow therapy to be proceed successfully. A sound knowledge and capability within either a voice dialogue approach or an ego-state approach is a necessity for a therapist seeking to work with this group of individuals. The reader is directed to the original source materials for these approaches, as a sound knowledge of their methodologies is an *essential* skill when working with this client group.

Resources for Voice Dialogue and the Psychology of Selves and Ego-State Work in EMDR Therapy

The following resources are recommended for further reading in relation to the voice dialogue and ego-state approaches when working with IConN 3 cases (Forgash & Copeley, 2008; Johnson, 1986; McCarthy-Jones, 2012; Romme & Escher, 2000; Romme, 1996, 2009; Rothschild, 2000, 2003; Stone & Stone, 1989; Watkins, 1993, 1998):

- Romme, M., & Escher, S. (2000). *Making sense of voices: The mental health professional's guide to working with voice-hearers.* London, England: Mind Publications.
- Romme, M. A. J. (1996). *Understanding voices: Coping with auditory hallucinations and confusing realities.* Limburg, Germany: Rijksuniversiteit Maastricht.
- Romme, M. A. J. (2009). *Living with voices: 50 stories of recovery.* Ross-on-Wye, England: PCCS Books in association with Birmingham City University.
- McCarthy-Jones, S. (2012). *Hearing voices: The histories, causes, and meanings of auditory verbal hallucinations.* Cambridge, England: Cambridge University Press.
- Stone, H., & Stone, S. (1989). *Embracing our selves: The voice dialogue manual.* San Rafael, CA: New World Library. http://www.voicedialogue.org
- John Kent is an excellent teacher/facilitator located in the United Kingdom; he is one of the senior teachers of the voice dialogue approach. He is the only person to have developed an online training program; see http://www.voicedialogue .org.uk/home.
- I also recommend Hal Stone's daughter's website. She is one of the senior teachers of the voice dialogue approach and is active in networking for the voice dialogue community; see http://voicedialogueconnection.com.
- Forgash, C., & Copeley, M. (2008). *Healing the heart of trauma and dissociation with EMDR and ego state therapy.* New York, NY: Springer Publishing Company.
- Johnson, R. A. (1986). *Inner work: Using dreams and active imagination for personal growth.* San Francisco, CA: Harper & Row.
- Rothschild, B. (2003). *The body remembers casebook: Unifying methods and models in the treatment of trauma and PTSD.* New York, NY: W. W. Norton.
- Watkins, H. H. (1993). Ego-state therapy: An overview. *American Journal of Clinical Hypnosis, 35*(4), 232–240.
- Watkins, J. (1998). *Hearing voices: A common human experience.* Melbourne, Australia: Hill of Content.

I also want to invite people who are interested in learning more about what individuals with lived experience and the professionals who support them are saying to explore Phil Borges and Kevin Tomlinson's new documentary *CRAZY-WISE*. It contains the voices of many experts through lived experience, in addition to professionals and healers. Certainly it is a film that will make you think, and that can only be a good thing, in my opinion. The film is the record of a journey that any one of us could take. Phil Borges acts as our "everyman" as we journey with him, asking the following questions:

1. What do traditional cultures have to teach us about mental health?
2. What do people with lived experience of ill mental health have to tell us?
3. Is there validity to the paradigm that teaches that there is spiritual/personal growth through the trauma of the experiences we label as mental illness?

Check out the information and blog at http://crazywisefilm.com/#about
    The Hearing Voices Network and the Icarus Project both carry the message that the emancipation of people with lived experience of these phenomena is what will truly bring hope for healing. More information about the Icarus project can be found at http://theicarusproject.net/
    If we accept that the voices and "psychotic" phenomena are a "peopled wound," then we need to listen to what the voices are telling us about the nature of the wound. These are real experiences, and we ought to treat them accordingly and with respect. If we will not listen to the voices, we will never learn the true nature of the wounding, and that means we cannot begin to facilitate the process of healing.

> "Without our stories, how will we know it's us? Without the
> stories of others, how will we know who they are?"
> —*Dudley Cocke, director of Roadside Theater*
> (*as quoted on the Icarus Project website*)

Key Points for IConN 3

1. Build a safe container for treatment using Caelian principles. Do the basics well.
2. Listen and allow clients to tell their stories and affirm them by acknowledging that these experiences are real. In particular, ensure that every "part"/self has the opportunity to do this.
3. Be actively neutral—neither confirm nor deny the person's beliefs; that is not your role. It is, however, important that clients know that you understand that their experiences are real. Avoid *epistemic hubris*—be gentle and respectful in attitude. In other words, be open-minded and openhearted enough to listen to the mythos/rationale that clients have for their experiences. Give space for them to explain why they believe what they believe. This is not the same as endorsing their beliefs, yet it works to restore their human dignity.
4. Ensure that you give enough time for each session.
5. Facilitate clients' connection with their emotions and understand how they feel about the reported experiences that they are having. Use the approach that you are familiar with—voice dialogue/ego state—to process the DMN by proxy.

6. Think of the person as a collective energy made up of a constituency of energy systems:
   a. Seek agreement from all of the parts/energy systems to do the therapeutic work.
   b. Reassure the system that no part will be annihilated.
   c. When they are present, find a way to work with perceived enemies/abusers.
7. Pay attention to the emotions you are experiencing in your body as the therapist.

REFERENCES

American Psychiatric Association. (2013). *Diagnostic and statistical manual of mental disorders* (5th ed.). Washington, DC: Author.

Boscolo, L. (1987). *Milan systemic family therapy: Conversations in theory and practice.* New York, NY: Basic Books.

Brown, B. (2012). *Daring greatly: How the courage to be vulnerable transforms the way we live, love, parent, and lead* (1st ed.). New York, NY: Gotham.

Burns, T. (2013). *Our necessary shadow. The nature and meaning of psychiatry.* London, England: Allen Lane.

DePrince, A. P., & Freyd, J. J. (2014). Trauma-induced dissociation. In M. J. Friedman, T. M. Keane, & P. A. Resick (Eds.), *Handbook of PTSD: Science and practice* (2nd ed., pp. 219–233). New York, NY: Guilford Press.

Fear, C. (2013). Recent developments in the management of delusional disorders. *Advances in Psychiatric Treatment, 19,* 212–220.

Fear, C., McMonagle, T., & Healy, D. (1998). Delusional disorders: Boundaries of a concept. *European Psychiatry, 13*(4), 210–218. doi:10.1016/S0924-9338(98)80006-0

Fear, C., Sharp, H., & Healy, D. (1996). Cognitive processes in delusional disorders. *British Journal of Psychiatry, 168*(1), 61–67.

Forgash, C., & Copeley, M. (2008). *Healing the heart of trauma and dissociation with EMDR and ego state therapy.* New York, NY: Springer Publishing Company.

Frank, J. D. (1961). *Persuasion and healing: A comparative study of psychotherapy.* Baltimore, MD: Johns Hopkins Press.

Freyd, J. J., & Birrell, P. (2013). *Blind to betrayal: Why we fool ourselves we aren't being fooled.* Hoboken, NJ: Wiley.

Holmesland, A. L., Seikkula, J., & Hopfenbeck, M. (2014). Inter-agency work in open dialogue: The significance of listening and authenticity. *Journal of Interprofessional Care, 28*(5), 433–439. doi:10.3109/13561820.2014.901939

Holmesland, A. L., Seikkula, J., Nilsen, O., Hopfenbeck, M., & Erik Arnkil, T. (2010). Open dialogues in social networks: Professional identity and transdisciplinary collaboration. *International Journal of Integrated Care, 10,* 1–14.

Johnson, R. A. (1986). *Inner work: Using dreams and active imagination for personal growth* (1st ed.). San Francisco, CA: Harper & Row.

Longden, E. (2013). The voices in my head. *TED Talks.* Retrieved from http://www.ted.com/talks/eleanor_longden_the_voices_in_my_head?language=en

McCarthy-Jones, S. (2012). *Hearing voices: The histories, causes, and meanings of auditory verbal hallucinations.* Cambridge, England: Cambridge University Press.

Romme, M. A. J. (1996). *Understanding voices: Coping with auditory hallucinations and confusing realities.* Limburg, Germany: Rijksuniversiteit Maastricht.

Romme, M. A. J. (2009). *Living with voices: 50 stories of recovery.* Ross-on-Wye, England: PCCS Books in association with Birmingham City University.

Romme, M. A. J., & Escher, S. (2000). *Making sense of voices: The mental health professional's guide to working with voice-hearers.* London, England: Mind Publications.

Rothschild, B. (2000). *The body remembers: The psychophysiology of trauma and trauma treatment.* New York, NY: W. W. Norton.

Rothschild, B. (2003). *The body remembers casebook: Unifying methods and models in the treatment of trauma and PTSD* (1st ed.). New York, NY: W. W. Norton.

Seikkula, J., & Alakare, B. (2004). [Open dialog: Alternative point of view in psychiatric patient care]. *Duodecim, 120*(3), 289–296.

Seikkula, J., & Olson, M. E. (2003). The open dialogue approach to acute psychosis: Its poetics and micropolitics. *Family Process, 42*(3), 403–418.

Shapiro, F. (2001). *Eye movement desensitization and reprocessing (EMDR): Basic principles, protocols, and procedures* (2nd ed.). New York, NY: Guilford Press.

Sharfstein, S. S. (2005, August 19). Big Pharma and American psychiatry: The good, the bad, and the ugly. *Psychiatric News, 3.* Retrieved from http://psychnews.psychiatryonline.org/doi/full/10.1176/pn.40.16.00400003

Stone, H., & Stone, S. (1989). *Embracing our selves: The voice dialogue manual.* San Rafael, CA: New World Library.

Walker, M. P., Liston, C., Hobson, J. A., & Stickgold, R. (2002). Cognitive flexibility across the sleep-wake cycle: REM-sleep enhancement of anagram problem solving. *Brain Research and Cognitive Brain Research, 14*(3), 317–324.

Watkins, H. H. (1993). Ego-state therapy: An overview. *American Journal of Clinical Hypnosis, 35*(4), 232–240.

Watkins, J. (1998). *Hearing voices: A common human experience.* Melbourne, Australia: Hill of Content.

Watkins, J. G. (2005). Over-resonance, the emaciation and destruction of Judy's self: Modifications to ego state theory. *Journal of Trauma and Dissociation, 6*(3), 1–9. doi:10.1300/J229v06n03_01

World Health Organization. (1993). *The ICD-10 classification of mental and behavioural disorders: Diagnostic criteria for research.* Geneva, Switzerland: Author.

TWELVE

EMDR Therapy + IConN 4 Category Case Examples

Intention: *To demonstrate to the reader, with clinical case material, the methodology for formulating cases using the AIP and IConN models in conjunction. To equip clinicians with the knowledge of how to target EMDR therapeutic endeavors within people diagnosed with schizophrenia or other psychoses.*

IConN 4

This is the fourth and final category of presentation within the Indicating Cognitions of Negative Networks (IConN) model. The psychotic phenomena cause distress and a functional impairment to the person, but the psychological pathogen (dysfunctional memory network, DMN) cannot be identified in the standard way, nor can it be tracked back across an *affect bridge*. There are no "heard voices" capable of being engaged in dialogue. What *can* be identified is a Gestalt that relates to psychotic material being presented, which possesses strong, and negatively valenced, emotion. It is this Gestalt, with its emotional energy, that is targeted in the reprocessing of IConN 4 category cases.

> "We cannot ignore the fact that a hallucinatory disposition is, to some extent, present in every psyche, and that schizophrenia, as well as other conditions, merely makes it manifest."
>
> —*Eugen Bleuler (1950)*

IConN 4 CASE: JANUS

Synopsis of Janus's History

In the case of Janus, eye movement desensitization and reprocessing (EMDR) therapy was successfully applied to a man who met the criteria for schizophrenia in the third edition, text revision of the *Diagnostic and Statistical*

Manual of Mental Disorders (*DSM-III-R*; American Psychiatric Association [APA] & American Psychiatric Association Work Group to Revise *DSM-III*, 1987). At the time of his referral to my service, he was 40 years of age and presented initially with issues regarding worsening domestic relationships and deterioration in his work performance, both felt to be associated with a decreased mood. Following his initial new-patient assessment he was diagnosed with *severe depression with psychosis*, Criterion F32.3 of the *International Classification of Diseases* (*ICD-10*; World Health Organization [WHO], 1993). Following this first meeting the client sent a typewritten letter disclosing the presence of psychotic phenomena that he had withheld "out of fear." Following the disclosure of psychotic symptoms by the client, a Structured Clinical Interview for *DSM-III-R* (SCID) was completed and the client was found to meet the criteria for schizophrenia that were used by Professor K. Kendler in the Irish Schizophrenia Triad Study (ISTS).

Presenting Issues at the Time of Janus's Psychiatric Assessment

- The client had presented to his general practitioner (GP) with low mood.
- Worsening of relationships in the home.
- Obsessive-compulsive behaviors: Janus reported intrusive thoughts to step off the curb into traffic; these were not associated with suicidal drives. He would have to repeat a route if he failed to touch all the lampposts along it, and the number 7 held special significance for him.
- Deterioration in work performance in a man who was premorbidly a capable employee.
- Significant sleep disturbance with initial insomnia and early-morning wakening.
- Poor concentration, decreased attention, and poor motivation.
- Poor appetite with associated weight loss.
- The initial presentation included delusions of reference, persecution, passivity, and grandiosity, as well as religious delusions.
- Auditory hallucinations were present, including "a malevolent chuckling" and command hallucinations that tell him to hurt work colleagues. He worries that when he resists the voice telling him to hurt his work colleagues, the voices might tell him to hurt his family. This has led to him self-harming on several occasions.
- At the time of initial presentation, the main distressing phenomena were a delusional belief and its associated hallucinatory experiences, which the client recorded in a letter stating, "My thoughts hang out of my head in a balloon where everyone can see them, attached to my brain on a string. I try to cut the string with my hand but it doesn't always work, so I don't like going out of the house." These phenomena had a significant functional impact on the client, resulting in social isolation and withdrawal from activities of daily living, as he believed all of his innermost thoughts were easily observable to those around him.

The following are extracts from the client's completed SCID:

- He was fully orientated and cognitively intact on testing.
- There were delusions of reference, persecution, passivity, and grandiosity, as well as religious delusions.

- Auditory hallucinations, including command hallucinations, were present.
- He reported that his first psychotic phenomena occurred at 12 years of age.
- When the psychotic phenomena were at their worst, they had a moderate effect on his level of functioning.
- The longest duration of active psychotic phenomena was 22 years.
- He described being prodromal from 11 years of age. (*He later revealed that his mother tried to shoot his father at this time. Initially this was disclosed as "arguments and parents fighting."*)
- Psychological precipitants: child sexual abuse; home environment.
- Insidious onset reported (>6 months).
- Scores positive for depression (he reports his worst depression as being at 12 years of age).
- Reports "low mood" for most of life.
- No mania; no schizoaffective phenomena.
- Major depression and delusions/hallucinations co-occurred.
- Delusions/hallucinations were present when *not* depressed (24 months on the longest occasion).
- No alcohol dependence.
- No illicit drug use.
- Level of functioning across lifetime: moderately good.
- Moderately full life; secured full-time employment in a skilled job.
- Significant deterioration in function at times of psychosis.

Considering these responses in the SCID, plus the available history, the client met criteria for a *DSM-III-R* diagnosis of schizophrenia.

Janus also completed the Dissociative Experiences Scale (DES) (Bernstein & Putnam, 1986), which is a valid and reliable tool for the measurement of dissociation recommended for use by clinicians in the accredited EMDR training. The DES can be used to screen for the presence of dissociative experiences in clinical and nonclinical populations (Putnam et al., 1996). It is noted in the literature that DES scores above 30 are almost always associated with *DSM-III-R* diagnoses of multiple personality disorder (MPD) or posttraumatic stress disorder (PTSD; Ross, 1991). At initial presentation the client completed the DES and scored 33.

History of Presenting Issues and Treatment

Janus presented with issues at work and deterioration in the quality of relationships with his family at home. The GP thought these issues were related to "past experiences" in his personal history and secondary to depression. Janus stated that he attended mainly because of encouragement from his wife, who was increasingly worried about his behavior. Originally, after his initial assessment, Janus's case was formulated within a biological model as psychosis initially and schizophrenia latterly. As such, the treatment plan was medication-focused at this point. Psychological therapies were not a part of the treatment plan until the medication had failed to ameliorate the phenomena significantly. At that stage I reformulated Janus's case within a trauma model and naturally then considered the options for psychotherapy, which included EMDR therapy.

Initially, Janus minimized the trauma aspect of his personal history. This is not at all unusual, because for the person this is "normal." When Janus spoke of his parents fighting, he spoke of it as a typical parental disagreement, but he was actually referring to occasions that included violence with a knife and a firearm. Janus eventually disclosed a history that included emotional and physical abuse by a violent, alcoholic father and described having experienced child sexual abuse (CSA) as a 12-year-old, at the hands of a family "friend." Janus had also experienced trauma within his family of origin. The specifics of this are related to the social context of Northern Ireland at the time: He had witnessed his mother try to shoot his father during an argument. There was access to a firearm in the home, as the wider social context required his father to carry a personal protection weapon. His mother also stabbed his father on another occasion. Janus eventually described occasions when he and his brother, as children, seriously discussed shooting their father because of his violent behavior in the home. Janus reported hearing voices from his teenage years on, and he described having had a conversation, prior to his initial assessment, with a man he later found out had been dead for many years.

Janus had never previously consulted any professionals about his mental health and had functioned effectively in work and at home. Collateral history confirmed this. His coping strategy was dissociation and denial. This is very typical of the Northern Ireland context and the stoicism of the Ulster-Scots tradition (Curran & Miller, 2001).

Case Formulation

At presentation, Janus was a 40-year-old man who reported depression and impairment in the workplace and at home. Although he had never attended a mental health professional for any issues prior to this presentation, he described hearing voices from his teenage years on after witnessing serious violence between his parents. On SCID assessment he presented a phenomenological picture consistent with the *DSM-II-R* criteria for schizophrenia. His DES was 33. He had previously held down a successful career and maintained a family life with children. He had become increasingly dysfunctional and socially isolated because of an increase in hallucinations and associated delusional beliefs.

Diagnosis

Janus was ultimately diagnosed as having recognizable psychiatric illness in the form of schizophrenia (see further discussion of this in the following section).

ROSS'S CRITERIA FOR DISSOCIATIVE SCHIZOPHRENIA

I have explored the phenomenology of schizophrenia and dissociation earlier in the book. Janus met the criteria that Kendler had set for the Irish Schizophrenia

Triad Study. Janus also met the criteria proposed by Ross (2004) for a type of schizophrenia that he refers to as *dissociative schizophrenia*, in which the clinical picture is dominated *by at least three* of the following:

1. Dissociative amnesia (including what he reports as a "brown study"[1])	*Yes*
2. Depersonalization	*Yes*
3. The presence of two or more distinct identities or personality states	*No*
4. Auditory hallucinations	*Yes*
5. Extensive comorbidity	*Yes*
6. Severe childhood trauma	*Yes*

Progress in Treatment

Initial assessment: Following this appointment Janus was diagnosed with depression, moderate severity, with obsessive-compulsive phenomena present. The Seroxat (paroxetine) that he had been prescribed by his GP at 20 mg for the previous 8 weeks, was increased to 30 mg and then, after a further week, increased to 40 mg. Seroquel (quetiapine), the atypical antipsychotic, was added at an anxiolytic dose, 25 mg, at night.

By the time of his next review appointment he had written to me, detailing a number of psychotic phenomena, such as auditory hallucinations, which included command hallucinations that he attributed to "the devil." Thought broadcast was described at interview and was reported alongside the delusional belief that he could read the minds of others; at the assessment this belief was held at the strength of an overvalued idea. Patient was off work on sick leave. Accordingly, following *ICD-10* guidelines, because of the evidence of psychosis, Janus's diagnosis became depression, severe severity, with psychosis.

Medication: By the next appointment his Seroquel (quetiapine) had been increased gradually to 150 mg twice daily (an efficacious antipsychotic treatment dose). On this dose he reported a decrease in the auditory hallucinations but continued to experience visual hallucinations, "like the shadow of a rat," which

---

[1] *A brown study:* This was a phrase that Janus recalled his mother using in reference to him as a boy. The phrase *brown study* is not often used in modern-day speech, but refers to a person being in a gloomy daydream. For me his description of his staring off into space for long periods of time sounded dissociative and would be in keeping with his DES scoring. This usage is well illustrated by the following two well-known pieces of literature:

Melville, H. (1851). *Moby-Dick; or The whale*. London, England: Richard Bentley.
"So gathering up the shavings with another grin, and throwing them into the great stove in the middle of the room, he went about his business, and left me in a *brown study*." (Melville & Melville, 1851, p. 21)
Doyle, A. C. (1893). *The adventures of Sherlock Holmes*. Leipzig, Germany: Bernhard Tauchnitz.
["The Adventure of the Resident Patient"] "Finding that Holmes was too absorbed for conversation, I had tossed aside the barren paper, and leaning back in my chair, *I fell into a brown study*. Suddenly my companion's voice broke in upon my thoughts." (Doyle, 1893, p. 761)

he experienced as occurring in the periphery of his vision. He continued to have the delusion and associated hallucinatory experience that his neighbors could see his thoughts as they floated around his head in speech bubbles, attached to his brain by a string, while he was cutting the grass. His Seroquel (quetiapine) was increased to 150 mg in the morning and 300 mg at night; Seroxat (paroxetine) was increased to 60 mg daily.

Upon subsequent review there had been no change to his delusional beliefs, but he was not as distressed by them. His Seroquel (quetiapine) was increased to 300 mg twice daily.

A computed tomography (CT) brain scan was completed to rule out any intracranial pathology; no abnormality was detected. Janus continued to report "malevolent chuckling," which he thought was connected with intrusive thoughts about harming his loved ones. Janus attributed this to "the devil." At this point we discussed the use of naltrexone for dissociation as per the work of Ulrich F. Lanius; Janus agreed to the off-license use of naltrexone, 25 mg.

By the 5-month time point from his disclosure of the psychotic phenomena, Janus felt "more in control" and reported that the psychotic phenomena were "lessening." Naltrexone was increased to 50 mg daily. At this point psychoeducation was completed, detailing psychological responses to trauma, the AIP model (Shapiro, Kaslow, & Maxfield, 2007), and dissociation. He agreed to the completion of the SCID.

Janus continued to report losing time, reporting that he had some days that "don't fit together." Usually this was occurring two or three times per month. Naltrexone was increased to 100 mg daily.

Due to his continued lack of function despite active treatment, he was medically retired from work.

At the 7-month time point Janus reported a continued low mood and was fearful that he would harm someone. Zispin (mirtazapine) 15 mg was added to his medication regimen. Following this, despite feeling physically unwell (blood pressure increase and an increase in weight), Janus reported feeling more settled: "I've had the unusual experience of happiness." He consented to proceed with EMDR therapy, which was explained to him and linked with earlier psychoeducation, with the reiteration of adaptive information processing (AIP) model and inclusion of the Tribrain model (MacLean, 1990).

The safe/calm place exercise was taught to Janus; he was asked to bring up an image of a place that elicited a positive feeling of well-being characterized by feeling safe and calm. While concentrating on the safe place image he selected, Janus appeared to become completely immersed in the experience and was felt by me to be dissociating. I switched to shorter sets of bilateral stimulation (eye movements) and noted that the dissociation lessened. The image, emotions, and physical sensations of the safe/calm place were then installed through simultaneous pairing with bilateral stimulation in the form of eye movements (Shapiro, 2001). Janus reported that he experienced this as a non-threatening way to introduce EMDR. A secondary safe/calm place was then developed with Janus using the room outside of time and space, with the three doors marked "past," "present," and "future." A good response to both safe/calm places was noted.

Janus participated in nine therapy sessions over 10 months, within an EMDR paradigm and with ongoing follow-up that included a review of his medication. Three of these nine sessions entailed EMDR reprocessing, with the remainder consisting of an initial assessment, history taking, and psychoeducation. The psychoeducation for Janus within the IConN approach included a description of the EMDR therapy paradigm, the AIP model of Shapiro (Shapiro et al., 2007), and MacLean's Tribrain model (MacLean, 1990).

There were three sequential targets in the EMDR reprocessing sessions:

1. *The delusion/hallucination that his neighbors could see his thoughts when he was cutting the grass.* In this case the target within the EMDR process was the psychotic phenomena and the associated emotion that was felt in his body, which Janus associated with the phenomena. This is an example of an IConN 4 category target.

In this case Janus found that he could not reduce the experience down to a specific discrete target. He experienced the *general Gestalt of the complex psychotic phenomena* that consisted of visual hallucinatory elements (the thoughts in speech bubbles; the strings from his brain), the delusional beliefs (that the neighbors could see the hallucinations he saw; that his thoughts could be read by people as they floated around his head), and the negative cognitions (NCs) and negatively valenced emotional charge that the experiences held.

> Target: general Gestalt of the complex psychotic phenomena—"speech bubbles above his head"
> Body: Chest
> Emotion: "exposed," "standing like a little boy in the garden"
> NC: "I am vulnerable"; Subjective Units of Distress Scale (SUDS) score = 10/10
> Positive cognition (PC): "I am able to protect myself"; Validity of Cognition (VoC) scale score = 1/7

Janus was able to process this with the standard model to a SUDS score of 0/10 and a VoC of 7/7. The most important thing to consider when targeting a Gestalt is that although it may feel very nebulous and therefore not a clear target, if the person has a clear connection to the felt sense that accompanies the phenomena then it can be reprocessed, as in this case.

2. *An episode of overwhelming emotion when at work.* This was a traditional target within the standard eight-phase protocol.

> Target: Last time he was at work
> Body: Head—"sensation of being overloaded"
> Emotion: Anger—"there's not a big enough word for it"
> NC: "I am not in control"; SUDS = 11/10 [Score given by Janus]
> PC: "I am in control"; VoC = 1/7

Janus was able to process this with the standard model to a SUDS score of 1/10 and a VoC of 7/7.

3. *His relationship with his abusive father.* This was a traditional target within the standard eight-phase protocol.

During the third reprocessing session, Janus was stuck on the dynamic with his father that he experienced as a boy. I utilized a noncognitive interweave, which I borrowed from the field of mythopoetic experiential men's work, called a "clearing." I invited Janus to stand and picture that he was facing his father. He first gave me the data—information about his father that was observable and factual. Next I asked him to tell me about the stories that he told himself about his father, the negative judgments. Finally, I had Janus tell me how those stories made him feel. This process enabled Janus to experience a catharsis; Janus saw that his "bottomless anger" was coming from the anger he had around his own sense of being judged as inferior and that he was not in control—both things that he saw mirrored in his father. Janus processed two NC/PC groups related to his father.

Target: Seeing his father standing in front of him
Body: Head
Emotion: Anger
NC: "I am not in control"; SUDS = "Don't know"
PC: "I am in control"

As we processed the target, Janus recalled deciding as a 7- or 8-year-old that he would not cry again, as that was the only thing that he "had over" his parents. It was his proof to himself that he was able to have some control of his life. As I was unable to obtain a SUDS or VoC score, we primarily focused on the emotion felt in his body and worked until the body scan was neutral.

Progress After EMDR Reprocessing

After the first EMDR reprocessing session, Janus was less dissociated and reported feeling more self-aware. The second session advanced his sense of integration, and following the last reprocessing session he was no longer delusional. The Dissociative Experiences Scale (DES) (Bernstein & Putnam, 1986) is felt to be a valid and reliable tool for the measurement of dissociation (Ross, Norton, & Anderson, 1988) and it was used to track response to treatment.

DES

The DES is useful for screening and tracking treatment outcomes (Ross et al., 2008). The DES score for Janus was 33 at the start of treatment, which decreased to 20 following commencement of medication and further decreased to 11 after all EMDR reprocessing sessions were complete. By the 1-month time point after the EMDR reprocessing sessions, this had further decreased to 3.

Since being medication- and symptom-free, Janus has been followed up 12 times over 88 months. In this time period Janus has experienced stressful personal life events, which can be classed as the normal vicissitudes of life and not qualifying as "Criterion A" trauma events. Janus has completed higher-level education and has secured work in skilled employment. There has been no return of any psychiatric pathology and he has now been free of any obsessive-compulsive or psychotic phenomena for 7½ years.

Note Regarding Medication

In the case of Janus, psychological and pharmacological treatments were applied to the issues presented. However, when we look at his response to the treatment plan, examining how the phenomenology did or did not respond to medication, we see that the medication did not resolve the psychotic phenomena. At times Janus reported some decrease in symptomology, but it never resolved completely with the medication alone. Three classes of medication were utilized and all except one were used within their United Kingdom license; the naltrexone was used for an off-license indication:

1. **Antidepressants**: Janus was prescribed the selective serotonin reuptake inhibitor (SSRI) Seroxat (paroxetine) by his GP. He was taking 20 mg once daily and this was increased over 2 weeks in 10-mg increments to 40 mg daily. In just over 1 month from the initial assessment Janus was taking 60 mg daily, and remained on this dose for 18 months. Subsequently, mirtazapine, a tetracyclic antidepressant, was added after 8 months and he remained on this for 5 months.
2. **Antipsychotic**: Quetiapine was prescribed following the new-patient assessment. Initially this was prescribed as an anxiolytic but then quickly increased to antipsychotic treatment doses once psychotic phenomena were identified. The dose was titrated up to the maximum dose of 300 mg twice daily in just over 3 months, and Janus remained on this dose for 8 months before it was then gradually withdrawn over about a 6-week period.
3. **Medication to limit dissociation:** Naltrexone was prescribed after I was introduced to the concept, following a discussion with Ulrich Lanius at an EMDR International Association (EMDRIA) conference. It is proposed that low-dose naltrexone is effective in decreasing the level of dissociation and can facilitate psychotherapy (Lanius, 2005). Janus was given the lowest available dose of naltrexone, but as a compounding pharmacist was not readily accessible for me at the time the lowest dose available was utilized—starting at 25 mg daily, this was increased over a 2-month period to 100 mg daily and continued for just under 9 months. (I now have access to the services of a compounding pharmacist and typically use naltrexone doses in the range of 1 mg to 3 mg.)

ICoNN 4 CASE: DYSMORPHOPHOBIA—WILLIAM

We noted that in William's case several DMNs were successfully identified and targeted for reprocessing using ICoNN 2 methodology. When attempting to develop the target for a current issue about two work colleagues who made jokes about his hair, he could only access the Gestalt of the events. Although he reported a good relationship with both men and didn't think that they were bullying him or being intentionally malicious, he was conscious of adopting passive adaptive behavior: laughing it off, only to ruminate on what had been said later in the day.

Helping the person to feel safe enough to connect to powerful and distressing material is vital. Clients will never choose to be vulnerable and reveal information to you if they feel unsafe. In this category of cases I always ensure that in addition to a standard safe/calm place, I also develop the past–present–future room, in accordance with the script outlined previously. This will act as an important secondary safe/calm place, and I install this with BLS. This was also done with Janus. Recall the adage "you've got to feel to heal"; allow how the person experiences his or her emotion (i.e., in the body) guide you both to the DMN.

PWM: As you stand in the room with the three doors, past, present, and future, notice how you are feeling. We have been exploring how you feel when your work colleagues banter with you about your hair. Notice what comes up for you now in your body. Notice if you feel an impulse to look behind one of the doors in particular. [DAS/BLS] What comes up for you right now?

W^{m}:   *I'm drawn to the past: it's 4 years ago. I'm studying for exams and pulling my hair out in anger.*

PWM: Go with that. [DAS/BLS] What comes up for you right now?

W^{m}:   *I'm at my desk now at work and I see one of the men* [who he perceives joke at his expense]. *He has a pen in his hair.*

PWM: Go with that. [DAS/BLS] What comes up for you right now?

W^{m}:   *Strong emotions are coming up.*

At this stage the target appeared to stabilize around this memory network and we now developed this as a target for reprocessing.

Target: William at his desk
Body: Chest and head
Emotion: Anger and shame
NC: "I am not acceptable"; SUDS = 7/10
PC: He was unable to articulate one, so we proceeded to desensitization.

PWM: See yourself sitting at your desk. Connect to the emotions of shame and anger that you feel in your chest and head. Now bring up the NC: "I am not acceptable." Go with that. [DAS/BLS] What comes up for you right now?

W^{m}:   *I'm less popular.*

PWM: Go with that. [DAS/BLS] What comes up for you right now?

W^{m}:   *I'm out of the loop.*

PWM: Go with that. [DAS/BLS] What comes up for you right now?

W^{m}:   *I don't want to look old… don't want to look ugly again.*

[Processing stalls at this point.]

PWM: [**Interweave:**] Who do you believe is judging you as "ugly"?

W^{m}:   *Don't know.*

PWM: [*Mythos Interweave—the diamond (see "Mythos Interweave—The Diamond" section):*] Go with that. [DAS/BLS] What comes up for you right now?

W^{m}:   *Bald people are not so cool.*

PWM: Go with that. [DAS/BLS] What comes up for you right now?

W^(m):   *I remember being assertive and speaking my mind. I can make good choices. Their opinion does not make me unacceptable.*

PWM: Go with that. [DAS/BLS] What comes up for you right now?

W^(m):   *I think both men are jealous of me having such a beautiful wife. They are insecure. [SUDS = 5/10]*

PWM: Go with that. [DAS/BLS] What comes up for you right now?

W^(m):   *I feel sympathy for them. [SUDS = 3/10]*

Please note that although the session proved to be incomplete, with the SUDS score coming down to 3/10, at subsequent review, William reported that the target was neutral—SUDS = 0. This was supported by collateral information from his wife, who noted that he was much improved functionally. He reported that in work he would no longer just laugh and leave. He was now able to let what was said just "go in one ear and out the other."

Mythos Interweave—The Diamond

Mythos/storytelling can prove to be a very useful method of interweave. In my opinion, it accesses the more abstract right-brain method of processing and can perhaps facilitate problem solving, much in the way that dreaming does. The diamond script is as follows:

Imagine that you are like a diamond. A diamond's character is made up of the different facets it has gained during the cutting and polishing process. No two stones are exactly the same, just like a person. We too have different facets, and just as different facets sparkle in the light, different aspects of who we are sparkle and shine. People we meet and experiences we have are like a cut diamond being held in different positions within a beam of light. We are not one facet, but the sum of all of our facets.

After using this mythos interweave with William, he concluded that he had other aspects of who he was, apart from his hair, and this facilitated a positive shift in processing.

RELATIONAL/INTERSUBJECTIVE INTERWEAVE

The following is a description of the relational interweave written by Mark Dworkin, who developed relational EMDR and emphasized the importance of the relational imperative in EMDR therapy. These are very useful tools in maintaining attunement when working in psychosis. I commend his work to you.

Randi—The Wronged Woman

By Mark Dworkin

Randi is a 44-year-old, Catholic, professional woman. She has been divorced for 7 years due to her husband's infidelity. This led her to become severely depressed. She works as a manager in a bank, and has two grown children whom she describes as "the reason I go on living." She had worked with an analytically oriented therapist with partial success but still found herself hypervigilant in her next relationship, always being on guard for any "perceived slights." Her therapist, sensing that Randi needed more than "talk therapy," referred her to this author (M. Dworkin), telling me that she was sure that Randi only needed a few "EMDR" sessions (meaning that the therapist expected me to begin EMDR reprocessing in my first session with Randi). She entered EMDR treatment with this expectation and was disappointed that I had to evaluate her and "get to know her a little better." She seemed to accept my explanation of the need to get an AIP-informed history (phase 1), and the need to prepare her (phase 2) for the active reprocessing phases of EMDR psychotherapy (phases 3–6), but was convinced that after one or two evaluation sessions we could begin reprocessing traumatic memories, although my "social brain" (Cozolino, 2002, 2014), which includes the mirror neuron system, informed me dissociatively that she wasn't ready. My countertransference to her demands was to capitulate and begin re-processing her traumas. My DMNs overrode my adaptive ones because of my fear of rejection, and activated my DMNs to behave subservient to her demands.

Although I could slow her down somewhat with explanations she could temporarily accept, she complained that she knew that her childhood issues had been resolved and that she needed to work on the pain of her husband's infidelity. Her DMNs, as it turned out, had to do with another man disappointing her—her father, her husband, and me. Her mirror neuron system evaluated me as another man in a string of men who would betray her. Her behavior was to hy-pervigilantly demand what she wanted, regardless of my "good intentions." At a certain point she even said to me, "Stop treating me like I'm some kind of fragile patient. Gloria [her previous therapist] told you that I can take it!" Although I evaluated her traumatic childhood memories as being quite active, she was insistent on working on what she wanted to work on. I explained EMDR; I ad-ministered the Dissociative Experience Scale (Carlson et al., 1993), and her score was expectedly low; she went through her safe/calm place experience (being at Sunday Mass at the church of her childhood), with all the completed steps successfully; she learned the stop signal; she demonstrated stress management techniques that Gloria had taught her; she indicated understanding of the train metaphor; and she "seemed" to understand and demonstrate the mindfulness necessary for successful EMDR reprocessing. Still, an inner voice kept on scream-ing, "stop, slow down, the bridge is out," but I believed that I was being too cautious, and that perhaps she was right. However, she was subsymbolically transmitting her "helpless little girl" memory networks that were the result of her "profound neglect in childhood" memory networks, and she suggested that we approach her painful rejection slowly. Randi suffered from a dismissive at-tachment disorder and experienced me as dismissing her once again, rather than accepting what I believed to be my compassionate and attuned caution to her need to rush into reprocessing her betrayal trauma. I accepted her need to focus on what she needed to primarily more so that she could "get what she was pay-ing for" (and not be dismissed), but in doing so my DMNs of wanting to be liked and not rejected caused me to become behaviorally subservient to her "entitled child" behavior, based upon her DMNs of profound childhood neglect.

I considered this a "now moment," and my "moment of meeting" (Stern, 2004) was to explain and give her an informed consent lecture. I was un-aware of how my rejection and subservient memory networks were activated.

I nonconsciously avoided my anxiety, and was colluding with Randi to avoid her dismissive patterns of interacting, and my unfinished disorganized attachment disorder (hostile/self-referential type). One could also consider this an example of concordant countertransference (Racker, 1968/1982). She insisted on starting with the following memory: The private detective she hired to follow her husband reported to her that she had been correct and gave her pictures he had taken of her husband and his lover in a compromising position.

Target: Seeing the photo of them kissing
NC: "I can't stand this."
PC: "I can move on."
VoC = 2/7
Emotions: Shame, humiliation, and trembling rage
SUDS = 10/10
Body: All over

She insisted on the eye scan at a high speed, and that it be kept on for long periods of time. Her initial associations were, "Nothing is happening at all." This went on for two sets. At this moment I experienced a pervasive feeling of anxiety and defeat in my chest. I used my containment skills and asked her to notice what was happening in her body.

"Nothing" was her reply. I had her go back to target and scan the picture for more details (one of the ways of facilitating blocked reprocessing). I asked her to notice any changes to the "target memory." She stated that she did not notice anything different. Whereas, in hindsight, I should have asked her to either focus on more of the target memory or less (I was not sure whether she was over- or underaccessing her memory), I was cowed by her increasing agitation. (In my book *EMDR and the Relational Imperative*, I recommend reprocessing her transference to me; I did not suggest this because I was in a dysfunctional state [countertransference to mother]). We began reprocessing the target memory, even though she stated that she had not noticed any differences in that memory. Again she reported that nothing was happening. She was in a somatically dissociated state, and reported that she felt nothing different.

I realized that I had dissociated my analytic training that stressed that any rupture between client and clinician was a function of both persons' subjectivity. I asked Randi to go inside and ask herself what DMNs that might have been encoded earlier in her life mirrored what might be happening between us. She then had an intense intrusion of DMNs holding painful memories of her father's emotional abuse and neglect of her being projected onto me. Even though she could access these dysfunctional memories, she stated, "Don't you understand? I feel humiliated and you are not helping."

I knew that my failure and rejection memories encoded dysfunctionally had been activated even more strongly. I used a compartmentalization strategy, a variation of the Korn and Leeds Resource and Development Strategy (Dworkin, 2005), and empowered my action tendencies to return to a prolonged reflective state (van der Hart, Nijenhuis, & Steele, 2006) where I could mentalize (Fonagy, 2002) Randi attacking me without my becoming countertransferentially activated.

The Relational/Intersubjective Interweave Used With Randi

I realized that by "pushing my agenda" of facilitating linkages to her past traumas, which she was not ready to deal with, I was re-creating an enactment of dismissing her again, like her parents and ex-husband. I realized that my somatic experience—a pervasive feeling of anxiety and defeat in my chest—was her role in our enactment of her feelings of defeat. I was dissociatively the embodiment of the dismissive attachments she had as a child, and in her marriage. This enactment prevented us from making any progress until it had been remediated by a "moment of meeting" (Stern, 2004). A moment of meeting is a spontaneous creation by the clinician aimed at releasing both parties of the enactment the clinician and client are stuck in.

I tuned into my somatic awareness of her DMNs of pervasive experience of anxiety and defeat, listening internally to her statement, "Don't you understand? I feel humiliated and you are not helping." Now that I had compartmentalized my DMNs I was able resonate with her pain. *This is the first step in the relational interweave.*

Using a "relational interweave" (Dworkin, 2005, 2015)—which is a variant of the cognitive interweave, when there is a block between client and clinician because of being trapped in an enactment—I admitted to Randi that although I believed that I may have been attuned to her pain, something in me didn't feel right, and therefore she had a point when she shared her anger with me for not understanding her pain and humiliation. I owned this as my problem and I then commented about my experience of her "nothingness," letting her know that I had a sense that the "nothing" she had been experiencing might have to do with the lack of connection she experienced as a child with her father, as an adult with her husband, and with me *now*, and I asked her if she could reflect on my thoughts. She became reflective; tears came to her eyes, and she shrugged her shoulders. That was enough of a response (because it indicated that there was a small opening in her blocked reprocessing) for me to ask her to just notice what the dyadic interaction was like for her in this *now* moment (my adaptive abilities meeting her DMNs).

Eye movements (EMs), a form of BLS, which is part of the desensitization phase, *are the second step in the relational interweave*, which proceeded as follows:

Randi: [Began to sob bitterly, first condemning herself for "putting me through hell."]
[*Author's comment:* Although I could have said, "Go with that," as is the instruction when the clinician notices a change indicating reprocessing, I believed—correctly—that her response was another now moment because she had a pattern of being harsh on others, or herself. I realized that another "moment of meeting" was necessary. I chose to share my experience, in the moment, with Randi.]
Me: Randi, I'm OK with your criticism of me [I was]. I think that my part was pushing my agenda to make linkages to your childhood activations. That's not what *you* needed right now. Am I close to what your experience is?
Randi: [Nodding her head "yes"] Yes, that fits.
Me: Just notice that. [I started another set of EMs]

Randi: I never told Frank [her ex-husband] what a bastard he was, because until this moment, I had been frozen into the role of being the "good little girl" who did not deserve to stand up for herself.

Me: Go with that. [EMs]

She continued reprocessing her childhood parental neglect—their fighting, her mother's fighting with her sister, and her needing to always be the peacemaker.

ICoNN 4 CASE: EVA

Synopsis of Eva's History

This is the case of a woman, whom we will call Eva, age 50. She was referred by her GP, who had seen her for a "long history of depressive symptomatology, anxiety and very strong depersonalization symptoms. Worst after most recent child born, hasn't really engaged well in attempted treatment of depression in the past." Eva described becoming suddenly aware that four of her children were "not real" and not actually her own children.

Presenting Issues at the Time of Eva's Psychiatric Assessment

- Depressive symptoms of low mood
- Self-blame and guilt about not loving her children enough
- The Capgras phenomena described in relation to four of her six children: "They look like my children, but they don't feel real; they're not my children"
- Dissociative symptoms were present, including derealization
- Delusions of persecution: she believed that God was punishing her

History of Presenting Issues and Treatment

When Eva's first child was born, she described that as she "felt around him" she got the feeling that he had in some way been "replaced" and that this was *not* actually her son; yet she had to raise him as such. This led to strong feelings of distress, and she believed that God was punishing her. She stated, "I think what is wrong with me is a lack of love." She attended sessions with counselors and a community psychiatric nurse (CPN), but experienced no relief. She had six children in all. The second child was born without any issues or related mental disorder. Shortly after her third child was born, her father died suddenly. She described leaving the baby with a babysitter, and when she returned to pick up the child, she noted, "I felt like it wasn't my baby." She described it as, "I can't get no feeling from my head to my heart." She told me that as she raised the children she had this ongoing belief that they were not really hers, so, she said: "I had to fight to love them and show love. Now I feel hurt [because she blames herself for not loving them enough]." This belief was connected to the related thought, "Someone else had mine and were mistreating them." The next child was born by Caesarean and she had no related mental disorder. At the birth of the next child, when the midwife took the child away to do a heel-prick test, Eva believes that the midwife brought back a different child: "Looked like my child but wasn't. I just thought, it's happening again." With the next child things were OK until the child was 2 years old, when, after leaving the child in the car to make a quick trip into a shop, she returned to feel that the child had been replaced.

On psychiatric assessment her mood was found to be low. This low mood was secondary to the conflict that she felt about having to raise children as her own, whom she believed were not. She reported thoughts that the people who had her children might be mistreating them, and was fearful that if she wasn't a "good enough" mother to the replacements this would get worse. She experienced doing so as an "extreme effort." Consequently she judged herself as not having done a good enough job. These phenomena resulted in a significant and substantial functional impact, which was consistent with the Capgras delusion.

DES

The DES was completed and she scored 26.4.

Case Formulation

Eva's psychiatric disorder had occurred in a premorbidly healthy and well-adjusted woman, with the first onset being related to having her first child. All other episodes of the Capgras delusion were either closely related to or subsequent to the birth of her children, but were not manifest on every occasion. There was no significant trauma history other than the sudden death of her father, and she believed that she coped and grieved normally for him. In particular, there were several touchstone moments within the chain of events. She could point to the specific moment when her "real" children had been "replaced": the onset of the Capgras phenomenon. These beliefs were held with delusional intensity and had proved resistant to attempted therapy in the past. The touchstone moments were ICoNN for the associated DMN. Initially the main priority was successful engagement and the commencement of constructing a safe container for treatment. This was achieved.

Diagnosis

A full psychiatric assessment, which included history taking and mental state examination, was completed. The *ICD-10* classifies Capgras as a *delusional disorder* (F22.0; WHO, 1993), although it is not specifically named within the nosological system. The *ICD-10* defines *delusional disorder* (F22.0; WHO, 1993, p. 97) as follows: "A disorder characterized by the development either of a single delusion or of a set of related delusions that are usually persistent and sometimes lifelong. The content of the delusion or delusions is very variable." Similarly, the most recent iteration of the *DSM*, the *DSM-5*, does not specifically include Capgras syndrome among its nomenclature, but codifies it as a *delusional disorder* (297.1; APA, 2013).

Capgras Delusion—A Brief Description and Neuropsychological Considerations

As previously noted in the discussion of the Cotard's syndrome case, neuropsychologically, Cotard's syndrome and Capgras syndrome are viewed as related disorders. Christodoulou suggests that we consider them both to be a part of a group of disorders that he classifies as *delusional misidentification syndromes*, which he describes in his book of the same name (G. N. E. Christodoulou, 1986). He has conducted research and published several key papers in this area (G. N. Christodoulou, 1986a, 1986b; Christodoulou, 1991; Christodoulou & Malliara-Loulakaki, 1981; Christodoulou, Margariti, Kontaxakis, & Christodoulou, 2009; Lykouras et al., 2008; Papageorgiou et al., 2005; Papageorgiou, Ventouras, Lykouras, Uzunoglu, & Christodoulou, 2003; Papageorgiou et al., 2004). The remaining disorders in the group are as follows:

1. *The Fregoli delusion*: The person believes that various different people are actually the same person in disguise (Christodoulou, 1976; Lykouras, Typaldou, Gournellis, Vaslamatzis, & Christodoulou, 2002; Papageorgiou, Lykouras, Ventouras, Uzunoglu, & Christodoulou, 2002).
2. *Intermetamorphosis*: The person is convinced that various people are able to swap identities, but maintain the same appearance (Malliaras, Kossovitsa, & Christodoulou, 1978).
3. *Subjective doubles*: The person believes that he or she has a doppelgänger (*double*) who is going about living an independent existence (Christodoulou, 1978a, 1978b).

The anatomical representation of love, affection, and attachment in the human brain is unknown. The recognition of facial expression and the emotional content or prosody of language is primarily mediated by the right hemisphere. Delusions and psychosis may be associated with right-hemisphere injury, and psychiatric disorders are more frequent after right-sided lesions. Two specific delusional disorders, Capgras delusion and reduplicative paramnesia, have also been linked with lesions of the right hemisphere (Anderson, Camp, & Filley, 1998). In respect to such delusional systems,

> research has shown that delusions are often the product of identifiable neurologic disease, particularly when the delusions have a specific theme or are confined to one topic-monosymptomatic or content-specific delusions. . . . **The review demonstrates that when adequate diagnostic workups are conducted, a high proportion of such delusions are found to have a neurologic basis. Lesions of the frontal lobes and the right hemisphere are shown to be critical to the development and persistence of many content-specific delusions** [emphasis added]. (Malloy & Richardson, 1994, p. 455)

Given this association with organic pathology, a magnetic resonance imaging (MRI) scan of Eva's brain was completed, which was normal. In the book *Phantoms in the Brain* (Ramachandran & Blakeslee, 1998), an underlying biological explanation of these phenomena is lucidly discussed; however, the phenomena manifested here had no evidence of biological change on MRI and the improvement in symptoms was rapid. I propose that this was achievable because in these cases there was no organic damage to the relevant pathways in the brain, and therefore the change was an electrochemical shift in signal management and not, at least in the first instance, a physical one. I propose that this shift takes place, under the facilitation of the DAS/BLS of EMDR therapy, in a structurally intact but functionally dysregulated system. It seems likely that Eva's depression and the associated deficit in reasoning, rigidity of thinking, and cognitive distortions allowed her beliefs to persist as long as they did (Gerrans, 2000).

Treatment

Phases 1 and 2 were completed per standard protocol. Following her initial psychiatric assessment, given the level of distress, Eva was offered medication. She accepted pregabalin 75 mg at night as an anxiolytic. She never increased beyond this small dose to the normal starting treatment dose of 75 mg twice daily. In this first session I focused on generating a strong therapeutic alliance and was actively neutral. Eva responded that she felt helped and heard by the end of the session. Subsequently, she stated at review, "I feel less unreal," and although the dissociation and Capgras delusion remained present, she was hopeful that something could be done. She believed that I "understood" what she was experiencing.

Progress

After informing her that the MRI was normal, I completed some psychoeducation focusing on the *normalization* of the experiences that she was describing to me. This increased the therapeutic alliance, and she consented to proceed with the planned EMDR therapy. The standard psychoeducation elements, which had not already been covered, were discussed. The safe/calm place was completed with EMs, and she responded very well to this.

IConN 4 Target
Rather than targeting the specific touchstone moments, we targeted the Gestalt of her experience of the Capgras delusion.

EMDR Treatment

There was one session of EMDR reprocessing.

Target: The Gestalt of her experience of the Capgras delusion

We developed the past–present–future room, with the three doors, and I asked her which door she felt drawn to. She stated the past. We went into the past, and on review of the targets identified as touchstones in previous sessions, she described that she felt there had been a shift with one of the children. I asked her to bring up the internal visualization of the child and check in with the NC and how she experienced that in her body.

NC: "She's not mine"; SUDS = 0/10
PC: "She's mine" VoC = 7/7

PWM: Picture your daughter. Now bring up the PC—"She's mine." Go with that. [DAS/BLS] What comes up for you right now?
Eva: *She's mine.* [Big, beaming smile]

PWM: Go with that. [DAS/BLS] What comes up for you right now?
Eva: *She's mine. I have no doubt that she is mine.*

Next we reviewed the other children, and two had SUDS scores of 0/10 and VoC scores of 6½/7. After one set of EMs holding the PC and the internal image of the child, the VoC rose to 7.

The last child was reviewed:

NC: "He's not mine"; SUDS = 6/10
PC: "He's mine"; VoC = 5/7
PWM: Go with that. [DAS/BLS] What comes up for you right now?
Eva: *He's mine! . . . that's brilliant, he's mine.*

PWM: So in the past you now feel clearly that the children are all yours. Can you check how that feels in the other rooms too?
Eva: *OK, they're mine.* [Big smile]

After the EMDR reprocessing session was completed, we closed in the standard way.

Note Regarding Medication

Although an anxiolytic (pregabalin) was used in the treatment of this case, it is notable that the dose was low—no higher than 75 mg daily.

TAKE-HOME FOR ICoNN 4 CASES

The initial phases 1 and 2 were completed according to the guidance described in a previous chapter. The case of Janus is a good example of how history and information about phenomenology can unfold over many sessions, rather than be gathered all at once in a new-client assessment. Janus felt more comfortable writing some of his experiences down, but even this was very challenging for him. We must remember how difficult it is for the person to reveal these experiences. Consider how Janus ended his letter to me: "I am almost physically sick with fear and dread over writing this down." As therapists, we need to make therapy a safe place to share such information, a place free of shame and judgment. Janus had a supportive family and group of friends, and this community of support helped him to feel safe enough to reveal the phenomenology that he did in his letter. These other people, who were important to Janus, helped enable him to build a robust therapeutic alliance with me. This proved to be a strong enough container to work with his psychosis. This partnership involving the person experiencing the psychosis, the people who are important to the individual, and the professionals working with the individual is a central tenet of the open dialogue approach (Seikkula & Olson, 2003), which I have commented on earlier. Together we are stronger.

Janus presents with targets in the ICoNN 1 and ICoNN 4 categories. In respect to the second and third targets, the DMN could be identified and was reprocessed according to the standard eight-phase, three-pronged protocol of EMDR therapy. In the case of these targets, no adaptation was required for phases 3 to 7 (de Bont et al., 2013; van den Berg et al., 2015; van den Berg, van der Vleugel, & Staring, 2010; van den Berg, van der Vleugel, Staring, de Bont, & de Jongh, 2013; van den Berg et al., 2014; van der Vleugel, van den Berg, & Staring, 2012). In the case of Janus, when the DMNs were processed the psychotic symptoms resolved, and Janus has remained medication- and symptom-free for the last 7½ years. This is what we would expect to find, considering the current literature (Gonzalez, Mosquera, & Moskowitz, 2012; van der Hart, Groenendijk, Gonzalez, Mosquera, & Solomon, 2014). Similarly, when we target and process the DMN associated with the Gestalt connected to the negatively valenced emotion being experienced, as in the cases of William and Eva, we see the psychosis resolve. This can remit quickly because the shift is an electrochemical one, and so, in Eva's case, the one session of EMDR reprocessing was capable of processing the related targets of Capgras delusions with her three children.

Key Points for IConN 4

1. Build a safe container for treatment using Caelian principles.
2. Build partnerships with the people who are important supports to the clients seeking help.
3. Listen and allow clients to tell their stories—this may occur over many sessions.
4. Be actively neutral.
5. Facilitate clients' connection with their feelings—you've got to feel to heal.
6. Pay attention to the emotions you are experiencing in your body as the therapist, and be especially vigilant toward your attunement with the person in therapy.
7. Utilize the key aspects of relational EMDR therapy.
8. Use relational/intersubjective interweaves to repair any mis-attunement between the therapist and the client; do so at the first possible opportunity.
9. Adhere to the standard eight-phase, three-pronged protocol where possible.

REFERENCES

American Psychiatric Association. (2013). *Diagnostic and statistical manual of mental disorders* (5th ed.). Washington, DC: Author.
American Psychiatric Association & American Psychiatric Association Work Group to Revise *DSM-III*. (1987). *Diagnostic and statistical manual of mental disorders: DSM-III-R* (3rd ed.). Washington, DC: American Psychiatric Association.
Anderson, C. A., Camp, J., & Filley, C. M. (1998). Erotomania after aneurysmal subarachnoid hemorrhage: Case report and literature review. *Journal of Neuropsychiatry, 10*(3), 330–337.
Bernstein, E. M., & Putnam, F. W. (1986). Development, reliability, and validity of a dissociation scale. *Journal of Nervous and Mental Disorders, 174*(12), 727–735.
Bleuler, E. (1950). *Dementia praecox; or, The group of schizophrenias.* New York, NY: International Universities Press.
Carlson, E. B., Putnam, F. W., Ross, C. A., Torem, M., Coons, P., Dill, D. L., . . . Braun, B. G. (1993). Validity of the Dissociative Experiences Scale in screening for multiple

personality disorder: A multicenter study. *American Journal of Psychiatry, 150*(7), 1030–1036. doi:10.1176/ajp.150.7.1030

Christodoulou, G. N. (1976). Delusional hyper-identifications of the Fregoli type. Organic pathogenetic contributors. *Acta Psychiatrica Scandinavica, 54*(5), 305–314.

Christodoulou, G. N. (1978a). Course and prognosis of the syndrome of doubles. *Journal of Nervous and Mental Disorders, 166*(1), 68–72.

Christodoulou, G. N. (1978b). Syndrome of subjective doubles. *American Journal of Psychiatry, 135*(2), 249–251.

Christodoulou, G. N. (1986a). Course and outcome of the delusional misidentification syndromes. *Bibliotheca Psychiatrica, 164,* 143–148.

Christodoulou, G. N. (1986b). Role of depersonalization-derealization phenomena in the delusional misidentification syndromes. *Bibliotheca Psychiatrica, 164,* 99–104.

Christodoulou, G. N. (1991). The delusional misidentification syndromes. *British Journal of Psychiatry, 14*(Suppl.), 65–69.

Christodoulou, G. N., & Malliara-Loulakaki, S. (1981). Delusional misidentification syndromes and cerebral "dysrhythmia." *Psychiatric Clinic (Basel), 14*(4), 245–251.

Christodoulou, G. N., Margariti, M., Kontaxakis, V. P., & Christodoulou, N. G. (2009). The delusional misidentification syndromes: Strange, fascinating, and instructive. *Current Psychiatry Reports, 11*(3), 185–189.

Christodoulou, G. N. E. (1986). *The delusional misidentification syndromes.* Basel, Switzerland: Karger.

Cozolino, L. J. (2002). *The neuroscience of psychotherapy: Building and rebuilding the human brain.* New York, NY: W. W. Norton.

Cozolino, L. J. (2014). *The neuroscience of human relationships: Attachment and the developing social brain* (2nd ed.). New York, NY: W. W. Norton.

Curran, P. S., & Miller, P. W. (2001). Psychiatric implications of chronic civilian strife or war: Northern Ireland. *Advances in Psychiatric Treatment, 7*(1), 73–80.

de Bont, P. A., van den Berg, D. P., van der Vleugel, B. M., de Roos, C., Mulder, C. L., Becker, E. S., . . . van Minnen, A. (2013). A multi-site single blind clinical study to compare the effects of prolonged exposure, eye movement desensitization and reprocessing and waiting list on patients with a current diagnosis of psychosis and comorbid post traumatic stress disorder: Study protocol for the randomized controlled trial Treating Trauma in Psychosis. *Trials, 14,* 151. doi:10.1186/1745-6215-14-151

Doyle, A. C. (1893). *The adventures of Sherlock Holmes.* Leipzig, Germany: Bernhard Tauchnitz.

Dworkin, M. (2005). *EMDR and the relational imperative: The therapeutic relationship in EMDR treatment.* New York, NY: Routledge.

Dworkin, M. (2015). *Relational EMDR: The synergy of procedure, therapeutic attachment, and intersubjectivity—implications for an expanded conceptualization of adaptive information processing and EMDR psychotherapy.* Retrieved from http://emdr-web.org/relational-emdr/

Fonagy, P. (2002). *Affect regulation mentalization, and the development of the self.* New York, NY: Other Press.

Gerrans, P. (2000). Refining the explanation of Cotard's delusion. *Mind & Language, 15*(1), 111–122. doi:10.1111/1468-0017.00125

Gonzalez, A., Mosquera, D., & Moskowitz, A. (2012). *[EMDR in psychosis and severe mental disorders].* Paper presented at the annual meeting of EMDR Europe Association, Madrid, Spain.

Lanius, U. F. (2005). EMDR processing with dissociative clients: Adjunctive use of opioid antagonists. In R. Shapiro (Ed.), *EMDR solutions: Pathways to healing* (pp. 121–146). New York, NY: W. W. Norton.

Lykouras, L., Typaldou, M., Gournellis, R., Vaslamatzis, G., & Christodoulou, G. N. (2002). Coexistence of Capgras and Fregoli syndromes in a single patient: Clinical, neuroimaging and neuropsychological findings. *European Psychiatry, 17*(4), 234–235.

Lykouras, L., Typaldou, M., Mourtzouchou, P., Oulis, P., Koutsaftis, C., Dokianaki, F., . . . Christodoulou, C. (2008). Neuropsychological relationships in paranoid schizophrenia with and without delusional misidentification syndromes: A comparative study. *Progress in Neuropsychopharmacology and Biological Psychiatry, 32*(6), 1445–1448. doi:10.1016/j.pnpbp.2008.04.012

MacLean, P. D. (1990). *The triune brain in evolution: Role in paleocerebral functions.* New York, NY: Plenum Press.

Malliaras, D. E., Kossovitsa, Y. T., & Christodoulou, G. N. (1978). Organic contributors to the intermetamorphosis syndrome. *American Journal of Psychiatry, 135*(8), 985–987.

Malloy, P., & Richardson, E. (1994). The frontal lobes and content-specific delusions. *Journal of Neuropsychiatry and Clinical Neuroscience, 6*(4), 455–466.

Melville, H. (1851). *Moby-Dick; or The whale.* London, England: Richard Bentley.

Papageorgiou, C., Lykouras, L., Alevizos, B., Ventouras, E., Mourtzouchou, P., Uzunoglu, N., . . . Rabavilas, A. (2005). Psychophysiological differences in schizophrenics with and without delusional misidentification syndromes: A P300 study. *Progress in Neuropsychopharmacology and Biological Psychiatry, 29*(4), 593–601. doi:10.1016/j.pnpbp.2005.01.016

Papageorgiou, C., Lykouras, L., Ventouras, E., Uzunoglu, N., & Christodoulou, G. N. (2002). Abnormal P300 in a case of delusional misidentification with coinciding Capgras and Fregoli symptoms. *Progress in Neuropsychopharmacology and Biological Psychiatry, 26*(4), 805–810.

Papageorgiou, C., Ventouras, E., Lykouras, L., Uzunoglu, N., & Christodoulou, G. N. (2003). Psychophysiological evidence for altered information processing in delusional misidentification syndromes. *Progress in Neuropsychopharmacology and Biological Psychiatry, 27*(3), 365–372. doi: 10.1016/S0278-5846(02)00353-6

Papageorgiou, C. C., Alevizos, B., Ventouras, E., Kontopantelis, E., Uzunoglu, N., & Christodoulou, G. (2004). Psychophysiological correlates of patients with delusional misidentification syndromes and psychotic major depression. *Journal of Affective Disorders, 81*(2), 147–152. doi:10.1016/S0165-0327(03)00136-8

Putnam, F. W., Carlson, E. B., Ross, C. A., Anderson, G., Clark, P., Torem, M., . . . Braun, B. G. (1996). Patterns of dissociation in clinical and nonclinical samples. *Journal of Nervous and Mental Disorders, 184*(11), 673–679.

Racker, H. (1982). *Transference and counter-transference.* London, England: Maresfield Reprints. (Original work published 1968)

Ramachandran, V. S., & Blakeslee, S. (1998). *Phantoms in the brain: Human nature and the architecture of the mind.* London, England: Fourth Estate.

Ross, C. A. (1991). Epidemiology of multiple personality disorder and dissociation. *Psychiatric Clinics of North America, 14*(3), 503–517.

Ross, C. A. (2004). *Schizophrenia: Innovations in diagnosis and treatment.* Binghamton, NY: Haworth Maltreatment and Trauma.

Ross, C. A., Keyes, B. B., Yan, H., Wang, Z., Zou, Z., Xu, Y., . . . Xiao, Z. (2008). A cross-cultural test of the trauma model of dissociation. *Journal of Trauma Dissociation, 9*(1), 35–49.

Ross, C. A., Norton, G. R., & Anderson, G. (1988). The Dissociative Experiences Scale: A replication study. *Dissociation, 1*(3), 21–22.

Seikkula, J., & Olson, M. E. (2003). The open dialogue approach to acute psychosis: Its poetics and micropolitics. *Family Process, 42*(3), 403–418.

Shapiro, F. (2001). *Eye movement desensitization and reprocessing (EMDR): Basic principles, protocols, and procedures* (2nd ed.). New York, NY: Guilford Press.

Shapiro, F., Kaslow, F. W., & Maxfield, L. (2007). *Handbook of EMDR and family therapy processes.* Hoboken, NJ: John Wiley & Sons.

Stern, D. N. (2004). *The present moment in psychotherapy and everyday life.* New York, NY: W. W. Norton.

van den Berg, D. P., de Bont, P. A., van der Vleugel, B. M., de Roos, C., de Jongh, A., Van Minnen, A., & van der Gaag, M. (2015). Prolonged exposure vs eye movement desensitization and reprocessing vs waiting list for posttraumatic stress disorder in patients with a psychotic disorder: A randomized clinical trial. *JAMA Psychiatry.* doi:10.1001/jamapsychiatry.2014.2637

van den Berg, D. P. G., van der Vleugel, B. M., & Staring, A. (2010). [Trauma, psychosis, PTSD, and the use of EMDR]. *Directieve Therapie, 30*(4), 303–328. doi:10.1007/s12433-010-0242-9

van den Berg, D. P. G., van der Vleugel, B. M., Staring, A. B. P., de Bont, P. A. J., & de Jongh, A. (2013). EMDR in psychosis: Guidelines for conceptualization and treatment. *Journal of EMDR Practice and Research, 7*(4), 208–224.

van den Berg, D. P. G., van der Vleugel, B. M., Staring, A. B. P., de Bont, P. A. J., & de Jongh, A. (2014). [EMDR in psychosis: Guidelines for conceptualization and treatment]. *Journal of EMDR Practice and Research, 8*(3), E67–E84. doi:10.1891/1933-3196.8.3.E67

van der Hart, O., Groenendijk, M., Gonzalez, A., Mosquera, D., & Solomon, R. (2014). Dissociation of the personality and EMDR therapy in complex trauma-related disorders: Applications in phases 2 and 3 treatment. *Journal of EMDR Practice and Research, 8*(1), 33–48. doi:10.1891/1933-3196.8.1.33

van der Hart, O., Nijenhuis, E. R. S., & Steele, K. (2006). *The haunted self: Structural dissociation and the treatment of chronic traumatization* (1st ed.). New York, NY: W. W. Norton.

van der Vleugel, B. M., van den Berg, D. P., & Staring, A. B. P. (2012). Trauma, psychosis, post-traumatic stress disorder and the application of EMDR. *Rivista di Psichiatria, 47*(2, Suppl. 1), 33S–38S. doi: 10.1708/1071.11737

World Health Organization. (1993). *The ICD-10 classification of mental and behavioural disorders: Diagnostic criteria for research.* Geneva, Switzerland: Author.

The INCBLOT Archive

Τί έστιν ἀλήθεια (What is truth?)
(John 18:38)

Intention: *To create and curate a space where we can gather and share stories of success, detailing cases where EMDR therapy is being efficaciously employed for the benefit of people who are experiencing psychosis, including schizophrenia. I aspire to co-create a repository of information with you, which can be used to improve our clinical endeavors in this area of EMDR therapy's practice.*

DO YOU SEE WHAT I SEE?

One of the things I hope to achieve in writing this book is that we inspire each other. The word *inspire* literally means "to breathe into." The original usage of the word made reference to the Divine and had connotations of imparting a truth or idea. I want us to breathe life into the psychotherapy of psychosis. I hope that we can share our truth and the ideas that we have regarding the use of eye movement desensitization and reprocessing (EMDR) therapy as psychotherapy for psychosis and schizophrenia. All too often people fail to realize the wonder of the things that they are doing on an everyday basis and therefore fail to see the need to share their experiences.

> "Men go abroad to wonder at the height of mountains, the
> huge waves of the sea, the long course of rivers, the vast
> compass of the ocean, the circular motion of the stars, but they
> pass by themselves and they don't even notice."
> —*St. Augustine*

Each time after presenting on the Indicating Cognitions of Negative Networks (IConN) model at EMDR therapy conferences, people have come up to me and often shared wonderful experiences that they have had of doing work with psychosis. Although we can aim for the gold standard of the randomized controlled trial (RCT), there is much to be gained from single case reports and case series.

LOOK AT HOW FAR WE HAVE COME

As we have seen, EMDR therapy can be used safely in patients diagnosed with psychosis and schizophrenia (van den Berg, van der Vleugel, Staring, de Bont, & de Jongh, 2013).

IConn 1 Category Case

In Paul's case, an IConN 1 category case of Cotard's syndrome, he had a clearly identifiable trauma and the dysfunctional memory network (DMN) was therefore readily identified and processed using the standard eight-phase, three-pronged protocol (Shapiro, 1989; Shapiro & Maxfield, 2002). In this first case, the formulation gained from an adaptive information processing (AIP) perspective stated that the trauma generated a DMN that was producing the posttraumatic stress disorder (PTSD), depression, and psychosis. AIP theory hypothesizes that if this DMN is reprocessed, then the phenomenology, including the psychosis, ought to abate or resolve completely. In this case we witnessed the psychosis resolve completely and not return, even when there was a relapse of depression during a time of later stress.

IConn 2 Category Cases

In the IConN 2 category cases that we outlined, we discussed two people with body dysmorphophobia, one of whom had limited insight and the other who held a delusional system that he was totally convinced of. Both were successfully engaged without the need to "persuade" them of the falseness of their beliefs and the veracity of a therapist's alternative view. The negative emotional valence that is associated with the psychotic material was engaged and used to guide the therapist, and the person experiencing the phenomena, back to the DMN. This could then be processed using the standard reprocessing phases of the EMDR model. According to AIP theory, this too would be anticipated to result in the decrease or complete resolution of the delusional phenomena. In these cases we witnessed that the clients no longer believed the body dysmorphic delusions, which did not return for as long as the cases were followed up.

IConn 3 Category Case

In the case of Oscar, we have been able to see that some of the work using EMDR therapy in psychosis can be prolonged over several years. Oscar had a diagnosis of dissociative identity disorder (DID) and met Ross's criteria for dissociative schizophrenia (Ross, 2004, 2013). He remains in active treatment, with an improving level of unity among the voices, which has resulted in improved function and decreased level of suffering. The therapist's ability to work in an attuned manner in the intersubjective is vitally important in this sort of work. When we are born, we have the potential to develop and mature into an innate information processing system—the AIP system. This maturation process requires the dynamic of community and the relationships of others to develop normally. This mature system is what we as therapists engage as we attune to clients and their "peopled wounds" (McCarthy-Jones, 2012). Progress can be made, and even small steps can have a huge impact on the client who experiences the truth of the adage that small things are not necessarily trivial.

IConn 4 Category Cases

In the IConn 4 category case of Janus, we described schizophrenia meeting the criteria in the third edition, text revision of the *Diagnostic and Statistical Manual of Mental Disorders* (*DSM-III-R,* American Psychiatric Association, 1987). The DMNs that were identifiable were targeted within the standard model, and the residual material was targeted using the IConn methodology by targeting the Gestalt of the psychotic material with negative emotional valence. The outcome was a complete resolution of the psychotic material that allowed for the subsequent controlled withdrawal of all medication, and Janus has been followed up for nearly 8 years at the time of this writing. Janus remains symptom-free and medication-free to the present day and has been able to undertake tertiary-level education, and recently was successful in re-entering the workplace at a professional level. Janus's level of working is higher than that engaged in premorbidly, which he became incapable of managing due to his psychotic experiences. Janus has summed up his growth, throughout the therapeutic journey and with his psychotic experiences, as follows: "I would say that you gave me my life back, but I don't know what that would mean. I didn't have a life. You have helped me to find a life." In the case of Eva, we saw how a shift can occur very rapidly in some individuals, even after many years of persistent and seemingly untreatable delusions. She has finally been able to own the belief that these are her children. I wish you could see her smile. For me that memory is priceless.

We see in these cases that people can have targets that fall into one or several of the IConn categories. Be attentive to that and respond accordingly. Remain attuned and in the intersubjective.

> "If you want to go fast, go alone; if you want to go far, go together."
> —*African proverb*

As I draw our literary journey to a close I invite you all on a further journey because, as the proverb indicates, together we can go further: toward our goal of helping bring hope to people who present with these experiences and who are seeking aid. "Together" is the state and trait that humanity was made for: unity but not uniformity.

So, I Have This Plan. . .

I want us to begin to gather together and share our case histories and the experiences of using EMDR therapy for psychosis. I hope that those who are experts-through-lived-experience will also join this expedition. This is about connection, and there's not going to be lots of laborious form filling and boring meetings. This is *dreaming* in community, and we are going to do that through the INCBLOT Archive. Let me explain a bit more . . .

INCBLOT = INTERNATIONAL COLLABORATION BRINGING LOCAL OUTCOMES TOGETHER

"The Universe is made up of stories, not of atoms."

—*Muriel Rukeyser (1913–1980)*

In the sleep cycle, the majority of dreaming occurs in the rapid eye movement (REM) stage of sleep. This essential time for the human brain allows for some house cleaning to occur, and it also facilitates interconnectivity within the brain. This interconnectivity allows for areas in the brain to connect that do not usually associate, and this maximizes our capacity for problem solving. *So now we are going to associate, where perhaps we don't usually, and do some dreamtime problem solving of our own.*

I would love to hear your thoughts and reactions to the book. Please get in touch using the contact details at the end of the discussion.

THE FIRST INCBLOT IN THE INCBLOT ARCHIVE

Every journey starts with a single step. Here is the first INCBLOT for the INCBLOT Archive. It comes from James (Jim) W. Cole, EdD, psychologist and approved EMDR therapy consultant in Ellensburg, Washington. After I had spoken about this work at a conference, Jim contacted me with the following encouraging message:

11/29/12

Paul,

After hearing you I started trying EMDR with a woman who was psychotic and now she has lost all of the voices in her head. You were right with your encouragement. We made the voices the targets and now they are gone.

Jim Cole

You can imagine how excited I was to receive that message. I do not want you to feel that you need to write a detailed academic paper and send it to me. Send brief messages at first and let's start a dialogue. Jim and I kept in touch and he sent me this update:

5/30/13

I continue to work using EMDR with the client I described before. She has had the longest period ever without a psychotic episode and her most recent episode was the shortest and least severe. Oh, and at the same time she lost 35 pounds.

Jim Cole

Even better! One of the major problems with the modern medications used in the treatment of schizophrenia and psychosis is their metabolic effects. So now I got a bit more proactive and sent a few questions:

1. **Why was the person consulting you?**
   The client was rather traumatized by having experienced 20 or more involuntary commitments. Some of these were experiences where they put her in jail rather than taking her to a hospital. Once she would not leave a pub and was charged with trespassing and taken to jail where she stayed for a few days. She was having her menstruation and she was not being given any hygiene supplies.

2. **At what stage did she disclose the voice-hearing to you?**
   There was no hesitation in discussing the voices. She was experiencing these voices almost continually.

3. **Was there one or more voices?**
   There were many voices; some would come to her at the same time and others would be alone when they spoke to her. Many were verbally abusive but this was not true of all of the voices.

4. **Were these described as being heard as she hears you speak or as if the voices were inside her head?**
   [NOT ANSWERED]

5. **Did the person describe dialoguing with the voices prior to consulting with you?**
   Yes, these voices had been experienced for a long time before coming in to see me.

6. **How did you work therapeutically with the person using EMDR therapy?**
   Initially we worked on the trauma of her repeated arrests and her repeated involuntary commitments. These traumatic events were creating a number of symptoms, which could easily have been diagnosed as posttraumatic stress disorder.

   Following the work with the involuntary commitments we worked to reduce the power of the abuse that she was receiving from the abusive voices. They were degrading her continually and calling her a racist. She has very strong values about not being prejudiced, and the voices clearly knew how to punish her. This woman reports that she had been molested as a child and then she was sent to a boarding school that she reports as being very abusive, with a great deal of corporal punishment. (I did a little bit of investigating and the school had been shut down after one student died.) She worked for a while as a topless dancer and then she was a prostitute working the streets near a military base. As we continued to work I started to work with the voices as if they were clients, having her translate. [She began] seeing their messages as in some way her own voice and her own meanings and feelings about herself; [we continued] working with the voices in this way and using EMDR the whole time.

7. **Please share any negative cognitions (NCs) that were associated with the voices.**
   I did not keep records of the NCs; however, they were all critical and abusive.

8. **Did the dialogue with the voices reveal a DMN that you targeted subsequently?**
   Yes.

9. **What was the therapeutic outcome?**
   I saw her on the street and stopped to visit with her some months ago and she wanted me to meet her family and she talked about her life having turned around considerably.

She had a long history of drug usage and I suspect there was some lingering damage from the meth; however, she appeared to be in a relatively happy mood and enjoying the people around her that she wanted to have me meet.

5/11/15

I just saw that ex-client & she reported that she has had no voices since August 2013.

Jim Cole

My hope is that as we begin to share and dialogue about the experiences with our clients, as Jim has so generously done, we can develop case series and design further studies in this vital area of study and practice. *No contribution is too small.*

Jim Cole has created the first INCBLOT. Will <u>YOU</u> be the next one? I hope so.

Contact Details:
E-mail: INCBLOT.archive@icloud.com

Please contact me to share your experiences. Together we can do more.

"A human being is a part of the whole called by us universe,
a part limited in time and space. He experiences himself, his
thoughts and feeling as something separated from the rest, a
kind of optical delusion of his consciousness. This delusion is
a kind of prison for us, restricting us to our personal desires
and to affection for a few persons nearest to us. Our task
must be to free ourselves from this prison by widening our
circle of compassion to embrace all living creatures and the
whole of nature in its beauty."
—*Albert Einstein, in letter of condolence to*
Mr. Marcus on the death of his son (1950)

יחד (Together)

REFERENCES

American Psychiatric Association. (1987). *Diagnostic and statistical manual of mental disorders* (3rd ed., rev.). Washington, DC: Author.

Einstein, A. (1950, December 2). [Letter of condolence]. Retrieved from http://www.letters ofnote.com/2011/11/delusion.html

McCarthy-Jones, S. (2012). *Hearing voices: The histories, causes, and meanings of auditory verbal hallucinations.* Cambridge, England: Cambridge University Press.

Ross, C. (2013). *Psychosis, trauma, dissociation, and EMDR.* Paper presented at the 18th EMDR International Association Conference, Austin, TX.

Ross, C. A. (2004). *Schizophrenia: Innovations in diagnosis and treatment.* Binghamton, NY: Haworth Maltreatment & Trauma Press.

Shapiro, F. (1989). Eye movement desensitization: A new treatment for post-traumatic stress disorder. *Journal of Behavioral Therapy and Experimental Psychiatry, 20*(3), 211–217.

Shapiro, F., & Maxfield, L. (2002). Eye movement desensitization and reprocessing (EMDR): Information processing in the treatment of trauma. *Journal of Clinical Psychology, 58*(8), 933–946. doi:10.1002/jclp.10068

van den Berg, D. P. G., van der Vleugel, B. M., Staring, A. B. P., de Bont, P. A. J., & de Jongh, A. (2013). EMDR in psychosis: Guidelines for conceptualization and treatment. *Journal of EMDR Practice and Research, 7*(4), 208–224.

Neurobiology and Stochastic Resonance: Going Deeper

This section is to inform therapists who have clients who want more detail on the proposed science of the eye movement desensitization and reprocessing (EMDR) method. It will not be necessary to go into such detail with all clients, but better to have this knowledge and not need it, than to need it and not have it; so here is a summary of the latest research and publications.

THALAMIC ACTIVITY AND PTSD

In patients with posttraumatic stress disorder (PTSD), where the naturally occurring noise from descending cortico-thalamic feedback is presumed to be unavailable due to a decrease in thalamic activity (Bergmann, 2008; Sartory et al., 2013; Yan et al., 2013) seen in PTSD, the dual attention stimulation/bilateral stimulation (DAS/BLS) of EMDR therapy could be generating a random (*stochastic*) signal at the thalamic level. Stochastic resonance (SR) in this setting would presumably facilitate the sensing of a signal that would otherwise be subthreshold. In other words, a further signal is transmitted that would otherwise not be. The principle of boosting an undetectable signal by having it resonate with added white noise is an area of intense research (Moss, Ward, & Sannita, 2004). So although noise may seem a worthless thing in one context, it can be the essential phenomenon for generating a meaningful signal in another. This observation has led one researcher in this area to state, "One man's noise is another man's signal" (Kosko, 2006).

REVIEW OF PROPOSED MECHANISMS OF ACTION OF DAS/BLS ELEMENT OF EMDR THERAPY

DAS/BLS is the element of the EMDR method that raises the most questions, controversy, and derision. One of the earliest and most influential authors who examined the effects of eye movements and their role within EMDR therapy states, "A major bar to the further acceptance of EMDR as a treatment and as an inviting research topic stems from the fact that workers still cannot see how eye movements can cause the reported clinical changes" (MacCulloch, 2006). This point is well made and we need to address this issue appropriately for our colleagues, our patients, and ourselves. The first paper published that explores a possible mechanism of action for DAS/BLS in EMDR therapy (Denny, 1995) suggests that the orienting reflex (OR) is engaged by the DAS/BLS through the use of eye movements. The orienting reflex is a reflex system where an organism becomes more sensitive to a novel stimulus when it first perceives it. This OR system is in turn proposed to inhibit the disturbance a person links with traumatic memories. Further examination of OR led to the proposal of an extinction model, which suggests that the OR system facilitates a reappraisal of, and subsequent change in, the neuronal model of the unconditional stimulus (Armstrong & Vaughan, 1996). In classical (Pavlovian) conditioning, the unconditioned stimulus is one that, naturally and automatically, triggers a response. In the EMDR therapy method the unconditioned stimulus is the trauma data. As with many of the attempts to understand the mechanism of EMDR therapy's efficacy, the proposed models built upon an existing knowledge base, which is taken from classical conditioning. In my opinion, the shortcoming of doing so for these models is that EMDR therapy is examined through a lens that sees it only as a variant or close relative of cognitive behavioral therapy (CBT). The same foundational thinking is seen in the paper by MacCulloch and Feldman (1996), which submits that DAS/BLS in the form of eye movements (EMs) facilitates a de-arousal of traumatic memories through classical Pavlovian conditioning, "by engaging positive visceral components of the investigatory reflex." In other words, the "novel" signal that DAS/BLS provides engages the innate reflex to investigate. This is the experience we can all identify with when we have turned suddenly to see what has just moved in the periphery of our visual field. This investigatory reflex is modeled as being hardwired to respond in a binary fashion, deciding either "threat" or "no threat" as the outcome of investigation. By re-experiencing the trauma data in a safe environment, as the DAS/BLS is being used to trigger the "no threat" outcome of the investigatory reflex, trauma data are desensitized. This was the first proposed mechanism that I was taught and that I used in the psychoeducation of my clients for many years. At this stage it is good to note that even the best model for how EMDR therapy works is still only a model. How you as the therapist utilize the model will denote its value.

QUESTION AND ANSWER WITH A CLIENT

In my opinion, as we describe the model of therapy and the current underlying scientific knowledge, we are demonstrating to our clients that we are familiar with and capable of applying the method to their problems. If clients pose a question that you cannot answer, I recommend an honest approach, such as, "I can't answer that right now; let me check and get back to you." This type of open approach means that you are not painting yourself as a perfect therapist who knows all. We all have gaps in our knowledge or even experience blanks for the basics on certain days. By demonstrating that we can answer the questions raised by our clients through supervision, consultation, or further research, we gain their confidence and trust. No one will believe you if say you have all the answers; I would not place my trust in such a therapist. Even when I had explained the extinction model to some clients, they would press me for more information, and it was at this stage that I would resort to the "experience paradigm." In the experience paradigm I would state something along the lines of, "We do not have all the explanations as to why EMDR therapy works, but I can say that I have observed it working in clients with a similar clinical picture to yours. The therapy does not work because you 'believe' in it, so let's go forward together with questioning minds." I found this an effective method that I still use, because although our models are more developed than when I started practicing EMDR therapy with clients, they remain models.

RECONSOLIDATION AND PROCESSING OF THE TRAUMA MEMORY DATA

Feedback from a substantial number of clinical hours with patients who have been treated successfully with EMDR therapy tells us that the traumatic flashback images that were so unavoidable *before* treatment become transformed, faded, or absent. They are no longer available for conscious access *after* successful treatment. This suggests that it is reconsolidation and processing of the trauma memory data that occurs with EMDR reprocessing, rather than the creation of a competing extinction memory, which would overwrite the previous disturbing trauma memory. Therefore, given the clinical descriptions by patients, the reconsolidation model is much more plausible than the extinction model, which has more to do with a CBT paradigm than the adaptive information processing (AIP) model of EMDR therapy. This is a very important area of distinction that we, as EMDR therapists, ought to understand clearly. It will aid us in our endeavor to answer a question that is often posed by colleague and client alike: "How does EMDR therapy differ from CBT?" Essentially the reconsolidation model proposes that the trauma memory data that existed before treatment with EMDR therapy are metabolized by the AIP system, facilitated by DAS/BLS, and as a consequence the data no longer exist in that form after EMDR reprocessing.

RESEARCH FOCUSES ON EYE MOVEMENTS

Following these initial papers, the literature next began to focus more intensely on research into EMs and their effects. These studies proposed that EMs interfered with the vividness of traumatic material in the visuospatial sketchpad of working memory (Andrade, Kavanagh, & Baddeley, 1997) and decreased both the emotionality and vividness of a trauma memory (Leer, Engelhard, & van den Hout, 2014). Work that explored the possible neurobiological means through which the de-arousal of the intense emotions linked with trauma memory occurred during hypnotic dissociation was presented by Corrigan (2002). Corrigan's work was based on observations of activity in the subdivisions of the anterior cingulate cortex, which is a part of the brain's limbic system. It is hypothesized that the ventral (affective) subdivision of the anterior cingulate gyrus is stimulated by DAS/BLS. This stimulation is proposed to result in its own subsequent deactivation, which in turn would allow stimulation and resultant activation of the dorsal (cognitive)

• **FIGURE A.1 DAS/BLS Stimulation in the EMDR Method**

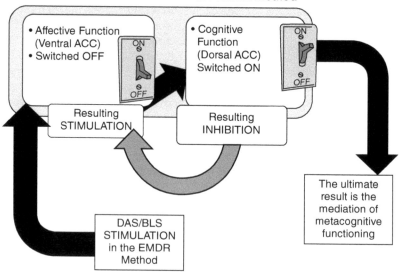

subdivision of the anterior cingulate. Once the cognitive subdivision is activated by DAS/BLS, this is believed to lead to *reciprocal inhibition* of the anterior cingulate cortex (ACC; see Figure A.1). Think of it in this way: A signal decreases the emotionality that in turn increases the capacity for thinking and reasoning, and this further decreases the emotionality. Other functions, such as dual attention and error monitoring, are known to activate dorsal regions of the anterior cingulate cortex, and we know that this area mediates metacognition (i.e., our thinking about how we think). In other words, by focusing on two targets and seeking errors, we stimulate the cognitive area of the ACC, which, it is proposed, then facilitates clients' capacity to think about *how* they are thinking; we refer to this as metacognition. Neurobiological interest in these brain regions is consistent with later work (Kaye, 2007) suggesting that EMs utilize error monitoring to reverse the suppression of the dorsal (cognitive) subdivision of the ACC by lowering activity of the ventral (affective) subdivision. In other words, we are proposing that DAS/BLS switches off the emotional area of the ACC, which then switches on the thinking area of the ACC. This would thus result in further inhibition of the emotional area—all of which would improve the higher executive functioning in the brain. This is the proposed "reciprocal inhibition" that Corrigan (2002) describes. Problem solving, the sequencing of tasks, and similar activities are traditionally thought of as higher executive functions of the brain. The de-arousing effect of EMs is consistent with the *reassurance reflex model* of EMDR proposed by MacCulloch and Feldman in their two subsequent papers (Barrowcliff, Gray, Freeman, & MacCulloch, 2004; Barrowcliff, Gray, MacCulloch, Freeman, & MacCulloch, 2003). They emphasise that de-arousal is not simply due to distraction by EMs. Another model hypothesized that EMDR therapy de-arouses "fear memories." The reduction of the activity (depotentiation) of limbic synapses is proposed to result from low-frequency stimulation, and this may be a mechanism through which EMDR therapy quenches or modifies "fear memory" (Rasolkhani-Kalhorn & Harper, 2006).

INTEGRATION

Much of this preceding work has focused on various proposed roles and functions of specific brain areas and isolated neurobiological systems. However, we know that, in vivo, such systems do not operate in isolation. It is not surprising that an expert in EMDR therapy was the first to suggest that DAS/BLS had an integrative role in the brain, presenting a model that is neurodynamic in character and in keeping with the AIP model (Bergmann, 1998). In my opinion, Uri Bergmann has been one of the most influential contributors to this area of EMDR therapy research and publication. I recommend his book to all readers seeking to delve deeper into this aspect of EMDR therapy. His contribution notes that the connection of structures within the brain and their integrated functions are characterized by synchronous electrical activity in the gamma band frequency (40 Hz). Initially it was proposed that DAS/BLS reset septal pacemaker cells, which would then enable the resynchronization of the connectivity between the right and left cerebral hemispheres (Bergmann, 1998). In other words, we are proposing that the activity between the two halves of the brain is returned to a synchronized form of communication, which is characterized by neural activity operating at 40 Hz. Later work by the same author posits a role for the activation of the lateral cerebellum. This area of the brain functions as an association area, which is believed to have projections to the ventro-lateral and central-lateral thalamic nuclei. Nuclei in this sense are collections of nerve cells in the brain and spinal cord in which nerve fibers form connections. Activation of these areas is theorized to facilitate repair and integration of somatosensory, memorial, cognitive, frontal lobe, and synchronized hemispheric function, which we know are disrupted in PTSD (Bergmann, 2008). The ventro-lateral thalamic nucleus is postulated to send connections to the dorsolateral prefrontal cortex, which activates this region. Bergmann (2008) proposed that DAS/BLS facilitates the process that metabolizes traumatic memory into general semantic memory, allowing integration with other neocortical networks. It is postulated that a related surge in acetylcholine (a neurotransmitter) is created as a consequence of DAS/BLS, which can then facilitate rapid eye movement (REM)–like physiological systems. This REM-like state is proposed to be capable of decreasing the strength of hippocampally mediated episodic memories and amygdaloid-mediated negative affect, which we see in PTSD (Stickgold, 2002). Sleep researchers at Harvard Medical School explored this area of overlap. During REM sleep, compared with non-REM sleep, there is a much wider activation of more distant associations (Stickgold, Fosse, & Walker, 2002; Walker, Brakefield, Morgan, Hobson, & Stickgold, 2002; Walker, Liston, Hobson, & Stickgold, 2002), and this is postulated to facilitate problem solving. In some ways this phenomenon is like the central information processing areas of the brain using the "phone a friend" option of the well-known TV quiz show, where participants "dial out" and get new information from more distant regions, which facilitates the finding of a solution. This problem-solving function of sleep activity is in keeping with the expectation fulfilment theory (ExFT) of dreaming as outlined by the researchers who have developed the "human givens" approach (Griffin & Tyrrell, 2006). These researchers describe dreaming as the deepest trance-like state humans can enter. They summarize three essential principles as being necessary to properly understand the ExFT of dreaming:

1. Dreams are metaphorical translations of waking expectations.
2. Only expectations that cause emotional arousals that are not acted upon during the day become dreams during sleep.
3. Dreaming deactivates that emotional arousal by completing the expectation pattern metaphorically, freeing the brain to respond afresh to each new day (Griffin & Tyrrell, 2006).

This proposed neural exploration of wider associations is characteristic of REM memory processing and EMDR but is not seen in exposure therapy, which focuses on the trauma memory. This is another very important difference between the therapy methods currently advocated in the treatment of traumatic memories: trauma-focused CBT and EMDR therapy (National Institute for Health and Care Excellence [NICE], 2005). As we have examined earlier, it is proposed that the wider involvement of brain regions draws in maximal neurodynamic resources to facilitate information processing. Integration of brain function has been the focus of the latest research, which proposes that EMDR therapy enables the integration of dissociated aspects of traumatic memories, resulting in a decrease in the hyperarousal symptoms we see in PTSD (Farina et al., 2014).

JIM KNIPE'S SUMMARY OF THE RESEARCH

Knipe summarizes the research into DAS/BLS differently from the research just described, by exploring the proposed consequences of DAS/BLS (Knipe, 2015):

1. EMs generate an increase in the vividness of episodic memory retrieval and expansion of association networks (Christman, Garvey, Propper, & Phaneuf, 2003) following 30 seconds of horizontal saccadic eye movements (but not smooth pursuit or vertical eye movements).
2. EMs during EMDR therapy are observed to activate cholinergic and inhibit sympathetic systems. This pattern of activity has similarities with the configuration observed during REM sleep (Elofsson, von Scheele, Theorell, & Sondergaard, 2008). An increase in parasympathetic tone follows EMDR therapy (Sack, Lempa, & Lamprecht, 2007). Another study showed distinct changes during EMDR therapy for a range of autonomic measures, which included respiratory rate, heart rate, systolic blood pressure (this was observed to increase during early sets, but invariably declined during abreactions, and decreased overall), fingertip skin temperature, and the galvanic skin response—all consistently showed a clear "relaxation response." Therefore, it was understandably proposed that EMDR facilitates desensitization by reciprocal inhibition, through the pairing of emotional distress with an unlearned or "compelled" relaxation response (Wilson, Silver, Covi, & Foster, 1996).

3. EMs (and, to a lesser degree, alternating tones) were found to reduce the mental avoidance of disturbing material by "taxing" working memory, while also decreasing the "emotionality" of the targeted memory network (de Jongh, Ernst, Marques, & Hornsveld, 2013). This built on earlier work that supported a working memory account of EMDR therapy, which found that DAS/BLS in the form of alternating beeps was inferior to eye movements in reducing the emotionality of negative memories (Hornsveld et al., 2010; van den Hout et al., 2011).

4. EMs result in activation of the parasympathetic elements of the OR (MacCulloch & Feldman, 1996; Sack et al., 2007).

5. EMs result in a decrease in interhemispheric gamma electroencephalogram (EEG) coherence in the frontal areas, leading to a reduction in traumatic memory intrusions (Propper, Pierce, Geisler, Christman, & Bellorado, 2007).

6. An increase in the capacity for "distancing and noticing" is facilitated by EMs, with a significant reduction in distress at posttreatment and at follow-up (Lee & Drummond, 2008). The effects of the EM element of EMDR therapy were reported as different from those of other exposure-based therapies (Lee & Cuijpers, 2013, 2014).

7. BLS facilitates the slow thinking that could result in an increased capacity for an objective assessment (Kahneman, 2011). Imagine two people and one is saying something that is blatantly incorrect. The other one might say, "Stop for a moment and think about what you just said." The slowing-down aspect of BLS is not only useful in resolving the distortion of posttraumatic disturbance (being afraid when there is no risk), but is also as helpful in realizing the short-sightedness of a psychological defense (such as getting an avoidance urge) (Knipe, personal communication, 2014).

All of these effects of DAS/BLS in general and of EMs in particular are hypothesized to enhance adaptive information processing and facilitate adaptive resolution of a "trauma memory" (Knipe, 2015).

STOCHASTIC RESONANCE—A PROPOSED MECHANISM OF ACTION

The leitmotif of efficacy as a return to an integrated, functional connection between both sides of the brain seems fundamental to the efficacy of EMDR therapy. It is logical, therefore, to search for a ubiquitous mechanism in nature that could facilitate such interconnectivity. I believe that the postulated mechanism of SR is an excellent candidate for the neurobiological mechanism that enables such organization of information, and as such it deserves further exploration. As we have seen, the DAS/BLS element has no widely agreed definitive mechanism of action to explain the rapid efficacy of EMDR therapy. A likely candidate that explains the efficacy of DAS/BLS will be an innate, biological mechanism that will most likely be found in many natural systems, including the human nervous system. As I have already stated, it is my belief that SR meets these criteria. Here a model is proposed where this innate mechanism makes what we speculate to be unintelligible signals, which constitute a dysfunctional memory network (DMN), intelligible. In EMDR therapy terms, we model a DMN as being the unprocessed data and sensory information that result from trauma.

The proposed mechanism of SR also helps us to generate a meaningful model explaining why the DAS/BLS element facilitates the encoding of memories in the neocortex. This model sits upon the proposition that functional encoding is characterized by neural interconnectivity. This push to cultivate an interconnected neurological state is believed to be a reparative adaptation to the deactivation of the thalamus. Daniel Siegel created the acronym *FACES* to describe the brain in an integrated and functionally optimal state: "When you are not traumatized, your brain is integrated in creating a Flexible, Adaptive, and Coherent flow that is Energized and Stable" (Siegel & Buczynski, 2014). "FACES is what well-being is" (Siegel & Buczynski, 2014). Activity in the thalamus is decreased in PTSD patients as compared with non-PTSD patients (Bergmann, 2008; Sartory et al., 2013; Yan et al., 2013), so it is not surprising to observe that SR operates at this influential brain region.

A form of signal "gating" is also believed to occur at the thalamic level. This gating function would be an adaptive function that could protect the higher neocortical systems in times of trauma. *Gating* is when the neural system functions as a gate, allowing some signals through (gate open) and blocking others (gate closed). Although it initially may appear counterintuitive, random (*stochastic*) neuronal "noise" at the level of the thalamus has been observed to help *filter* an incoming signal and is proposed to act to control the focus and sensitivity of the system (Béhuret, Deleuze, Gomez, Fregnac, & Bal, 2013). This model, which utilizes SR, looks upon thalamic noise as the phenomenon that is controlling what is passed on, and it would also be the mechanism involved in the gating function. A naturally occurring stochastic signal is believed to be normally present in the form of descending cortico-thalamic feedback (Béhuret et al., 2013). However, this innate stochastic signal could very well be blocked in trauma, as we know there is down-regulation of the thalamus (Bergmann, 2008). I propose that when we introduce a stochastic signal through the application of DAS/BLS within EMDR therapy, we may be returning normal functioning to the innate information processing system of the brain through the proposed phenomenon of SR.

WHAT EXACTLY IS STOCHASTIC RESONANCE?

SR is a proposed model where a signal that is too weak to be picked up by a sensor is boosted by the addition of random noise. Therefore the original signal, rather than being drowned out, is detected. In physics, resonance can be defined as a dynamic that results in a sound becoming louder or lasting longer through the synchronous vibration of another object in the same proximity. If one of two tuning forks that are pitched at the same resonant frequency is struck, the other will begin to vibrate, due to resonance.

LET ME TELL YOU A STORY. . .

Consider the following metaphorical story as a word picture for the modeled behavior of SR:

a. *Simon* is the signal coming into the thalamus.
b. *Lilly* is the limbic system.

c. *Neo* is the neocortex.
d. *The wall* is the thalamus.
e. The *single box* is a specific boosting signal—but this is not available in the natural system.
f. The *many boxes* thrown over at multiple points along the whole length of the wall constitute a stochastic (*random*) signal, and the box that lands in front of Simon allows him to boost himself above the level of the wall and be "sensed" by his friends—this is the process of SR.

Simon wants to send a message to Lilly and Neo but a 6-foot wall blocks his direct line of sight. One way around this would be for Simon to raise his height; then he could see over the wall and communicate with his friends. However, the problem is what to use to raise Simon above the height of the wall. Lilly and Neo could throw a box over the wall at the point on the wall where Simon is standing, but they do not know where that is. So let us imagine that they are able to throw boxes over the wall throughout its entire length. Simon would invariably get one of the many boxes and be able to transmit his message to Lilly and Neo.

Normally, Simon's friends are the ones to throw the boxes over the wall—this is the presumed natural stochastic signal of descending cortico-thalamic feedback. However, in trauma we know that thalamic activity is thought to be decreased and the descending cortico-thalamic noise may be reduced, or not available at all. This is thought to be most true for the thalamic projections of the perigenual anterior cingulate cortex (Corrigan, personal communication, 2014), the part that is most consistently shown to be deactivated in PTSD (Vogt & Laureys, 2009). This means Simon has no way to boost himself above the wall and therefore no communication can take place with his friends. The DAS/BLS of EMDR therapy is proposed to provide a replacement for the absent "boxes" from an outside source (*Simon's side of the wall*); this would allow him to boost himself and communicate as usual. This model suggests that the facilitation occurs through the phenomenon of SR. See Figure A.2.

The phenomenon that has been modeled as SR is widely observed throughout nature in biological, physical, and electromagnetic systems. Several

• **FIGURE A.2 Scenarios of Signal Transmission**

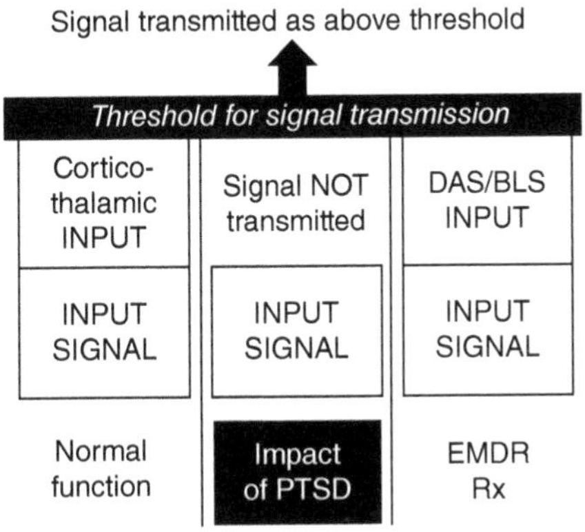

Signal transmitted as above threshold

Threshold for signal transmission		
Cortico-thalamic INPUT	Signal NOT transmitted	DAS/BLS INPUT
INPUT SIGNAL	INPUT SIGNAL	INPUT SIGNAL
Normal function	Impact of PTSD	EMDR Rx

organisms, including humans, are known to exhibit in their tissues what we characterize as SR (Kosko, 2006). The first observed SR phenomenon was described in the visual neurons of cats. In humans, SR is observed in muscle spindles and has a demonstrable behavioral impact in the human balance system, which is where I first encountered it. However, SR has not been previously defined or explored in relation to the neurobiology of EMDR therapy in general nor for the DAS/BLS elements in particular. Further examples of helpful noise in humans are modeled in the literature: in the hippocampal CA3-CA1 model, where SR is proposed as a mechanism through which memories are recalled (Yoshida, Hayashi, Tateno, & Ishizuka, 2002); and in attention deficit hyperactivity disorder (ADHD), where moderate noise induces SR, and this is believed to be responsible for improved cognitive performance (Söderlund, Sikstrom, & Smart, 2007). A stochastic signal can be externally input into the nervous system. In the case of one foot device, an initial study describes an improved balance in humans, which is believed to result from a randomly vibrating gel insole (Priplata, Niemi, Harry, Lipsitz, & Collins, 2003). The research team that developed this device demonstrated that their randomly vibrating insoles could ameliorate age-related impairments in balance control, and I believe that this is an example of "helpful noise" that could well be operating through SR (Priplata et al., 2003). For me, SR is a plausible candidate as a proposed innate mechanism that would help to explain the efficacy and importance of the DAS/BLS elements within the EMDR therapy, if we model DAS/BLS as a stochastic signal. In presenting this model to clients seeking EMDR therapy, we give them what I consider to be a plausible model for how the DAS/BLS element provides helpful noise to the neural system.

SR AND THE NEUROBIOLOGICAL UNDERSTANDING OF HOW MENTAL HEALTH PATHOLOGY ARISES IN TRAUMA

We understand from neuroimaging studies (Sartory et al., 2013) that the thalamus is a vital brain structure in the integration of perceptual, somatosensory, memorial, and cognitive processes. This proposed function is referred to as *thalamo-cortical-temporal binding,* and it is a model in which data are normally metabolized into a functional memory network in the neocortex (Bergmann, 2008). In psychological trauma, we hypothesise that the subthreshold signal of a traumatic memory needs to be detected before thalamo-cortical-temporal binding can happen. Normally, we presume that the innate stochastic feedback from the descending cortico-thalamic pathways facilitates behavior in the neural bioelectric system, what we model as SR (Béhuret et al., 2013). This model is offered as a plausible explanation as to how a subthreshold signal in PTSD patients can be boosted at thalamic level. However, in psychological trauma we have modeled this descending cortico-thalamic feedback as not being available and, as a consequence, processing would be effectively blocked—*like the wall in our story.* This modeling of a failure in our innate information processing system is, I believe, neurobiologically consistent with what EMDR therapy posits in the AIP model (Shapiro, 2007).

SR AND THE PREDICTION OF SUCCESSFUL CLINICAL OUTCOMES

It is a logical proposal, when we consider the current body of neurobiological literature, that increasing thalamic activity is an important component in the effective treatment of PTSD. Given that the activity in the thalamo-cortical tracts is reported to be decreased in PTSD as compared with non-PTSD controls (Bergmann, 2008) and that the proposed phenomenon of SR is described as resulting in an increase in the activity of this brain area, SR becomes a plausible candidate for the efficacy of DAS/BLS in EMDR therapy. The model of SR explains how a stochastic signal would facilitate the synchronization of neuronal oscillation and coherence in the brain. We are aware that such a coherent state is believed to be established by activity in the gamma-band wave frequency of 40 Hz, which DAS/BLS also generates (Bergmann, 2008; Reinker, Puil, & Miura, 2004). In other words, in our model we are suggesting that the boosting that occurs for the signal (*Simon*) allows it to be sensed and communicated onward through the thalamus (*the wall*) to the limbic (*Lilly*) and neocortical (*Neo*) areas by the facilitatory effects of DAS/BLS (*the boxes*), which create the AIP equivalent of "white noise" at the thalamic level. One research group has proposed that in both age-related states and brain disorders that feature memory deficits linked to abnormal functioning in the mesolimbic region, this "white noise" may facilitate learning through the restoration of functioning in the mesolimbic system (Rausch, Bauch, & Bunzeck, 2014).

SR AND THALAMIC GATING

In the Tribrain model we describe sensory information as being relayed to the cerebral cortex through the thalamus, which functions as the primary gateway for all sensory input signals on their way to the neocortex. A research team has created a realistic hybrid retino-thalamo-cortical pathway by mixing biological cells and simulated circuits to allow detailed study of this neural dynamic (Béhuret et al., 2013). We have already modeled a normally occurring, descending cortico-thalamic feedback in the form of *noise* from the cortex (higher brain centers) to thalamic synapses. Researchers injected a stochastic (*random*) mixture of excitatory and inhibitory signals to the hybrid pathway model. The analysis of the impact of the simulated cortico-thalamic feedback on the overall efficiency of signal transfer highlighted a previously unidentified control mechanism that they observed to be functioning at the thalamic level. This control mechanism was believed to result from the collective resonance of all thalamic relay neurons. The study reported that the efficiency with which signals are transmitted increases when the level of correlation across thalamic cells decreases. This suggests that the transfer efficiency of relay cells could be selectively amplified when they become simultaneously desynchronized by the cortical feedback. In other words, when the relay cells are not in synchronous activity because of feedback from the higher centers, they become better able to forward information. When contemplating how this may function, in vivo, in the human brain, it appears plausible that this mechanism of regulation at the thalamic level could direct the focus of perception to specific thalamic subassemblies. This would mean that the appropriate input lines to the cortex could be selected according to the descending influence of cortical signal (Béhuret et al., 2013). This is very important, as not only are we proposing that stochastic noise may facilitate the transmission of signal, but also that it may have a role in the brain's capacity to focus on certain inputs while ignoring others.

SYNTHESIS

Considering the previous discussion, I believe that we can argue the following model: DAS/BLS induces a stochastic signal similar to one that is naturally present in the thalamo-cortical system (Béhuret et al., 2013) as descending cortico-thalamic feedback. In psychological trauma, this stochastic signal in the thalamo-cortical system allows sensing and transmission of an incoming signal to occur via the phenomenon of SR (Melloni et al., 2007). DAS/BLS is observed to result in the activation of the ventrolateral and central-lateral thalamic nuclei. The activation of the ventrolateral nucleus crucially facilitates the activation of the dorsolateral prefrontal cortex, which is described as being disrupted in PTSD (Bergmann, 2008). Bergmann further unpacks for us the importance of this area of the brain as follows:

> This dorsolateral prefrontal part of the brain brings a more analytic and appropriate response to emotional impulses, modulating the amygdala and other limbic areas (LeDoux, 1986). The presence of circuits noted above connecting the amygdala to the prefrontal lobes implies that the signals of emotion, anxiety, anger, and terror generated in the amygdala can cause decreased activation in the dorsolateral area, sabotaging the ability of the prefrontal lobe to maintain working memory and homeostasis (Selemon, Goldmanrakic, & Tamminga, 1995). (Bergmann, 2008)

Essentially, what is being modeled here is a shift from a disconnected state to a functionally interconnected state between these important brain areas. Such a shift would be clinically characterized by a rapid shift from dysfunction to function. The fact that this is an electrochemical shift in signal management and not primarily a structural change in brain tissue helps to explain the speed of change that is observed in patients treated with EMDR therapy (Solomon & Shapiro, 2008). These observations and the previously proposed modeling show how the DAS/BLS of EMDR therapy could bring online and connect areas of the brain that are vital for the healthy processing of information. The function of DAS/BLS within these proposals is the facilitation, repair, and integration of somatosensory, memorial, cognitive, and synchronized hemispheric functions. This synchronization of neuronal oscillation is described as occurring at the 40-Hz (gamma band) frequency of oscillation in the thalamo-cortical system. All neuronal activity is linked with electrical charges in some manner. Not only does this represent communication between nerve cells, it is "the electrical glue that allows the brain to organize itself functionally" (Bergmann, 2008; Llinás, 2001). Neural synchrony represents an electrical interconnectedness of the brain's neuronal systems, which operate at the 40-Hz frequency (the gamma wave band), and this is also thought to be the mechanism through which SR operates (Melloni et al.,

2007). The importance of this frequency is underlined by the observation that the thalamo-cortical system has an intrinsic 40-Hz oscillatory activity, which, it is posited, serves to mediate global temporal mapping by scanning for, targeting, and synchronizing the activity of the various neuronal assemblies (Bergmann, 2008). In this paradigm we can model a healthy memory, which represents successfully "metabolized" data, as being stored as a coherent "melody" of neuronal activity in the brain, oscillating at 40 Hz. It is the belief of this author that the phenomenon of SR facilitates this process. If SR is successfully induced in the thalamus through DAS/BLS, we see increased activity in this area, with a clinically significant response to EMDR therapy. Further study is warranted that could look for the occurrence of SR in the thalamus and thus examine if its presence resulted in increased thalamic activity, which is believed to be a marker of the efficacy of EMDR therapy in PTSD.

THE ISSUE OF BILATERALITY

Corrigan, in a personal communication (2014) discussing this issue, notes a potential weakness of the sensory stimulation model (Bergmann, 2010; Lanius, Paulsen, & Corrigan, 2014) in its lack of applicability to the alternating bilaterality of DAS/BLS. In regard to the proposed mechanism of SR, if an incoming signal is sufficient to induce interconnectivity through SR, does the bilaterality of the DAS/BLS signal induce SR more than a nonalternating stimulus? This is a valid question. Béhuret et al. (2013) observed that level 6 cortical neurons that project to the thalamus had a greater response to whisker deflections when the motor cortex was focally enhanced. This cortico-thalamic feedback represents a stochastic (random) signal that facilitates signal filtering and transmission at the level of the thalamus (Béhuret et al., 2013; Melloni et al., 2007). Activity in level 6 of the cortex may thus influence cortical sensory responses indirectly through cortico-thalamic feedback projections (Béhuret et al., 2013). If we include consideration of the earlier models that suggest a role for the OR in the efficacy of EMDR (Armstrong & Vaughan, 1996; Denny, 1995; MacCulloch & Feldman, 1996; Sack et al., 2007), the orienting response will result in an increased cortico-thalamic signal (Béhuret et al., 2013). This is not just true for input from the motor cortex. In the six-stage valence-code processing model of Vogt and Laureys (2009), signal transition through the cingulate from posterior to anterior results in orienting to any stimulus. This overt or covert orienting allows the brain to make an assessment in respect to memories, self-significance, motor impulse requirement, and, at the level of the anterior cingulate cortex, autonomic nervous system outputs (Corrigan, personal communication, 2014). All of these cingulate areas are believed to have extensive connections with the thalamus, especially the intralaminar and midline nuclei. This means that it is feasible for DAS/BLS to trigger cingulate activity throughout its entire length via the OR to visual, oculomotor, tactile, or auditory inputs (Shibata & Yukie, 2009). This would go some way toward explaining the efficacy of all of the various forms of DAS/BLS currently utilized in EMDR therapy and not necessitate that the model be limited to EMs.

The visual system shows active and constant feedback. This is due to the role of the cortex in predicting future sensory inputs, an important survival function. It is thought that this cortico-thalamic feedback modulates thalamic activity, and it may be doing so through the phenomenon of SR. As a patient is asked to follow the DAS/BLS stimulus, the cortical system, which predicts future sensory input, will be understandably active. In other words, we are proposing that DAS/BLS switches on the system in the higher, more advanced brain centers that are responsible for predicting the future course of behaviors. As attention typically amplifies neuronal responses evoked by task-relevant stimuli, while attenuating responses to irrelevant distractors (Béhuret et al., 2013), it seems likely that the bilaterality of the DAS/BLS would amplify the SR effect more than a constant, nonalternating stimulus. This is what appears to have been observed by Herkt et al. (2014) when they compared three groups: bilateral alternating stimulation in the form of auditory tones, bilateral simultaneous auditory tones, and no additional stimulation. The results show that the effects for alternating BLS were greater than those for simultaneous BLS, which was in turn greater than no additional stimulation (Herkt et al., 2014). This is consistent with the modeling that views increased thalamic activity as facilitating the repair and integration of somatosensory, memorial, cognitive, and synchronized hemispheric functions. This functional interconnectedness amongst these important brain regions is reputed to potentiate rapid shifts from a DMN to an integrated functional memory. This type of rapid shift is indeed what we observe in a client successfully treated with EMDR therapy.

REFERENCES

Andrade, J., Kavanagh, D., & Baddeley, A. (1997). Eye-movements and visual imagery: A working memory approach to the treatment of post-traumatic stress disorder. *British Journal of Clinical Psychology, 36*(Pt. 2), 209–223.

Armstrong, M., & Vaughan, K. (1996). An orienting response model of eye movement desensitization. *Journal of Behavior Therapy and Experimental Psychiatry, 27*, 21–32.

Barrowcliff, A., Gray, N., Freeman, T. C. A., & MacCulloch, M. J. (2004). Eye-movements reduce the vividness, emotional valence and electrodermal arousal associated with negative autobiographical memories. *Journal of Forensic Psychiatry and Psychology, 15*, 325–345.

Barrowcliff, A., Gray, N., MacCulloch, S., Freeman, T., & MacCulloch, M. (2003). Horizontal rhythmical eye movements consistently diminish the arousal provoked by auditory stimuli. *British Journal of Clinical Psychology, 42*, 289–302.

Béhuret, S., Deleuze, C., Gomez, L., Fregnac, Y., & Bal, T. (2013). Cortically-controlled population stochastic facilitation as a plausible substrate for guiding sensory transfer across the thalamic gateway. *PLoS Computational Biology, 9*, e1003401.

Bergmann, U. (1998). Speculations on the neurobiology of EMDR. *Traumatology, 4*, 4–16.

Bergmann, U. (2008). The neurobiology of EMDR: Exploring the thalamus and neural integration. *Journal of EMDR Practice and Research, 2*, 300–314.

Bergmann, U. (2010). EMDR's neurobiological mechanisms of action: A survey of 20 years of searching. *Journal of EMDR Practice and Research, 4*, 22–42.

Christman, S. D., Garvey, K. J., Propper, R. E., & Phaneuf, K. A. (2003). Bilateral eye movements enhance the retrieval of episodic memories. *Neuropsychology, 17*, 221–229.

Corrigan, F. (2002). Mindfulness, dissociation, EMDR and the anterior cingulate cortex: A hypothesis. *Contemporary Hypnosis, 19*, 8–17.

de Jongh, A., Ernst, R., Marques, L., & Hornsveld, H. (2013). The impact of eye movements and tones on disturbing memories involving PTSD and other mental disorders. *Journal of Behavior Therapy and Experimental Psychiatry, 44, 477–483*.

Denny, N. (1995). An orienting reflex/external inhibition model of EMDR and thought field therapy. *Traumatology, 1, 1–6*.

Elofsson, U. O., von Scheele, B., Theorell, T., & Sondergaard, H. P. (2008). Physiological correlates of eye movement desensitization and reprocessing. *Journal of Anxiety Disorders, 22, 622–634*.

Farina, B., Imperatori, C., Quintiliani, M. I., Castelli Gattinara, P., Onofri, A., Lepore, M., . . . Della Marca, G. (2014). Neurophysiological correlates of eye movement desensitization and reprocessing sessions: Preliminary evidence for traumatic memories integration. *Clinical Physiology and Functional Imaging*. doi: 10.1111/cpf.12184

Griffin, J., & Tyrrell, I. (2006). *Dreaming reality: How dreaming keeps us sane, or can drive us mad*. Chalvington, England: Human Givens Publishing.

Herkt, D., Tumani, V., Gron, G., Kammer, T., Hofmann, A., & Abler, B. (2014). Facilitating access to emotions: Neural signature of EMDR stimulation. *PLoS One, 9, e106350*.

Hornsveld, H. K., Landwehr, F., Stein, W., Stomp, M. P. H., Smeets, M. A. M., & van den Hout, M. A. (2010). Emotionality of loss-related memories is reduced after recall plus eye movements but not after recall plus music or recall only. *Journal of EMDR Practice and Research, 3, 106–112*.

Kahneman, D. (2011). *Thinking, fast and slow*. New York, NY: Macmillan.

Kaye, B. (2007). Reversing reciprocal suppression in the anterior cingulate cortex: A hypothetical model to explain EMDR effectiveness. *Journal of EMDR Practice and Research, 1, 88–99*.

Knipe, J. (2015). *EMDR toolbox: Theory and treatment of complex PTSD and dissociation*. New York, NY: Springer Publishing Company.

Kosko, B. (2006). *Noise*. New York, NY: Viking.

Lanius, U. F., Paulsen, S. L., & Corrigan, F. M. (Eds.). (2014). *Neurobiology and treatment of traumatic dissociation: Towards an embodied self*. New York, NY: Springer Publishing Company.

Lee, C. W., & Cuijpers, P. (2013). A meta-analysis of the contribution of eye movements in processing emotional memories. *Journal of Behavior Therapy and Experimental Psychiatry, 44, 231–239*.

Lee, C. W., & Cuijpers, P. (2014). What does the data say about the importance of eye movement in EMDR? *Journal of Behavior Therapy and Experimental Psychiatry, 45, 226–228*.

Lee, C. W., & Drummond, P. D. (2008). Effects of eye movement versus therapist instructions on the processing of distressing memories. *Journal of Anxiety Disorders, 22, 801–808*.

Leer, A., Engelhard, I. M., & van den Hout, M. A. (2014). How eye movements in EMDR work: Changes in memory vividness and emotionality. *Journal of Behavior Therapy and Experimental Psychiatry, 45, 396–401*.

Llinás, R. R. (2001). *I of the vortex: From neurons to self*. Cambridge, MA: MIT Press.

MacCulloch, M. (2006). Effects of EMDR on previously abused child molesters: Theoretical reviews and preliminary findings from Ricci, Clayton, and Shapiro. *Journal of Forensic Psychiatry and Psychology, 17, 531–537*.

MacCulloch, M. J., & Feldman, P. (1996). Eye movement desensitisation treatment utilises the positive visceral element of the investigatory reflex to inhibit the memories of post-traumatic stress disorder: A theoretical analysis. *British Journal of Psychiatry, 169, 571–579*.

Melloni, L., Molina, C., Pena, M., Torres, D., Singer, W., & Rodriguez, E. (2007). Synchronization of neural activity across cortical areas correlates with conscious perception. *Journal of Neuroscience, 27, 2858–2865*.

Moss, F., Ward, L. M., & Sannita, W. G. (2004). Stochastic resonance and sensory information processing: A tutorial and review of application. *Clinical Neurophysiology, 115,* 267–281.

National Institute for Health and Care Excellence. (2005). *Post-traumatic stress disorder (PTSD): The management of PTSD in adults and children in primary and secondary care. Clinical Guideline 26.* London, England: Author.

Priplata, A. A., Niemi, J. B., Harry, J. D., Lipsitz, L. A., & Collins, J. J. (2003). Vibrating insoles and balance control in elderly people. *Lancet, 362,* 1123–1124.

Propper, R. E., Pierce, J., Geisler, M. W., Christman, S. D., & Bellorado, N. (2007). Effect of bilateral eye movements on frontal interhemispheric gamma EEG coherence: Implications for EMDR therapy. *Journal of Nervous and Mental Disease,* 785–788.

Rasolkhani-Kalhorn, T., & Harper, M. L. (2006). EMDR and low frequency stimulation of the brain. *Traumatology, 12,* 9–26.

Rausch, V. H., Bauch, E. M., & Bunzeck, N. (2014). White noise improves learning by modulating activity in dopaminergic midbrain regions and right superior temporal sulcus. *Journal of Cognitive Neuroscience, 26,* 1469–1480.

Reinker, S., Puil, E., & Miura, R. M. (2004). Membrane resonance and stochastic resonance modulate firing patterns of thalamocortical neurons. *Journal of Computational Neuroscience, 16,* 15–25.

Sack, M., Lempa, W., & Lamprecht, F. (2007). Assessment of psychophysiological stress reactions during a traumatic reminder in patients treated with EMDR. *Journal of EMDR Practice and Research, 1,* 15–23.

Sartory, G., Cwik, J., Knuppertz, H., Schurholt, B., Lebens, M., Seitz, R. J., & Schulze, R. (2013). In search of the trauma memory: A meta-analysis of functional neuroimaging studies of symptom provocation in posttraumatic stress disorder (PTSD). *PLoS One, 8,* e58150.

Shapiro, F. (2007). EMDR, adaptive information processing, and case conceptualization. *Journal of EMDR Practice and Research, 1,* 68–87.

Shibata, H., & Yukie, M. (2009). Thalamocingulate connections in the monkey. In B. A. Vogt (Ed.), *Cingulate neurobiology and disease.* New York, NY: Oxford University Press.

Siegel, D., & Buczynski, R. (2014). *The neurobiology of trauma treatment: How brain science can lead to more targeted interventions for patients healing from trauma.* Retrieved from http://www.nicabm.com/treatingtrauma2014/a1-transcript-sample/?del=11.14.14LTsampleemailunreg

Söderlund, G., Sikstrom, S., & Smart, A. (2007). Listen to the noise: Noise is beneficial for cognitive performance in ADHD. *Journal of Child Psychology and Psychiatry, 48,* 840–847.

Solomon, R. M., & Shapiro, F. (2008). EMDR and the adaptive information processing model. *Journal of EMDR Practice and Research, 2,* 315–325.

Stickgold, R. (2002). EMDR: A putative neurobiological mechanism of action. *Journal of Clinical Psychology, 58,* 61–75.

Stickgold, R., Fosse, R., & Walker, M. P. (2002). Linking brain and behavior in sleep-dependent learning and memory consolidation. *Proceedings of the National Academy of Sciences, 99,* 16519–16521.

van den Hout, M. A., Engelhard, I. M., Rijkeboer, M. M., Koekebakker, J., Hornsveld, H., Leer, A., . . . Akse, N. (2011). EMDR: Eye movements superior to beeps in taxing working memory and reducing vividness of recollections. *Behaviour Research and Therapy, 49,* 92–98.

Vogt, B. A., & Laureys, S. (2009). The primate posterior cingulate gyrus: Connections, sensorimotor orientation, gateway to limbic processing. In B. A. Vogt (Ed.), *Cingulate neurobiology and disease.* New York, NY: Oxford University Press.

Walker, M. P., Brakefield, T., Morgan, A., Hobson, J. A., & Stickgold, R. (2002). Practice with sleep makes perfect: Sleep-dependent motor skill learning. *Neuron, 35,* 205–211.

Walker, M. P., Liston, C., Hobson, J. A., & Stickgold, R. (2002). Cognitive flexibility across the sleep-wake cycle: REM-sleep enhancement of anagram problem solving. *Brain Research. Cognitive Brain Research, 14*, 317–324.

Wilson, D. L., Silver, S. M., Covi, W. G., & Foster, S. (1996). Eye movement desensitization and reprocessing: Effectiveness and autonomic correlates. *Journal of Behavior Therapy and Experimental Psychiatry, 27*, 219–229.

Yan, X., Brown, A. D., Lazar, M., Cressman, V. L., Henn-Haase, C., Neylan, T. C., . . . Marmar, C. R. (2013). Spontaneous brain activity in combat related PTSD. *Neuroscience Letters, 547*, 1–5.

Yoshida, M., Hayashi, H., Tateno, K., & Ishizuka, S. (2002). Stochastic resonance in the hippocampal CA3-CA1 model: A possible memory recall mechanism. *Neural Networks, 15*, 1171–1183.

Index

active imagination, 105, 192
adaptive information processing (AIP)
    model, xxiii–xxiv, xxv, xxvi, 10–11,
    28, 38, 64, 67, 77, 78–79, 81, 84,
    86–89, 92, 97, 104, 111, 113, 115, 117,
    124, 130, 131, 135, 137–139, 146,
    148, 151, 152, 156–157, 165, 193,
    212, 232, 241, 248, 249
affect bridge, 94, 155, 156, 157, 173, 177–
    178, 185–186, 188, 191, 207
altered consciousness, 25–26, 151
apparent normal part (ANP), in structural
    dissociation model, 27, 28
Armed Forces Act of 2006, 3
Armed Forces Day, 3
assessment phase, of EMDR therapy, 92–93
    IConN modifications to, 155–157
attachment, 9, 12, 13, 27, 67, 68, 95, 182,
    193, 198, 223
attention seeking, 28
attunement, 34, 80–81, 95, 148–149, 150,
    153, 156, 160, 164, 200, 217, 218,
    220, 226, 232, 233
auditory hallucinations, 10, 31, 44, 102, 103,
    126, 127, 134, 135, 208, 209, 211
avatar therapy, 103, 104–105, 127, 136
aware ego, 106, 154, 155, 157, 163, 165
axial age, 136

behavioral psychotherapy, 70
bilateral stimulation (BLS), 66, 85–86, 88–
    89, 90, 92, 94, 96, 107, 152, 157–159,
    191, 198–199, 216–217, 224–225,
    245–252
    bilaterality of, 251–252
    for body dysmorphophobia,
        178–181, 185
    consequences of, 244–245
    mechanism of action, 239–240

body dysmorphophobia, 149, 173–188, 232
body scan phase, of EMDR therapy, 96
    IConN modifications to, 159–160
brain, trauma effect on, 13–14
British Psychological Society (BPS), 24, 102,
    126–129, 134
    Division of Clinical Psychology, 106, 154
brown study, 211

CAEL, 71, 82–84, 149, 150, 153, 194, 199
Capgras delusion, 168, 222–225
case formulation, xxiv, 47, 60, 97, 102, 103,
    127, 131, 145–161, 167, 176, 183,
    196, 210, 222
Central Intelligence Agency (CIA), 150
childhood physical abuse (CPA), 12
childhood sexual abuse (CSA), 12
children of Holocaust survivors,
    posttraumatic stress disorder
    in, 8–9
chlorpromazine, for schizophrenia, 128
classical (Pavlovian) conditioning, 240
Clinical Resource Efficiency Support Team
    (CREST), xix, xxiii
closure phase, of EMDR therapy, 97
    IConN modifications to, 160
clozapine, for schizophrenia, 112, 135
cognition
    negative, 65, 84, 92, 97, 115, 152, 157,
        167, 177, 179, 180, 196, 213, 214,
        216, 224, 225
    positive, 66, 92, 96, 97, 115, 152, 158–159,
        160, 177, 179–181, 213, 214, 216,
        224, 225
cognitive behavioral therapy (CBT)
    benefits of, 126–128
    for psychosis, 123–129, 138
    for schizophrenia, 66–67, 102, 104, 105,
        110, 111, 240, 241

community, importance in EMDR
therapy, 151–152
community mental health team
(CMHT), 123
community psychiatric nurse (CPN),
123, 221
compassionate pluralistic psychiatry, 147
complexes, 68, 79
computed tomography (CT), for
schizophrenia, 45
core relational schemas, 68
cortical translations, 92, 158
Cotard's syndrome, 166, 167–171,
222–223, 232
credibility gap, in treatment
preparation, 86

deep cognitive structures, 68
delusion(s), 103, 112, 166, 208–214
Capgras, 168, 222–225
defined, 168
Fregoli, 223
of grandiosity, 125, 208
of passivity, 208
of persecution, 125, 208, 221
of reference, 208
religious, 208
dementia dissecans (insanity of
dissociation), 29
dementia praecox, 7, 15, 30, 33, 69
dementia sejunctiva (insanity of
dissociation), 29
desensitization phase, of EMDR
therapy, 93–96
IConN modifications to, 157–158
Diagnostic and Statistical Manual of Mental
Disorders (DSM), xxxvii, 24, 130,
132, 133, 168
Fifth Edition (DSM-5), 4, 28, 31, 34,
112–113, 133, 137, 164, 167, 174,
176, 183, 196, 222
First Edition (DSM-I), 3
Fourth Edition (DSM-IV), 33, 137, 167
Fourth Edition–Revised (DSM-IV-R),
33, 137
Second Edition (DSM-II), 3, 31, 44
Second Edition–Revised (DSM-II-R), 210
Third Edition (DSM-III), xxx, 3, 4, 31, 44,
45, 133, 137
Third Edition–Revised (DSM-III-R), xxx,
31, 44, 45, 133, 137, 207–226, 233

diagnostic labels, 25
dialogism, 200
diathesis, 3, 24, 68
diathesis–stress model, 4, 5, 14, 24
diet, and schizophrenia, 8
disintegration, 70
dissociation, 25–29
definition of, 25
extreme, 26–27
historical context of, 28–29
insanity of, 29
pathological, 26
psychosis, 29
dissociative disorder, schizophrenia
as, 29–30
Dissociative Experiences Scale (DES), 6,
110, 209, 210, 214, 222
dissociative identity disorder (DID), 5, 6,
11, 27, 28, 32, 133–134, 165, 232
dissociative schizophrenia, 5, 32–33, 210–215
criteria for, 131–132, 134
Ross's criteria for, 210–211, 232
dissoziationsprozess (process of
dissociation), 29
divided self, 105–107
EMDR therapy and, 106–107
DTNBP1 mutation, and schizophrenia, 47
dual attention stimulation (DAS), 66,
85–86, 88–89, 90, 92, 94, 96, 107,
152, 157, 158, 159, 191, 198–199,
216–217, 224–225, 245–252
bilaterality of, 251–252
for body dysmorphophobia,
178–181, 185
consequences of, 244–245
mechanism of action, 239–240
dysfunctional memory network (DMN),
xxiv, xxv, xxvi, 10, 11, 25, 28, 34–35,
36, 37, 64–66, 68, 77, 78–79, 83, 84,
88, 92–94, 97, 104, 111–114, 124,
130–132, 136–137, 138, 147–151,
154–160, 164, 167, 173, 176, 177,
179, 180, 182–187, 191, 207, 215,
216, 218–219, 222, 225, 226, 232,
233, 245
dysfunctional psychological pathogen, 68
dysmorphophobia, 215–217

ego-state therapy, 106–107, 157, 191, 192,
197–198
resources for, 203–204

emoting, 92, 158
emotional part (EP), in structural
    dissociation model, 27, 28
epigenetics, 7–8, 15
epistasis, 7, 31
epistemic hubris, 165, 204
European Society for Trauma and
    Dissociation (ESTD), 133
expressed emotion (EE), 128–129, 151
eye movement desensitization and
    reprocessing (EMDR) therapy, xxiii,
    75–97, 145–147
adaptive information processing
    model. See adaptive information
    processing model
assessment, 92–93
bilateral stimulation. See bilateral
    stimulation
body scan, 96
case examples, 173–188, 191–205,
    207–226
closure, 97
for Cotard's syndrome, 169
desensitization, 93–96
distinguished from ICoNN model,
    147–148
divided self and, 106–107
dual attention stimulation. See dual
    attention stimulation
focus of research, 241–243
history and treatment
    planning, 78–84
installation, 96
integration, 243–244
intersubjective space, 35–36,
    69, 199–200
preparation, 85–92
for psychosis, 107–116
    suitability of, 129–135
question and answer with client,
    240–241
rationale for using, 103–104
re-evaluation, 97
reasons for using, 101–105
relational imperative
    of, 81, 150, 157
right target for, getting, xxv–xxvi
for schizophrenia, 63–64, 65, 66
thalamic activity and PTSD, 239
trauma memory data, reconsolidation
    and processing of, 241

FACES (Flexible, Adaptive, and
    Coherent flow that is Energized
    and Stable), 246
familiality, as history-taking approach,
    44–45
family, importance in EMDR therapy,
    151–152
fantasy, 28
fixed ideas, 68, 79
flash-forwards, 111
Foundation Resonance, 153
Fregoli delusion, 223

genetic epidemiology
    on island of Ireland, 45
    of schizophrenia, 30–31
Genetic Epidemiology of Mental Illness
    in Northern Ireland (GEMINI),
    44, 45, 125
Gestalt of schizophrenia, 33–34, 36, 153,
    155–160, 179, 184, 186, 207, 213, 215,
    224, 226, 233
grandiose delusions, 125, 208
gross stress reaction, 3

hallucination, 6, 34, 52, 59, 64, 158, 193, 196,
    210, 213
    auditory, 10, 31, 44, 102, 103, 112,
        126, 127, 134, 135, 195, 208,
        209, 211
    command, 208, 209, 211
Hearing Voices Network, 106, 124, 153–154,
    192, 204
Hero's Journey, The, 65
history-taking approach to schizophrenia,
    43–60, 81–84
    case formulation/diagnosis, 60
    familiality, 44–45
    family history, 55
    family psychiatric history, 54
    forensic history, 56
    ICoNN modifications to, 148–149
    Irish Schizophrenia Triad Study, 44, 45
    listening, 43, 81
    medication (current), 55
    mental state examination, 57–60
    past medical history, 54
    past psychiatric history, 53–54
    personal history, 56–57
    presenting problems, 49–50
    presenting problems, history of, 50–53

history-taking approach to
schizophrenia (*cont.*)
social history, 55–56
Structured Clinical Interview for
DSM-III-R, 45, 46–47

INCBLOT (International Collaboration
Bringing Local Outcomes Together)
Archive, 234–236
Indicating Cognitions of Negative
Networks (IConN) model, xxvii,
xxix, xxx, 10, 11, 25, 34, 64, 66, 71,
81, 97, 103, 104, 111, 112, 116, 130–
131, 132, 135, 138, 139, 145–161, 231
case examples, 163–171, 173–188,
191–205, 207–226
distinguished from EMDR therapy,
147–148
modifications, 148–161
assessment, 155–157
body scan, 159–160
closure, 160
desensitization, 157–158
history taking, 148–149
installation, 158–159
preparation, 149–155
re-evaluation, 160–161
treatment planning, 149
installation phase, of EMDR therapy, 96
IConN modifications to, 158–159
intermetamorphosis, 223
internal working models, 68
*International Classification of Diseases
(ICD)*, xxvii, 24, 130, 132, 133
ICD-10, xxx, 4, 28, 34, 132, 137, 167–168,
174, 176, 183, 196, 208, 211, 222
ICD-11, 31
intersubjective interweaves. *See* relational
interweaves
intersubjective space, 35–36, 69, 199–200
Irish High-Density Schizophrenia Family
Study, 45
Irish Schizophrenia Triad Study
(ISTS), 44, 45, 208

language use, in schizophrenia, 35
law of conservation of energy, 107
Life of Pi, 11
limbic system, 88
listening, as history-taking approach, 43, 81
logos, 76

Maastricht approach, 153, 154, 157, 199
magnetic resonance imaging (MRI), for
schizophrenia, 46
"Medical 203," 3, 24
mental disorders
history of nomenclature in, 24–25
medical model of, 24
mental state examination, 57–60, 84, 133,
167, 176, 183, 196, 222
metaphor, 65, 79, 86, 89, 91, 154–155,
196, 197
monasticism, 43
multifactorial polygenic model of
schizophrenia, 31
multiple personality disorder (MPD), 209
myth, 67, 72, 81, 87, 92, 138–139, 147, 151,
152, 164, 192
mythopoeia, 65–66
mythopoetics, 196–197
mythos, 66, 72, 76, 104, 130, 131, 138, 151,
152, 204, 216
interweave, 217

naltrexone, for dissociative schizophrenia,
103, 212, 215
negative cognition (NC), 65, 68, 84, 92, 97,
115, 152, 157, 167, 177, 179, 180, 185,
186, 196, 213, 214, 216, 224, 225
negative schizophrenia, 6
neuroses, 102
nonaffective psychosis, 45
nosology of schizophrenia, 6–7, 23–24
nostalgia, 2

oligogenic model of
schizophrenia, 7, 31
open dialogue approach, 200–201
organ of emotion, 149, 153, 158, 159

persecutory delusions, 125, 208, 221
phenomenology, 23
phenotype, definition of, 30
pluralistic psychiatric practice, 164
pointlessness, 27
polyphony, 200, 201
positive cognition (PC), 66, 92, 96, 97, 115,
152, 158–159, 160, 177, 179, 180,
185, 186, 213, 214, 216, 224, 225
positive schizophrenia, 6
Post-Traumatic Growth Inventory
(PTGI), 116

posttraumatic stress disorder (PTSD), 11,
85, 86, 103, 104, 209, 232
    birth of, 4–5
    in children of Holocaust survivors, 8–9
    comorbid, 131
    "gatekeeper" criterion for, 4, 137
    thalamic activity and, 239
praecox-feeling (praecox Gefühl), 33, 36,
157, 160
pregabalin, for dissociative
    schizophrenia, 224, 225
preparation phase, of EMDR
    therapy, 85–92
    ICoNN modifications to, 149–155
primum non nocere, 125
prodromal period, 110
psychiatric training, earliest days
    of, 128–129
psychoeducation, 86, 152–153, 213
psychology of the aware ego. *See* voice
    dialogue approach
psychosis, xxvi
    as adaptation, 135–137
    cognitive behavioral therapy for,
        123–129
    dissociation, 29
    EMDR therapy for, 107–116
    history of, 102
    nonaffective, 45
    pathology-level, 12, 13
    reactive dissociative, 32, 33
    and schizophrenia, 29–32
psychotherapy
    behavioral, 70
    paradigm, for schizophrenia, 67–72

Quantum Brain model, 83, 87

railway spine, 2
re-evaluation phase, of EMDR
    therapy, 97
    ICoNN modifications to, 160–161
reactive dissociative psychosis,
    32, 33
relational EMDR therapy, 81
relational imperative, of EMDR therapy,
    69, 150, 157
relational interweaves, 95, 217–221
room, as safe/calm place, 90–91
Roscommon Family Study, 44, 45
Rule of St. Benedict, 43

safe/calm place exercise, teaching, 90
schizodissociative disorder, 5
schizophrenia, xxvi
    as biological brain disease, 45–46
    diet and, 8
    dissociative, 32–33, 131–132,
        210–215, 232
    as dissociative disorder, 29–30
    dissociative heart of, 6
    DSM-III-R criteria for, 207–226, 233
    epigenetic transmission of risk, 8
    genetic epidemiology of, 30–31
    Gestalt of. *See* Gestalt of schizophrenia
    as group of disorders, 5–6, 31–32
    history of, 102
    history-taking approach to, 43–60, 81–84
    intersubjective space, 35–36
    multifactorial polygenic model of, 31
    negative, 6
    nosology of, 6–7, 23–24
    oligogenic model of, 7, 31
    positive, 6
    psychosis and, 29–32
    smoking and, 8
    and trauma, relationship between, 9–10
    traumagenic neurodevelopmental
        model of, 14–15
    treatment-resistant, 102–103, 126, 127
    use of language in, 35
schizophrenic taint, 33–34
sejunctionpsychose (dissociation
    psychosis), 29
selves, 197–198
Seroquel (quetiapine), for dissociative
    schizophrenia, 211–212
Seroxat (paroxetine), for dissociative
    schizophrenia, 212, 215
"shaman's advantage," 71
shell shock, 2–3, 70
smoking, and schizophrenia, 8
soldier's heart, 2
somatic (physical) illness, 23–24
stochastic resonance (SR), 89, 92, 239,
    245–252
    bilaterality, 251–252
    defined, 246
    synthesis, 250–251
    and thalamic gating, 249–250
    thalamo-cortical-temporal binding
        and, 248
Stockholm syndrome, 201

stop signal, teaching, 89–90
stress–vulnerability model, 14–15
Structured Clinical Interview for
    DSM-III-R (SCID), 45, 46–47,
    208–209, 210
subjective doubles syndrome, 223
Subjective Units of Distress Scale (SUDS),
    93, 94, 157, 177, 181, 184–186, 214,
    216, 217, 224, 225
suicidal ideation, 27

thalamic activity, and posttraumatic stress
    disorder, 239
thalamic gating, stochastic resonance and,
    249–250
thalamo-cortical-temporal binding, 248
therapeutic alliance, 80, 85–86, 95, 187
therapeutic interweaves, 95–96
therapeutic window, 70
TICES strategies, 91
tolerance of uncertainty, 200
trauma, xxvi
    effect on brain, 13–14
    memory data, reconsolidation and
        processing of, 241
    modern nosological classifications
        of, 3–4
    phenomena as, 112–113
    psychological impact nomenclature,
        history of, 1–3
    and psychosis, 108–109
    role of, 11–12

and schizophrenia, relationship
    between, 9–10
    treatment as, 114–116
traumagenic neurodevelopmental (TN)
    model, of schizophrenia, 14–15
treatment as usual (TAU), 111
treatment planning phase, of EMDR
    therapy, 84
    ICoNN modifications to, 149
treatment-resistant schizophrenia,
    102–103, 126, 127
trench warfare, 126
Tribrain model, 152, 212, 213, 249
Triune Brain model, 83, 86, 87–88, 92

unintegration, 70

Validity of Cognition (VoC) scale, 92, 96,
    158, 177, 185, 186, 213
voice dialogue approach, 106, 154, 157,
    191–205
    dialogism, 200
    polyphony, 200, 201
    resources for, 203–204
    tolerance of uncertainty, 200

war neurosis, 2–3
Wizard of Oz, The, xxx, 10, 64–66, 157,
    197, 201

Zispin (mirtazapine), for dissociative
    schizophrenia, 212, 215

Lightning Source UK Ltd.
Milton Keynes UK
UKHW021902191020
371860UK00011B/108